Thomas Goldschmidt

AF287621

View-Based Textual Modelling

The Karlsruhe Series on Software Design and Quality

Volume 6

Chair Software Design and Quality
Faculty of Computer Science
Karlsruhe Institute of Technology

and

Software Engineering Division
Research Center for Information Technology (FZI), Karlsruhe

Editor: Prof. Dr. Ralf Reussner

View-Based Textual Modelling

by
Thomas Goldschmidt

Dissertation, Karlsruher Institut für Technologie
Fakultät für Informatik,
Tag der mündlichen Prüfung: 24.11.2010

Impressum

Karlsruher Institut für Technologie (KIT)
KIT Scientific Publishing
Straße am Forum 2
D-76131 Karlsruhe
www.ksp.kit.edu

KIT – Universität des Landes Baden-Württemberg und nationales
Forschungszentrum in der Helmholtz-Gemeinschaft

KIT Scientific Publishing 2011
Print on Demand

ISSN 1867-0067
ISBN 978-3-86644-642-7

View-Based Textual Modelling

Zur Erlangung des akademischen Grades eines

Doktors der Ingenieurwissenschaften

von der Fakultät für Informatik
des Karlsruher Instituts für Technologie (KIT)

genehmigte

Dissertation

von

Thomas Goldschmidt
aus Emmendingen

Tag der mündlichen Prüfung: 24. November 2010

Erster Gutachter: Prof. Dr. Ralf Reussner
                                Karlsruher Institut für Technologie (KIT)

Zweiter Gutachter: Prof. Dr. Colin Atkinson
                                Universität Mannheim

Abstract

The main goal of model-driven software development (MDSD) is to make software development more efficient. By raising the level of abstraction and employing model transformations and generators, the productivity of developers should by improved. The use of multiple views on a central model shall enable the different roles involved in a software development process to focus on their specific tasks. For example, separating the dynamic and static parts of a system into different views allows to work more focussed on the respective areas. Such as separation is, in graphical modelling languages, such as the Unified Modelling Language (UML), a well established and central concept since many years. An additional aspect that is in the focus of MDSD is the development and use of Domain Specific Languages (DSLs). Within DSLs also different aspects of the software under development and the different involved roles are involved in the development process. While graphical DSLs are in use for a certain time now, also more and more textual DSLs emerge.

However, the area of view-based modelling in conjunction with domain specific metamodels and languages has not been investigated to a large extent. Especially the synchronisation of overlapping or partial views on central model in combination with textual modelling languages is a challenge that is yet to be solved. Model transformations are means for synchronising view models with their underlying models. However, problems occur if such transformations are to be used with partially incomplete or inconsistent views but where those part that are consistent should be synchronised anyway.

In the area of textual modelling, the concept of view-based modelling is, in contrast to graphical modelling, currently only weakly supported. It is, for example, not yet possible to explicitly define partial view types or multiple views on common model elements which might even show different parts of the model element while hiding other parts. Furthermore, specific problems occur whenever such views are modified and a compiler analyses the textual views to translate them into their corresponding model representation. Partial views may only show a certain part of the attributes and associations. With the use of traditional textual modelling approaches, the compiler will, depending on the changes made, possibly create a new model element instance for the changed textual representation. This will then result in the loss of all information that is currently not inside this textual view.

This thesis presents an approach which allows for the easy and rapid creation of textual, view-based modelling languages as well as the synchronisation between multiple views on a central model. To achieve this goal, this thesis comprises a comprehensive analysis and classification of existing approaches for view-based as well as textual modelling. Based on this analysis an existing textual modelling approach is extended with the capabilities to define textual view types. In addition, this thesis contributes an approach for representing textual views that may be partial, selective or overlapping. Concerning the problem of (partial) synchronisation of inconsistent or incomplete textual views an approach is introduced that allows for the specification of model transformations in a way that they are able to retain specific modifications to their target models. Based in these, so called retainment policies, algorithms have been developed which retain temporary inconsistent parts as well as manual formatting within the textual views. The approach developed in this thesis has been validated against formal properties of view-based modelling as well as in the context of several industrial case studies.

Zusammenfassung

Modellgetriebene Software-Entwicklung (MDSD) hat es zum Ziel, die Software-Entwicklung effizienter zu gestalten. Durch die Erhöhung des Abstraktionsniveaus so wie den Einsatz von Transformationen und Generatoren soll die Produktivität gesteigert werden. Durch Benutzung multipler Sichten auf ein zentrales Modell soll es ermöglicht werden, die verschiedenen Aspekte der Software wie zum Beispiel die statischen und dynamischen Teile sowie die am Entwicklungsprozess beteiligten Rollen spezifisch zu unterstützen. Eine solche Aufteilung ist in Standardmodellierungssprachen wie z.B. der Unified Modelling Language (UML) bereits seit Langem ein zentrales Konzept. Ein weiterer Aspekt der im Fokus der MDSD steht ist die Entwicklung sowie der Einsatz Domänen-spezifischer Sprachen (DSL). Auch hier sind verschiedenste Aspekte der zu entwickelnden Software und diverse verschiedene Rollen am Entwicklungsprozess beteiligt. Verstärkt wird hier auch der Einsatz von textuellen Modellierungssprachen, neben traditionellen graphischen Modellierungssprachen gewünscht.

Der Bereich der sichtenbasierten Modellierung gerade im Zusammenhang mit domänenspezifischen Metamodellen und Sprachen ist jedoch noch wenig untersucht. Es ist beispielsweise nicht möglich, explizite Teilsichttypen zu erzeugen oder mehrere textuelle Sichten auf gemeinsame Modellelemente zu erzeugen, welche evtl. sogar unterschiedliche Teile der Elemente zeigen während sie bestimmte andere verbergen. Gerade die Synchronisierung von überlappenden oder Teilsichten auf ein zentrales Modell stellt eine große Herausforderung dar. Modelltransformationen bieten hier die Möglichkeit, verschiedene Sichten mit deren darunterliegenden Modellen abzugleichen und zu aktualisieren. Probleme entstehen jedoch, wenn diese Transformationen während der Entwicklungsphase auf noch unfertigen oder teils inkonsistenten Sichten arbeiten und trotzdem Teile des Modells aktualisiert werden sollen. Im Bereich der textuellen Modellierung ist das Sichtenkonzept im Vergleich zur graphischen Modellierung noch kaum unterstützt. Spezielle Probleme entstehen hier zudem, wenn textuelle Sichten durch einen Übersetzer analysiert und in die entsprechende Modellrepräsentation übersetzt werden sollen. Partielle Sichten zeigen jedoch nur einen Teil der Attribute und Assoziationen eines Modellelements. Wird nun eine textuelle Sicht geändert und vom Übersetzer neu eingelesen, führt dies im Standardfall dazu, dass auch die entsprechenden Modellelemente neu instanziiert werden und somit alle Teile des Elements verloren gehen, welche nicht in der aktuellen Sicht enthalten sind.

In dieser Arbeit wird ein Verfahren vorgestellt, welches es erlaubt, textuelle, sichtenbasierte Modellierungsprachen einfach und schnell zu entwickeln sowie die Synchronisierung von multiplen Sichten auf ein zentrales Modell durchzuführen. Um dies zu erreichen, wird zunächst eine Analyse und Klassifikation der verschiedenen Arten und Möglichkeiten in der sichtenbasierten Modellierung gegeben. Basierend auf dieser Analyse wird ein bereits existierender Ansatz zur Erstellung von textuellen Modellierungssprachen um die Möglichkeit der Definition von Sichten erweitert. Bezüglich des Problems der (Teil-)Synchronisierung von inkonsistenten Sichten und Modellen wird ein Ansatz eingeführt, welcher es erlaubt, Modelltransformationen derart zu spezifizieren und auszuführen, dass bestimmte Bereiche im Zielmodell der Transformation erhalten bleiben. Auf Basis dieser Erhaltungsregeln sind Algorithmen entwickelt worden, welche beim Einsatz textueller Sichten Formatierungen sowie temporär inkonsistente Bereiche über Änderungen hinweg erhalten. Der in dieser Arbeit entwickelte Ansatz wurde mit Hilfe mehrerer industrieller Fallstudien validiert.

Acknowledgment

First of all, I would like to thank my advisers Reussner and Colin Atkinson for their support. Ralf laid the foundation for my PhD work and provided me a very pleasant and productive working atmosphere. Colin supported my work with his expertise in view-based modelling. A special thank goes to Axel Uhl from SAP AG. He was the one initiating the collaboration with SAP AG and my work on this thesis. He also was one of the major discussion partners giving knowledgeable feedback and always asking one question further and deeper into the details and problems of the topic. Furthermore, I would like to thank Steffen Becker for the supervision and support. He provided me very constructive feedback and innovative ideas.

The members of the Software Engineering (SE) group at FZI as well as the members of the Chair Software Design & Quality (SDQ) from KIT helped me due to their feedback in many "doctoral rounds". Especially Martin Küster who also wrote his diploma thesis within the context of my work and then joined the SE group had a major influence on my work. Klaus Krogmann and Michael Kuperberg helped me in the finalisation phase of my thesis by reviewing the thesis and giving detailed and constructive feedback. Furthermore, Mircea Trifu who gave me the necessary freedom during the final phase of the creation of this thesis despite the many projects he required people working in.

The implementation of FURCAS would not have been possible without many students and external collaborators helping me to create a running version of FURCAS. Therefore, I thank Philipp Meier, Christian Siani, Thibault Kruse, Stephan Erb and Armagan Kilic for their collaboration in the FURCAS project.

Finally, I would like to thank my girlfriend Petra Ackermann, as without her I wouldn't have achieved all of this. Especially during the many weekends I spent writing this thesis, she always supported me in this task.

Contents

List of Figures

List of Tables

List of Listings

Chapter 1.

Introduction

Engineers and experts of a certain domain think and express themselves mostly and most efficiently using terms of their, often very specific domain. To allow for better communication of programmers and experts as well as for giving experts the possibility to create applications using their common terms and vocabulary specifically tailored languages need to be provided. The multitude of languages that such an approach implies was the motivation to find means of rapid and efficient language engineering approaches. To find solutions for this problem, the research field of Domain Specific Languages (DSLs) emerged. DSLs are languages in computer science, that serve as means of formulating solutions for strictly defined, technical problems in a predefined domain. Due to their focus on a specific domain, these languages allow experts in such as specific domain to be more productive than with the use of a traditional programming languages [vDK98]. The higher level of abstraction of the language allows developers to perform optimisations and maintainability tasks on the abstraction level of the domain [MP99]. DSLs are also often tightly coupled to the concepts of model-driven engineering [Kle09]. The use of model-driven engineering with its generative techniques and commonly defined metamodels allows for building tool-chains and efficient development environments based on a common basis. In this area a common practice is the use of views to allow for the tackling of a problem from different view points and different roles each with a specific focus. On the other hand, there are more and more textual DSLs emerging. However, textual DSLs in combination with view-based modelling has not been tackled in research to a satisfying extent. This thesis introduces an approach, called FURCAS, that allows for the specification of view-based textual modelling languages including the representation of textual views and means for the synchronisation of textual views with their underlying models.

1.1. Motivation

Domain specific languages (DSLs) and more specific DSL workbenches, have been perceived as a major step towards creating software in strictly defined domains in more efficient way [vDK98, vDKV00, Fow05]. This is due to the raised level of abstraction on which the software is developed, which allows domain experts to communicate with developers on the same level. Due to the focus on aspects that are specific for each domain the efficiency of software development can be increased. However, this advantage can only be exploited if the language keeps a strong focus and avoids to include too generic aspects [Hud98]. An additional advantage of DSLs is that they make domain knowledge more explicit and thus more reusable and long-living. Through the use of transformations domain specific models, representing that knowledge can transform these models into further models for different purposes.

Martin Fowler [Fow05] envisioned a DSL approach that allows users to freely define new languages which are fully integrated with each other. He argued that the primary source of information should be a persistent abstract representation on which the three main parts of a language workbench, the data schema, the editors as well as generators or interpreters are based. More specific, he envisioned as a consequence of this central abstract representation that language users will manipulate the DSL through a projectional editor. Finally, as Fowler perceives the creation of applications a creative task he argues that a language workbench should persist incomplete or contradictory information in its abstract representation. This would improve the way developers achieve their tasks. Fowler also motivated the use of views within DSLs. A key aspect that he mentioned is that there is no need to show all information all the time. The projection and selection of elements that are shown in an editor should be reduced to what is necessary for the current task a developer works on.

Tackling a problem from different sides or views allows for a well structured development process. However, switching between views may also leave them in inconsistent states. Still, this inconsistency is not considered to hinder the productivity of developers working with views. From the area of view-based modelling the existence of inconsistency between views is accepted and even exploited by developers [FKN+92]. With the use of multiple views developers tend to really use the different views for very distinct purposes and are able to move rapidly between them. Consistency is only required at certain stages and should therefore not be enforced by a view-based approach.

This also may explain the failure of early approaches for projectional, language oriented editors. These approaches did not allow the developer to write and persist syntactically or semantically incorrect programs. This reduced the freedom of developers and therefore also their creativity.

However, with the multi-view paradigm for modelling which was already present in graphical modelling since some time ago the resurrection of projectional textual editors seemed to take place. Language workbenches such as the JetBrains Meta Programming System [Jet] gain more and more attention not only from academic but also from industrial users. However, despite MPS is a projectional editor approach it does not account for partiality or overlapping of the models that are created.

Especially the combination of allowing a certain degree of freedom in the process of working with a DLSs with the aspects of partiality and overlapping views poses challenges that are yet unsolved. This includes the specification of textual view types that only expose certain parts of an underlying model to the developer in a respective view. This implies that precautions need to be arranged for the way such textual views are edited synchronised with the underlying model. For example, the view synchronisation process cannot simply re-create an element from the current textual representation as the information given there may only resemble a part of that element. Thus, an intelligent incremental update approach is required that ensures the retainment of partially viewed elements throughout the editing process.

Having a Universally Unique Identifiers (UUIDs) based model repository poses some additional requirements to the implementation of a CTS approach. UUIDs for model elements and therefore also links between model elements that are based on these UUIDs links unfold several advantages in a large-scale setup [Uhl08]. Especially for distributed and parallel model development this identification mechanism is important. Imagine in a key attribute based repository one user changes the key attribute of an element that is referenced from several other elements that he does not necessarily have under control or perhaps does not even know about. All references to this element will break. This problem does not occur with UUID based identification. However, UUID based identification comes at a price that currently not all repository and tool implementations are willing to pay. Caution is therefore required in selecting the right infrastructure components for an enterprise modelling setup. There are several issues that have to be tackled when handling UUID based elements, though especially when a CTS should be developed that does not store these IDs explicitly in the textual representation as well.

While its UUID remains stable across the life time of a model element, some repositories allow the key attributes to change their values. For example, the Web Tools Platform (WTP) built in Eclipse with EMF uses names for identifying model elements. Element references can break if elements change their name and referring elements are not covered by the refactoring. UUID-based references are not affected by such changes and from this perspective work better in a large-scale environment where owners of an artefact do not always know all of the artefact's users or referrers. Beyond that, UUIDs can get "lost" if elements are accidentally deleted. It then depends on the tools and the capabilities of the repository how this case gets handled and what this means to references pointing to the UUID which now has disappeared.

In textual syntaxes identification through UUIDs becomes problematic for several reasons:

- **Storage mechanism:** If a model artefact is stored using the concrete syntax only, there needs to be the possibility to store these IDs somewhere in the text. However, during development a developer should not see these IDs as they contradict the crisp textual view and make it confusing. On the other hand, if the artefact is solely stored as model, other problems concerning the update from text to model arise (see below).

- **Model updates:** Updating existing models is an inherent problem of textual notations. In graphical or forms-based modelling only a comparably small set of changes may occur that can easily be wrapped into command structures that are executed in a transactional way, transforming the model from one consistent state to another. In a textual editor this is very difficult, especially when IDs are not present in the textual representation. A small change, e.g., adding an opening bracket in the text may alter the whole structure of the text, making it difficult to identify which elements in the model are meant to be kept and which are not.

- **Creation and deletion of model elements:** In a graphical editor there are explicit commands to create and delete model elements. Within a textual editor this is difficult mostly because the creation or deletion of model elements is done implicitly. For example, if the name of an element is changed in the textual syntax it may either mean that the old element should be deleted and a new one should be created, or a simple rename of the existing model element may have been intended.

A solution that lets transformations produce stable UUIDs for new model elements was proposed in [Uhl08]. For example, such an approach may use the ID of the source element and some transformation ID to compute the ID of the target element. However, if text is used as source there is no stable ID for a source element, just properties derived directly from the textual representation, such as a name attribute. Hence, no stable ID for a target element can be computed and the only way to keep the identity is to rely on incremental updates of the model.

A survey on existing concrete textual modelling approaches by Goldschmidt et al. [GBU08] revealed that current approaches for textual modelling are not suitable for view-based modelling nor do they account for UUID based identifiers as they do not allow for explicitly defining concrete textual syntaxes that are partial w.r.t. to the employed metamodel. Furthermore, they do not incorporate incremental update techniques which are a basic requirement for the synchronisation of multiple views with their underlying model.

A solution approach to this problem, which is called FURCAS, is presented in this thesis. FURCAS is based on an existing template, based approach for specifying textual concrete syntaxes, introduced by Jouault et al. in 2006 [JB06b, JBK06] which is called Textual Concrete Syntax (TCS). As TCS is already template based it serves as good starting point for view-based textual modelling approach. This thesis presents concepts and realisations on the extension of that template based approach which allow for the definition of textual views. This includes the possibility to explicitly define the scope of a template as partial or complete w.r.t. the metamodel element it represents as well as extensive support defining lookup rules and model construction rules with the use of the Object Constraint Language (OCL). To account for the bidirectionality of the view type definitions FURCAS includes an approach for automatically inverting parametrised OCL queries.

This thesis furthermore introduces a textual decorator model which allows for the representation of partial views on a single underlying model. This approach non-intrusively attaches the textual representation to the model elements and thus enables the use of multiple, overlapping views on common model elements. This decorator model is capable of representing and storing temporary inconsistent textual representations which enable developers to creatively and iteratively work with the provided editors.

Based on these two foundations for textual view-based modelling, this thesis furthermore, contributes an incremental update approach for the synchronisation of views with their model and vice-versa. This approach makes use of incremental lexing and parsing

5

techniques with the combination of novel algorithms that handle the reuse and merging of the textual representation and the model. Additionally, this synchronisation process accounts for the retainment of temporary inconsistent textual representations as well as manual changes made to the layout of the textual view. To achieve this FURCAS relies on a novel approach for specifying so called *RetainmentPolicies* for model transformations, which are also a contribution of this thesis. With these rules it is possible to explicitly define which rules or which areas in a target model should allow for external changes in their respective target models. These areas are then protected from changes that are propagated from subsequent executions of the transformation.

With the use of this synchronisation approach, this thesis also solves the problem of UUID retainment of model elements within textual syntaxes. For this, this thesis will show that the UUID retainment problem can be reduced to the partial view problem and therefore be solved with the very same means.

Finally, this thesis contains a validation of the presented concepts on different levels. First, FURCAS is validated formally against predefined properties of view types and views in view-based modelling. Second, industrial case studies have been performed to validate the applicability and usability of FURCAS in practice.

1.2. Application Scenario

The application scenario targeted in this thesis is the engineering of complex DSLs with multiple aspects and/or roles involved. Complex DSLs with a large, expressive metamodels require the focus on different aspects or roles to exploit the main advantage of DSLs, which is their focus on a specific domain and the ability to be as concise as possible in creating domain constructs. FURCAS allows to tailor specific textual view types for certain aspects of a DSL or for different roles.

FURCAS supports this by helping language engineers to create explicit partial and/or overlapping textual view types using specific concepts of view-based modelling. This process is supported by guiding language engineers in the process of defining partial and/or combined view types for a DSL. Explicit design decisions, making specific parts of a view type partial or complete avoid errors in language specifications that would hinder the rapid development of the DSL. For example, view types may be explicitly defined as complete w.r.t. an element of the DSL, which means that all possible instances of this element can be viewed and created with the view type. During the development of this view type FURCAS checks whether this constraint is fulfilled and if not the language engineer will receive direct feedback concerning an error in this specification.

Especially Through its powerful OCL model construction rules FURCAS makes it possible to define concise view types while keeping constructing complex models in the background. By reusing OCL for several parts of the view type specification language FURCAS reduces the learning effort as large and complex metamodels will most probably already use a multitude of OCL constructs, either for constraint or operation body implementations [Uhl07, Uhl08].

As it is likely that, in complex and large scale DSLs and projects developed with the DSL more than one tool will interact with a central model, the concrete textual syntaxes for views developed with FURCAS are non-intrusive w.r.t. the underlying domain model. This feature also allows for a clear separation and storage of concrete and abstract syntax.

Traditionally, language engineers were only able to create view-based languages for graphical view-based modelling. With FURCAS this limitation is removed and *view-based textual* modelling becomes possible.

1.3. Scientific Contributions

The main contributions of this thesis reside on different levels within the whole area of model-driven and domain specific language engineering. Figure 1.1 gives an overview on the the different areas this thesis contributes to. These different layers are given by the generality of the contribution made by a specific part of this thesis:

1.3.1. Model Transformations

In the area of round-trip and incremental transformations this thesis contributes the *RetainmentPolicies* approach [GBU08]. This approach can be applied wherever incremental transformations take place. Given a transformation that transforms a given source model to a target model. In some scenarios these target models are also target to modifications from external sources. For example other transformations may modify the same target model in a different way. Furthermore, a modeller may want to refine the results of the transformation by adding additional elements or by modifying certain default properties the transformation has set. With the use of traditional transformation approaches this would not be possible, a transformation that is run a second time would probably remove elements that were added manually and recreate those elements

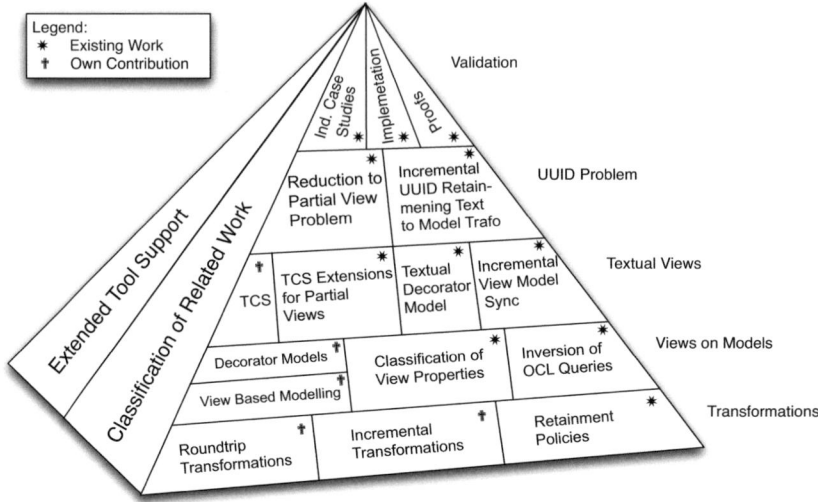

Figure 1.1.: Foundations and contributions of this thesis.

that were deleted. With the use of *RetainmentPolicies* transformation developers may specify that in certain cases modifications to the target model should be retained even though the transformation would normally overwrite them. The approach introduced in this thesis is based on the identification of target model changes that can be found by the use of the transformation trace that a transformation engine created during the execution of a transformation.

1.3.2. View-Based Modelling

This thesis contributes to the generic area of view-based modelling by defining a taxonomy of concepts and properties of view points, view types and views. This taxonomy defines properties, such as partiality or completeness of views types or the synchronisation properties for views. This taxonomy is encompasses formal definitions of the respective properties based on a formalisation of the artefacts of model-driven engineering provided by Amelunxen and Schürr [AS07] and Hettel et al. [HLR08].

Additionally an approach for automatically inverting parametrised OCL queries is introduced in this thesis. One of the main purposes of OCL is the use as model query language. For this purpose it is sometimes necessary to define queries that can be parametrised by certain values. FURCAS makes use of such queries for the resolving of model elements that are linked from textual views. However, if we want to consider such a specification not only as query but also, bidirectionally, as computation directive for the valued which where used in the query these queries need to be inverted. This thesis provides an approach that, if certain assumptions are fulfilled, allows for the automatic inversion of such queries.

1.3.3. Textual Modelling

This thesis introduces the notion of textual view-based modelling [GBU09b]. This novel approach combines the aspects of textual modelling with those of view-based modelling. The FURCAS approach [GBU09a] contributes to the area of textual modelling on several levels. First, by extending the template based textual modelling approach TCS [JBK06, JB06b] this thesis contributes an approach for defining partial and overlapping textual view types. This part of FURCAS furthermore, includes an approach that automatically determines whether a template is capable of representing all possible model instances or not. This is important as view types in FURCAS can be defined to explicitly be partial or complete w.r.t. their corresponding class in the metamodel. FURCAS also makes intensive use of OCL expressions for different purposes, such as: resolving of model elements based on parametrised queries or for formulating advanced model construction rules directly within the templates.

The second major contribution to the area of textual modelling is the textual decorator model of FURCAS. This decorator model is capable of representing textual views on models that may be partial or selective. Furthermore, temporary inconsistent views can also be represented and stored with this, so called TextBlocks model approach [GBU09b].

Finally, FURCAS provides an incremental synchronisation approach for its textual views [Gol08, GBU10]. This approach serves as mediator between the textual views and their underlying models. This process also accounts for the retainment of partially viewed model elements and translates textual modifications made to the TextBlocks model in a way that elements that this kind of elements are kept so that the information which is currently not available in the partial view is not lost.

1.3.4. UUID Retainment

The incremental update process of FURCAS also contributions to the solution of the UUID retainment problem [Gol08]. This thesis shows that the UUID retainment problem can be reduced to the partial view problem and therefore be solved by the means of FURCAS. This reduction is done based on the idea that a UUID is nothing else than an attribute that every model element implicitly owns. By making this attribute explicit and declaring each view type partial w.r.t. this attribute allows to use the same solution as FURCAS provides for partial views.

1.4. Structure

This thesis is structured in eight chapters:

Chapter 2 introduces foundations and work related to the concepts presented in this thesis. Work in this area stems from three different areas: First model-driven engineering, where a trend towards textual modelling languages emerged during recent years. Second, view based modelling approaches which deal with the general idea of tackling a problem that is modelled from different angles with different foci. And third, grammar based language engineering with a strong focus on incremental transformation techniques. Section 2.1.1 gives a brief overview on the concepts of model-driven engineering. More specific, concepts such as metamodels, models and transformations are introduced here. Additionally some formal foundations for these concepts are laid on which later-on introduced formalisations base. Section 2.1.2 focuses on domain specific languages (DSLs) and gives a brief overview on the history as well as the different areas of application of DSLs. Section 2.1.3 introduces the area of concrete textual syntaxes for models. It gives an overview on the basic structure of components (such as parsers and editors) such approaches have in common. A specific approach, called Textual Concrete Syntax (TCS) is presented in greater detail in this Section, as it will serve as foundation of the FURCAS approach presented in later chapters of this thesis. The rest of Chapter 2 deals with related work in the three different areas, starting from approaches of view-based modelling in Section 2.2, over approaches for view synchronisation in Section 2.3 and grammar based language engineering approaches in Section 2.4, and finally in Section 2.5 concrete textual language approaches for models. In this last area of related work a detailled classification scheme is introduced defining the features along which the CTS approaches were examined. This scheme serves as basis for a detailled analysis of the multitude of approaches existing in this area of research.

Chapter 3 introduces an approach for the retainment of external modifications in models which are at the same time targets for model transformations. Section 3.5 starts by classifying the changes that may occur in models that are worth to be retained. Based on this classification, Section 3.6 presents a formally backed approach for identifying changes to target models based on the trace of a transformation. The remainder of Chapter 3 deals with the introduction (Section 3.7), definition of the formal semantics (Section 3.9) and realisation (Section 3.11) of the so called *RetainmentPolicies* approach. This approach serves as basis for several transformations presented in later chapters.

Chapter 4 analyses the area of view-based modelling in general. It introduces the three-fold taxonomy of *viewpoints*, *view types* and *views* in Section 4.3 which defines the different levels of view-based modelling. Additionally it discusses the advantages and disadvantages of view-based modelling with a single underlying model versus the synchronisaiton of specific view models with each other. Section 4.4 defines the different properties of view types, such as partiality and completness and expresses formally what a view-based approach needs to support for the different properties to be fulfilled. Section 4.5 enters the next level of the taxonomy and explains the properties of views in greater detail. Special focus is also laid on the the synchronisation properties for views with their underlying model. Finally, Section 4.6 gives a short overview on different patterns of view types as their appear in practice.

Chapter 5 starts to introduce the FURCAS approach, which is a central contribution of this thesis. This chapter consists of two major Sections, Section 5.3 which deals with the definition of an approach to specify textual view types and Section 5.4 which handles the problem of how to represent textual views. Within the former Section, Subsection 5.3.2 deals with the features which FURCAS introduces to extend the TCS approach, which serves as basis for the view type definitions of FURCAS, with capabilities that allow for the definition of textual view types. Subsection 5.3.3, deals with the specific problems of how OCL queries, which are used in the FURCAS view type definitions, can be automatically inverted to resolve them

11

to unknown parameters. As last part of the FURCAS view type definition approach, Subsection 5.3.4 introduces advanced model construction rules which allow for the definition of complex textual modelling languages without the additional use of model transformations. The second part of this Chapter first introduces a decorator approach for textual models in Subsection 5.4.3. This approach serves as basis for the representation of temporary inconsistent textual views as well as the possibility to make use of the selectiveness property which are presented in Sections 5.4.4 and 5.4.5 respectively.

Chapter 6 deals with the problem of view synchronisation within the textual view approach of FURCAS. Section 6.3 handles the incremental synchronisations form the textual representation to the underlying model. It presents a multi-phased, incremental update approach which utilises incremental lexing and parsing techniques in combination with special reuse and merging rules. This approach allows for the retainment of model elements which are only partially viewed in a textual representation and avoids the loss of information when such model elements are edited from different views simultaneously. Section 6.4 gives a brief overview on a so called, OCL impact analysis approach which allows for the efficient re-evaluation of the OCL based constructs of the FURCAS view type specification. Section 6.5 shows how the special problem of retaining UUIDs of model elements in textual modelling approaches can be reduced to the partial view problem that is dealt with by FURCAS anyways. The last Section 6.6, completes the presented view synchronisation approach by providing a solution for the model to textual representation direction. It pays special attention to the problem of how manually adapted layout and the manual selection of elements within a view can be solved.

Chapter 7 shows in proofs and case studies the validity of the contributions of this thesis. Section 7.1 presents proofs that FURCAS fulfils certain properties of view based modelling as they were introduced in Chapter 4. This includes the properties for view types as well as views. Section 7.2 deals with critical modifications to the textual representations which are hard to handle by FURCAS and gives guidelines on how interaction with textual views in FURCAS is done in the best way. Finally, Section 7.3 presents the results of several industrial case studies performed to validate the FURCAS approach. To evaluate the use of certain view specific features of FURCAS, a metrics suite, defined using the Goal, Question, Metric approach is introduced. The metrics are gathered and analysed for the different case studies.

Chapter 8 concludes this thesis. It gives a summary of the results of this thesis in Section 7.1 and discusses the limitations of the FURCAS approach in Section 8.2. Section 8.3 finally poses some questions that are still to be solved, w.r.t. view-based textual modelling.

Chapter 2.
Foundations and Related Work

Related work relevant to this thesis mainly stems from two different areas. First, view-based modelling, which relates mainly to the graphical modelling as well as the synchronisation of views in general. And second, textual modelling languages, which is currently a field of research that is tackled by many different groups. Foundations for both of these areas are model-driven engineering and domain specific modelling languages. Foundations (Section 2.1) as well as competing approaches (Sections 2.2 to 2.5) will be introduced and discussed in this chapter.

2.1. Foundations

Model-driven engineering, domain specific languages and concrete textual syntaxes are the main areas on whichs foundations this thesis relies on. Model-driven engineering and domain specific languages are often closely related resulting in domain specific modelling languages. Both areas require an interface with which developers can interact, this is, in both cases, called the concrete syntax. As this thesis more specifically makes contributions in the area of concrete *textual* syntaxes, the third main area, for which foundations are laid in this chapter, is the area of concrete textual syntaxes.

2.1.1. Model-Driven Engineering

Model-driven engineering (MDE) or more specific model-driven software development aims at raising the abstraction level within software development and with that the productivity of software engineers that create the software. Models are central to this approach and are not only used for design and documentation purposes. Model transformations and generators translate models into other models and code. By this, for example, error prone tasks like writing boiler plate code can be automated, leveraging the productivity of software engineers.

15

2.1.1.1. Models and Metamodels

The main artifacts in MDE are called models. A common definition of the term *model* is, according to [Mod07]:

"A formal representation of entities and relationships in the real world (abstraction) with a certain correspondence (isomorphism) for a certain purpose (pragmatics)."

A classical definition of a model stems from a more generic source, the "common model theory" by Stachowiak [Sta73]. He defines a model by three main characteristics: abstraction, isomorphism and pragmatism. *Abstraction* means that a model hides certain parts of its real world correspondent. Which of the attributes of a real world object are acutally removed depends on the *pragmatic* goal for which a model is used. The relation between the real world object and its model can be seen as a projection from the object to the model in which the unconsidered attributes are excluded. Still, this projection has to be *isomorphic* as the model should still allow to draw conclusions from the model that can be translated to the real world object. Again, these conclusions are considered w.r.t. the goal for which the model is created. Finally, the *pragmatism* of the model is given by its purpose, the actual goal for which a model is created. Thus, models are not models for their own sake but always need to serve a certain purpose.

A metamodel characterises the set of models that is called the metamodel's instances. A metamodel defines the constructs that are allowed to build models conforming to that metamodel with.

Ernst [Ern99] defines a metamodel as follows:

"A metamodel is a precise definition of the constructs and rules needed for creating semantic models."

A similar definition is given by Kleppe [Kle09]:

"A metamodel is a model used to specify a language"

However, as Kleppe also writes about software language engineering, a metamodel in this specific case is better to be called an *abstract syntax model*, as in software language engineering further models of models, and therefore also metamodels are present. These other metamodels are those that define the concrete syntax as well as the semantics definition of a language. Thus, in the remainder of this thesis, the unqualified use of the term metamodel will always refer to the metamodel as the definition of the abstract syntax of a language.

A central task in MDE is the process of creating such metamodels for a modelling language, which is also called metamodelling. Kleppe [Kle09] even calls the role of the abstract syntax or the metamodel as "of critical importance" as it is the "pivot between various concrete syntaxes of the same language, as well as between the syntactical structure of a [..][program] and its meaning". For creating new modelling languages, first their central concepts should be defined on an abstract level. Kleppe and also other authors therefore propagate that the metamodel should be developed as first artefact when creating a new language. As it resembles the conepts of its target domain, it supposed to undergo more infrequent changes than the languages user interfaces, i.e., the concrete syntaxes.

The Meta Object Facility (MOF) – a Standard for Metamodelling   The Meta Object Facility (MOF) [Obj02, Obj06] is a meta-metamodel, defined as a standard by the Object Management Group (OMG), which is used for the definition of metamodels. Initially stemming from the UML [Obj10b], the MOF inherits several concepts from UML. Mainly, MOF uses class diagrams with its main constructs classes, attributes and associations as basis. However, MOF resides one meta-level above UML. UML being a metamodel can therefore be expressed using means of its meta-metamodel MOF.

With version 2.0 of the MOF specification [Obj06] two different flavours of the MOF exist: the Essential MOF (EMOF) and the Complete (CMOF). The most important difference between EMOF and CMOF is that CMOF contains associations as first level entities wheras EMOF only knows the concepts of a class' properties which may refer to other classes. The remainder of this thesis will use the concept of first level associations, as it allows to define more expressive and better extensible metamodels. However, in general, the concepts presented in this thesis are also applicable to EMOF. Then, all features explicitly referring to first level associations will not be available. Especially non-intrusive extensions to existing metamodels are not then not possible anymore in the desired way. To have a navigable reference to an element EMOF requires to add a property to the source class.

To omit technical but irrelevant details, the meta-metamodel used for the definition of metamodels used in this thesis is an that of the MOF version 1.4 [Obj02]. Being the ancestor of the newer MOF it is somehow a unification of the basic concepts of both EMOF and CMOF whith a more practical focus. The parts of this meta-metamodel, which are relevant for the remainder of this thesis are depicted in Figure 2.1.

The Object Constraint Language (OCL)   The Object Constraint Language (OCL) [Obj10a] constitutes the means for the definition of constraints and several other expres-

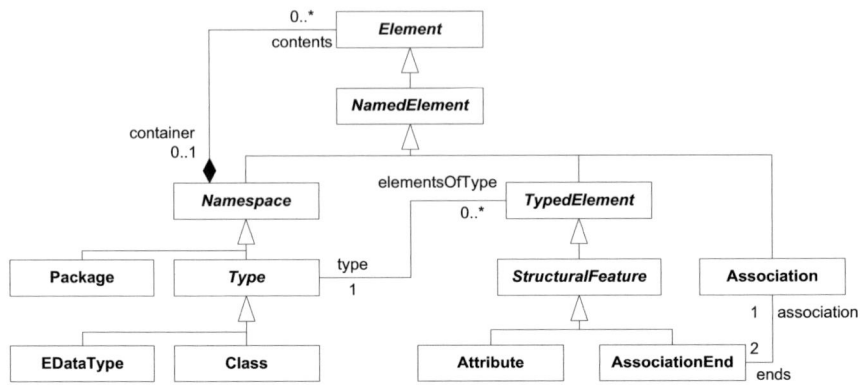

Figure 2.1.: The main components of the Meta Object Facility meta-metamodel.

sions in MOF based metamodels. The expressive power of OCL is equal to a three-level Kleene logic with equality [BW02]. OCL can not only be used to define constraints in metamodels but also to define queries over a model. Nearly every modern metamodelling environment nowadays has support for defining and evaluating OCL expressions.

Running Example   The following running example will serve to explain the concepts of MDE. A company wants to design their own modelling language to describe their business. The metamodel for this example is depicted in Figure 2.2. The modelling language provides concepts such as `BusinessEntity` which can be used to express things like customer, sales order or stock. Relations between these entities are expressed using `Associations`. For example, a customer may be related to one or more adresses using an association between both. To be able to employ a loosely coupled type system the company decides to use the concept of `TypeDefinitions` to the metamodel (cf. Section 7.3.2.1 for a detailed description on this concept).

Furthermore it is possible to define `MethodSignatures` for entities that can be used to compute values (by using a `Block` as `MethodImplementations`) or access associated entities (by using `AssociationEndNavigations` as `MethodImplementations`).

18

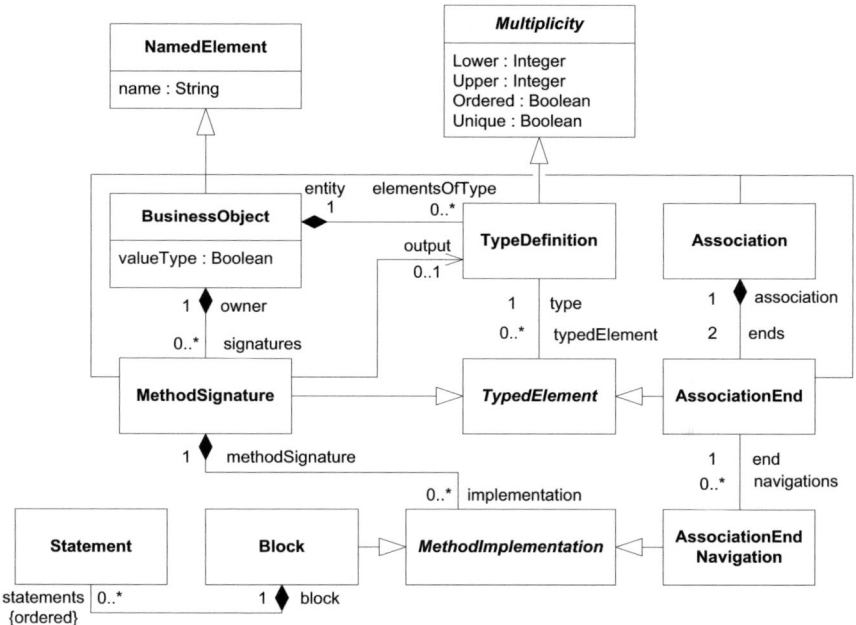

Figure 2.2.: Metamodel of an Example Modelling Language

2.1.1.2. Formal Definitions of Modelling Concepts

The remainder of this thesis will use several formal definitions that give a clear under-standing of views and view types as well as novel features introduced for the devel-opment of retainment policies for model transformations. To base these definitions on a solid, formal ground, first a few basic definitions need to be introduced. As there are several formalisations of model driven constructs [AS07, Gar09, Het10] this section will clearly define the structure and semantics of models, meta-models and transformations on which the concepts introduced in this thesis are based.

Formalisation Basis For the formalisation of properties of the modelling concepts such as model, meta-model and transformation, the following Definition 2.1 introduces a basic set of notational conventions used throughout the remainder of this thesis. A quick reference for the used formal representations used throughout this thesis is given in Appendix A for quick lookup.

Definition 2.1 (Basic Definitions). $\perp$ *denotes the undefined state*

$\mathbb{N}^+$ *denotes the set of positive natural numbers including ∞ and excluding 0.*

$\mathbb{N}_0^+$ *denotes the set of positive natural numbers including ∞ and 0.*

$\mathbb{N}^\perp := \mathbb{N}_0^+ \cup \perp$ *denotes the set of positive natural numbers including 0 ,∞ and an undefined state.*

$\mathbb{B} := \{true, false\}$ *denotes the set of logical values.*

$\mathbb{D} := \{first, second\}$ *denotes a set of values for the distinction between the first and the second end of an association.*

$proj_n(x_1, ..., x_n, ..., x_m) = x_n$ *denotes the n-th element in a given tuple.*

$\mathcal{P}(X)$ *denotes the powerset of a given set X*

$\mathcal{B}(X)$ *denotes set of all multi-sets over a given set X*

$\#(X)$ *denotes the cardinality of a given set or tuple X*

$\#_y(X)$ *denotes the cardinality of element y in a given multi-set X*

r^* *denotes the reflexive transitive closure of a binary relation r and a set-valued function (which is another representation of a binary relation)*

r^+ *denotes the transitive closure of a binary relation r*

$$e \in T \text{ where } T \text{ is a tuple means} \quad \begin{cases} e \in \bigcup_{n=1..\#(T)} proj_n(T), & \text{if } proj_n(T) \text{ is a set} \\ \varnothing, & \text{else} \end{cases}$$

$\exists e_1 \in E_1, ..., e_n \in E_n|...$ *is shorthand for* $\exists e_1 \in E_1|(...|\exists e_n \in E_n|(...)...)$ *(Same applies for* $\forall e_1 \in E_1, ..., e_n \in E_n|...$*).*

Metamodels and Models To define make formal statements on the relation between models and views, a formal understanding of models, metamodels and transformations is required. The following definitions are based on the formalisation of models, metamodels and transformations given by Amelunxen and Schürr in [AS07] plus minor enhancements to include the definition of attributes.

Definition 2.2 (Metamodel). *A metamodel MM is a tuple*

$$MM := (C, A, P, \Xi, first, second, attributes, isOrdered, isComposite, constraints)$$

where

C *is the finite set of classes,*

A *is the finite set of associations (for sake of brevity, I consider all associations as navigable in both directions),*

P *is the finite set of attributes,*

Ξ *denotes a set of metamodel constraints,*

$first : A \rightarrow C$ *is the mapping of associations to their first end,*

$second : A \rightarrow C$ *is the mapping of associations to their second end,*

$attributes : C \rightarrow P$ *is the mapping of classes to their attributes,*

$isComposite : A \times \mathbb{D} \rightarrow \mathbb{B}$ *returns the information whether an end of a given association is a composite end or not,*

$constraints : C \rightarrow \mathcal{P}(\Xi)$ *returns the set of constraints that are defined for given class.*

Using the running example from Page 18, the corresponding formal metamodel MM_e would consist of the following sets:

$C_e = \{$ *NamedElement, BusinessEntity, Multiplicity, TypeDefinition, Association, MethodSignature, TypedElement, AssociationEnd, MethodImplementation, AssociationEndNavigation, Block, BlockStatement* $\}$

$A_e = \{$ *Entity_ElementsOfType, Type_TypedElement, Association_Ends, Owner_Signatures, MethodSignature_Implementation, End_Navigations, Block_Statements* $\}$

$P_e = \{$ *Name, ValueType, Upper, Lower, Ordered, Unique* $\}$

Definition 2.3 (Model)**.** *Let MM be a metamodel and let the alphabets*

O_{MM} *denote the infinite set of possible object IDs for all classes $c \in C$, where $C :=$ $proj_1(MM)$,*

L_{MM} *denote the infinite set of possible link IDs for all associations $a \in A$, where $A :=$ $proj_2(MM)$,*

V_{MM} *denote the infinite set of possible values for all attributes $p \in P$, where $P :=$ $proj_3(MM)$.*

Then a model is defined as follows

$$M = \big(O, L, V, class, association, attribute, firstObject, secondObject, compositeLinks \\ , childObjects, compositeParent, value, orderL, orderV \big)$$

where

$O \subset O_{MM}$ *denotes the finite set of the model's object IDs,*

$L \subset L_{MM}$ *denotes the finite set of the model's link IDs,*

$V \subset V_{MM}$ *denotes the finite set of the model's attribute values ,*

$class : O \to C$ *returns the class $c \in C$ of a given object $o \in O$,*

$association : L \to A$ *returns the association $a \in A$ of a given link $l \in L$,*

$attribute : V \to P$ *returns the attribute $p \in P$ of a given attribute value $v \in V$,*

$firstObject : L \to O$ *returns the first object $o \in O$ for a given link $l \in L$,*

$secondObject : L \to O$ *returns the second object $o \in O$ for a given link $l \in L$,*

$compositeLinks : O \to \mathcal{P}(L)$ *returns the links in which a given object acts as composite object,*

$childObjects : O \to \mathcal{P}(O)$ *returns all child objects for a given composite object,*

$compositeParent : O \to \mathcal{P}(O)$ *returns the composite parent object for a given child object,*

$value : O \times A \to \mathcal{P}(O)$ *returns the attribute value for a given object and attribute,*

$orderL \subseteq L \times L$ *is a strict partial order on L where $(l_1, l_2) \in orderL \iff l_1$ occurs directly before l_2.*

$orderV \subseteq V \times V$ *is a strict partial order on V where $(v_1, v_2) \in orderV \iff v_1$ occurs directly before v_2.*

Furthermore, $Models_{MM}$ denotes the set of all (consistent) models for a given metamodel MM as defined above.

An example model for metamodel MM_e is given in Figure 2.1.1.2 and the following sets.

O_e = { *Customer : BusinessEntity, Address : BusinessEntity, CustomerHasAdresses : Association, customer : AssociationEnd, addresses : AssociationEnd, customerType : TypeDefinition, addressesType : TypeDefinition* }

L_e = { *Customer - customerType, customerType - customer, customer - CustomerHasAdresses, CustomerHasAdresses - addresses, addresses - addressesType, addressesType - Address*}

V_c = { *"Customer", "Address", "CustomerHasAdresses", "addresses", 0, -1, false, true, "customer", 1, 1, false, false, true* }

Model Changes   Hettel et al. [HLR08] give a complete definition of types of changes that may be applied to a model. They distinguish between *Atomic Changes* which refer to exactly one atomic modification and *Complex Changes* which are composites of atomic changes. Definition 2.4 is a slight modification to the original definition given by Hettel et al., as it also includes changes to the ordering of association links.

Definition 2.4 (Atomic Change). *An atomic change δ is defined the minimal set of changes to a tuple element of a model M. The application of a change δ to a model M resulting in a model M' is denoted as: $M' = \delta M$.*

There are six different atomic changes:

δ_o^+ *creating an instance o,*

δ_o^- *deleting an instance o,*

δ_{l,o_1,o_2}^+ *creating a link l between instances o_1 and o_2,*

δ_{l,o_1,o_2}^- *deleting a link l between instances o_1 and o_2,*

δ_{l_1,l_2}^o *change of ordering of a link l_1 which is swapped with l_2 if $association(l)$ is ordered at its first or second end,*

$\delta_{o,a,v}^s$ *setting attribute a of instance o to value v,*

$\delta_{o,a,v}^u$ *unsetting attribute a of instance o for value v,*

δ_{o,a,v_1,v_2}^o *change of order of value v_1 of attribute a of instance o which is swapped with v_2 if $isOrdered(a) = true$,*

Furthermore, $Changes_{MM}$ denotes the set of all possible changes for a given metamodel MM.

The element that is the actual change is retrieved from a change δ by applying the function $element : Changes_{MM} \to Models_{MM}$ to the change. For the creation or deletion of model elements $element$ yields o. For creation or deletions of links it yields l and for changes of attribute values the value v will be returned. For changes in the order of links or attribute values the corresponding tuple (l_1, l_2) or (v_1, v_2) from $orderL$ or $orderV$ will be returned respectively.

For unsetting an attribute by a change $\delta_{o,a,v}^u$ the value v needs to be given, as for a multi valued attribute it needs to be distinguished which of its value should be unset.

Definition 2.5 (Complex Change). *A complex change Δ is defined as set of atomic changes where each change Δ is composed of a sequence of atomic changes $\delta_1, ..., \delta_n$ such that*

$$\Delta M = \delta_1 \circ \cdots \circ \delta_n M = M'$$

where ∘ is a sequencing operator and δ_1 to δ_b are atomic changes applied to M; M' is the resulting model after change Δ was applied.

All possible changes that can be applied to models of metamodel MM denoted as $Changes_{MM}$ can be partitioned into the disjoint sets of changes by their atomic change type as defined in Definition 2.4:

$$Changes_{MM} = \Delta_o^+ \cup \Delta_o^- \cup \Delta_{l,o_1,o_2}^+ \cup \Delta_{l,o_1,o_2}^- \cup \Delta_{l_1,l_2}^o \cup \Delta_{o,a,v}^s \cup \Delta_{o,a}^u \cup \Delta_{o,a,v_1,v_2}^o$$

2.1.1.3. Transformations

Model transformations are another central artefact within MDE. There purpose is to translate model instances of one metamodel into model instances of other (or the same) metamodel. Alternatively, a model transformation can also be an inplace transformation making all modifications directly in the source model. Mens [MG06] defines a *model transformation* as an automatic generation of one or more target models from one or more source models according to a *transformation definition*. The *definition of a transformation* consists of set of transformation rules which describe the way a transformation is executed. A *transformation rule* describes, in detail, how or which elements of the target models are transformed.

A model transformation may either be specified in an imperative or in a declarative manner [CH06]. Imperative model transformations contain rules that have a well defined sequential call hierarchy and describe the way *how* a target model is created. In contrast to that, a declarative model transformation only defines *what* should be the result of the transformation. Rules in declarative model transformations define pre- and post-conditions, i.e., which rules need to be fulfilled before certain other rules will hold.

Query/View/Transformation (QVT) – a Standard for Model Transformation

The OMG defines a standard for model transformations called Query/View/Transformation (QVT) [Obj11]. This standard relates to the MOF as basis for metamodelling and models. The QVT specification defines three languages, the *Operational Mappings* language which is an imperative transformtion language, the *Relations* language which is declarative and the *Core* language, which is also declarative but resides on a lower level. The *Core* language is targeted as a base language which should be executable by a virtual machine for model transformations. The specification furthermore contributes a mapping from the *Relations* language to the *Core* language.

Formal Definitions of Model Transformations Amelunxen and Schürr [AS07] base their formal definition of model transformations on the concept of morphism between models. Definition 2.6 given by these authors states the meaning of a morphism between models. They state that "a model can be considered being homomorphic to a second model if all objects and all links of the first model can be mapped onto objects and links of the second model, in such a way, that the classes and associations of the mapped objects and links remain unchanged in the second model".

Definition 2.6 (Model Morphism). *Let MM_1, MM_2 be metamodels and let $M_1 \in Models_{MM_1}, M_2 \in Models_{MM_2}$. Then a model morphism $h : M_1 \to M_2$ is a triple of functions $h = (h_O, h_L, h_V)$ that maps M_1 onto M_2 where,*

$$h_O : O_1 \to O_2$$
$$h_L : L_1 \to L_2$$
$$h_V : V_1 \to V_2$$

$$\forall o \in O_1 \mid class_2(h_O(o)) = class_1(o)$$
$$\forall l \in L_1 \mid association_2(h_L(l)) = association_L(l)$$
$$\forall l \in L_1 \mid h_o(firstObject_1(l)) = firstObject_2(h_L(l))$$
$$\forall l \in L_1 \mid h_o(secondObject_1(l)) = secondObject_2(h_L(l))$$
$$\forall v \in V_1 \mid value_2(h_L(v)) = value_L(v)$$

Furthermore, $Morphisms_{MM_1, MM_2}(M_1, M_2)$ denotes the set of all possible model morphisms between two given models $M_1 \in Models_{MM_1}, M_2 \in Models_{MM_2}$ for the given metamodels MM_1 and MM_2.

Definition 2.7 (Transformation). *Let MM_1, MM_2 be metamodels and let $M_1 \in Models_{MM_1}, M_2 \in Models_{MM_2}$. Then a exogenous transformation T is a pair of model(s) (patterns) $T := (M_l, M_r)$. Furthermore, $Transformations_{MM} := (Models_{MM_1} \times Models_{MM_2})$ denotes the set of all transformations for a pair of given metamodels MM_1, MM_2. Additionally, we define*

25

$leftModelPattern_T := proj_1(T)$ *with* $T \in Transformations_{MM_1,MM_2}$
$rightModelPattern_T := proj_2(T)$ *with* $T \in Transformations_{MM_1,MM_2}$

Short hand for $left$- *and* $rightModelPattern$ *is* lmp *and* rmp *respectively.*

For an endogenous transformation the same definition applies with $MM_1 = MM_2$.

Based on this morphism and a basic definition of model patterns within transformations, as given in Definition 2.7, Amelunxen and Schürr define the application of a transformation to a source and target model as presented in Definition 2.8. The exact conditions under which $(M_1, M_2) \in \leadsto_T$ holds are not listed here, as this exact relationship is not important in the scope of this thesis. However, basically two models are element of this relation if there is a *model morphism* between them according to Definition 2.6.

Definition 2.8 (Application of a Transformation). *Let* MM_l, MM_2 *be a metamodels and let* $M_1 \in Models_{MM_l}, M_2 \in Models_{MM_2}, T \in Transformations_{MM}$ *and* $M_l = leftModelPattern_T, M_r = rightModelPattern_T$ *whereas* M_2 *is one possible result of the application of* T *to* M_1. *Then a transformation* T *defines a binary relation* $\leadsto_T \subseteq Models_{MM_1} \times Models_{MM_2}$.

The short-hand writing $\leadsto_T(e_1)$ *will be used to yield the element* e_2 *from* $(e_1, e_2) \in \leadsto_T$ *and vice-versa* $\leadsto_T(e_2) = e_1$.

The function $\leadsto_T^\Delta: Models_{MM_1} \times Models_{MM_2} \to Changes_{MM_2}$ *yields the set of changes that the transformation applies to a target model during its application.*

For further details on the above definitions refer to [AS07].

2.1.2. Domain Specific Languages

In literature, there is no common understanding of what *exactly* a domain specific language is adn what their main purpose is. Kleppe [Kle09] values domain specific languages as useful by saying that "Developers are applying DSLs to improve productivity and quality in a wide range of areas, such as finance, combat simulation, macro scripting, image generation, and more." On the other hand she criticises the there is too less practical experience in this area: "But until now, there have been few practical resources that explain how DSLs work and how to construct them for optimal use.".

Other authors provide similar but slightly different definitions of DSLs. Kolovos et al. [KPKP06] state that "DSLs show an increased correspondence of language constructs to domain concepts when contrasted with general purpose languages [...] [and are] often computationally incomplete.". This statement points out that DSLs are mostly only a part of a system, i.e., that part on which domain experts and developers might work jointly to produce results in an efficient way, without having to worry about a common vocabulary.

According to Krahn [Kra10], the main aspects of a DSL can be condensed into the following characteristics:

- The language focusses on specific application domain. The main purpose of the language is based on the semantic aspects of this domain as opposed to the technical realisation of a problem.

- If a DSL is executable, its expressive power is constrained as much as the domain allows. This is mostly less than the ability for universal computation.

- A DSL allows to solve the problems of a domain in a compact way.

However, the mentioned criteria do not allow a sharp distinction between General Purpose Languages (GPLs) and DSLs. In some scenarios, a DSL can even evolve to become a GPL [JB06a]. Much more important than this distinction is that with the constraint of its expressive power a language may increase the productivity of its users. Therefore, the most important aspect when building a DSL is its strict focus on the application domain [Hud98].

The main components of a DSL comprises the following four elements [HR04]:

- The *abstract syntax*, which defines the basic structure as well as the conceptual elements of a language. This is often done using means of metamodelling. It serves as the central data structure in which the programs written in the language are internally represented, analysed or transformed. It also serves as starting point for code generation or as basis for an interpreter for that language. In some approaches also programs are stored in their abstract syntax. Examples are the Meta Programming System approach [Jet] or the IPSEN approach [Nag96]. The abstract syntax also referred to as the machine representation of a program.

- One or more *concrete syntaxes*, which define the way for humans interact with the language. Concrete syntaxes may have different forms, such as: graphical, textual, forms- or tree-based. Additionally, the concrete syntax often constrains the set of possible language instances developers may create. In a view-based

DSL approach, concrete syntaxes may also be partial w.r.t. to the metamodel or overlapping w.r.t. to other syntaxes. In this case they are also called view types.

- The *context conditions* of a language are checkable conditions that constrain the set of licit instances of a language. These rules complete the abstract and concrete syntax with additional constraints which cannot be directly expressed using means of the abstract and concrete syntax formalisms. For a metamodel based approach, these are called metamodel constraints, which are, in the case of MOF [Obj06] based metamodels expressed using the Object Constraint Language [Obj10a]. These context conditions shall impede the creation of language instances for which no well-defined semantics exist.

- Finally, each language needs to define its semantics which defines its meaning. Different techniques may be employed to define the semantics. For example, denotational semantics [SS71] which defines the semantics using means of mathematics. Alternatively, the semantics may be defined using operational semantics [Plo04], which is based on the step-wise change of the states of an abstract state machine. Especially in the use of DLSs, also transformational semantics [Pep79] are often used which defines the semantics based on a transformation to a different language for which the semantics are already defined. Especially DSLs are often translated into GPLs such as Java. These semantics are also based on the abstract syntax of the language and are thus independent from employed the concrete syntax.

2.1.3. Concrete Textual Syntaxes

Software languages consist of different notions of syntaxes. First, there is the abstract syntax which defines the concepts and abstract entities that are expressed by the language. The abstract syntax is not intended to be edited directly by a user working with the language. It is merely an internal representation that is used by the software that deals with the language. The abstract syntax in modelling languages is mostly defined by the metamodel of the language.

Editing and viewing of models is done using a concrete syntax. The concrete syntax is intended to be used by developers to interact with model instances. There are different types of concrete syntaxes. A concrete syntax may be graphical, textual, forms-based, tree-based, or any other form that is suited for user interactivity. Furthermore, there may be more than one concrete syntax for an abstract syntax. For example, some parts of a metamodel may be best to be edited in a graphical syntax whereas others are best presented in a forms-based way.

Several basic components are needed to provide a comprehensive tooling for a CTS approach. To be able to relate constructs from a metamodel to elements of a CTS, a mapping between the metamodel and the definition of this syntax is needed. The definition of a textual syntax is provided by a grammar. To translate the textual syntax to its model representation, a *lexer*, a *parser* as well as a component that is responsible for the *semantic analysis* (type checking, resolving of references, etc.) are needed. Even for an approach that directly edits the model without having an explicit *parser* component for the grammar, a similar component is needed that decides how the text is translated into model elements. For reasons of convenience we will call all kinds and combinations of components that implement the translation form text to model a *parser*. The backward transformation, from model to text, is provided by an *emitter*. Both components can be generated using the above-mentioned mapping definition.

2.1.3.1. General Components of a CTS Approach

An overview of these components is depicted in Fig. 2.3. This figure shows that the CTS framework uses the information that is provided in the mapping definition to generate the parser, emitter and editor components. For example, the mapping could define that a UML class c is represented in the concrete syntax using the following template: `class <c.name> { <call to templates for contents of c> }`.
The framework could then generate a parser that recognises this structure and instantiates a UML class when parsing this pattern and setting the name property accordingly. Furthermore, an emitter can use this template to translate an existing UML class into its textual representation.

The grammar⇔metamodel mapping can also be used to generate an editor for the language represented by the metamodel. This editor can then use the generated parser and emitter to modify the text and the model. This editor is then also responsible for keeping the text and the model in sync, e.g., by calling the parser every time the text has changed. Based on the mapping definition several features of the editor can be generated, such as syntax highlighting, auto-completion or error reporting. Refactoring actions can also be provided with this editor. Having the model as well as the text in its direct access such an editor could, e.g, provide a rename action which updates the name property of

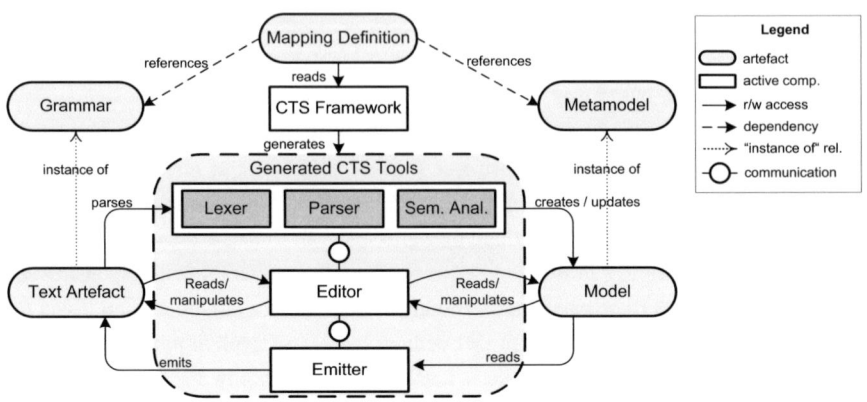

Figure 2.3.: General structure of a CTS framework

an element on the model and then uses the emitter to update all occurrences of this name in the text.

2.1.3.2. TCS

For the FURCAS approach TCS was chosen as a basis because it fitted best the posed requirements. A more detailed explanation will be conducted in Chapter 5. Being the foundation for FURCAS the concepts and elements of TCS are described here in greater detail.

TCS defines a metamodel for textual concrete syntax mappings for metamodels. It is based on templates that define how a specific textual structure is mapped to the metamodel. Figure 2.4 shows the basic strucure of the TCS metamodel. For example a `ClassTemplate` directly references the `Class` from its corresponding metamodel. Each `ClassTemplate` may then contain several `SequenceElements` that may themselves refer to properties of the respective `Class`. Furthermore, it is possible to define several alternatives within a `ClassTemplate` that give additional possibilities to represent the corresponding class in multiple ways.

A TCS concrete syntax mapping can be translated into a grammar for a parser generator, i.e., ANTLR [PQ95] which comes with TCS. In fact, each `ClassTemplate` of the mapping corresponds to a generated production rule in the grammar. `SequenceElements` of the templates that refer to properties from the metamodel

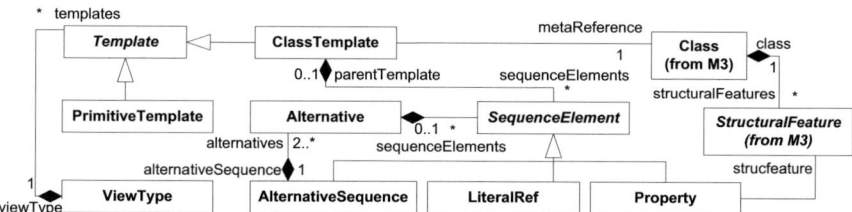

Figure 2.4.: The basic structure of a TCS Mapping.

```
 1  syntax BOsAndMethods {
 2   primitiveTemplate identifier for PrimitiveTypes::String
 3    default using NAME:
 4             value = "unescapeString(%token%)";
 5   template BusinessObject
 6    : "bo" name methodSignatures {separator = ";"}
 7    ;
 8
 9   template MethodSignature
10    : name "(" ")"
11    ;
12  }
```

Listing 2.1: Example TCS mapping.

for which's type also a template is defined are translated into calls to the corresponding production rules.

An example for the mapping to grammar transformation, based on a simple "classes and method signatures" syntax, based on the running example metamodel given in Figure 2.1.1.2, is given below in Listings 2.1 and 2.2. In this case, ANLTR is used as target grammar language. The transformation creates an ANTLR grammar rule for each template in the TCS mapping. Additionally for abstract templates the transformation generates a production rule including all subclasses as alternatives.

ClassTemplate For each class in a metamodel, a language engineer may define one ClassTemplate (more than one if using modes, see paragraph **References in Template Sequences** below). This ClassTemplate defines how the class will be represented as text. The classifier is referenced using the classifier name, which may be qualified using a '::' notation such as RootPackage::SubPackage::MyClass.

31

```
 1  grammar BOsAndMethods;
 2
 3  identifier returns[Object ret2] @init{java.lang.Object ret=null;}
 4  :
 5  (ast=NAME {ret = unescapeString( ast.getText());})
 6  {
 7  ret2=ret;
 8  }
 9  ;
10
11  businessobjects_businessobject returns[Object ret2]
12  @init{
13    List<String> metaType=list("businessObjects","BusinessObject");
14    ret = onEnterTemplateRule(metaType); }
15  :
16  'class' temp=identifier {setProperty(ret, "name", temp);}
17  ( ( temp=businessobjects_methodsignature
18      {setProperty(ret, "methodSignatures", temp);}
19    ( ';' temp=businessobjects_methodsignature
20      {setProperty(ret, "methodSignatures", temp);} )*
21  { ret2 = commitCreation(ret); }
22  ;
23
24  businessobjects_methodsignature returns[Object ret2]
25  @init{
26    List<String> metaType=list("businessObjects","MethodSignature");
27    ret = onEnterTemplateRule(metaType); }
28  :
29  temp=identifier {setProperty(ret, "name", temp);}
30  '(' ')'
31  { ret2 = commitCreation(ret); }
32  ;
```

Listing 2.2: Example TCS mapping translated to an ANTLR grammar.

However, if the unqualified name is unique in the Metamodel, it is possible to omit the packages.

Properties of metamodel elements that should appear in the textual syntax can by referred to by their name. If their type is a primitive type, then a suitable `PrimitiveTemplate` as above will has to exist in the syntax. If the property has another class as its type, the `ClassTemplate` for the model elements type will be used to represent that property's value (and must be defined as well). See the `properties` paragraph for more details and options.

The following are examples for primitive properties:

```
1  template Person
2    : "Person" "=" firstname lastname "."
3    ;
4
5  template Year
6    : "year" "=" value
7    ;
```

Not all templates of a syntax definition refer to concrete classes with a syntax contribution. *Abstract* `ClassTemplates` are usually used with abstract classes, or with operators (see **operators** paragraph). The templates in the syntax for abstract classes need to be stated explicitly so that it can be distinguished which parts of the inheritance hierarchy are to be included in the syntax. If all levels of hierarchy need to be specified the keyword `deep` can be defined in addition.

```
1  template Person abstract;
2
3  -- if MalePerson does extend Person in metamodel
4  template MalePerson
5    : "Mr." lastname
6    ;
7    </pre>
```

PrimitiveTemplate   This kind of template is used to define how primitive values are mapped from and to the textual concrete syntax. This for example includes the conversion of values to their primitive value, e.g., from the string representing a number "42" to the integer 42.

Some examples for `PrimitiveTemplates` are:

33

```
1 primitiveTemplate identifier for String default using NAME:
2   value = "%token%";
3
4 primitiveTemplate boolean for Boolean default using INT:
5   value = "Boolean.valueOf(%token%)";
6
7 primitiveTemplate integerSymbol for Integer default using INT:
8   value = "Integer.valueOf(%token%)";
9
10 primitiveTemplate floatSymbol for Double default using FLOAT:
11   value = "Double.valueOf(%token%)";
```

For each datatype in the metamodel that is used in a syntax definition, there must be one `default` primitive template, denoted by the `default` keyword. In some cases, it is necessary to have more than one primitiveTemplate for a datatype, for example if the language uses different representations of a primitive type. To use alternative primitiveTemplates one can specify to use them using the "as" property argument:

```
1 primitiveTemplate identifier for String default using NAME:
2 value = "%token%";
3
4 primitiveTemplate specialIdentifier for String using SPECIAL_NAME:
5 value = "%token%";
6
7 template SomeType
8   : someField{as=specialIdentifier}
9   ;
```

OperatorTemplate An extended feature of TCS is the possibility to explicitly define operators and their precedences. This allows for an easy creation of expression constructs in the TCS mappings. As starting point serves a super class for which the operator hierarchy should apply. This class is annotated with the definition of a so called operator list. The operator list defines what operators, such as $+$, $-$, $*$ or $/$ the expression allows. Furthermore, it defines the precedence levels using explicit priorities for the different operators.

For each combination of operator and class from the metamodel an operator template can be defined. This is then the template that will be called when a certain operator is matched in the textual representation. Depending on the text on the right hand side the parser will then choose the corresponding operator template for that part of the text and the operator.

In addition to the handling of operators and their priorities, operator templates can also be used to resolve the left recursion problem. As the current generators for TCS rely on LL-based parser generator frameworks, such as ANTLR, templates that recur on their left hand side cannot be directly expressed in the grammar. To resolve this problem, TCS' operator templates also suit this purpose. By simply declaring the token on the right of the recursion as an operator, the generator will create grammar production rules to that no left recursion occurs anymore.

Keywords and Symbols Literals such as keywords and symbols may occur in two different ways within a TCS mapping. First, directly as a string in a template or second as explicitly named symbol where the symbolic name is then used in the templates. For the latter case TCS uses so called `LiterRef` elements in the templates which refer to the corresponding symbols. Internally, however, TCS will also create symbols for the directly declared strings in the templates and create the corresponding `LiteralRefs` for them.

LiteralRef By writing the name of a symbol or keyword in the template, a language engineer will create a subclass of the `SequenceElement` class called `LiteralRef`. This element refers to the corresponding symbol in the TCS mapping. In the generated parser these `LiteralRef` will refer to lexer rules matching for example the keyword "class" or an opening or closing parenthesis "(" or ")".

Alternative A template may define more than one possible representation at once. The use of `Alternatives` enables this possibility. If the alternative is postfixed with a "*", e.g., `[[ elem1 | elem2 ]]*` the contents of the alternative may occur more than once and in an arbitrary order. For example a template would then also match text such as `elem1 elem1 elem2 elem1`.

The following example illustrates the use of an `Alternative` element within a template:

```
1 template Author
2   : "author" "="
3       [[ "{" name "}" | "\"" name "\"" ]]
4   ;
```

35

Functions and FunctionCalls Common parts of templates are a typical case where a reuse concept is useful. TCS provides the concept of Functions and FunctionCalls for this case. Functions may be declared on a given base class. All template for classes inheriting from this base class can then use this function to include common parts of the syntax definition.

The following example illustrates the use of Functions and FunctionCalls:

```
1 template Book
2   : publisher $hasAuthorAndTitle
3   ;
4 template Article
5   : journal $hasAuthorAndTitle
6   ;
7 function hasAuthorAndTitle(BibItemWithAuthorAndTitle) :
8   : [[ author | title ]]*
9   ;
```

Property Properties in TCS are used to define which properties of a class should be represented in a syntax. By writing their name within the template body this inclusion is performed. There is a number of options available for properties, all of which go into curly brackets after the property. These are called PropertyArguments. The most important argument types are the following:

As and Mode: For primitive datatypes it is possible to define more than one PrimitiveTemplate defining different formats in which the same datatype may be represented in the textual syntax in different places. To use a specific non-default PrimitiveTemplate for a primitive property, the as-PropertyArgument, e.g., as=primitiveTemplateName, may be used. Furthermore, there may be cases where specialized ClassTemplates exist, these are called *moded* ClassTemplates. To ensure a Property of a non-primitive type is textually represented using a special *moded* ClassTemplate, the mode can be specified using mode=modeName. If a specialized template (e.g., template for a subclass) should be called it is also possible to directly specify this in the as-clause.

RefersTo: TCS supports the creation of cross-references between elements by their identifiers. In this case a language engineer would add the feature name of the reference in the template's body for the referring class, but add different arguments in curly brackets: The key for the reference is a property that will represent the reference target in the text. This must be a primitive property, as its value needs to be directly representable in the textual representation.

The following example illustrates the use of `refersTo`:

```
1 template Article
2  : "article" "{" author{refersTo=name} "}"
3  ;
4 template Author
5  : "author" "=" name "."
6  ;
```

In the case above, an author would have to be defined somewhere else in the model, else the reference could not be resolved. An example textual representation using these templates would be:

```
1 article { "John"}
2 author = "John".
```

Conditionals In some situations parts of the textual representation depend on certain values of a model elements properties. To achieve this, a language engineer may use so called `Conditionals` in a template's body.

For example, for boolean types attributes of a class, the following is possible:

```
1 template Person
2 : (isProfessor ? "Prof") firstname lastname
3 ;
```

For making a comparison, an additional "else" part can be specified:

```
1 template Person
2 : (gender="male" ? "Mr" : "Ms") firstname lastname
3 ;
```

Or for optional attributes the predifined `isDefined()` function can be used:

```
1 template Person
2 : (isDefined(title) ? title) firstname lastname
3 ;
```

Alternatives   In some situations it might be necessary that more than one syntax is allowed to represent the very same class. This is where `Alternatives` come into play. A language developer may define that certain areas within a template can be expressed in different ways. To achieve this, the alternative sequence elements are enclosed within a list of alternatives: `[[ alternative1 | alternative2 ]]`. It is furthermore possible to nest these alternatives into each other.

The following listing is an example for the use of the `Alternative` construct:

```
1  template AlternatingProperties :
2  "Alternating elements:"
3  [[ altA | altB ]]* ;
4
5  template AltA : "a" ;
6  template AltB : "b" ;
```

PropertyInit   `PropertyInits` are declarations to initialize features of model elements which have no representation in the textual syntax, similar to default values. TCS supports two kinds of `PropertyInits`, initialization of property values using using primitive literals, and initialization using lookups. Primitive literals assign values to properties that have a corresponding primitive type.

```
1  template Wife
2  : "Mrs." name {{gender="female", isAdult=true, isMarried=true}}
3  ;
```

It is also possible to use lookups to assign values that already exist somewhere in the model to a property. The path navigation expression used within the `lookIn` traverses the model by subsequently navigating over the dot separated properties.

```
1  template Something
2  : {{property = lookIn('#context.property')}}
3  ;
```

Mode   If a `Class` should be treated differently within a certain context an additional mode designator may be specified. This allows to define multiple templates for one class of the metamodel. Thus, it is possible to define alternative syntaxes for the same class. A mode is entered when a `Property` denotes its name. The templates that are called from this property needs to be present in the given mode and is used at this place.

2.2. Existing Approaches for View-Based Modelling

Building views on underlying data has been researched in the context of relational and object-oriented databases thoroughly. An introduction to views in relational databases is given in [Cod91] . Therein, a view is defined as a virtual database deduced from an actual persistent database. A view is actually a subset of this database and cannot contain more data than the underlying database. The definition of a view consists of an algorithm or a query specifying which data belongs to the view and a schema definition.

A classification of views within object-oriented databases can be found in [SLT91]. Views in object-oriented databases are classes using an additional query. Updatable views in object-oriented databases have to be object preserving. This means that views are working with the base objects and updates to objects in a view are equivalent to a direct update of the base objects. Regarding the kind of query used for the view definition, there are different kinds of views: selection views, difference views, union views, intersection views, join views, projection views and extend views. These kinds of views are formally defined by mathematical set operations.

The concepts and solutions that where developed within the databases area can serve as a basis and source for the analysis of views in MDE. However, having a strong focus on interaction with humans views in MDE need to be tackled from a different angle.

A classification of views in software architectures in general is given by Clements et al. in [Cle03]. A complex software architecture is conveyed by a set of views with every view representing a subset of the architecture. Which view type is chosen depends on the goal of the documentation. E.g. if one needs information about the portability of a system, one will use a view showing the applicability/deployability of an architecture to different platforms. However, Clements does neither tackle the different properties of views and view types nor does he give any hints on how a view type is constructed based on a general metamodelling approach. The definitions of views and view types are given on an architectural level which cannot be mapped to general view-based modelling.

A general approach for so called "viewpoint-oriented systems engineering" (VOSE) was introduced by Finkelstein et al. in [FKN+92]. They describe a framework which allows for the use of multiple perspectives in system development. They introduce the term of "viewpoints" to partition the system specification which they encompass with a development method as well as formal representations. Furthermore, they introduce an approach for mapping the views to a common underlying data model. However, textual views are not considered this approach.

A relation between different viewpoints which is particularly interesting for MDA is shown in [DQPvS03]. Therein an approach helping designers to relate different viewpoints of different stakeholder to avoid inconsistent models is presented. A view is therefore defined as a mental image of a stakeholder focusing on specific concerns of a system. To relate the different view points, they introduce the Interaction System Design Language (ISDL).

However, these approaches fail to thoroughly investigate and identify the properties of views in the context of MDE. Even though the IEEE 1471-200 standard defines what the terms view and viewpoint in the context of software architectures mean, the term view is often used ambiguously and with different flavours in different domains. At last, there is neither a precise definition of the properties of views in the context of modelling nor a comprehensive description of the relation between a view and its model.

Work on formalisation of MDE has been introduced by Amelunxen and Schürr in [AS07]. They present a formalisation of (meta-)models and transformations. Hettel [HLR08], furthermore, introduces formalisations of model changes and partial transformations. However, a both papers do not include a formal representation of views in MDE.

In practice, several approaches have been developed that allow to define explicitly holistic, partial or combined graphical views for models. A prominent example for graphical modelling is the Graphical Modelling Framework (GMF)[Ecl10b]. GMF, as part of the Eclipse Modelling Framework (EMF), provides means to define and generate partial as well as complete view types for EMF-based [Ecl10c] metamodels. However, GMF and other approaches were mostly driven in a pragmatic manner, lacking a sound and distinct basis concerning the construction of the view aspects. Thus, building views with these approaches requires a lot of additional manual effort and understanding to implement explicitly view-based models.

Garcia [Gar08] presented an approach that allows to define bidirectional transformations to employ a view synchronisation process. However, properties if views, such as partial, selective etc., are not considered by Garcia.

2.3. Existing Approaches for the Synchronisation of Views

Synchronisation of views with their underlying model is problem that has been tackled within different existing approaches. The approaches stem from different non-model driven areas, namely program inversion, data synchronisation as well as virtual view update. Additionally there are approaches that are based on model transformation (such as graph-grammar based transformation or QVT-Relations). These approaches will be evaluated here, with respect to the synchronisation properties defined in Section 4.5.3.1.

If a view is *complete* w.r.t. the underlying model, i.e., both can be completely reconstructed from each other, it is possible to employ approaches that do function inversion. An approach that presents a solution for this problem is given for so called *dual syntaxes* [BMS08]. The approach defines a visual language which pretty prints Abstract Syntax Trees (ASTs) accompanied by an XML-based syntax that is used for storing data and interchange with other tools. Both are complete views on the underlying data which are kept in sync automatically.

From the area of functional programming an approach for *program inversion* was introduced by Matsuda et al. [MHN+07] that for a given function $f(x_1, ..., x_n)$, determines its reverse so that $x_1, ..., x_n$ are given as output parameters. This approach implements the principles of bidirectional view transformations as presented in Section 4.5.3.1. Further usage of this approach for bidirectional transformations of XML documents as well as an approach for a mainstream language for view definition have been published in [LHT+07b] and [LHT07a] respectively. However, even though supporting textual views, problems that occur around partial and overlapping views as well as retainable, non displayed parts of the model(e.g., UUIDs) are not tackled by the approach.

Data synchronisation tries to solve problems when intermittently connected data sources (file-systems or address books on mobile and stationary devices) should be kept in sync. One representative of this area is the Focal language which was contributed by the Harmony project [FGM+07] introducing the concept of *lenses* as bidirectional transformations. Focal operates on tree-structured data such as XML and provides strong support for robustness and statically analysable synchronisations. However, on the other hand neither support for intermediately inconsistent states, nor means for retainment of certain elements (i.e., UUIDs) and protection of externally changed areas is provided.

A combined reference model- and view-based approach was introduced by Ehrig et al. in [EHTE97]. In this work the authors introduce the formal notions of views and view-relations based on graphs and graph-transformations. However, they do not consider overlapping and/or partial views explicitly, nor do they give an overview on possible formal properties of view based approaches. In addition, no textual views are considered.

Triple-graph grammars (TGG) as well as QVT-Relations with their support for bidirectional transformations also serve as foundation for several approaches that try to solve the view-update problem. Erche et al. [EWH07] identify that language specifications created based on metamodels do not include the connection between the concrete and abstract syntax. For this purpose they propose to employ QVT-Relations in order to bridge this gap. However, Erche et al. do not give hints to whether their approach can cope with partial view definitions or fulfils the requirements for bidirectional view transformations as proposed by Matsuda et al. [MHN⁺07]. Furthermore, the presented approach is not generic enough to be employed for textual view as well.

Sabetzadeh et al. [SE06] published an approach for view synchronisation that is able to cope with incomplete and inconsistent views on a single underlying model. They introduce a formalism, called annotated graphs, with a built-in annotation scheme for expressing incompleteness and inconsistency in views. Furthermore, they show provide a general algorithm for merging views with arbitrary interconnections. Sabetzadeh et al. provide a systematic way to represent the traceability information that is required for tracing the merged elements of a view back to their sources in the common model. However, the approach presented in their work only allows for the use of graph-based graphical views and does not include a notion of textual views.

Garcia [Gar08, Gar09] introduced an approach called Declarative Model View Controller (DMVC) which allows to define and statically analyse synchronisation transformation for view models.

In other, more specific domains such as the modelling of component-based software systems the concept of the idea of having a central model with different views on it has become popular [AS08]. The goal of this approach is to provide support for on-the-fly view generation for graphical as well as textual views. However, the actual approach is not elaborated within the paper. Atkinson et al. only handle very specific views that are implemented manually. Their approach supports different kinds of views (static component view, dynamic and allocation view as well as a textual view for the Java language) but has no capabilities for defining new views. Furthermore, it is not planned in [AS08] to provide support for persistent views (retaining all format information).

Andres et al. [PALG08], extended their multi-view DSL approach called AToM with textual DSLs. The approach is based on TGGs and allows for the generation of parsers and transformations from a grammar like specification. Even though, the approach uses TGGs, Andres et al. do not claim that their approach works bidirectionally for textual DSLs. Furthermore, problems that arise due to partial and overlapping textual views are also not tackled by AToM.

2.4. Existing Approaches for Language Engineering

In the area of compiler construction many approaches were developed that deal with incremental transformation of concrete and abstract syntax trees in general.

Attribute grammars can be used to specify context-dependant language features in a modular, declarative way. Traditional language-based editors use the derived attributed abstract syntax trees to internally represent programs. Many different algorithms have been developed that allow the incremental evaluation of these attributes upon local changes to this tree. The main goal of these algorithms was to make this evaluation optimal concerning time.

The following sections will shortly explain some of these approaches. However, as they operate on a different technical level, they are not analysed according to the classification scheme presented in Secion 2.5.1.

Mentor [DGHKL84] allows for the specification of a programming language using different means of specifications. With Centaur [BCD+89] the same authors present a next iteration of the approach with enhanced features. Using Centaur it becomes possible to define the *natural semantics* [Kah87] of a language with the use of Typol [Des84]. Centaur translates both, the specification as well as the programs, to Prolog which allows for type checking but on the down side results in a quite bad runtime behaviour.

The Cornell Program Synthesizer approach to incremental attribute evaluation presented by Reps et al. in [RTD83] is based on a certain model of input. In this model all actions that are performed in a language-based editor are mapped to the atomic functions *replace subtree* and *move cursor*. Using these basic operations the Reps et al. present algorithms that allow to identify the optimal set as well as order of attributes that need to be re-evaluated based upon the given changes. The Synthesizer Generator [RT84, RT89] is based on this approach and allows to automatically generate such a language-based editor for new languages. The approach uses attribute grammars to formulate the rules of a language.

The Programming System Generator [SH86] uses so called context-relations [Sne91] to define type inference rules for a language. In comparison to natural semantics, the context-relations approach is less flexible, does not allow to create forward references but enables for the evaluation of incomplete programs.

IPSEN [Nag96] is an approach that can be used to create tightly coupled development environments for languages. A special feature of this approach is the use of the graph replacement system PROGRES [Sch90] which allows for complex transformations. Furthermore, IPSEN allowed to define textual as well as graphical languages.

ASF+SDF [vdBHvD$^+$01] is a grammar based framework that allows for the the definition of a vast range of different languages. Is uses the formalism called Abstract Specification Formalism (ASF) for the specification of the abstract syntax. Additionally, the Syntax Definition Formalism allows for the specification of the concrete syntax including the mapping to the ASF-data structures. The use of scannerless parsing makes this approach capable of creating modular and reusable languages.

2.5. Existing Concrete Textual Syntax Modelling Approaches

The closest area of related work of this thesis stems from the area of textual modelling. This area defines metamodels as basis for their abstract syntax and provide different techniques on how to define a concrete textual syntax. As most of these approaches have a different focus and different capabilities, in order to classify them, this section first introduces a classification schema for this kind of approach. Based on this comprehensive schema, existing CTS approaches were analysed [GBU08].

2.5.1. Classification Schema

To be able to compare and classify different approaches that exist for the creation of a concrete textual syntax for a metamodel a systematic list of possible features of such an approach is needed. Feature diagrams [SHT06] were chosen to provide an overview on the available features. Figure 2.5 depicts a feature diagram of the features considered in this survey. The features shown in this figure are discussed in detail in the following subsections. How and if these features are provided by the actual approaches is shown in Tab. 2.1.

2.5.1.1. Supported Meta-metamodels (M_3)

Current approaches are based on different meta-metamodels: Ecore [Ecl10c], different versions of MOF 1.4 [Obj02] or 2.0 [Obj06] or the Kermeta meta-metamodel [MFJ05] used by Sintaks [JBK06]. Based on the capabilities of the meta-metamodels also the supported features of the textual syntax approaches vary. For example, MOF 1.4 uses UUIDs (in this case called MOFID) to identify model elements where Ecore uses designated key attributes. Because of these different approaches also the implementation

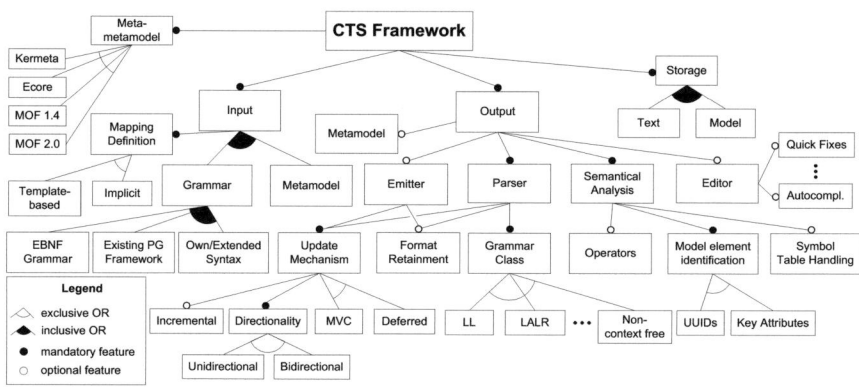

Figure 2.5.: Feature Diagram of all considered features

based on one of these meta-metamodels needs to support the respective identification mechanism (see Sect. 2.5.3 for a detailed discussion on this problem).

2.5.1.2. Input and Output

Depending on the use case for a textual language and its editor, different artifacts may already exist or need to be created. Possible combinations are:

1. Existing language specification, e.g. with a formal grammar, no metamodel exists. This is a typical use case when existing languages, i.e. Domain Specific Languages (DSL), should be integrated into a model driven development environment.

2. Existing metamodel, no specification for concrete syntax. For the development of a new concrete syntax based on an existing metamodel this is an important use case.

3. Both, concrete syntax definition and metamodel exist. For this use case the mapping definition needs to be flexible enough to bridge larger gaps between concrete and abstract syntax (e.g., OCL).

For frameworks which use a grammar as input it should also be distinguished if it is possible to use standard (E)BNF grammars or if a proprietary definition for the CTS constructs is needed. For approaches that specify the concrete syntax based on an existing metamodel a template-based approach that defines how each metamodel element is represented as text may be used. The components needed to translate back and forth between text and model—namely parser and emitter—are considered an output of the CTS framework. This is closely connected to the bidirectionality support of an approach because it is clear that if it only supports one direction, one of these components is not needed. For example, an approach only supporting the translation from the textual syntax to the model representation would not generate an emitter.

In Tab. 2.1 the following abbreviations denote the input and output parts of the CTS frameworks: E=Emitter, G=EBNF grammar, G_{pg}=Reuse of an existing parser generator grammar definition, G_s=Proprietary grammar definition, M_2=Metamodel, P=Parser, T=Templates for the concrete syntax.

2.5.1.3. Update Mechanism

There are two main possibilities how changes of the text can be reflected in the model. First, a Model View Controller (MVC) like approach may be used. Using an MVC-based editor, all changes to the textual representation are directly reflected in the model and vice versa. This means that there are only atomic commands that transform the model from one consistent state to another. Hence, it is at every point in time consistent. Second, a deferred update approach may be used. The parser is called from time to time or when the text is saved. However, intermediate states of the text may then be out of sync with the model because it may not always be possible to parse the text without syntactical errors. Such an approach is for instance used in the background parsing implementation of the Eclipse JDT project.

These approaches are identified in Tab. 2.1 by: mvc=Model View Controller, bg=Background parsing.

2.5.1.4. Incrementality

If the translation between text and model is done incrementally, only the necessary elements are changed rather than the whole text or model. For example, model elements are kept, if possible, when the text is re-parsed. Vice versa, changes to the model would only cause the necessary parts of the text to be updated. Especially when dealing with models in which model elements are identified by a UUID an incremental update approach becomes more desirable. Here, incrementality is important to keep the UUIDs of the model elements stable so that references from other models outside the current scope do not break. Therefore it is important not to re-create model elements every time a model is updated from its CTS. A detailed discussion on the issues that arise when using a CTS approach on top of a UUID-based repository is performed in Sect. 2.5.3. Even in a non UUID-based environment incrementality becomes important as soon as the textual representation reaches a certain size. Lexing, parsing, semantical analysis and instantiating model elements for the whole text causes a significant performance overhead.

In Tab. 2.1 the following abbreviations are used to distinguish these possibilities: y=Full support for incremental parsing/updating, n=No support for incremental updates, $y([p|e])$=Support only for incremental parsing(p) or emitting(e).

2.5.1.5. Format Retainment

If an emitter is used to translate models to their textual representation, users would expect that the format information of the text, such as whitespaces, is preserved. Furthermore, elements that are only present in the concrete syntax and not in the metamodel, as for example comments, also need to be retained. Especially when the textual representation is not explicitly stored but rather derived from the actual model (c.f., Sect. 2.5.1.12) format information has to be stored in addition to the model.

Possible values for this feature in Tab. 2.1 are the following: y=Format is retained upon re-emitting, n=No format retainment support.

2.5.1.6. Directionality

Bidirectional transformations between the abstract model representation and its CTS means that it is also possible to update existing textual representations if the model has changed. An initial emitter that produces a default text for a model can easily be produced using the information from the grammar or mapping definition. For a more sophisticated emitter, knowledge about formatting rules and format retainment is needed.

For updating existing representations, it would be expected that the user-defined format is retained. Imagine a textual editor that is used to create queries on business objects. Now an attribute in the business object model is renamed. This means that all references in the queries need to be updated. Hence, the queries need to be re-emitted from the model. For this case it would be desirable that the queries' format looks exactly the same as before that change rather than having the default format.

There are some difficult cases that should be considered: Imagine a series of inline "//" comments that the user aligned nicely. When the length of the identifier changes, it will be tricky to know what the user wanted with the formatting: aligned comments or a specific number of spaces/tabs between the last character of the statement and the "//" marker. Hence, perhaps there needs to be the possibility to specify the behaviour of such formatting rules within the mapping definition.

The following values are possible for this feature in Tab. 2.1: y=Completely bidirectional transformation, n=No bidirectionality supported, i=Creation of textual representation only initially.

2.5.1.7. Grammars Class

The parser component of an approach needs to have a grammar defined to be able to handle the textual input of the concrete syntax. Possible grammar classes are those of general-purpose programming languages such as LL or LALR [Muc97]. However, it might be possible that even non context-free grammars may be used as input. Another possibility where no grammar in a usual form is needed would be a pseudo text editing approach. In such an approach no text file is edited but all modifications are directly applied to the model using an MVC approach (c.f., Sect. 2.5.1.3).

The following grammar classes are considered for Tab. 2.1: LL(1/k/*), SLR, LR, LALR, ncf=Non-context free, dir.=Direct editing.

2.5.1.8. Semantical Analysis

After the parser has analysed the structure of the text document links between the resulting elements need to be created. For example, a method call expression in an OCL constraint that was just parsed needs to be linked to the corresponding operation model element. To represent these links, two different concepts may be used by the model repository, either by their UUID or by designated key attributes (c.f., Sect. 2.5.3). As the choice of one of these mechanisms has a great impact on the implementation of the CTS approach (also see Sect. 2.5.3) this feature is also listed in this classification schema.

The following abbreviations are used in Tab. 2.1: UUID=Identification via UUID, KeyAttr.=Identification by designated key attributes.

2.5.1.9. Operators

Especially in mathematical expressions the use infix operators is widely spread. During the semantical analysis the priorities, arities and associativities of such expressions habe to be resolved. To be able to automatically translate a textual representation of such an expression into its abstract model this information needs to be present in the mapping definition. If such an automated support is present this allows the gap between the metamodel and the grammar to be much bigger. For approaches that generate a metamodel from the mapping definition this feature is mostly implicitly supported since the operator precedence is then directly encoded in the generated metamodel.

In Tab. 2.1 a y means that explicit support for operators is built into the framework, p means partial support exists and n means that a manual translation is needed.

2.5.1.10. Symbol Table

A symbol table is needed to handle the resolving of references within the textual syntax. As there is, mostly, only the containment hierarchy explicitely present within a CTS a symbol table is needed during the parsing process to resolve other references that are stated using e.g., named references. The support for custom namespace contexts (such as blocks in Java) can also be an important feature of the employed symbol table.

Possible values for this feature in Tab. 2.1 are the following: y=full support including custom contexts, p=partial support without additional contexts, n=no built-in symbol table.

2.5.1.11. Features of the Generated Editor

Most approaches also generate a comfortable editor for the concrete syntax. Functionality that is based on the abstract syntax (such as auto-completion or error reporting) can be provided based on the model. If the tool also supports bidirectional transformation, refactoring support (such as renaming, etc.) may be easily implemented using the model. Other possible features are syntax highlighting or quick fixes.

Table 2.2 shows an overview on the features of the generated editors of each framework. The following features are considered: auto-completion, syntax highlighting, refactoring, error markers and quick fixes.

2.5.1.12. Storage mechanism

Having two kinds of representation, i.e. concrete textual syntax or abstract model, there are several possibilities to store the model. First, the model may be stored just using the concrete syntax. Second, only the abstract model is stored and the textual representation is derived on the fly whenever the textual editor opens the model. Then formatting information needs to be stored additionally to the model (c.f., Sect. 2.5.1.5). Third, both representations could be stored independent from each other. However, this means in most cases that they are not kept in sync with each other. Fourth, a hybrid approach may be implemented that stores the format information and merges them with the model when it is loaded into the editor. This additional format storage may then again be represented as an annotation model to the actual model or as some kind of textual template.

These different possibilities are identified in Tab. 2.1 using the following abbreviations: text=The textual representation is stored, mod.=The model is stored, both=Both representations are stored, hyb.=Hybrid storage approach.

2.5.2. Classification of Existing Concrete Textual Syntax Approaches

According to the classification schema presented in Sect. 2.5.1, several approaches were evaluated that present a possibility to create a model based CTS. Table 2.1 lists the supported features of each approach. Table 2.2 shows the features of a potentially generated editor. All evaluations were based on the cited works and prototypes that were available at the time of writing. Future work proposals of these sources were not considered.

2.5.2.1. Bridging Grammarware and Modelware

Grammar-based approaches are used to automatically generate a metamodel for the CTS. Those metamodels are closely related to the grammar elements for which they were created. This inherently causes the metamodel to be relatively large. Reduction rules can be used to reduce the amount of metamodel elements that are produced for elements in the grammar.

For example, a trivial mapping would generate a class c_{nt_k} for each non-terminal nt_k in the grammar as well as one class c_{alt_i} for each alternative alt_i of nt_k. Furthermore, an association ref_{alt_i} would be generated that connects the c_{alt_i} to their c_{nt_k}. The c_{alt_i} then reference the corresponding c_{nt_j} for the referenced non-terminals nt_j of alt_i. One reasonable reduction rule for this scenario is: if nt_k references only alt_i with only one referenced non-terminal each, the ref_{alt_i} as well as c_{alt_i} could be omitted, reducing the whole structure to a direct generalisation between the c_{nt_j} and c_{nt_k}.

Some of these reduction rules can be applied automatically during the metamodel generation, while others need additional information given as annotations to the grammars.

Table 2.1.: Comparison of related approaches.

Name(s)	Ref.	Input	Output	Bid.	Updates	Inc.	Grammars	Format	M_3	Ident.	Oper.	Symb. Tab.	Storage
Bridging GW and MW	[WK05]	G	M_2, P, E	y	bg	n	LL(k)	n	Ecore	KeyAttr.	*n/a*	p	both
Frodo	[Kar07]	G or G_{PG}, M_2, T[a]	P, E	y	bg	n	LL(*)	n	Ecore	KeyAttr.	n	p	both
Gr. Bsd. Code Transf.	[Gol06]	G_{PG}[b]	M_2, P, E	y	bg	n	LALR(1)	y	MOF 1.4	KeyAttr.	*n/a*	p	both
Gymnast	[GS07]	G	M_2, P, E	y[c]	bg	n	LL(k/*)	y	Ecore	KeyAttr.	*n/a*	n	both
HUTN	[Obj04]	M_2	G, P, E	y	bg/mvc[d]	n	*n/a*[d]	n	MOF 1.4	KeyAttr.	n	p	*n/a*[d]
MPS	[Jet]	G_s	M_2, P, E	y	mvc	y?[e]	*n/a*	y	prop.	UUID	y	y	mod.
MontiCore	[KRV07a]	$I(M_2, G)$[f]	P, E	y	bg	n	LL(k)	n	Ecore	KeyAttr.	n	y	text
TCS	[JBK06]	M_2, T	G, P, E	y	bg	n	LL(*)	n	Ecore	KeyAttr.	y	y	both
Sintaks	[Fon07]	M_2, T	G, P, E	y	bg	n	LL(*)	n	Kermeta	KeyAttr.	p	p	both
TEF	[Sch07]	M_2, T	G, P	n	bg	n	*LR	n	Ecore	KeyAttr.	y	y	text[g]
xText	[Fou10]	G_s	M_2, P	n	bg	n	LL(*)	n	Ecore	KeyAttr.	y	p	text

Legend:

Input/Output: E=Emitter, G=Grammar, G_s=Own Grammar Definition, G_{pg}=Reuse of parser generator framework grammar definition, M_2=Metamodel, P=Parser, T=Templates for the CS

Updates: bg=Background parsing, mvc.=Model View Controller based

Storage: mod.=Model

[a]Frodo allows the import of standard EBNF or ANTLR grammars that can then be annotated with mapping rules.

[b]Currently there are implementations for SableCC and ANTLR

[c]Navigation only, no transformation from model to text.

[d]This depends on the actual implementation of the HUTN standard.

[e]Supported somehow due to MVC approach.

[f]The metamodel as well as the concrete syntax are defined within the same file.

[g]It is possible to directly access the underlying model via a special implementation of the Eclipse DocumentProvider interface.

Wimmer and Kramler [WK05] present such an approach. A multi-phase automatic generation that facilitates reduction rules as well as manual annotations reduces this amount to make the resulting metamodel more usable. The reduction steps that are applied during these phases then also implicitly define the mapping between the mapping definition. The main area where such an approach is useful is the Architecture Driven Modernisation (ADM)[Obj] where existing legacy code is analysed for migration, documentation or gathering of metrics.

2.5.2.2. Frodo

Frodo [Kar07] was developed with the goal to provide a unified solution for the creation of a DSL. This approach presents an end-to-end solution for textual DSLs, providing support for the creation of a CTS as well as back-end support for the target DSL. It also makes initial attempts to derive a debugging support from the mapping specification. Frodo supports several sources for the definition of the CTS. Either a grammar metamodel may be specified or a specific grammar for a supported parser generator (currently ANTLR) could be used. An implicit mapping from the grammar to the DSL metamodel is automatically created. This is done by matching the names of classes and attributes to elements in the grammar rules. Additional mapping rules, such as those needed for the resolving of references between model elements can be specified on the grammar metamodel.

2.5.2.3. Grammar Based Code Transformation for MDA

The approach elaborated in [Gol06], similar to **Bridging Grammarware and Modelware**, also relies on reduction and annotations to the grammar. However, this approach additionally facilitates the storage of format information as a decorator model attached to the actual model.

2.5.2.4. Sintaks (TCSSL)

Fondement [Fon07] presents an bidirectional approach that generates a parser (based on the ANTLR parser generator) and an emitter (using the JET template engine). The mapping definition is created using the MOF concrete syntax. For complex mappings which need several passes, e.g., for resolving references or performing type checking, a multiple pass analysis can be integrated into the mapping. The main idea of this approach is to have an n-pass architecture for the transformation from code to model. Intermediate models are hereby treated as models decorated with refinements. Model transformations are then used to subsequently transform these models and finally create the abstract model that then conforms to the target metamodel.

2.5.2.5. MontiCore

Another approach to integrate a textual concrete syntax with a corresponding metamodel is presented by Krahn et al. in [KRV07a]. This approach facilitates an integrated definition where the abstract syntax (the metamodel) is also defined within a grammar like definition of the concrete syntax. For simple languages and especially for languages where only one form of presentation, i.e. the textual syntax, is used, this approach seems to be promising. However, if a metamodel may have several presentation forms, or if only parts of the metamodel are represented as text, the tight integration of concrete and abstract syntax this approach promotes does not seem to be applicable. MontiCore allows the composition and inheritance of different languages and provides a comfortable support for generating editors from these composite specifications [KRV07b].

2.5.2.6. HUTN

The Human-Usable Text Notation (HUTN) approach [Obj04], now specified as a standard by the Object Management Group (OMG) can be used to generate a standard textual language for a given metamodel. It focuses on an easy-to-understand syntax as well as the completeness of the language (it is able to represent all possible metamodel instances). Furthermore all languages, though each language is different, conform to a single style and structure and it is not possible to define an own syntax for a metamodel. In HUTN a grammar for a metamodel, including parser and emitter is generated.

There were currently only two implementations for HUTN. An early implementation was developed by the DSTC, named TokTok. However, this implementation is not available anymore. Another implementation was developed by Muller and Hassenforder [MH05], who examined the applicability of HUTN as a bridge between models and concrete syntaxes. They identified several flaws in the specification that make it difficult to use.

2.5.2.7. TEF

The first version of the Textual Editing Framework (TEF) presented in [Sch07] was based on an MVC updating approach. Inherent problems with this concept (see Sect. 2.5.3) led to the choice of background parsing as the final method for updating the model. An interesting feature of TEF that is not directly mentioned in the classification schema is the possibility to define multiple syntactic constructs for the same metamodel element. Vice-versa, it is also possible to use the same notation for different elements by providing a semantic function that selects the correct function based on the context.

2.5.2.8. JetBrains MPS

JetBrains developed a framework called Meta Programming System (MPS) [Jet, Dim05] that allows to define languages that consist of syntactical elements that look like dynamically-arranged tables or forms. This means, that the elements of the language are predefined boxes which can be filled with a value. MPS follows the MVC updating approach that allows for direct editing of the underlying model. This allows the editor to easily provide features such as syntax highlighting or code completion. However, it is not possible to write code that does not conform to the language. Hence, a copy, paste, adapt process is not possible in this approach.

2.5.2.9. xText

Developed as part of the openArchitectureWare (oAW) framework, xText [Fou10] allows the definition of a CTS within the oAW context. xText generates an intermediate metamodel for the concrete syntax from the mapping specification. For this reason the framework provides an EBNF-like definition language which facilitates features like the possibility to specify identity properties or abstract classes. A translation into an instance of the intended target metamodel needs to be done by developing a model to model transformation from this intermediate language into the target abstract syntax. Having such an intermediate metamodel complicates the bidirectional mapping as an additional transformation for the backward transformation is needed.

2.5.2.10. Gymnast

Garcia and Sentossa present an approach called Gymnast in [GS07], which similar to xText generates an intermediate language on which the editor is based. Refactorings,

Table 2.2.: Editor capabilities

Name	Reference(s)	Autocomp.	Err. mark.	Refact. supp.	Quick fixes
Frodo	[Kar07]	n	?[a]	n	n
Gymnast	[GS07]	y	y	y	n
MPS	[Jet]	y	y[b]	y	y
MontiCore	[KRV07b]	y	y	y	n
TCS	[JBK06]	n	y	n	n
TEF	[Sch07]	y	y	y	n
xText	[Fou10]	y	y	y	n

[a]This feature could not be evaluated.
[b]No syntactic errors possible because of resolute MVC concept.

occurrence markings, etc., are provided by the generated editor based. As this work's main focus is on the generation of the editor and its functionality, a mapping to an existing target metamodel has to be developed in addition to the generated tools.

2.5.2.11. TCS

A similar technique is presented in [JBK06]. This approach also provides a generic editor for the syntaxes handled by TCS. For each syntax that is defined using TCS, there is also a definition that can be registered in the editor. Within this definition, it can, for example, be specified how the syntax highlighting should be done. This editor uses text-to-model trace-links that are created during parsing to allow hyperlinks and hovers for references within the text. However, currently these links are implemented as attributes (column and line number of the corresponding text) on a mandatory base class (LocatedElement) for all metamodel elements handled by a TCS editor. If the metamodel classes do not extend these class, the trace functionality is disabled. In later versions of TCS, this issue might be resolved. The mapping definition of a TCS syntax is tightly coupled to the metamodel, which means that for each element in the metamodel there is one rule describing its textual notation. This tight coupling makes the definition of a syntax relatively easy. With the use of so called operator templates TCS furthermore allows to resolve left recursions [Muc97] as they occur in LL grammars.

2.5.2.12. Other Approaches

A recently emerged project on eclipse.org that also aims to tackle the development of CTSs is the **Eclipse IMP** [FCS+10]. However, the current focus of the project lies on the easy development of an editor and not on the integration with a model repository. Still, it was stated in the project's declaration of intent that an integration with EMF is projected. Furthermore, there is an eclipse.org project called **Textual Modelling Framework (TMF)**[Fou] that currently regroups TCS and xText under a common architecture. A different approach is followed by Intentional Software's **Intentional Programming** [Sim07]. Here, it seems to be possible to directly edit the model using a text editor. Multiple syntaxes, also textual ones, can be defined and handled even in the same editor. However, being a proprietary approach, the integration with existing standards-based repositories may be problematic.

2.5.3. Discussion

Current CTS implementations span a continuum between text and model affine-frameworks. On the text-end-side there are tools that stem from conventional programming languages. The idea to create development tools that are based on a model rather than on plain text was already developed before model-driven development became prominent. The IDE of Smalltalk systems follows a similar paradigm. Code artifacts are also Smalltalk objects that are edited using a specialised editor. Especially considering refactoring, this is a great advantage. Another example where boundaries between a textual and a model view on code are starting to blur is the Eclipse Java Development Tools (JDT) project. Even though the Java source files are still stored as plain text files, JDT uses indexes and meta-data in the background to be able to provide comprehensive refactoring, navigation and error reporting capabilities. Many tools that were considered here (such as Gymnast or xText) focus on this end of the spectrum. On the other end of this spectrum, there are tools such as the MPS framework treating text as a sequence of frames or compartments containing text blocks. While text-based issues such as diff or merge are solved on text artifacts, solutions for these problems are still immature concerning models. Vice versa, issues that can easily be or are already solved on models, such as the usage of UUIDs for references or partial and combined views on models are challenges that none of the currently available CTS approaches is able to handle.

As it can be seen in Tab. 2.1 support for incremental model updates is currently not widely available. Only MPS provides some support for this. Furthermore, none of the approaches under evaluation support the UUID identification mechanism for model elements. Even HUTN, which is an OMG standard explicitly specifies that key attributes need to be specified in order to realise model element identification. That lack of these features complicates the application of these approaches in certain environments. The next sections discuss some of the yet untreated issues.

2.5.3.1. Universally Unique Identifiers

The UUID retainment problem, as discussed in the introduction of this thesis (cf. Section 1.1), is also not tackled by any of the presented CTS approaches. Some kind of incremental update mechanism is required to solve this problem, which none of the existing approaches includes. Otherwise, UUIDs of model elements will get lost upon the re-transformation of the textual representation to the model. MPS, not relying on parser techniques, avoids this problem by employing a MVC-like approach for model updates. However, also MPS does not guarantee that UUIDs will be retained.

2.5.3.2. Update Mechanism

Many of the aforementioned problems may be solved by employing an MVC-based update mechanism. However, there are still other problematic constructs in this concept. Consider for example an expressions such as "(a+b)*c": At the time of typing the expression in the parentheses, it can not be known that the model that actually should be created would have the "*" expression as root node and the parenthesised expression only as a subnode. A discussion of the advantages and disadvantages of the MVC and the background parsing approach can be found in [Sch07].

Closely related to the update issue is the general problem of incremental updates. In compiler construction literature this problem was already discussed. For example, Wagner [Wag98] developed a methodology that allows incremental lexing as well as parsing. Furthermore, Reps et. al. [RTD83] present an incremental process that allows incremental updates to the attributed trees that result from the semantical analysis. However, such techniques were not adopted by any of the CTS frameworks under evaluation.

2.5.3.3. Partial and Combined Views

One advantage of graphical modelling is that it is easily possible to define partial views on models. This means that it is possible to create diagrams that highlight only a specific aspect of the model while hiding other parts. for example, in UML one diagram may be used to display an inheritance hierarchy of classes only while another diagram is used to show the associations between these classes. Defining models with a CTS should also include the possibility to do this. However, this imposes that there are two different modes for deleting elements. One, which deletes only the text and another which deletes the model element from the text *and* the model. Using only standard text editing techniques (typing characters and using backspace or delete to remove them) there is no possibility to distinguish between both commands.

None of the approaches analysed above deals with the possibility to explicitly define partial or overlapping view types on the underlying metamodel. Therefore, also no support for custom selections of elements within the textual representation (cf. Section 4.5.1) is given.

Chapter 3.

Retainment Policies for Model Transformations

Models that are used in a model-driven environment are at the same time subject to modification by users as well as automated transformations. As the transformations in such an environment should aim to support the modellers in their work, it should be possible to configure them in a way that best fits the requirements of a modeller with respect to the changes that they perform to the model.

One such requirement is, as depicted in Figure 3.1, the retainment of changes that a modeller applies to the target model of a transformation (or a part thereof). In some scenarios it becomes necessary that those changes to target models should be preserved rather than overwritten by a re-execution of the transformation. One of the most prominent cases for such a requirement is the creation of an initial or default model using a model transformation that is then refined by the modeller. Of course, those refinements should not be overwritten if the transformation is re-executed. However, simply omitting the re-execution is also not practicable as maybe a lot of additional default model elements should be created by the transformation due to additional elements in the source model of the transformation.

This issue becomes even more important when multiple transformations have the same model as their target model. In this case model elements that are considered to be created/modified by more than one transformation can cause conflicts as well as inconsistencies. If for example, one transformation is responsible for creating a certain element in the target model, whereas another transformation contains rules that would delete the same model element, executing both transformations leads to different results depending on the order in which the transformations are executed.

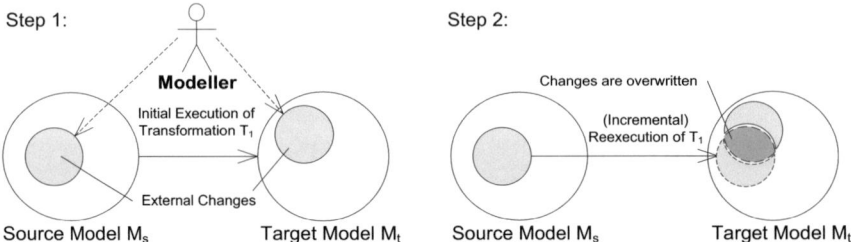

Figure 3.1.: Step 1: Initial execution of T_1 produces M_t from M_s. A modeller applies changes to both M_s and M_t. Step 2: Changes in M_t will be overwritten by the reexecution of T.

3.1. Scientific Challenges

From these findings the following scientific challenges can be derived:

- In order to support retainment of external changes to target models, first an approach needs to be defined that allows for the identification of these changes.

- How can external changes in target models be preserved when the target model is also subject to modification by a transformation? A generic solution ought to be found that supports the specification of how the transformation should deal with these changes as soon at it is re-executed.

- How can the solution be defined in a generic way so that it is applicable to the multitude of model transformation approaches that currently exists. The solution shall be agnostic w.r.t. the employed model transformation technique and shall be defined on an abstract level.

- Assuming, the retainment is controlled by some kind of rules, i.e., so called retainment rules, how can these retainment rules be attached and declared in an easy to use and intuitive way? The way of specifying these rules should be possible without needing to extend the transformation language.

- How to define a framework that supports the execution of model transformations including the defined semantics of the attached retainment policies.

3.2. Contributions

This thesis contributes an approach that allows to define generic rules for model transformations that define how to deal with external changes to the transformation's target model.

- The first contribution of this chapter is an approach that deals with the problem of identifying arbitrary external changes to models that are, at the same time, source or target models of automated model transformations. In this thesis, a change identification approach is introduced that is based on the record of the transformation that is created during its execution, which is called *trace of the transformation*. The approach is defined on an abstract level, based on the formal semantics of a transformation's definition and execution.

- Second, the approach presented in this thesis introduces means for the specification of so-called *Retainment Policies* that can be declared to describe how changes to a target model shall be treated upon re-execution of a transformation.

- The semantics of these retainment policies are defined in an abstract and formal way which allows to transfer them to arbitrary model transformation approaches.

- Included in the presented approach is also a way to attach the retainment policies to either transformation rules or directly to certain areas of the involved models. Based on these defined scopes, an approach is presented that dynamically reconfigures the employed transformation according to the rules and their defined scopes.

- A new *higher-order transformation* is presented that automatically modifies the existing transformation in a way that includes the semantics of the attached retainment policies. Concretely, a realisation of the retainment policies approach for the OMG's standard for model transformations, called Query, View, Transformation (QVT) [Obj11] is given.

In this chapter, first a classification of model changes is introduced. This thesis provides an approach that allows for detection of target model changes based on the execution trace of a transformation which is presented afterwards. For each kind of change special *retainment policies* are introduced that may be attached to either elements in the target model or transformations themselves. These policies allow for a distinctive treatment of changes to a transformation's target model. Additionally, this thesis presents

61

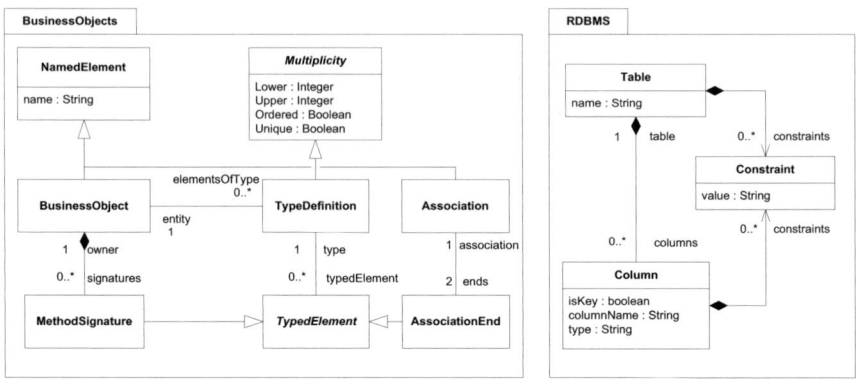

Figure 3.2.: Metamodels of business objects and relational databases showing the elements relevant for the running example.

the formal semantics of these policies and uses them to reason about completeness and conflict resolution.

3.3. Running Example

The running example that will be used to explain all kinds of retainment scenarios employs a domain model representing business entities as well as associations between them as presented in Chapter 2 on Page 18 as source model. This model is transformed to a relational database target model used to store the data represented by the business entity model. The relevant parts of both metamodels are shown in Figure 3.2.

The example model, as depicted in Figure 3.3 consists of a simple business entity "Customer" having two associations, one to the business entity "PurchaseOrder" and one from "PurchaseOrder" to "Invoice". The relational database model is generated using the transformation T_{bo2db} shown in Listing 3.1.

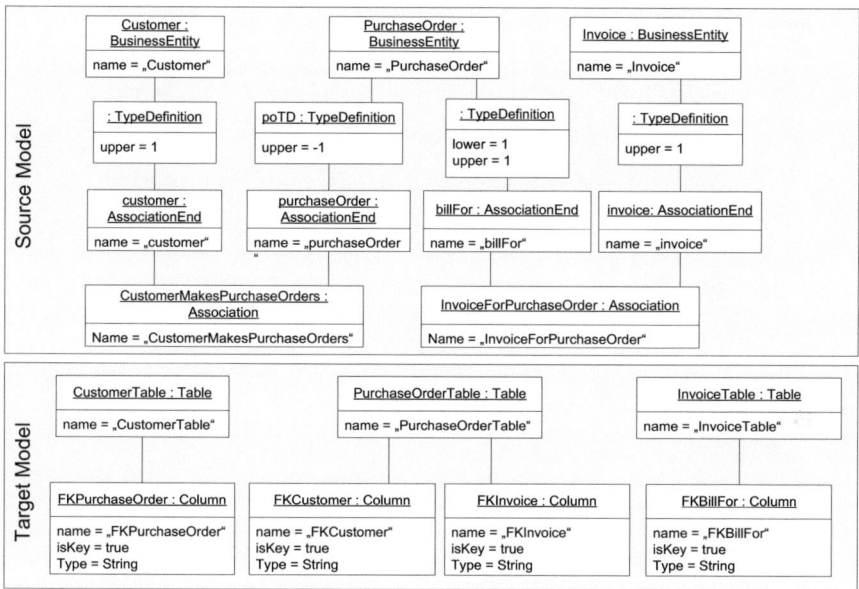

Figure 3.3.: Example model showing source and target model of a business entity model to relational database transformation.

A formal representation of the target model given in Figure 3.3 using Definition 2.3 is then the tuple as follows:

$$
M_t = \left(\begin{array}{l}
O = \{\text{CustomerTable, PurchaseOrderTable, InvoiceTable, FKCustomer,} \\
\qquad \text{FKPurchaseOrder, FKInvoice, FKBillFor}\}, \\
L = \{\text{CustomerTable} \leftrightarrow \text{FKPurchaseOrder,} \\
\qquad \text{PurchaseOrderTable} \leftrightarrow \text{FKCustomer,} \\
\qquad \text{PurchaseOrderTable} \leftrightarrow \text{FKInvoice, InvoiceTable} \leftrightarrow \text{FKBillFor}\}, \\
V = \{\text{``CustomerTable'', ``PurchaseOrderTable'', ``InvoiceTable'', \dots}\}, \\
orderL = \{(\text{PurchaseOrderTable} \leftrightarrow \text{FKCustomer,} \\
\qquad \text{PurchaseOrderTable} \leftrightarrow \text{FKInvoice})\} \\
orderV = \varnothing
\end{array} \right.
$$

63

```
 1  transformation BO2DB (bo : businessObjects, db : rdbms) {
 2    top relation BusinessObject2Table {
 3      checkonly domain bo myBo : businessObjects::BusinessObject{
 4        elementsOfType = td : businessObjects::TypeDefinition { }
 5      };
 6      enforce domain db table : rdbms::Table {
 7        tableName = myBo.name
 8      };
 9    };
10
11    top relation Association2ForeignKeyColumn {
12      checkonly domain bo assoc : businessObjects::Association{
13        ends = end : businessObjects::AssociationEnd {
14          type = td : businessObjects::TypeDefinition {
15            entity = bo : businessObjects::BusinessObject{}
16          }
17        }
18      };
19      enforce domain db keyColumn : rdbms::Column {
20        table = tab;                isKey = true;
21        name = 'FK' + end.name; type = 'String'
22      }
23      when {
24        BusinessOject2Table(myBo, tab);
25      }
26    }
27  }
```

Listing 3.1: Example Transformation: BusinessObjects to Relational Database Model.

A transformation that realises the mapping within the given example is sketched in Listing 3.1. The transformation is written in the QVT Relations language and consists of two top level relations BusinessOject2Table and Association2ForeignKeyColumn. While BusinessObject2Table creates a Table for each BusinessObject, Association2ForeignKeyColumn is responsible for the creation of one foreign key Column per Association within the corresponding target Table.

3.4. Assumptions for the Application of the Retainment Policy Approach

As there exists a multitude of model transformation approaches it is impossible to develop an approach that fits all of them equally. The *Retainment Policies* approach is based on some basic assumptions with respect to the employed model transformation approach. However, if these assumptions are fulfilled it can be applied to arbitrary model transformation approaches.

- **Unique Object Identities:** All elements involved in the model transformation have a UUID which is immutable and cannot be reconstructed in any case. This means, a newly created element will always have a new UUID. In distributed development this is an important requirement as links between elements that are currently not in the scope of the modelling environment might break upon changes to these elements.

- **No time component:** The time between subsequent executions of the transformation is not defined. Arbitrary changes might have been applied to the source as well as the target model between two subsequent transformation executions.

- **Unidirectional transformations:** The retainment policy approach presented in this chapter is based on having a distinct source and target model. For bidirectional transformations both "sides" can be considered source or target model. However, during the execution of a bidirectional transformation there are distinct source and target sides. Therefore, the presented approach – though being only active for one side at a time – is in general also applicable to bidirectional transformations.

3.5. Classification of Changes to Target Models

To be able to decide if a target model change should be retained or not, changes that can be applied to the target model need to be classified into different types of changes. For the formal description of the changes, the definitions of atomic and complex changes given in Chapter 2 on page 2.4 are used here.

3.5.1. Images of Transformations

A transformation is considered to be responsible for creating, deleting and updating elements that are in their *image*, meaning that they potentially could have been produced by the transformation. Elements that lie outside the image of the transformation are invisible to the transformation and will therefore be ignored during the execution of the transformation. Changes that lie *inside* the image of the transformation need to be detected in order to be handled by the transformation. Additionally, a target

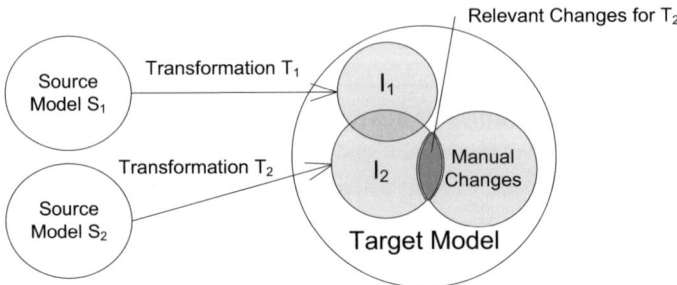

Figure 3.4.: Transformations may have different images within a target model. Transformation T_1 only "sees" the elements of the target model that lie in its image I_1 wheres T_2 only "sees" I_2. Therefore, the mannual changes to the target model are only relevant for T_2.

model may be handled and updated by more than one transformation. Figure 3.4 illustrates how different transformations have different images in the target model. Due to this determination the change detection distinguishes between two different types of changes, *relevant* changes and *non-relevant* changes. *Non-relevant* changes are changes that are not matched by the right model pattern of a transformation – e.g., δ_o^+ where $o \notin rightModelPattern(T)$ – are not relevant for a transformation. Second, *relevant* changes are those changes that are matched by the right model pattern of a transformation, e.g., δ_o^+ where $o \in rightModelPattern(T)$.

An approach on how to compute the set of relevant changes from a set of changes to the target model is presented by Hettel in [Het10]. However, Hettel does not consider that manual changes should be retained in target models. He is rather concerned with the synchronisation of these changes back to the source model. Furthermore, note that images of transformations may overlap and it is therefore possible that changes to the same element within a target model is considered *relevant* for several transformations at the same time.

Considering the running example from Figure 3.2 on page 62 and Listing 3.1 on page 64 it can easily be recognised that transformation T_{BO2DB} could never produce an instance of the class Constraint. Therefore, every change in the target model concerning an instance of Constraint would be automatically classified as a *non-relevant* change with respect to the BO2DB transformation because it is always outside the image of the transformation.

3.5.2. Consistent Changes

Atomic changes are by definition the minimal set of changes that can be applied to a model. However, it might still be possible that the application of an atomic change leads to consistency violations in a model. For example, the deletion of an element will cause all links that included this element to become inconsistent (cf. model consistency rules in [AS07]). In order to make the model consistent again, additional changes, in this case the deletion of all links that included the deleted element need to be performed. In order to reflect this set of changes the definition of a *complex change* is introduced. A complex change consists of the original atomic change plus all additional changes that are required to yield a consistent model.

Another example for an atomic change that is extended to be a *consistent change* is the creation of a model element a in the target model. This is followed by the creation of a link l that compositely attaches the created object a to another existing model element b. If l is not created a is considered a free floating element within the target model which might violate model constraints such as the requirement that there is only one "root" element per model[1].

Definition 3.1 (Consistent Change). *A consistent change ∇_δ is defined as a set of changes that need to be perfomed in addition to δ to keep the model to which δ is applied in a consistent state. This set is then defined as $\nabla = \delta \cup \Delta_f$ where*

δ is the original change and,
Δ_f is a complex change which is a set of subsequent changes

$$\left\{ \delta_i \in \Delta_f \mid \begin{pmatrix} \delta_i \text{ is required to hold the model in a consistent state,} & \vee \\ \delta_i \text{ is relevant for the context of } \delta, & \end{pmatrix} \right\}$$

Δ_f may also be the empty set $\varnothing$.

Furthermore, the set of all possible consistent changes of metamodel MM is denoted as ConsistentChanges$_{MM}$.

For example, considering again the running example model from Figure 3.3. The deletion of Column "FKInvoice" yields the deletion change $\delta^-_{\text{FKInvoice}}$. As there was also

---

[1]This is for example a constraint that applies to models in the Eclipse Modelling Environment (EMF) [Ecl10c]

a link Invoice $\leftrightarrow$ FKInvoice attached connecting FKInvoice to Invoice, the consistent change for $\delta^-_{\text{FKInvoice}}$ would be

$$\nabla_{\delta^-_{\text{FKInvoice}}} = \left\{ \delta^-_{\text{FKInvoice}}, \delta^-_{\text{Invoice}\leftrightarrow2\text{FKInvoice},\text{Invoice},\text{FKInvoice}} \right\}$$

The creation a `Column` ColAmount and adding it to the `column` property of the existing object Invoice by creating a link $\delta^+_{\text{Invoice}\leftrightarrow\text{ColAmount},\text{Invoice},\text{ColAmount}}$ will result in a consistent change

$$\nabla_{\delta^+_{\text{ColAmount}}} = \left\{ \delta^+_{\text{ColAmount}}, \delta^+_{\text{Invoice2ColAmount},\text{Invoice},\text{ColAmount}} \right\}$$

The function $consistentChanges$ that yields the set of consistent changes for a given set of changes is defined as $consistentChanges : \mathcal{P}(Changes_{MM}) \to \mathcal{P}(Changes_{MM})$.

3.6. Detection of Relevant Changes

In order to retain changes to the target model of a model transformation, the first thing that needs to be done is to identify those changes. Transformations should be enabled to individually react upon different kinds of small-grained external changes. Thus, it is a requirement to identify these modifications and make them available to the transformation.

3.6.1. Trace of a Transformation

To ensure traceability and to be able to compute actions that decide on the retainment of changes in the target model, the transformation runtime has to create a *transformation trace*. A trace can be seen as a record of the execution of the transformation run, it stores which rule was triggered by which element from the source model and which target model elements were produced by its execution. Many transformation approaches use implicit trace models that are automatically created during the execution of the transformation. For example, the Query/View/Transformation (QVT) [Obj11] specification states that for the relations as well as the operational language implicit trace classes are derived from the transformation rules. Other approaches such as triple graph grammars [HG09] use a so-called correspondence graph that resembles the trace between a source and a target model. These traces are then used to incrementally execute a transformation, updating only those elements in the target model where the corresponding elements in the source model have changed.

The granularity of these links is mostly defined on a per transformation rule basis. For example, in QVT Relations each relation implicitly defines a trace class that is instantiated each time the relation matches a source model / target model pattern. Hence, if multiple transformation act on the same models, each of them has its own trace model that refers to the elements that lie inside the image of the respective transformations.

Alternatively, trace models can be created by explicitly adding additional transformation rules to the transformation that create, read and update trace model. However, this technique is less common as it implies a large overhead when writing a transformation.

Based on the transformation trace, changes to the corresponding models can be detected. As the change detection mechanism used in the approach presented in this thesis also relies on trace models, and trace models mostly rely on some rule structure in the transformation, a formal description of the change detection also requires a formal representation of rules in transformations. The original formal definition of a transformation (cf. Definition 2.7 on page 25), as presented by Amelunxen et al. [AS07], does only introduce the notion of a transformation having a left and a right model pattern that define the transformation. To apply rule based trace models in this formalisation, a formal definition of a rule based transformation as well as the trace for a rule based transformation is given below. Based on these definitions the change detection approach will be defined in later sections.

Definition 3.2 (Rule-Based Transformation). *A rule-based transformation is defined as a transformation where the left and right model patterns are grouped into rules that are atomic with respect to their usage in the application of the transformation. For a rule based transformation the function $rules : Transformations_{MM} \rightarrow \mathcal{P}(Transformations_{MM})$ partitions the left and right model patterns of a transformation into a sequence of rules, which are pairs of smaller model patterns which represent the rules of a transformation. Therefore the definition of a rule-based transformation is given in the following way: $T := (M_l, M_r, rules)$.*

69

For example, the formal representation of the T_{bo2db} transformation applied to the business objects Customer and PurchaseOrder from the running example model, given in Section 3.3, consists of the following left and right model patterns:

$$lmp(T_{bo2db}) = \{Customer, PurchaseOrder, purchaseOrder, customer\}$$
$$rmp(T_{bo2db}) = \{CustomerTable, PurchaseOrderTable, FKPurchaseOrder,$$
$$FKCustomer\}$$

A partitioning into rules would result in a partitioning of the left model pattern into the two rules (the relations as they are present in the QVT-R representation of T_{bo2db}) $r_{BO2Table}$ and $r_{Association2FKColumn}$ where

$$rules(T_{bo2db}) = \{r_{BO2Table}, r_{Association2FKColumn}\}$$
$$lmp(r_{BO2Table}) = \{Customer, PurchaseOrder, Invoice\}$$
$$rmp(r_{BO2Table}) = \{CustomerTable, PurchaseOrderTable\}$$
$$lmp(r_{Association2FKColumn}) = \{customer, purchaseOrder\}$$
$$rmp(r_{Association2FKColumn}) = \{FKCustomer, FKPurchaseOrder\}$$

The partitioning left and right model patterns given by $rules$ partitions the transformation patterns in a ways such that the right model pattern of each rule is disjoint with the respective other rules. This is required to keep the semantics of the transformation. If there would be more than one rule having the right model pattern those element would be produced multiple times, once for each occurrence in a rule. This would change the semantics of a transformation producing exactly the model that is represented by its right model pattern.

In the running example from Listing 3.1, the partitioning of the left and right model patterns would be done according to the two relations. Each relation then represents a rule. For example relation `BusinessObject2Table`, the left model pattern is defined as

Definition 3.3 (Trace of a Transformation Application). *Let MM be a metamodel and let $M_s, M_t \in Models_{MM}$ be the source respectively target model of the transformation's application. Furthermore, let $\leadsto_T$ be the application of the transformation $T \in Transformations_{MM}$. Then a trace of a transformation application is a tuple:*

$$Trace = (T, M_l, M_r, \Theta, source, target, rule)$$

where

T denotes the transformation of which the trace is a record,
M_l, M_r *denote the source and target models of the transformation application,*
Θ *denotes a finite set of trace links,*
$source : \Theta \rightarrow \mathcal{P}(M_l)$ *yields the set of source elements of a trace link,*
$target : \Theta \rightarrow \mathcal{P}(M_r)$ *yields the set of target elements of a trace link.*
$rule : \Theta \rightarrow rules(T)$ *yields the rule from the transformation that was responsible for the*
   creation of the trace link.

Furthermore, $Traces_{T,MM}$ *denotes the set of all possible traces for a given transform-ation T and metamodel MM.*

3.6.1.1. Consistency Rules for the Trace of a Transformation

The information that is stored within a trace model needs to be kept up-to-date when the transformation performs changes to a target model. The following consistency rules have to be fulfilled in order to have a consistent trace model that can be used for change detection. For the trace to be consistent after a transformation run, the following consistency rules need to hold. These rules are given for each change type that is performed by the transformation during its run.

δ_o^+ : If an element o is added by the transformation, there also needs to be a trace link θ that refers to the element:

$$\forall r \in rules(T) : \exists \theta \in \Theta : rule(\theta) = r \wedge o \in rightModelPattern(r) \rightarrow o \in target(\theta)$$

The same applies analogously for link additions δ_{l,o_1,o_2}^+ and setting of attribute values $\delta_{o,a,v}^s$.

δ_o^- : If an element o is deleted by the transformation also the trace link that referred to the target element needs to be deleted:

$$\forall r \in rules(T) : \nexists \theta \in \Theta : rule(\theta) = r \wedge o \in rightModelPattern(r) \rightarrow o \in target(\theta)$$

The same applies analogously for link removals δ_{l,o_1,o_2}^+ as well as $\delta_{o,a,v}^s$.

71

$\delta^o_{l_1,l_2}$ For a change in ordering of links l_1, l_2 the corresponding order of tracelinks needs to be adapted accordingly.

$$\forall r \in rules(T) : \forall \theta_1 \theta_2 \in \Theta : (rule(\theta_1) = r \wedge rule(\theta_2) = r$$
$$\wedge\ l_1 \in target(\theta_1) \wedge l_2 \in target(\theta_2)) \rightarrow (\theta_1, \theta_2) \in projectOrderL(orderT)$$

Analogously for δ^o_{o,a,v_1,v_2} using $projectOrderV$ instead of $projectOrderL$.

- The same rules apply analogously using $source(\theta)$ for the source models of a transformation. With the difference that not the transformation applies the changes but the transformation reacts to the changes that are applied to its source model.

On the other hand, after external changes - either performed by a modeller or by a different transformation - are applied to a model involved, certain other consistency rules need to hold. For each type of change the consistency rules for the trace model are given below where Θ is the set of trace links before the change occurred and Θ' is the set of trace links after the change occurred. To realise these rules, first the equivalence between trace links have to be defined. Definition 3.4 denotes when this is the case.

Definition 3.4 (Equivalence of Trace Links). *A trace link θ is equivalent to a tracelink θ' if both refer to the same rule and either refer to the same source or target model element.*

$$\theta \equiv \theta' \iff$$
$$rule(\theta) = rule(\theta')$$
$$source(\theta) = source(\theta') \vee target(\theta) = target(\theta')$$

Using the definition of trace link equivalence the consistency rules on trace links that have to hold after the external changes have been performed to a model that is linked in a trace model can be defined as follows:

$\delta^-_o M_t$: Deleting an element o from the target model results in the removal of o from all trace links:

$$\forall (\theta \in \Theta, \theta' \in \Theta') : \theta \equiv \theta \wedge o \in target(\theta) \rightarrow o \notin target(\theta')$$

$\delta^-_{l,o_1,o_2} M_t$: Deletion of a link l from the target model leads to the removal of that link from all tracelinks that referred to l:

$$\forall (\theta \in \Theta, \theta' \in \Theta') : \theta \equiv \theta \wedge l \in target(\theta) \rightarrow l \notin target(\theta')$$

$\delta^u_{o,a,v} M_t$: Unsetting of an attribute value v leads to the removal of v from the trace values of each tracelink that contained that value:

$$\forall (\theta \in \Theta, \theta' \in \Theta') : \theta \equiv \theta \wedge v \in traceValue(\theta) \rightarrow v \notin traceValue(\theta')$$

all other changes: No additional consistency rules are defined for the other changes as those are either additional changes which are not represented in the trace anyway (e.g., δ^+_o) or do not affect the trace (e.g., $\delta^o_{l_1,l_2}$).

3.6.2. Detecting Model Changes Based on the Trace of a Transformation

External changes to a model can be made at an arbitrary point of time during the modelling process. From the view of a transformation engine changes to the target model can only be identified as soon as the transformation is re-executed with the given target model. Thus, in general a change detection can at the earliest be performed at the point where the transformation is executed a second (n-th, $n > 1$) time. During this transformation execution it can be decided whether a certain change in the target occurred. Whether a change can be detected or not, depends on how fine-grained the trace is created.

The goal of the following change detection definitions is to implement a function revealing all manual changes to a target model given a target model and a trace model. Therefore, for the identification of the set of changes that were applied to a target model we define the function $identifyTargetChanges : Models_{MM} \times Traces_{T,MM} \rightarrow Changes_{MM}$ which yields the set of manual changes to the target model since the last execution of the transformation.

In the following a definition of $identifyTargetChanges$ is given based on the changes that result from the application of $identifyTargetChanges$ to a target model M_t and a trace $Trace_{\rightarrow T}$.

3.6.2.1. Addition of Objects, Links and Values:

For the detection of additions of objects, links and values in the target model minimum trace capabilities are required. The storage of trace links, pointing to the source and target model elements as defined in Definition 3.3, is required. So that after a transformation T was executed the following holds: For each pair of elements e_s, e_t where e_s is from the source model and e_t was produced by the transformation in the target model, there has to exist a tracelink θ that refers to e_s as source and to e_t as target.

$$\forall e_s \in M_s, e_t \in M_t \mid ((e_s, e_t) \in \leadsto_T \rightarrow \exists \theta \in \Theta \mid (source(\theta) = e_s \wedge target(\theta) = e_t))$$

An addition of an object o to a target model M_t, can be identified in the following way: Let M_s be the source model of the transformation T resulting in model M_t and $Trace_{\leadsto_T}$ be the trace of the application of T to M_s. Then $identifyTargetChanges$ will return a change δ_o^+ (addition of element o to M_t) which has occurred iff

$$identifyTargetChanges(M_T, Trace) = \delta_o^+ \iff$$
$$\exists e_s \in M_s, r \in rules(T) \mid$$
$$(e_s \in leftModelPattern(r) \wedge o \in rightModelPattern(r) \rightarrow \forall \theta \in Trace \mid$$
$$rule(\theta) = r \rightarrow (e_s \in source(\theta) \rightarrow o \notin target(\theta)))$$

Change detection for δ_{l,o_1,o_2}^+ (addition of a link l which goes from o_1 and o_2) is defined analogously.

A change of an attribute value v can be identified analogously if the value of the attribute was *not* set initially. This kind of change is denoted as $\bar{\delta}_{o,a,v}^s$. $identifyTargetChanges$ identifies a change $\delta_{o,a,v}^s$ (setting of attribute a of element o to value v) as shown below.

$$identifyTargetChanges(M_t', Trace_{\leadsto_T}) = \bar{\delta}_{o,a,v}^s \iff$$
$$= \begin{cases} \delta_{o,a,v}^s, & \text{if } value(a, o) = \varnothing \\ \varnothing, & \text{else} \end{cases}$$

where $o \in O_i \wedge a \in attributes(class(o)) \wedge v \in V_i'$.

3.6.2.2. Changed Primitive Values

For the identification of changes to primitive valued attributes the value of the property as it was set by the transformation needs to be stored in the trace as well. Thus we need to extend the Definition 3.3 of $Trace$ by replacing Equation 3.3 with the following:

Definition 3.5 (Trace with Attribute Values).

$$Trace = (T, M_l, M_r, \Theta, TV, source, target, traceValue)$$

where

$TV \subseteq V_r$ *is a finite set of attribute values that where set during the application of the transformation,*

$traceValue : \{\theta \in \Theta \mid target(\theta) \in V_r\} \to TV$ *yields the attribute value that is linked by a given trace link θ.*

Now it is possible to also detect attribute value changes where the value of the attribute was set before. This kind of change is then defined as $\underline{\Delta}^s_{o,a,v} = \Delta^s_{o,a,v} \setminus \bar{\delta}^s_{o,a,v}$. The detection then works as follows: A change $\underline{\delta}^s_{o,a,v}$ has occurred iff

$$identify\,TargetChanges(M_T, Trace) = \underline{\delta}^s_{o,a,v} \iff$$
$$\exists e_s \in M_s \mid (e_s \in leftModelPattern(T) \land v \in rightModelPattern(T) \land$$
$$\forall \theta \in Trace \mid e_s \in source(\theta) \to (v \in target(\theta) \land v \neq trace\,Value(\theta)))$$

Changes $\delta^u_{o,a,v}$ (unsetting of an attribute a of element o which had value v) can be identified analogously.

3.6.2.3. Deletion of Elements from the Model

Robustness to dangling links is needed to detect deleted elements. If a trace holds a direct link to the target element and this elements gets deleted, the trace might be inconsistent. However, to be able to detect the deletion the trace must be kept in that way, having either a dangling reference or a NULL value for the target element. Thus it must be possible that $\exists \theta \in \Theta \mid (target(\theta) = \varnothing)$. If this is possible depends to a large extent on the model repository where the trace links are stored. In some implementations it might be the case that inconsistent links are not kept but immediately deleted after they are detected.

A change δ^-_o can be detected in the following way: A change occurred iff

$$identify\,TargetChanges(M'_t, Trace_{\rightsquigarrow T}) = \delta^-_o \iff$$

where

$$o \in O'_t \mid \exists e_s \in M_s, r \in rules(T) \mid (e_s \in leftModelPattern(r) \land o \in rightModelPattern(r) \land$$
$$\exists \theta \in Trace \mid e_s \in source(\theta) \to target(\theta) = \varnothing \land rule(\theta) = r)$$

Changes δ^-_{l,o_1,o_2} (removal of a link l from element o_1 to element o_2) can be identified analogously.

Furthermore, those inconsistent traces should not be deleted upon re-execution of the transformation as long as the deletion should be retained. Otherwise, if the trace is deleted during a subsequent transformation run because it was inconsistent the information that once an element existed will be lost and it will probably re-created if the transformation is re-executed the next time.

3.6.2.4. Ordering

To be able to compare the ordering of elements against a previous version this ordering needs also to be reflected within the trace. Thus Definition 3.5 has to be extended in the following way:

Definition 3.6 (Trace with Attribute Values and Ordering).

$$Trace = \big(T, M_l, M_r, \Theta, TV, source, target, traceValue, orderT, projectOrderL,$$
$$projectOrderV\big)$$

where

$orderT \subseteq \Theta \times \Theta$ *is a strict partial order defined on* Θ *where* $(\theta_1, \theta_2) \in orderT \iff \theta_1$ *occurs directly before* θ_2. *This defines the order in which the model objects, links or values where set in the target model according to the transformation.*

$projectOrderL : \Theta \times \Theta \to L \times L$ *projects the order as given in the tracelink to a strict partial order of links.*

$projectOrderV : \Theta \times \Theta \to V \times V$ *projects the order as given in the tracelink to a strict partial order of attribute values.*

Thus, it is now possible to detected changes in ordering, i.e. $\delta^o_{l_1,l_2}$ and δ^o_{o,a,v_1,v_2}. A change $\delta^o_{l_1,l_2}$ can be detected in the following way:

$$identifyTargetChanges(M_T, Trace) = \delta^o_{l,i} \iff$$
$$\exists l_1, l_2 \in L_t \mid (\forall \theta_1, \theta_2 \in Trace \mid ($$
$$l_1 \in target(\theta_1) \land l_2 \in target(\theta_2) \land (l_1, l_2) \in orderL \to (\theta_1, \theta_2) \notin orderT))$$

Changes δ^o_{o,a,v_1,v_2} can be identified analogously.

3.6.2.5. Identification of All Changes to a Target Model

Lemma 3.1. *Given the above change detection for all types of changes δ, it can be inferred that a detection of all types of atomic changes can be performed if the trace model is a rich enough.*

Proof. The proof of correctness of Lemma 3.1 relies on the change classifcation given by Hettel in [HLR09] which is also given in Section 2.1.1.2 on page 23. Per definition *identifyTargetChanges* is given for each kind of atomic change δ and its target domain is the set of all possible changes made to such models $Changes_{MM}$. As given by the definition of *Model* given in Definition 2.3 a model is a tuple of the sets O, L and V, the strict partial orders $orderL, orderV$, as well as the definition of several functions. Assuming the functions do not change at all, changes can only occur within the sets for elements O, links L and attribute values V and the orders $orderL, orderV$. Further assuming an atomic change consists at most of the addition or removal of an element of one of the sets or the change of order of two elements in one of the orders we can conclude by the following that all changes are mapped by the different types of δ given by Definition 2.4 as shown below.

$$\delta_o^+ O \qquad = O \cup o$$

$$\delta_o^- O \qquad = O \setminus o$$

$$\delta_{l,o_1,o_2}^+ L \qquad = L \cup l$$

$$\delta_{l,o_1,o_2}^- L \qquad = L \setminus l$$

$$\delta_{o,a,v}^s V \qquad = V \cup v$$

$$\delta_{o,a,v}^u V \qquad = V \setminus v$$

$$\delta_{l_1,l_2}^o orderL \qquad = orderL \setminus (l_2, l_1) \setminus \bigcup_{(l_a,l_b)\in orderL} (l_b = l_2 \vee l_a = l_1) \cup (l_1, l_2) \cup$$
$$\bigcup_{\{(l_b,l_1),(l_2,l_a)\}} ((l_a, l_b) \in orderL)$$

$$\delta_{v_1,v_2}^o orderV \qquad = orderV \setminus (v_2, v_1) \setminus \bigcup_{(v_a,v_b)\in orderV} (v_b = v_2 \vee v_a = v_1) \cup (v_1, v_2) \cup$$
$$\bigcup_{\{(v_b,v_1),(v_2,v_a)\}} ((v_a, v_b) \in orderV)$$

As $Changes_{MM}$ can be parted into disjoint sets of changes by their types

$$Changes_{MM} = \Delta_o^+ \cup \Delta_o^- \cup \Delta_{l,o_1,o_2}^+ \cup \Delta_{l,o_1,o_2}^- \cup \Delta_{l_1,l_2}^o \cup \Delta_{o,a,v}^s \cup \Delta_{o,a}^u \cup \Delta_{o,a,v_1,v_2}^o$$

and $identifyTargetChanges$ is surjective w.r.t. these sets, it is possible to conclude that $identifyTargetChanges$ is surjective concerning $Changes_{MM}$. $\square$

Lemma 3.2. *The change detection for a given tuple of source model M_s, target model M_t' and a trace model with attribute values and ordering $Trace$ (as defined in Definition 3.6). The given change detection approach finds a deterministic set of atomic changes that were applied to get from M_t to M_t'. Given that the change lies in the image of the transformation T. Formally this is expressed by:*

$$identifyTargetChanges(M_t', Trace_T) = \delta \iff M_t' = \delta M_t$$

Proof. The proof for correctness of Lemma 3.2 can be partitioned into each subtype of the change to identify δ. Because of Lemma 3.1 a change may only be one of the given types. Thus we identify the effect of each change event specific for each change detection definition given for $identifyTargetChanges$.

Generally, each partial definition of $identifyTargetChanges$ operates only on one of the disjoint sets O, L, V as well as the $Trace$ model. Therefore, we can show that as a distinct atomic change δ also only modifies one of these sets at the same time (cf. proof for Lemma 3.1) $identifyTargetChanges$ will also only result in exactly one identified change. In the following it will be shown that this is true for each kind of change δ. Furthermore, it will be shown that the identified change is always the correct one. Each partial definition of $identifyTargetChanges$ will be applied to M_t to show that.

Given a change δ_o^+ that adds the model element o to the target model M_t resulting in M_t' the result of the $identifyTargetChanges$ function is as follows.

Per definition the application of $\delta = \delta_o^+$ to M_t will result in $M_t' = M_t \cup \{o\}$. The partial definition if $identifyTargetChanges$ given for this type of change will therefore evaluate as follows:

$$identifyTargetChanges(M_T, Trace) = \delta_o^+ \iff$$
$$\exists r \in rules(T) \mid (\exists e_s \in M_s \mid e_s \in leftModelPattern(r) \wedge o \in rightModelPattern(r)) \rightarrow$$
$$(\forall \theta \in Trace \mid (rule(\theta) = r \wedge e_s \in source(\theta)) \rightarrow o \notin target(\theta))$$

Through the trace consistency rules for changes of type δ_o^+ defined in Section 3.6.1.1 it can be followed that the trace model is not affected by this type of change. Therefore, no trace link can refer to o: $\forall \theta \in \Theta \mid o \notin target(\theta)$. Combined with the previous formula it can be followed:

$$identify\,TargetChanges(M_T, Trace) = \delta_o^+ \iff$$
$$\exists r \in rules(T) \mid (\exists e_s \in M_s \mid e_s \in leftModelPattern(r) \wedge o \in rightModelPattern(r)) \rightarrow$$
$$(\forall \theta \in Trace \mid (rule(\theta) = r \wedge e_s \in source(\theta)) \rightarrow \textbf{true}) \iff$$
$$\exists r \in rules(T) \mid (\exists e_s \in M_s \mid e_s \in leftModelPattern(r) \wedge o \in rightModelPattern(r)) \rightarrow \textbf{true}$$

The change detection only has to work for changes that lie in the image of the transformation T. Therefore, it can be assumed that the element under change (e.g., o for a change δ_o^+) needs to be in the $rightModelPattern$ of T. From this assumption it can be followed that $\exists r \in rules(T) \mid e \in rightModelPattern(r)$. This leads to:

$$\exists r \in rules(T) \mid (\exists e_s \in M_s \mid e_s \in leftModelPattern(r) \wedge o \in rightModelPattern(r)) \rightarrow \textbf{true}$$

Due to the implication to $\textbf{true}$ it can be deduced that the expression is always true, which means that $identify\,TargetChanges(M_T, Trace) = \delta_o^+$ holds for a change δ_o^+.

The proofs for the change identification of the other types of change work analogously.

$\square$

Thus it can be argued, that if a tracing mechanism that is employed by a model transformation engine supports the traces as defined in Definition 3.6 all kinds of atomic changes can be detected.

3.6.2.6. Source Model Changes

A source change can be identified in the following through the comparison of the original target model and the target model as it would be produced by the re-application. After identifying all target changes it is possible to get the original target model M_t by the inverse application of the changes to the changed target model M_t'. This is denoted as:

$M_t = M_t' \Delta_t$ where $\Delta_t = identifyTargetChanges(M_t')$. A source model change $\delta_{o_s}^+$, with $o_s \in M_s$ occurred iff

$$\leadsto_T (M_s) \setminus M_t' \Delta_t \cup M_t' \setminus \leadsto_T (M_s) \Delta_t \neq \varnothing$$

For the identification of the set of changes that were applied to a *source* model we define the function $sourceChanges : Models_{MM} \times Traces_{T,MM} \rightarrow Changes_{MM}$ which yields the set of source changes since the last execution of the transformation.

3.7. Retainment Policies

To be able to provide means for specifying rules for target model retainment, a metamodel for so called *Retainment Policies* was derived. This metamodel, which is depicted in Figure 3.5, provides the class *RetainmentPolicy*. A *Retainment-Policy* can be seen as a rule on how a transformation should handle elements in the target model. A *RetainmentPolicy* defines which kind of retainment should be applied during the execution of the transformation. The different available kinds are enumerated by `RetainmentKind` as depicted in Figure 3.5. The usage of a specific `RetainmentKind` within a *RetainmentPolicy* can be set by using the `retainChanged` attribute of *RetainmentPolicy*. Note that *RetainmentPolicy* defines the transformation behaviour on a coarse-grained level. This is for example sufficient if all kinds of changes should be treated equally or if only a single valued property should be annotated with the policy. For the definition of more fine grained rules, the sub-class `TypeSpecificRetainmentPolicy` is used. This class allows to define `RetainmentKind`s for several types of changes such as addition, removal or changes in ordering. Especially for the use with multi-valued properties in the target model that should be controlled using the policy a `TypeSpecificRetainmentPolicy` needs to be used.

A *RetainmentPolicy* can be applied in different ways to either the transformation or specific elements in the target model. Thus, a retainment policy is considered a loosely coupled rule that in conjunction with a target and a transformation is used to decide whether manual changes to target models are overwritten once the transformation is re-executed. In practice, the policy may either be attached to elements from the target model or the transformation itself. Figure 3.6 illustrates the usage of `RetainmentPolicies` that are defined on the transformation as well as on the tar-

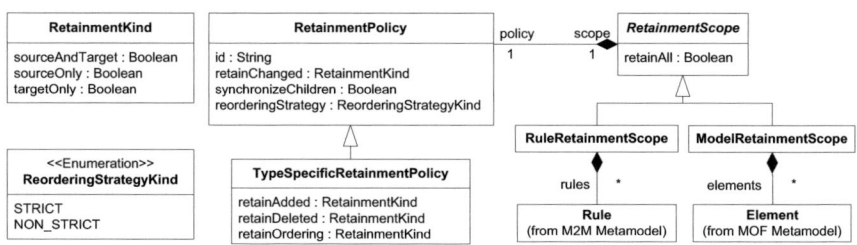

Figure 3.5.: Retainment Policies Metamodel

get model. Policies that are defined on the transformation implicitly map their scope to the respective elements which are matched or created by the transformation rule to which the policy is attached. In the running example, a retainment policy attached to the `BusinessObject2Table` relation would imply that all instances of `Table` are in the scope of this retainment policy. Policies that are defined directly on the target model are more specific as they are attached to specific elements for which they are then responsible. Again, taken from the running example, a policy attached to the `InvoiceTable` would only be valid for exactly this element. All other instances of `Table` would not be in the scope of the retainment policy. Thus, a reasonable default behaviour is that policies defined on target model elements overrule those defined in the transformation. Using this rule it is, for example possible to define a generic retainment policy for the `BusinessObject2Table` handling all instances of `Table` and then specifying a specifically different retainment policy for the `InvoiceTable`. Then this specific policy would overrule the generic one from the transformation for this specific `Table`.

As depicted in Figure 3.5 an additional attribute `synchronizeChildren` can be specified for a retainment policy. This option is a shortcut to specify that composite children of the annotated element or rules that get called to set subproperties within the containment hierarchy of the corresponding elements should be handled by the same retainment policy as the annotated element. If, in the running example, `synchronizeChildren` is set for a policy attached to the `BusinessObject2Table` relation this policy would also be used for all columns (because of the composite association between `Table` and `Column`) of the `Tables`.

If an ordering change should be retained or reapplied in the target model different strategies can be used. First, a *strict* reordering where elements, that where added in addition to those that were already ordered, are moved to the end of the order. And second, a *non-strict* ordering which denotes that additional elements are kept at their relative position and only the order of preexisting elements is retained in relation to each other. A reordering strategy is defined by the `reorderingStrategy` attribute of a `RetainmentPolicy` which is set to a literal of the `ReorderingStrategyKind` enumeration. A more detailed description on the reordering strategies is given in Section 3.9 where the formal semantics of the reordering are given.

A *RetainmentPolicy* can have two different types of scopes. Either its scope is defined using a `RuleRetainmentScope` which specifies for which rules of a transformation the *RetainmentPolicy* should be applied or it is directly attached to specific areas of the target model which should be retained in the specified way. The latter is specified by using a `ModelRetainmentScope` which references the elements that should be protected by the *RetainmentPolicy*. A `RetainmentScope` can additionally be configured in two different modes: (I) Having set `retainAll` to `false`, which specifies that each element in the scope is treated separately by the policy. (II) Having set `retainAll` to `false`, which denotes that as soon as a single element within the scope is considered to be retained, all elements within same scope are also retained in the same way. The latter is useful, for example, assuming a transformation that generates an initial behaviour model such as an activity model in UML. As soon as a modeller manually modifies this model and overwrites parts of the automatically generated activities the whole activity model should be considered to be retained in subsequent transformation runs. Otherwise, the transformation might destroy the modelled semantics even if it only overwrites changes that are not directly modified by the modeller.

For cases where a policy is specified on multiple elements and they contradict each other, a (semi-)automatic disambiguation has to be performed. This may either be done by configuring the transformation execution to use precedence rules, for example, "use target model policies only" or "prefer source model policies over transformation policies". A comprehensive analysis of conflicts and precedence rules is presented in Section 3.10.3.

During the the re-execution of the transformation, the `RetainmentPolicies` that are in the scope of the current execution are combined with the actual transformation. The transformation rules are modified according to the current policies and yield a new, temporary transformation. The actual semantics of the combination of a transformation with a retainment policy are described in Section 3.9. To be able to detect and react to target model changes the trace model of the previous transformation execution needs to

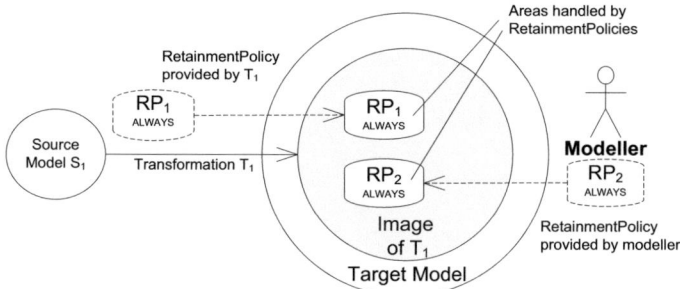

Figure 3.6.: **Application of a transformation with specified RetainmentPolicies.** Retainment-Policy RP_1 is provided by T_1 whereas RP_2 is explicitly defined by the modeller. Both policies cover a certain part of the target model. RP_1 as well as RP_2 are configured to retain any kind of change applied to the target model.

be consulted as an additional input for the modified transformation. Figures 3.7 and 3.8 illustrate this process.

Based on the given metamodel it is furthermore possible to define the formal semantics of each the retainment policies. First, the semantics of each RetainmentKind will be defined in Section 3.8. Then the formal semantics of each kind will in conjunction with the different attributes of TypeSpecificRetainmentPolicy will be elaborated. These formal definitions are then used to reason about completeness as well as conflict resolution of the policies.

3.8. Retainment Kinds

Before a transformation is re-executed there may exist several states of the source and the target model: the source model, the target model, or both models have changed. To be able to specify in which of the cases an element in the target model should be retained rather than overwritten by the transformation, the combination of each of the cases needs to be analysed. For each of these cases one *Retainment Kind* will be presented that allows the retainment of the target model for the corresponding cases.

For example, as illustrated in Figure 3.9, starting from a source model M_s and applying the transformation T will result in target model M_t. Then external modifications Δ are applied to M_t yielding a modified target model M_t'. Then the T is re-executed based on

83

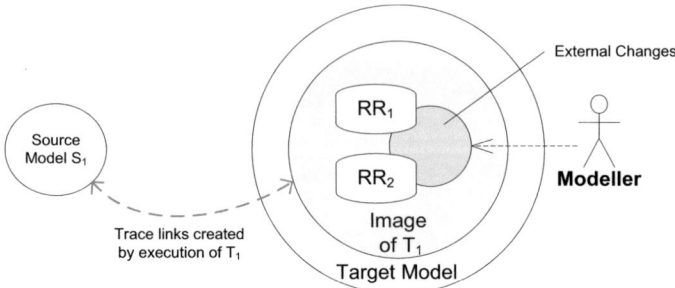

Figure 3.7.: **Elements in the target model changed.** RetainmentPolicy RP_1 is combined with T_1 to yield a modified transformation that is then used to update the model elements of the target model in this scope. The same applies for RP_2 and T_1. The *Trace Model* that was created during the previous transformation execution is used as additional input for the transformation when creating the temp transformation in the next step.

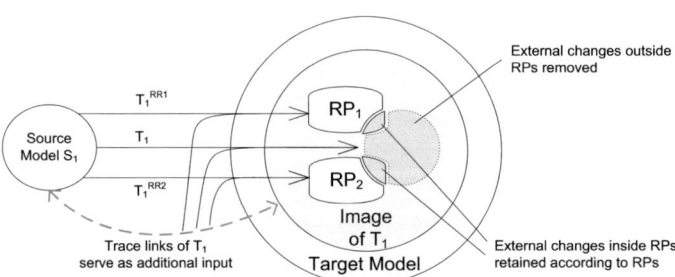

Figure 3.8.: **Deriving temporary transformations.** The result of the re-execution of T_1 is that external changes to the target model that were not protected by retainment policies were overwritten by the transformation (T_1) whereas those parts with a *Retainment-Policy* applied where retained (using the temporary transformations $T_1^{RP_1}$ and $T_1^{RP_2}$).

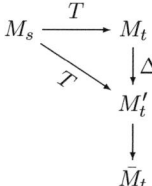

Figure 3.9.: Example scenario: the target model M_t is the result of the application of T to M_s. A change Δ is applied to M_t resulting in M_t' and the transformation is reexecuted using M_s as source and M_t' as target model. The final result is $\bar{M}_t$.

	target changed	target unchanged
source changed	$M_s \xrightarrow{T} M_t$ $\downarrow \quad \xrightarrow{T} \quad \downarrow$ $M_s' \xrightarrow{T} M_t'$	$M_s \xrightarrow{T} M_t$ $M_s' \nearrow \mathcal{T}$
source unchanged	$M_s \xrightarrow{T} M_t$ $\mathcal{T} \nearrow \quad \downarrow$ M_t'	$M_s \xrightarrow{\quad T \quad} M_t$ $\searrow \xrightarrow{T} \nearrow$

Table 3.1.: Different combinations of changes to source or target models.

the unchanged source model M_s now having M_t' as result. The application of T to M_t' will then result in the final target model $\bar{M}_t$.

Table 3.1 gives an overview on the possible combinations of source and target model changes. The final resulting model $\bar{M}_t$ is omitted in this table. As this table shows, there are four different scenarios in which a transformation can be re-applied. For each of these scenarios the transformation should be able to react by either applying the result of T or by retaining the current target model according to the retainment policies. However, the scenario of *source unchanged / target unchanged* can be omitted in this analysis as if both models are unchanged. The transformation would result exactly in M_t again and the result would be $M_t = \bar{M}_t$. Therefore, the *RetainmentKinds* will be characterised by the way how these three different scenarios are handed.

Having three different types of scenarios (source changed, target changed, source/target changed) and two types of reactions to these scenarios (retain target, apply transformation) results in 2^3 different combinations and thus in 8 different *RetainmentKinds*.

Retain target	never	if target changed exclusively	if source changed exclusively	if source *and* target changed	if source *xor* target changed	if target changed	if source changed	always
Short Symbol	∅	►	◄	■	◄►	■►	◄■	◄■►
$M_s \xrightarrow{T} M_t$ / $\downarrow \;\; \xrightarrow{T} \;\; \downarrow$ / $M_s' \xrightarrow{T} M_t'$	T	T	T	$\mathcal{F}$	T	$\mathcal{F}$	$\mathcal{F}$	$\mathcal{F}$
$M_s \xrightarrow{T} M_t$ / $\downarrow \;\;\; \nearrow T$ / M_s'	T	T	$\mathcal{F}$	T	$\mathcal{F}$	T	$\mathcal{F}$	$\mathcal{F}$
$M_s \xrightarrow{T} M_t$ / $\searrow T \;\;\downarrow$ / M_t'	T	$\mathcal{F}$	T	T	$\mathcal{F}$	$\mathcal{F}$	T	$\mathcal{F}$

(Left column label, rotated: Change Scenarios)

Table 3.2.: Possible reactions when re-executing a transformation depending on different combinations of changes to source or target models. T means the transformation will overwrite a target change. $\mathcal{F}$ denotes that the current target model element will be retained.

These possible reactions when re-applying T are shown in Table 3.2 for each of the scenarios. A reaction is either the application of T which is denoted by a cell having T as value or, if the target model is retained, the reaction is denoted by $\mathcal{F}$. The retention of changes in the target model can be understood intuitively, since these elements will be retained as they are. However, for those cases where the target model should be retained and there are no changes in the target model (row 2 in Table 3.2), the understanding is a bit more complicated. In this case a retention of the target model means that although changes to the source model have been made, they are not synchronised with the target model; the target model will be in the state as it was after the last execution of the transformation even though no external changes have been applied to it.

A *RetainmentKind* represents exactly one of the combinations given in Table 3.2. As illustrated in Figure 3.10, each RetainmentKind has three attributes defining in

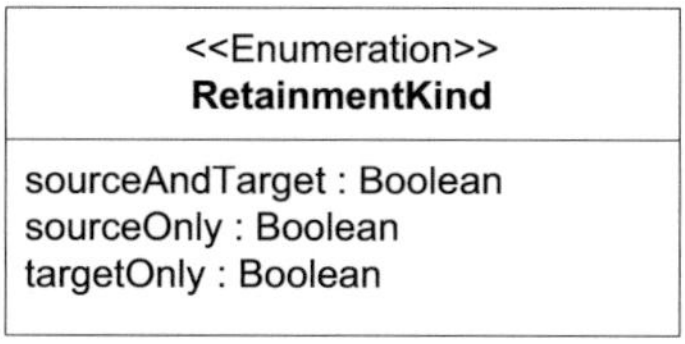

```
+-------------------------------------------+
|           <<Enumeration>>                 |
|           RetainmentKind                  |
+-------------------------------------------+
| sourceAndTarget : Boolean                 |
| sourceOnly : Boolean                      |
| targetOnly : Boolean                      |
+-------------------------------------------+
```

Figure 3.10.: The RetainmentKind class in detail.

which scenario which transformation reaction should be applied. This is comparable to QVT-R enforce, checkonly advices but more flexible since models changes of both models (source and target) are supported. The attribute `sourceAndTarget` is used to specify the reaction to changes where the source and the target model have changed at the same time. The attributes `sourceOnly` and `targetOnly` specify the reaction when only the source or the target model changed respectively. For example a `targetChangedExclusively(▶)` `RetainmentKind` would be represented as an instance of `RetainmentKind` having set `sourceAndTarget = false`, `sourceOnly = false` and `targetOnly = true`.

An overview on the application of each of the presented *RetainmentKinds* is illustrated in Figure 3.11.

3.9. Formal Semantics of Retainment Policies

The formal semantics of the different `RetainmentKinds` when used in a `RetainmentPolicy` are specified below. As introduced in Figure 3.1, M_s denotes the source model, M_s' denotes the modified source model respectively and M_t' denotes the manually changed target model. The final target model, being the result of the re-executed transformation with applied retainment policies, is denoted as $\bar{M}_t$. $Trace_T$ denotes the trace of the transformation execution that was recorded for the previous transformation execution. As a prerequisite for the definitions of the formal semantics of a *RetainmentPolicy*, Definitions 3.7 and 3.8 introduces the formal representation of a *RetainmentKind* and a *RetainmentPolicy*.

Definition 3.7 (Retainment Kinds). *The set of retainment kinds K is defined as*

$$K = \{\bot, \varnothing, \blacktriangleright, \blacktriangleleft, \blacksquare, \blacktriangleleft\blacktriangleright, \blacksquare\blacktriangleright, \blacktriangleleft\blacksquare, \blacktriangleleft\blacksquare\blacktriangleright\}$$

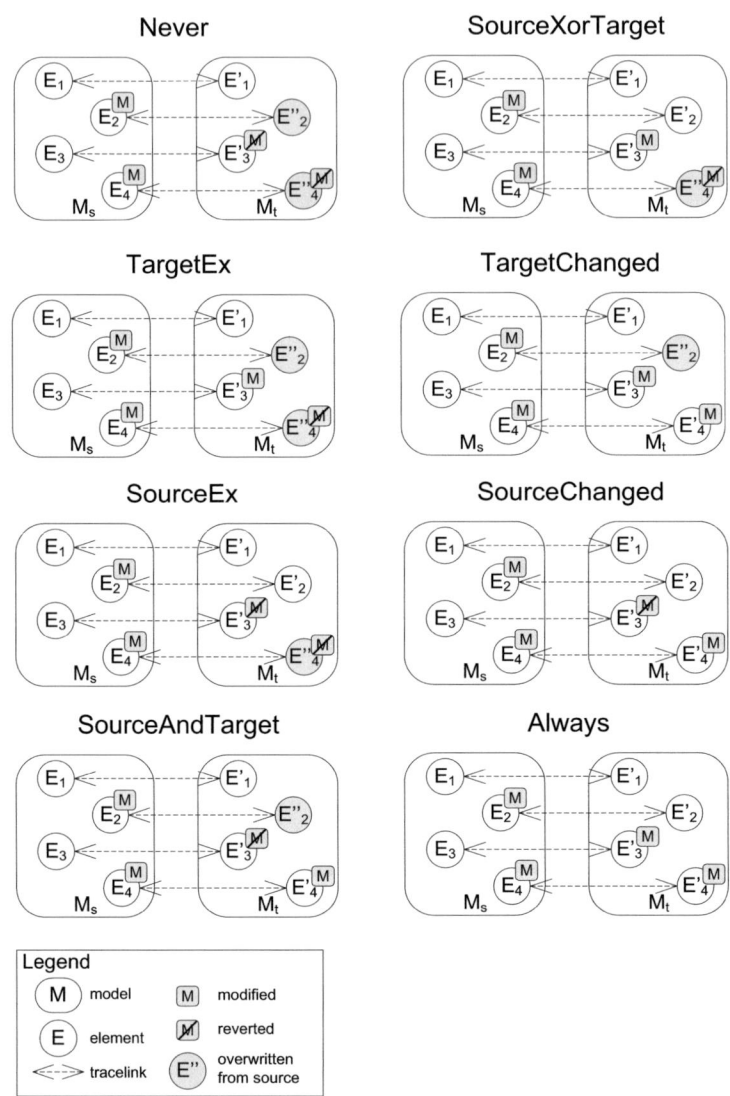

Figure 3.11.: The RetainmentKinds applied in a minimal example showing all possible combinations.

where

$\perp$ *is the* `NotSet` `RetainmentKind`,

$\varnothing$ *is the* `never` `RetainmentKind`,

$\blacktriangleright$ *is the* `targetChangedExclusively` `RetainmentKind`,

$\blacktriangleleft$ *is the* `sourceChangedExclusively` `RetainmentKind`,

$\blacksquare$ *is the* `sourceAndTargetChanges` `RetainmentKind`,

$\blacktriangleleft\blacktriangleright$ *is the* `sourceXorTargetChanged` `RetainmentKind`,

$\blacksquare\blacktriangleright$ *is the* `targetChanged` `RetainmentKind`,

$\blacktriangleleft\blacksquare$ *is the* `sourceChanged` `RetainmentKind`,

$\blacktriangleleft\blacksquare\blacktriangleright$ *is the* `always` `RetainmentKind`.

The application of a retainment kind in a transformation or a single transformation rule is denoted as $\rightsquigarrow_T^k$ or $\rightsquigarrow_r^k$ respectively. So for example, $\rightsquigarrow_T^{\blacksquare\blacktriangleright}$ means that for the application of transformation T the `targetChanged` `RetainmentKind` *is applied, which means that all external changes to the target model will be retained.*

Definition 3.8 (Retainment Policy). *A* RetainmentPolicy *R is a tuple*

$$R = (k, s, Scope, reorderingStrategy, retainAll)$$

where

$k \in K$ *is the* RetainmentKind *that defines the reactions to the different change scenarios.*

$Scope \subseteq M_s \cup M_t = Scope_m \cup Scope_r$ *is the scope of model elements in the source and target model $Scope_m$ and the rules of a transformation to which the policy is applied $Scope_r$. For the case of a* ModelRetainmentScope *these are exactly the elements that are defined using the* elements *property resulting in. For a* RuleRetainment-Scope *the scope $Scope$ is produced by a projection using the image of the rules defined by the* RuleRetainmentScope. *In this case the scope $Scope_r$ of a rule r is derived as follows:*

$$Scope_r = \bigcup\{e \in \cup M_t \mid e \in rightModelPattern(r)\}$$

$Scope_r$ is produced by building the unification of the elements that are in the image of the corresponding rule.

$reorderingStrategy \in reorderingStrategies$ *defines the reordering strategy to be used by the policy. The set $reorderingStrategies$ is defined as $\{strict, non-strict\}$.*

retainAll $\in \mathbb{B}$ *defines whether a single change in the scope will cause the whole scope to be treated as changed.*

Eventually, a decision on the retainment of target model elements is always based on:

- changes in the source model Δ_s,

- changes in the target model Δ_t,

- the transformation that is executed T as well as

- the retainment policy R which is responsible for the combination of Δ_s, Δ_t and T.

If more than one *RetainmentPolicy* matches an element in its scope conflicts may occur. Section 3.10.3 gives a detailed description on how these conflicts are handled and solved. In the following sections it is assumed that no conflicts are present or that they have already been resolved.

Running Example: For purposes of illustration, a set of changes is applied to the sample source and target models given in Section 3.3. These changes will be used in the explanations of the policies semantics. The source model is changed in the following way:

- $\delta^s_{PurchaseOrder,name,``PurchOrd"}$: Setting of the name attribute of PurchaseOrder to "PurchOrd".

- $\delta^+_{Address}$: The creation of a new BusinessEntity Address.

- $\delta^-_{purchaseOrder}, \delta^-_{:TypeDefinition}, \delta^-_{C2POpo,CustomerMakesPurchaseOrders,purchaseOrder}$, $\delta^-_{poTD,purchaseOrder,poTd}, \delta^-_{TDPO,poTD,PurchaseOrder}$: Deletion of the purchaseOrder AssociationEnd including its TypeDefinition and the its links.

The changes applied to the target model are the following:

- $\delta^s_{PurchaseOrderTable,name,``POTable"}$: Setting of the name attribute of PurchaseOrderT-able to "POTable".

- $\delta^-_{FKBillFor}$: Deletion of the Column *FKBillFor* from the Table InvoiceTable. The corresponding consistent change is

$$\nabla_{\delta^-_{FKBillFor}} = \left\{ \delta^-_{FKBillFor}, \delta^-_{InvoiceTable2FKBillFor,InvoiceTable,FKBillFor} \right\}$$

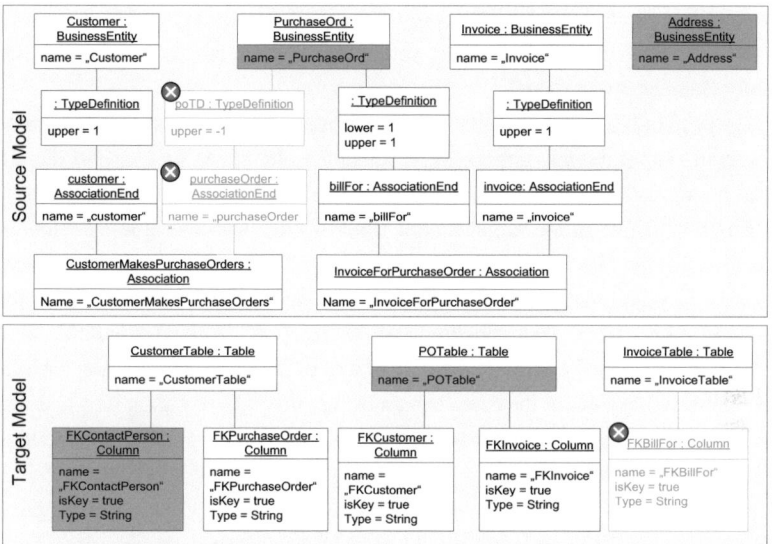

Figure 3.12.: Example model showing source and target model of a business entity model to relational database transformation after they were changed externally. Light grey elements with crosses were deleted. Elements in dark grey were changed or added.

which includes the removal of the link between the `InvoiceTable` and `FKBillFor`.

- $\delta^+_{FKContactPerson}$: Creation of a new `Column` FKContactPerson.

- $\delta^+_{cToCp,CustomerTable,FKContactPerson}$: Linking of FKContactPerson to the columns of CustomerTable.

These changes are illustrated in Figure 3.12, where light grey elements with crosses were deleted. Elements in dark grey were changed or added.

3.9.1. Determination of Change Sets

Derived from the three basic scenarios, shown in Table 3.2, for source and/or target model changes, it is possible to define certain types of *change sets*. These *change sets* are given as complex changes of the form $\Delta^{addition/deletion,source/target}_{type}$ that can be applied

91

to the modified target model M_t' to apply or revert a certain type of change. M_s and M_s' denote the source model, modified source model respectively and M_t' denotes the manually changed target model.

Changes can either be applied to the source model, then the transformation translates them into the target model. alternatively, the target model can be changed directly by external manipulations. For the determination of the change sets, it needs to be identified which elements in the target model would result from changed elements in the source model, after the transformation would have been re-executed, and which elements were externally changed. If an element e is identified to be in the set of changes $sourceChanges(M_s', Trace_T)$ or $identifyTargetChanges(M_t', Trace_T)$ it is either an addition of e to, a removal of e from a model M or a re-ordering of links or values within the model. Considering each of the cases separately results in the building blocks described below. The change sets defined here will then serve as basis for the definition of the different *RetainmentKinds*.

To account for the consistency of the model to which the changes are applied the *consistentChanges* function is applied to each of the different change sets. This will include changes such as the deletion of links when one if its linked elements is deleted in the set of changes.

The following change sets can be distinguished:

1) *Deletion of model elements or links or unsetting of attribute values* $(\delta_o^-, \delta_{l,o_1,o_2}^-, \delta_{o,a,v}^u)$:
   According to the trace model consistency rules defined in Section 3.6.1.1 on page 71 a deletion of an element from a model will also result in the deletion from every trace link that referenced that element. Thus, for any deletion type of change δ_o^- or δ_{l,o_1,o_2}^-, the source or target of the trace link will be empty; $source(\theta) = \varnothing$ or $target(\theta) = \varnothing$ respectively. Assuming that there are no external modifications to the trace links, every trace link having an empty source or target can be considered an indicator of a change on the source respectively target side. From these detected changes, depending on whether the change occurred on the source or target model, it is now possible to determine the effect such a change has on the target model:

   a) *Target deletion due to source change:* A model element o that should be deleted from the target model due to a change on the source model can be identified by analysing the transformation trace. This type of change is depicted in Figure 3.13. If o is in $target(\theta)$ of a trace link θ it was once created by a certain rule $r = rule(\theta)$ of the transformation T. During the application of the transformation, firstly, the

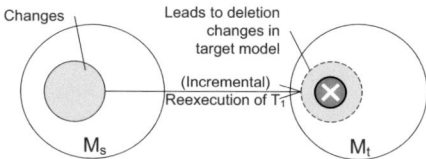

Figure 3.13.: Deletion in target model resulting from a source model change.

model element o will be deleted if the source of the trace link is empty due to a change on the source model side. Secondly, the element o will also be deleted if $source(\theta)$ is modified in a way that it is not anymore in the source model pattern[2] of r. In conclusion, the changes that are a deletion of a model element in the target $\Delta_o^{-,sourceChanges}$ due to changes in the source model are given as follows:

$$\Delta_o^{-,sourceChanges} = consistentChanges(\{\delta_o^- \in \Delta_o^- \cap \leadsto_T (M_s', M_t') \mid \exists \theta \in \Theta \mid (target(\theta) = o$$
$$\wedge (source(\theta) = \varnothing \vee source(\theta) \notin leftModelPattern(rule(\theta))\})$$

The set of deletion changes that are caused by changes to the source model $\Delta_o^{-,sourceChanges}$ is determined by building the intersection between the set of all possible model element deletion changes Δ_o^- and the set of changes resulting from the reapplication of the transformation $\leadsto_T (M_s', M_t')$. From this set, those changes are taken for which exists a tracelink that points to the corresponding model element in the target model $(target(\theta) = o)$ but the source element is either the empty set $(source(\theta) = \varnothing)$ or has left the source image of the transformation rule $(\notin leftModelPattern(rule(\theta))$.

The same applies analogously for links and results in $\Delta_{l,o_1,o_2}^{-,sourceChanges}$ and attribute values $\Delta_{o,a,v}^{u,sourceChanges}$.

Running Example: Applied to the changes performed in the running example this would result in

$$\Delta_o^{-,sourceChanges} = \{\delta_{FKPurchaseOrder}^-, \delta_{cToPO,CustomerTable,FKPurchaseOrder}^-\}$$

as a source change occurred $\delta_{purchaseOrder}^-$ which led to the nullification of the existing tracelink θ_{po} from purchaseOrder to FKPurchaseOrder, in turn, resulting in $source(\theta_{po}) = \varnothing$. Therefore, the corresponding target element $FKPurchaseOrder$

---

[2]See for example the execution semantics of TGGs [AS07] or QVT [Obj11]

would be considered to be deleted by the transformation. To ensure consistency $consistentChanges$ applied to this change will also include the deletion of the attached link $\delta^-_{cToPO,CustomerTable,FKPurchaseOrder}$ into the change set.

b) *External target deletion:* A model element o that was deleted in the target model can be detected using $identifyTargetChanges$ defined in the change detection approach in Section 3.6.2. Figure 3.14 illustrates this type of change. Thus, these changes $\Delta_o^{-,targetChanges}$ are given as:

$$\Delta_o^{-,targetChanges} = consistentChanges(\Delta_o^- \cap identifyTargetChanges(M_t', Trace_T))$$

The set of deletion target changes is determined by computing the *consistentChanges* of the intersection of the set of all possible model element addition changes Δ_o^+ with the set of external changes that have been identified in the target model using $identifyTargetChanges$. However, as these changes are already applied to the target model, additionally the possibility to let the application of the transformation undo these changes needs to be provided by the *RetainmentPolicy* approach. Due to the trace consistency semantics (cf. Section 3.6.1.1) and the unique object identity (cf. assumptions in Section 3.4) it is not possible to reconstruct a deleted object completely only using existing traces. However, it is possible to re-apply the transformation ($\leadsto_r (M_s', M_t')$) to the corresponding source element for which the deleted target model element was once created. The inversion of these changes is then given as:

$$\Delta_o^{-,targetChanges,-1} = consistentChanges(\bigcup_{r \in rules(T)} \delta \in \Delta_o^+ \cap \leadsto_r (M_s', M_t') \,|$$
$$\exists \theta \in \Theta \,|\, target(\theta) = \varnothing \wedge rule(\theta) = r)$$

The intersection of all possible model element addition changes (Δ_o^+) and the changes resulting from the reapplication of the transformation $\leadsto_r (M_s', M_t')$ is the starting point to build the the inverse change set $\Delta_o^{-,targetChanges,-1}$. From this intersection the union of those changes over all rules of the transformation $rules(T)$ is build for which a tracelink exists but the target of that link is the empty set ($target(\theta) = \varnothing$).

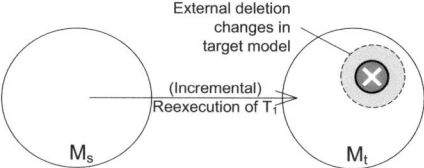

Figure 3.14.: External deletion in target model.

Running Example: For the changes applied in the running example, $\Delta_o^{-,targetChanges}$ would be:

$$\left\{ \delta_{FKBillFor}^-, \delta_{iToPO,Invoice,FKBillFor}^- \right\}$$

According to the transformation $FKBillFor$ would be created resulting in a change $\delta_{FKBillFor}^+$, therefore the inversion of the changes, including the determination of the inverted consistent changes, would be

$$\Delta_o^{-,targetChanges,-1} = \left\{ \delta_{FKBillFor}^+, \delta_{iToPO,Invoice,FKBillFor}^- \right\}$$

.

As links and attribute value do not have a unique identity, the set of inversion changes can be determined by simply using the complementary change type. The function $invert : Changes_{MM} \rightarrow Changes_{MM}$ gives the inverse change of these change types. For a given detected target change δ_{l,o_1,o_2}^- the inverted change is δ_{l,o_1,o_2}^+. Analogously the inversion of an attribute value change $\delta_{o,a,v}^u$ is $\delta_{o,a,v}^s$. This approach then yields the inversion change sets that can then be used to revert the external changes in the target model:

$$\Delta_{l,o_1,o_2}^{-,targetChanges,-1} = consistentChanges\left(\bigcup_{\delta \in \Delta_{l,o_1,o_2}^{-,targetChanges}} invert(\delta) \right)$$

and

$$\Delta_{o,a,v}^{u,targetChanges,-1} = consistentChanges\left(\bigcup_{\delta \in \Delta_{o,a,v}^{u,targetChanges}} invert(\delta) \right)$$

c) *Parallel source and target deletion changes:* If changes that result in a deletion of the element o in the target model $(\Delta_o^{-,targetChanges})$ are done in the source model and the target model in parallel, no inversion of the deletion in the target model is possible. The problem in this case is that both ends of the tracelink that was created between the source and target model elements are nullified. Therefore it is not possible anymore to identify what the original situation in the model was. This is an important limitation for of the retainment policy approach as it will not be possible to specify a policy that undoes this kind of changes to the target model. A retention of the change due to changes on either of both sides, on the other hand, is no problem as both will result in the same change $\delta^{-}o$.

2) *Creation of model elements or links or attribute values* $(\delta_o^+, \delta_{l,o_1,o_2}^+, \delta_{o,a,v}^{s,sourceChanges})$: Externally added model elements and links in the target model are handled differently – (I) they may be left untouched as long as they do not interfere with updates from source the source model or (II) the may be reverted in any case – depending on their semantics of the employed transformation approach. Most popular approaches such as QVT [Obj11] or Triple Graph Grammars [HG09] enforce the deletion of elements that do not have a corresponding match in the source model (see Section 7.10.2 Enforcement Semantics, in the QVT specification [Obj11]). However, to be able to handle both cases (I) and (II) independent from the underlying model transformation engine, the retainment policy approach needs the capability of reverting or retaining these additions.

a) *Target addition due to source change:* A model element o that should be created in the target model due to changes in the source model can be identified by analysing the trace model. This is actually the standard case for the application of an incremental model transformation based on traces, which is also depicted in Figure 3.15. If there is no pre-existing trace link that refers to the source element for which the target change should be applied, the target element will be newly created. In conclusion, the changes that cause a creation of a model element in the target $\Delta_o^{+,sourceChanges}$ due to changes in the source model are given as follows (analogously for links and the resulting changes $\Delta_{l,o_1,o_2}^{+,sourceChanges}$ and attribute values $\Delta_{o,a,v}^{s,sourceChanges}$):

$$\Delta_o^{+,sourceChanges} = consistentChanges(\{\delta \in \Delta_o^+ \cap \rightsquigarrow_T (M_s', M_t') \mid \nexists \theta \in \Theta \mid ($$
$$source(\theta) \in \bigcup_{\delta \in sourceChanges(M_t', Trace_T)} element(\delta))\})$$

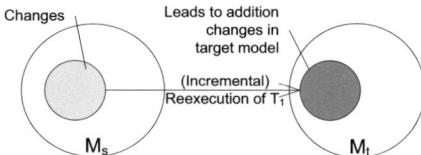

Figure 3.15.: Addition in target model resulting from a source model change.

The set of additional source changes is retrieved by intersecting the set of all additional model element changes Δ_o^+ with the set of changes that results from the reapplication of the transformation $\leadsto_T (M_s', M_t')$. From this intersection only those elements that do not have an existing tracelink to an element in the set of source changes are considered to be part of the resulting change set. Finally, the consistent changes are computed from those changes.

Running Example: Within the changes of the running example this selection will result in the following change set:

$$\Delta_o^{+,sourceChanges} = \{\delta_{AddressTable}^+\}$$

The corresponding source change $\delta_{Address}^+$ is the source for the `BO2Table` transformation rule and will therefore result in the creation of another `Table` element by the $\delta_{AddressTable}^+$ change.

b) *External target addition:* A model element o that was added to the target model can be detected using *identifyTargetChanges* defined in the change detection approach in Section 3.6.2. For illustration, Figure 3.16 depicts this change set. Thus, these changes $\Delta_o^{+,targetChanges}$ are given as:

$$\Delta_o^{+,targetChanges} = consistentChanges(\{\Delta_o^+ \cap$$
$$identifyTargetChanges(M_t', Trace_T)\})$$

The set of additional target changes is gained by building the consistent change set of the intersection between the identified target changes (*identifyTargetChanges*(M_t', *Trace$_T$*)) and the set of all possible model element addition changes Δ_o^+. However, as these changes are already applied to a modified target model, additionally the possibility to undo these changes needs to be provided by the retainment policy approach. The default behaviour of the transformation application would be to de-

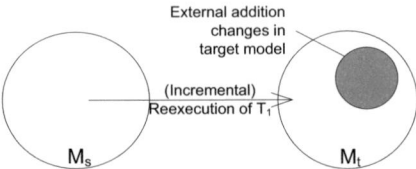

Figure 3.16.: External addition in target model.

lete the externally added element as there exists no corresponding element in the source model. Thus, it is possible to apply the needed inversion changes by applying the corresponding parts of T. The inversion of these changes is then given as:

$$\Delta_o^{+,targetChanges,-1} = consistentChanges(\{\delta_o^- \in \rightsquigarrow_T (M_s', M_t') \mid$$
$$\exists \delta_{o'}^+ \in \Delta_o^{+,targetChanges} \mid o = o'\})$$

The corresponding set of changes for the addition of links $\delta_{l,o_1,o_2}^{+,targetChanges,-1}$ is determined analogously. From the given sets of changes in the running example, the set of changes $\Delta_o^{+,targetChanges}$ is determined as:

$$\Delta_o^{+,targetChanges} = \{\delta_{FKContactPerson}^+\}$$

The corresponding set of inverted changes is then, including the determined consistent changes given as

$$\Delta_o^{-,targetChanges} = \{\delta_{FKContactPerson}^-, \delta_{cToCP,CustomerTable,FKContactPerson}^-\}$$

.

c) *Parallel source and target changes:* Applying changes that add model elements due to changes on the source model as well as having externally added model elements target model in parallel does not lead to any conflicts as long there is no restriction on the existence of elements. Such a restriction may be applied by a constraint on the target metamodel specifying that e.g., there may be only a certain amount of instances of a certain metamodel class at the same time. However, adding a link l through the transformation as well as directly in the target model may lead to conflicts:

- $upper(secondEnd(association(l))) = 1$: If the upper multiplicity of an association end is one, a conflict occurs if there is a change δ^+_{l',o_1,o_2} and another change with δ^+_{l',o_3,o_4} if $o_3 = o_1 \wedge o_4 \neq o_2$. Then it needs to be decided which link (existing via target / existing via source) should be used as there can only be one link at a time. This conflict does not occur if $o_4 = o_2$ as then both links would be the same.

- $isUnique(association(l)) \wedge isOrdered(association(l)) \wedge l \equiv l'$: If the association of the added link is unique as well as ordered, the addition of links may conflict with a parallel change δ^+_{l',o_1,o_2} if the order is not the same $order(l) \neq order(l')$. Due to the uniqueness, only one of the links may be in the link list and they have a different position, it needs be decided which position within the link list should be used. Thus, this conflict does not occur if $order(l) = order(l')$.

3) *Change in order of links or values:* For multi-valued, ordered associations or attributes, a reordering of the elements is also a change that needs to be retainable. Especially if a target model is created from an more abstract source model where ordering is not yet specified but the target model is then modified and a certain order is given, this order needs to be retained upon subsequent transformation runs. Insertions at specific positions to a property's collection can also be easily mapped to two atomic changes. First an addition of the new link and then a reordering to the desired position is performed. Thus, it is e.g. possible to allow for the addition of links but prevent them from reordering so that it is only possible to insert elements at the end of the link collection. In this thesis this strategy is called *strict* reordering. Note that this is only one possible strategy; it might also be enough to retain the ordering of existing elements so that insertions at arbitrary positions will not be harmful. In the context of this thesis, this strategy is called *non-strict* reordering. Formally the set of possible ordering strategies is given as $orderingStrategy = \{strict, non-strict\}$. The actual strategy which is to be used is given by the *RetainmentPolicy* in its *reorderingStrategy* tuple element. Assuming the ordering, that was applied in a previous transformation run, is represented within the trace as given by Definition 3.3, the function $determineOrder : \mathcal{P}(orderL) \times orderingStrategy \rightarrow \mathcal{P}(\Delta^o_{l_1,l_2})$ can be used to apply the ordering stored in the trace to the ordering in the model by using $determineOrder(projectOrderL(\Theta))$. This function also includes both ordering strategies defined in $orderingStrategy$.

a) *Order changes in target model due to source model changes:* The order in which the new elements are added to a target model does not imply that their corresponding source model patterns identified any changes. The order of elements in the target model may be determined by different factors:

(I) The ordering in the source model is copied. If corresponding elements in the source model are ordered, this order may be directly transferred by the transformation to the corresponding elements in the target model.

(II) If the source model elements are unordered the target model order may be random just depending on the (arbitrary) order of the execution of the transformation rules for the respective elements. Furthermore, it might be the case that the rules for creating and adding elements are not re-executed themselves, but the order in which they would have been called by the transformation did change. If the order of elements is not made explicit within these transformation rules, this change in execution order would then have led to a different order in which these elements were added to the target model.

(III) The order is specified in the transformation rules. Transformation rules may have been provided that order elements in the target model according to some criterion, such as e.g., the alphabetical order of their names.

To support each of these scenarios the reordering of elements the *determineOrdering* function is used to explicitly apply an ordering to the target model instead of depending on the ordering semantics of the underlying transformation approach. The set of order changes that are applied due to changes in the source model $\Delta_{l1,l2}^{o,sourceChanges}$, as depicted in Figure 3.17, can then be determined as follows.

$$\Delta_{l1,l2}^{o,sourceChanges} = consistentChanges(determineOrdering($$
$$\{\delta_{l1,l2}^{o} \in \leadsto_T (M'_s, M'_t) \mid (l1,l2) \notin projectOrderL(\Theta)\}, strict))$$

Each pair of links that is in the result of the application of the transformation $(\leadsto_T (M'_s, M'_t))$ is filtered by checking if it is already part of the order that is projected from the order of the tracelinks using *projectOrderL*. From this set the corresponding reordering changes are determined using *determineOrdering*.

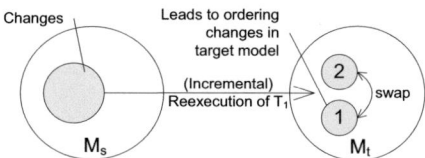

Figure 3.17.: Ordering change due to changes in source model.

Alternatively to the *strict* reordering strategy, also the *non − strict* strategy can be used.

b) *Target ordering change:* Changes in the order of links and attribute values in the target model are also identified by using the *identifyTargetChanges* function, which leads to the set of ordering changes $\Delta_{l1,l2}^{o,targetChanges}$ (illustrated in Figure 3.18) which is determined by filtering the identified target model changes by their type (by intersecting the set of all possible link order changes $\Delta_{l1,l1}^{o}$ with the set of changes identified in the target model using *identifyTargetChanges*):

$$\Delta_{l1,l2}^{o,targetChanges} = consistentChanges(\{\Delta_{l1,l2}^{o} \cap$$
$$identifyTargetChanges(M_t', Trace_T)\})$$

Using *determineOrder* the inversion change set for externally modified ordering in the target model $\Delta_{l1,l2}^{o,targetChanges,-1}$ can be defined as:

$$\Delta_{l1,l2}^{o,targetChanges,-1} = consistentChanges(determineOrder($$
$$projectOrderL(\Theta), strict))$$

Alternatively to the *strict* reordering strategy, also the *non − strict* strategy can be used.

If the ordering change is not the only change to the target model but there where external deletions or additions the order that was represented in the traces might not be fully re-applicable. For link deletions the ordering pairs that contain deleted links will not be part of the projection anyway as this would cause pairs having empty elements, such as $(l_1, \varnothing)$. For additions, if the *strict* reordering strategy is applied, the *consistentChanges* function ensures that externally added links

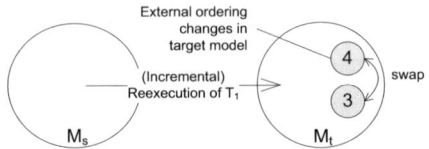

Figure 3.18.: External ordering change in target model.

are moved to the end of the order. In case of the $non-strict$ externally added elements will be kept are there relative position in the order.

c) *Parallel source and target changes:* A conflict between a source resulting ordering change $\delta^o_{l_1,l_2}$ and a target ordering change $\delta^o_{l_3,l_4}$ may occur if $l_1 = l_4$ and $l_2 = l_3$ which would invert each other.

Lemma 3.3. *For all types of changes to a source and a target model a corresponding set of changes can be given that either applies or reverts the change to or from the target model.*

Proof. Per Definition 2.3 a model consists of the sets O, L, V as well as the orders $orderL$ and $orderV$. Thus, an atomic change can only modify one of these sets at once. The sets $\Delta^{sourceChanges}$ and $\Delta^{targetChanges}$ defined above are defined for each such change on the source and target model respectively. Given the additional set of inverse changes $\Delta^{-1,targetChanges}$ for the changes applied through the re-application of the transformation it is possible to apply or revert any type of change to or from the target model. $\qquad\square$

3.9.2. Application of Change Sets for each RetainmentKind

The union of all change sets for the respective types is then built as follows. The set of changes that applies all changes that result from a change in the source model is defined by $\Delta^{sourceChanges}$ ($\Delta^{targetChanges}$ is defined analogously).

$$
\begin{aligned}
\Delta^{sourceChanges} =\ & \Delta^{-,sourceChanges}_o \cup \Delta^{+,sourceChanges}_o \cup \Delta^{-,sourceChanges}_{l,o_1,o_2} \\
& \cup \Delta^{+,sourceChanges}_{l,o_1,o_2} \cup \Delta^{s,sourceChanges}_{o,a,v} \cup \Delta^{u,sourceChanges}_{o,a,v} \\
& \cup \Delta^{o,sourceChanges}_{l_1,l_2} \cup \Delta^{o,sourceChanges}_{v_1,v_2}
\end{aligned}
$$

The set of changes that reverts all modifications to the target model is given as $\Delta^{targetChanges,-1}$.

$$\begin{aligned}
\Delta^{targetChanges,-1} \quad &= \Delta_o^{-,targetChanges,-1} \cup \Delta_o^{+,targetChanges,-1} \cup \Delta_{l,o_1,o_2}^{-,targetChanges,-1} \\
&\cup \Delta_{l,o_1,o_2}^{+,targetChanges,-1} \cup \Delta_{o,a,v}^{s,targetChanges,-1} \cup \Delta_{o,a,v}^{u,targetChanges,-1} \\
&\cup \Delta_{l_1,l_2}^{o,targetChanges,-1} \cup \Delta_{v_1,v_2}^{o,targetChanges,-1}
\end{aligned}$$

Based on the unified change sets, the following formal semantics of the different *RetainmentKinds* are defined based on a transformation T. For the sake of simplicity exactly one retainment policy R defining a retainment kind k will be used for the whole transformation. The scope of R is defined to be a rule retainment scope including all rules of T. The basic building blocks presented above will be used to define these semantics. The set of changes that is given by the application of a certain retainment kind is denoted as $\overset{k}{\Delta}$. For example, the set of changes that is applied by the application of the Never retainment policy is denoted as $\overset{\varnothing}{\Delta}$. In the following, these sets will be defined for each retainment kind so that the final resulting model $\bar{M}_t$ is given by:

$$\bar{M}_t = \leadsto_T^k \left(M_s', M_t' \right) \quad \Longleftrightarrow \quad \bar{M}_t = \overset{k}{\Delta} M_t'$$

3.9.2.1. Never ($\varnothing$)

All manual changes are overwritten when the transformation is re-executed. The result is the same – with respect to the image of the transformation – as if the initial transformation would have been re-applied. For the application within a transformation this policy is defined as the subsequent application of the following two change sets:

$$\overset{\varnothing}{\Delta} = \Delta^{targetChanges,-1} \circ \Delta^{sourceChanges}$$

Application Scenario: This type of retainment kind can be used for areas where changes to the target model would harm the consistency of the whole system. Therefore, any external change to the target model needs to be reverted. Furthermore, this retainment kind is useful for what can be called *master transformations*, that are responsible for the existence of certain parts of the target model where external changes migh occur in between, but as soon as the *master transformation* is re-executed all changes w.r.t. to the image of this transformation are reverted.

Running Example: For the running example, the result of the reapplication of the transformation using a globally applied `Never` *RetainmentPolicy* would result in all the changes to the target model being reverted plus the application of all changes that resulted from changes in the source model. Thus, the applied set of changes is given by:

$$
\overset{\varnothing}{\Delta} = \{\delta^+_{FKBillFor}, \delta^+_{Invoice2FKBillFor,InvoiceTable,FKBillFor}, \delta^-_{FKContactPerson},
$$
$$
\delta^-_{cpToC,CustomerTable,FKContactPerson}, \delta^u_{PurchaseOrderTable,name,``POTable"}\}
$$
$$
\circ \{\delta^s_{PurchaseOrderTable,name,``PurchOrdTable"}, \delta^+_{AddressTable}, \delta^-_{FKPurchaseOrder},
$$
$$
\delta^-_{cToPO,CustomerTable,FKPurchaseOrder}\}
$$

The resulting target model is the same as depicted in Figure 3.3 except for the deletion of `FKPurchaseOrder`, the new `Table` called `AddressTable` and the renaming of `PurchaseOrderTable` to "PurchOrdTable". Note that for the inversion of the deletion of `FKBillFor` also the dependent changes of the consistent change, namely the deletion of the link from `InvoiceTable` to `FKBillFor` has to be reverted by re-establishing this link.

3.9.2.2. Target changed exclusively (▶)

All manual changes that where applied to the target model are retained when the transformation is re-executed as long as there is no change in the source model that would overwrite this change. For the application within a transformation this policy is defined as:

$$
\overset{\blacktriangleright}{\Delta} = \Delta^{sourceChanges}
$$

Application Scenario: This retainment kind is quite useful for scenarios where no round-trip from the target back to the source model is performed but it should be possible to refine the target model to a certain extent. As Changes resulting from modified source models are still synchronised to the target model possibly overwriting external changes there the retainment kind is well fitted for forward engineering scenarios.

Running Example: For the running example, the result of the reapplication of the transformation using a globally applied `Target changed exclusively` *RetainmentPolicy* would result in all the changes to the target model being retained except those where a change from the source model overwrites it, plus the application of all changes

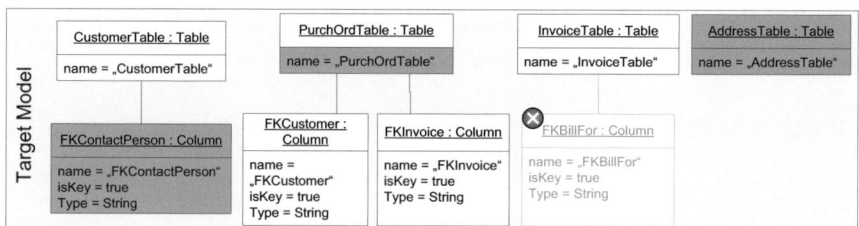

Figure 3.19.: Example: target model after re-applying the transformation using the `target changed exclusively` (▶) retainment policy.

that resulted from changes in the source model. Thus, the applied set of changes is given by:

$$\overset{\blacktriangleright}{\Delta} = \{\delta^s_{PurchaseOrderTable,name,"PurchOrdTable"}, \delta^+_{AddressTable}, \delta^-_{FKPurchaseOrder},$$
$$\delta^-_{cToPO,CustomerTable,FKPurchaseOrder}\}$$

The resulting target model is depicted in Figure 3.19. The changed regions are highlighted in dark grey. The Figure shows that the `FKPurchaseOrder` column has been deleted and an externally created new column `FKContactPerson` was retained. The name attribute of `PurchaseOrderTable` was changed in the target model but in parallel the corresponding source model changed. According to the semantics of the retainment policy, the synchronisation from the source model was preferred over the target model change. Additionally, the deletion of `FKBillFor` was also retained and a new table `AddressTable` was created as a result from the corresponding change in the source model.

3.9.2.3. Source changed exclusively (◀)

All changes to the target model will be reverted. The resulting target model will only have those elements synchronised from the source where a change was made in the target. Elements in the target model, that did not change and the corresponding source model element did change, will not be synchronised from the source. An untouched image of the transformation in the target model will not be synchronised from the source model. For the application within a transformation this policy is defined as:

$$\overset{\blacktriangleleft}{\Delta} = \Delta^{targetChanges,-1} \circ \left\{ \delta \in \Delta^{sourceChanges} \mid \exists \delta_t \in identifyTargetChanges\left(M'_t, Trace_T\right) \mid element(\delta) = element(\delta_t) \right\}$$

Application Scenario: Considering a model transformation that generates a view layout model from a domain model, this retainment kind is useful for re-applying the original layout if it is for example corrupted by external changes to the layout model. However, because only changed target elements are resynchronised from the source it is still possible to, for example, keep the initially generated layout that is uncorrupted intact.

Running Example: For the changes of the running example, the application of the `Source changed exclusively` retainment policy would result in the following changes being applied to M'_t :

$$\overset{\blacktriangleleft}{\Delta} = \left\{ \delta^+_{FKBillFor}, \delta^+_{Invoice2FKBillFor,InvoiceTable,FKBillFor}, \delta^-_{FKContactPerson}, \right.$$
$$\left. \delta^-_{cToCP,CustomerTable,FKContactPerson}, \delta^u_{PurchaseOrderTable,name,"POTable"} \right\}$$
$$\circ \left\{ \delta^s_{PurchaseOrderTable,name,"PurchOrdTable"} \right\}$$

According to these changes, the difference to the application of the `Never` retainment policy can be seen in the second set of changes. There, only the change that synchronises the name of the `PurchaseOrderTable` from the source model, by setting it to "PurchOrdTable", is present because this is the only change where the corresponding target model element did change in parallel.

3.9.2.4. Source and Target changed (■)

Only those external changes to the target model are retained for which there is a corresponding change in the source model that would overwrite this change. In other words, changes to the source model are synchronised to the target model except for elements where the target model changed. This is achieved by applying the $\ominus$ operator, which denotes the creation of the symmetric differences set, to the change sets $\Delta^{targetChanges,-1}$ and $\Delta^{sourceChanges}$. In conjunction with $element(\delta)$ this set is built using the affected elements of the change sets. For the application within a transformation this retainment kind is defined as follows.

$$\overset{\blacksquare}{\Delta} = \Delta^{targetChanges,-1} \underset{element(\delta)}{\ominus} \Delta^{sourceChanges}$$

Application Scenario: This retainment kind is useful when parallel changes to source and target models should be resolved manually whereas non-conflicting changes can be synchronised automatically. Keeping those elements untouched which are in a possible conflict state due to parallel source and target changes solves this problem.

Running Example: For the changes of the running example the application of the Source and Target changed retainment policy would result in the following changes being applied to M_t':

$$\overset{\blacksquare}{\Delta} = \{\delta^+_{FKBillFor}, \delta^+_{Invoice2FKBillFor,InvoiceTable,FKBillFor}, \delta^-_{FKContactPerson},$$
$$\delta^-_{cToCP,CustomerTable,FKContactPerson}, \delta^u_{PurchaseOrderTable,name,``POTable"}\}$$
$$\underset{element(\delta)}{\ominus} \{\delta^+_{AddressTable}, \delta^-_{FKPurchaseOrder}, \delta^-_{cToPO,CustomerTable,FKPurchaseOrder},$$
$$\delta^s_{PurchaseOrderTable,name,``PurchOrdTable"}\}$$
$$\Longleftrightarrow \overset{\blacksquare}{\Delta} = \{\delta^+_{FKBillFor}, \delta^+_{Invoice2FKBillFor,InvoiceTable,FKBillFor}, \delta^-_{FKContactPerson},$$
$$\delta^-_{cToCP,CustomerTable,FKContactPerson}, \delta^+_{AddressTable}, \delta^-_{FKPurchaseOrder},$$
$$\delta^-_{cToPO,CustomerTable,FKPurchaseOrder}\}$$

This example shows that the changes to the target model are reverted excluding the change that renamed PurchaseOrderTable to "POTable" as for this change the corresponding model element in the source model also changed ($\delta^s_{PurchaseOrder,name,``PurchOrd"}$). Therefore, $elements(\delta)$ returned the same element which, in turn, led to the removal of the changes from the resulting change set according to the $\ominus$-operator. Furthermore, all the changes from the source model are propagated to the target model.

3.9.2.5. Source xor Target changed(◀▶)

This option is the opposite of the Source and Target changed retainment kind. Elements in the target model are only retained if either the corresponding source model or the target model changed. Elements where both sides changed will be re-synchronised

107

from the source model. Formally expressed, the semantics of this retainment kind are defined as:

$$\overset{\blacktriangleleft\blacktriangleright}{\Delta} = \Delta^{sourceChanges} \underset{element(\delta)}{\cap} identifyTargetChanges(M'_t, Trace_T)$$

Application Scenario: This retainment kind finds application in resolving conflicts where source and target model changed in parallel, i.e. overwriting these changes by re-applying the transformation to those elements.

Running Example: Applied to the changes in the running example, this retainment kind yields the following set of changes:

$$\overset{\blacktriangleleft\blacktriangleright}{\Delta} = \{\delta^s_{PurchaseOrderTable,name,``POTable"}\}$$

The name of `PurchaseOrderTable` is the only element that changed on both sides. Therefore, this change is re-synchronised from the source model.

3.9.2.6. Target changed(■►)

If this retainment kind is applied, all changes to the target model will be retained; even if the corresponding source model did also change. Formally, this set of changes is determined as:

$$\overset{\blacksquare\blacktriangleright}{\Delta} = \Delta^{sourceChanges} \underset{element(\delta)}{\setminus} \Delta^{targetChanges}$$

Application Scenario: In scenarios where it is allowed to do manual refinements to target models this retainment is most useful. This way, it is possible to refine the target model in an arbitrary without having to worry that these changes will get lost upon subsequent transformation calls. Areas of the model where no external changes have been performed, however, will still be updated from the source model allowing to reuse the initial transformation to extend the manually refined target model in unchanged areas.

Running Example: Applied to the changes in the running example this retainment kind yields the following set of changes:

$$\overset{\blacksquare\blacktriangleright}{\Delta} = \{\delta^+_{AddressTable}, \delta^-_{FKPurchaseOrder}, \delta^-_{cToPO,CustomerTable,FKPurchaseOrder}\}$$

This change set shows that even though the name of `PurchaseOrderTable` would change also according to a source change all target model changes including this one are retained.

3.9.2.7. Source changed(◄■)

All kinds of changes that result from changes in the source model are not applied to the target model and external changes will be retained where the corresponding source element changed at the same time. However, all other external changes will be reverted. Formally, this set of changes is determined as:

$$\overset{\blacktriangleleft\blacksquare}{\Delta} = \Delta^{targetChanges,-1} \underset{element(\delta)}{\diagdown} \Delta^{sourceChanges}$$

Application Scenario: Using a transformation to only revert some changes in the target model and doing no transformation from source to target at all is, in practice, a very rare case. However, having the possibility to specify this case completes the *RetainmentPolicy* approach to be able to handle *all* scenarios.

Running Example: Applied to the changes in the running example this retainment kind yields the following set of changes:

$$\overset{\blacktriangleleft\blacksquare}{\Delta} = \{\delta^+_{FKBillFor}, \delta^+_{Invoice2FKBillFor,InvoiceTable,FKBillFor}, \delta^-_{FKContactPerson},$$
$$\delta^-_{cpToC,CustomerTable,FKContactPerson}\}$$

This change set shows that because the name of `PurchaseOrderTable` did change according to a change in the source model, only this renaming is retained and all other external changes are reverted.

3.9.2.8. Always(◄■►)

The semantics of this retainment kind is that the transformation will only produce the target model initially and will leave it untouched in any case. External changes to the target model will be allowed and no re-synchronisation from the source model will be performed in any case.

$$\overset{\blacktriangleleft\blacksquare\blacktriangleright}{\Delta} = \emptyset$$

Application Scenario: This retainment kind can be used to let a transformation create initial default models that are afterwards completely ignored by the transformation.

3.9.3. Completeness of RetainmentKinds

Having presented the formal semantics of all *RetainmentKinds* allows to reason about the completeness of the *RetainmentPolicy*-approach. Completeness can be ensured if all possible change combinations are mapped by the approach so that fine-grained decisions can be specified using *RetainmentPolicies*. Lemma 3.4 formulates the completeness of *RetainmentPolicies*.

Lemma 3.4. *All combinations of source and target model changes can be mapped using the* RetainmentPolicy *approach.*

Proof. By lemma 3.3 it is possible to give change sets for all types of changes that may be applied to the target model. As there are 8 possible combinations of source and target model changes and it is possible, and we defined for each of them a corresponding retainment kind we can argue that each type is mapped by the *RetainmentPolicy* approach. Furthermore, by comparing the change set definitions of the different retainment kinds to the possible intersections and unifications of the change the complete change sets given in lemma 3.3 can be produced. □

3.9.4. Formal Semantics of the retainAll Property

If the `retainAll` property of a *RetainmentPolicy* is set to true, all elements in the scope of a *RetainmentPolicy* are considered to be handled by the *RetainmentPolicy*. If, for example, a `Target changed` *RetainmentPolicy* is applied to a scope of three elements $\{a, b, c\}$ and one of it is changed, e.g., from a to a' this setting will cause also b and c to be retained, even if they did not change themselves. Semantically, the retainment of b and c can not be represented by the same *RetainmentPolicy* `Target changed`, as they did not change at all. Applying `Target changed` to the elements would not prevent them from being overwritten by changes resulting from the source model as they simply did not change.

Furthermore, in contrast to `Target changed`, imagine the same scenario but with the `Source changed exclusively` *RetainmentPolicy* applied. If a would to be retained because of source model changes but b and c do not have a corresponding source model change they cannot be retained by using the same `Source changed`

	Trigger Change	Mapped *RetainmentPolicy*	
∅	never	never	∅
►	target changed excl.	always	◄■►
◄	source changed excl.	source changed excl.	◄
■	source *and* target changed	source changed	◄
◄►	source *xor* target changed	source changed excl.	◄
■►	target changed	Always	◄■►
◄■	source changed	source changed	◄■
◄■►	always	Always	◄■►

Table 3.3.: *RetainmentPolicy* mapping for elements included in a `retainAll` retainment scope.

`exclusively` *RetainmentPolicy*. However, as the *RetainmentPolicy* only resembles retainment actions for source model changes, changes to the target model would still need to be reverted. Due to the semantics of retaining elements in the target model, the semantics of the `retainAll` property only are only extended w.r.t. ,*Retainment-Policies* that deal with target model changes. The following Table 3.3 presents mapping rules that translate a so called *trigger change RetainmentPolicy* into a *RetainmentPolicy* that can be applied to retain all other elements within the retainment scope.

For cases that retain default elements in the target model upon source changes the *retainAll* semantics is quite difficult to grasp. For example, assuming elements $\{a, b, c\}$ in the source model and the corresponding elements $\{a', b', c'\}$ in the target model. For simplicity, considering the transformation to be a simple one-to-one copy transformation. Deleting element a in the source model would then cause the deletion of its corresponding element a'. Applying, e.g., a `source changed exclusively` *RetainmentPolicy* to this scenario would prevent a' from also being deleted upon the deletion of a. However, as b and c did not change there is no retainment action to be done for these elements anyway. Thus, in this case the mapping from the *trigger change* to the mapped *RetainmentPolicy* is identical: `source changed exclusively`. Target changes to this area would then still be reverted as defined in the `source changed exclusively` *RetainmentPolicy*. The mapping applies analogously for `source xor target changed`. For cases where also a target change would be retained (`source and target changed`, `source changed`, the mapping leads to

Using this mapping, it is possible to specify how elements in a `retainAll`-scope are handled. For example, if a `target changed exclusively` *RetainmentPolicy* is specified to a changed target model element a, also having elements b and c in its scope these elements are treated as if an `always` *RetainmentPolicy* would have been applied to them.

Formally this mapping is defined as follows:

$$\Delta^{triggerChange}_k = changeSet_k \left(Scope_{R_{elements(\delta)}} \cap \overset{k}{\Delta} \right)$$

$$\overset{k}{\Delta} = \Delta^{triggerChange}_k \cup \left(changeSet_{mapped(k)} \left(Scope_{R_{elements(\delta)}} \setminus \Delta^{triggerChange}_k \right) \right)$$

where $mapped(k)$ gives the retainment kind mapped using Table 3.3.

3.10. Type Specific Retainment Policies

Specifying a retainment policy using one of the retainment kinds given above allows to define rules for change retainment on a coarse-grained level for all types of changes. However, it cannot yet be distinguished between the actual type of the change that should be retained or not. All types of changes, i.e., addition, deletion and change in ordering of elements are handled the same way according to the specified *RetainmentPolicy*. In many cases, changes to the target model should not be handled equally. For example, it should be possible to specify that deletions of elements in the target model should be allowed (i.e., retained), whereas external additions are not.

In the running example (cf. page 62), it could be required that deletions of generated columns within a table are allowed. Therefore, a *RetainmentPolicy* using a `target changed` *RetainmentKind* is attached to the transformation rule which is responsible for creating columns from association ends. However, this would also imply that all columns added to the target table would be retained. However, this might not be the intended behaviour. Therefore, to enable the *RetainmentPolicies* to distinguish between change types a more fine-grained type of *RetainmentPolicy* is introduced.

To be able to specify retainment in a more fine-grained way, a *TypeSpecificRetainmentPolicy* (cf. Figure 3.20) can to be used. The semantics of the inherited (from *RetainmentPolicy*) `retainChange` attribute changes slightly in the context of this class. If `retainChange` set to a specific *RetainmentKind*, this setting includes the handling of all types of changes, namely adding, removing of elements as well as changes in ordering. As long as the other `retain*`-attributes are set to `NOT_SET`, this value is used

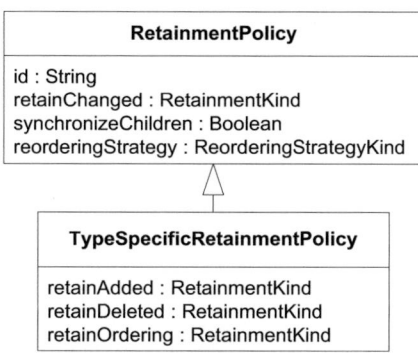

Figure 3.20.: Type specific retainment policy.

for all kinds of changes. If any of the other attributes is set to a value different than NOT_SET, this will overrule the setting in retainChange.

To achieve the intended behaviour of the example given above, a *TypeSpecificRetainmentPolicy* can be specified defining for retainChange the never *RetainmentKind*. To account for the retainment of deletions from the respective part of the target model, the retainRemoved attribute of the *TypeSpecificRetainmentPolicy* is set to target change. This allows to only retain deletions of columns in the target table whereas all other types of changes, i.e., the addition of columns and ordering changes therein are reverted.

3.10.1. Formal Semantics of Type Specific Retainment Policies

The combination of the attribute values for retainAdded, rertainDeleted, retain- Ordering given in a TypeSpecificRetainmentPolicy with a *RetainmentKind* results in a new formal entity called *Type Specific Retainment Kind*, which is defined as:

Definition 3.9 (Type Specific Retainment Kind). *A collection retainment kind is a tuple* $TK = (k, CT)$ *where*

$k \in K$ *is a retainment kind,*
$CT \subseteq \{+, -, o\}$ *is a specific type of change operation, where*

+ *denotes the addition of an object, link or attribute value and is specified by* `retainAdded`,

− *denotes the deletion of an object, link or attribute value and is specified by* `retainRemoved` *and*

o *denotes the change of ordering of a link or an attribute value in a collection and is specified by* `retainOrderingChanged`.

A type specific retainment kind is written in shorthand in the following way: k^{CT}. So that for example, $\blacktriangleleft\blacksquare\blacktriangleright^{\{+\}}$ denotes the type specific retainment kind $TK = (\blacktriangleleft\blacksquare\blacktriangleright, \{+\})$, which defines that the `RetainAdded` property of a *TypeSpecificRetainmentPolicy* has been set to `always`.

In combination with a rule to which a retainment policy is attached, a specific type of change can be derived. For example, a type specific retainment policy $\blacktriangleleft\blacksquare\blacktriangleright^{\{+,o\}}$ is attached to a rule that is responsible for creating links of an association a between model elements of the classes c_1 and c_2. Then the actual change types, to which the policy is specific, are $\Delta^+_{l,o_1,o_2} \cup \Delta^o_{l_1,l_2}$.

These actual change sets are given by a function

$$changeSetsByType : \mathcal{P}(\{+,-,o\}) \rightarrow \mathcal{P}(Changes_{MM})$$

.

Recall that the specification of type specific retainment settings may be used in combination with a specific complementary setting of `RetainChange`. Thus, the semantics of the type specific retainment kinds will be described based on the setting of `RetainChange` = $k_1 \in RetainmentKinds$. The semantics of a type specific retainment kind are defined as follows, where k_2 represents a type specific retainment kind.

$$
\begin{aligned}
\overset{k_1,k_2^{CT}}{\Delta} =&\, changeSets_{k_2}((\Delta^{sourceChange} \cup \Delta^{targetChange}) \cap changeSetsByType(CT)) \\
&\cup changeSets_{k_1}((\Delta^{sourceChange} \cup \Delta^{targetChange}) \\
&\cap (Changes_{MM} \smallsetminus changeSetsByType(CT)))
\end{aligned}
$$

The change set determined for k_2 is filtered by the included element's type, i.e., by intersecting this change set with the set of all changes of the specific types CT defined in r_2. From this intersection, the actual change set, according to the given *RetainmentKind* k_2 is determined using $changeSets_{k_2}()$. The resulting change set is unified with the analogously determined change set for the rest of the changes that are not of the types given in CT.

In the running example, an application of a type specific retainment policy with retainChanged = Never($\emptyset$) in combination with a type specific retainment kind retainAdded = Target Changed($\blacksquare\blacktriangleright^+$) would then result in the following change set:

$$
\Delta^{\emptyset,\blacksquare\blacktriangleright^+} = \{\delta^+_{FKBillFor}, \delta^+_{Invoice2FKBillFor,InvoiceTable,FKBillFor},
$$
$$
\delta^-_{cpToC,CustomerTable,FKContactPerson}, \delta^u_{PurchaseOrderTable,name,``POTable"}\}
$$
$$
\circ \{\delta^s_{PurchaseOrderTable,name,``PurchOrdTable"}, \delta^+_{AddressTable}, \delta^-_{FKPurchaseOrder},
$$
$$
\delta^-_{cToPO,CustomerTable,FKPurchaseOrder}\}
$$

This example shows that the externally added Column FKContactPerson was retained by the additional type specific retainment policy whereas all other external changes were reverted.

3.10.2. Completeness of Type Specific Retainment Policies

Lemma 3.5. *Using* TypeSpecificRetainmentPolicies *each type of change in each combination of source target model change can be retained or reverted from the target model.*

Proof. Due to lemma 3.4 all changes to either a source or target model can be separately applied to a target model. By intersecting the sets that make up a model defined in Definition 2.3 with the change sets of the different retainment kinds it is thus possible to restrict these change sets to a specific type of change as only changes of the given set will be left over. □

3.10.3. Conflicts Between Retainment Policies

Conflicts between several *RetainmentPolicies* may occur if they are specified on the same scope but declaring different kinds. For example, if two *RetainmentPolicies* R_1 and R_2 are defined over the same element in the target model a, but R_1 declares an always *RetainmentKind* whereas R_2 declares a never *RetainmentKind* it is not possible to fulfil both policies at the same time.

3.10.3.1. Conflict Detection

A conflict can be detected by intersecting the change sets of the respective policy over the elements in their scopes thus a set of potential conflicts $\Delta^{conflicts}$ is produced:

$$Delta^{conflicts,R_1,R_2} = \bigcup_{e \in Scope_{R_1} \cap Scope_{R_2}} changeSet_{R_1}(e) \underset{element(\delta)}{\cap} changeSet_{R_2}(e)$$

If $\Delta^{conflicts}$ contains changes that are inverse w.r.t. each other they are considered to be in conflict. For example, if $\Delta^{conflicts}$ contains a change δ_o^+ as well as a change δ_o^- a conflict is present. This detection can be expressed as follows:

$$R_1, R_2 \text{ are in conflict w.r.t. an element } e \iff$$
$$\exists \delta_1, \delta_2 \; in \Delta^{conflicts,R_1,R_2} : \delta_1 = invert(\delta_2)$$

3.10.3.2. Conflict Resolution

Resolution of *RetainmentPolicy*-conflicts can be performed on multiple levels.

1. An *RetainmentPolicy* that is attached via a model retainment scope always over-rules a *RetainmentPolicy* defined via a rules retainment scope.

2. More specific *RetainmentPolicies* overrule less specific ones. This resolution mostly accounts for rules *RetainmentPolicies* that are (I) applied to a certain scope using the `synchroniseChildren` properties having child elements that have additional *RetainmentPolicies* on their own and (II) *RetainmentPolicies* that are attached to rules which are transitively called by other rules. In the latter case the *RetainmentPolicies* attached to the called rules overrule those of specified at the callees side. For example, consider a `never` *RetainmentPolicy* attached to the *BusinessObject2Table* rule given in the running example from page 62 and a `always` policy attached to the *Association2ForeignKeyColumn* rule. The `synchroniseChildren` property being set, would imply that all children of the first rule would also have the `never` policy applied. This would, however, conflict with the specified `always` *RetainmentPolicy*. Hence, this conflict can be resolved by only using the most specific policy for the elements under conflict.

3. As a final point to resolve conflicts manual precedences amongst *Retainment-Policies* can be specified by explicitly configuring them to *overrule* each other.

These overruling is represented in the *RetainmentPolicy*-metamodel by the *Overrules* association.

3.11. Realisation of Retainment Policies Using QVT Relations

A realisation of the retainment policies approaches for QVT Relations (QVT-R), the OMG's declarative model transformation approach is presented here. QVT-R includes some features on which the semantics of the retainment policies can be based. For example, QVT-R already includes the concept of checkonly/enforce domains. According to the specification, checkonly defines for a rule's domain that the pattern represented in the checkonly domain is only checked for and the model is not enforced to hold the pattern. This semantics are irrespective of the direction in which the transformation is executed. Thus, also if the transformation is executed in the checkonly domain's direction the pattern within this domain will not be applied to the current target model. This fits the semantics of the `always` retainment policy. However, this check is always performed based on the current target model and no distinction is made between an original and a modified target model.

Furthermore, QVT-R supports the *default values* specification within enforce domains. These patterns are only used when the transformation is executed in enforcement mode and do not play a role when the transformation is checking the model. This is useful if the transformation is used bidirectionally. However, these default values do not have the semantics of default values w.r.t. external changes to the target model. Each time the transformation is executed in the enforced domain's direction, the default values will be re-applied to the corresponding elements in the target model. Thus it is not possible to realise the, for example the `source changed exclusively` *RetainmentPolicy* using this standard construct.

The most important feature which allows for the realisation of the retainment policy approach for QVT-R, is the trace model that is created during the transformation's execution. This allows to write transformation rules that directly operate on the trace model to check which elements were created by the transformation by which other elements.

3.11.1. Applying RetainmentPolicies to a QVT-R Transformation

As *RetainmentPolicies* reference to transformation rules to determine their retainment semantics using a rule retainment scope, an approach to attach them to these rules needs to be provided. Furthermore, *RetainmentPolicies* have to be taken into account during execution of the transformation. This requires to interpret them during the runtime of the transformation. Thus, a solution for applying their semantics needs to be provided in addition.

One can think of different possibilities on how *RetainmentPolicies* can be represented in transformation rules.

- **Extension of the QVT-R grammar:** The existing concrete and abstract syntax is extended by *RetainmentPolicies*. Rules can be directly written in the concrete syntax having their own constructs in the concrete as well as abstract syntax. The advantage of this approach is that editors can directly support the new constructs and they are directly represented in the abstract syntax of the transformation. However, the resulting transformation language would not be standard compliant anymore; requiring special support in editors as well as runtime.

- **Annotation as decorator model on the abstract syntax:** A less invasive approach can be realised using a decorator model. This model can be attached to the unmodified abstract syntax of the transformation, annotating its rules with *RetainmentPolicies*. Thus, there is no need to extend the QVT grammar and editors. However, the QVT transformation needs to be available and accessible from within the editing environment in order to let a developer attach the *RetainmentPolicies*.

- **Using annotations within the concrete syntax of QVT:** Allowing to write annotations within comments of the original transformation that are then later-on processed by an additional parser and attached to the abstract syntax of the transformation is an extension of the previous approach. This extension allows to define *RetainmentPolicies* directly at the places where they are going to be used later, i.e., the comments that can be written at arbitrary places within the transformation.

The last approach was taken in the realisation of this thesis as it seems to be the most easy to use as well as less invasive one. An additional parser is provided to parse annotations that are written in the comments of the transformation. The grammar used for this parser is shown in Listing 3.2. The syntax allows to define *RetainmentPolicies* as well as *TypeSpecificRetainmentPolicies*. The scope of a *RetainmentPolicy* can be defined in two different ways:

1. A scope can be defined by enclosing transformation rules within within a two annotations, starting with a the definition of the *RetainmentPolicy* followed by a

```
28 single_line_annotation ::= '--' rp_scope
29 multi_line_annotation ::= '/*' rp_scope '*/'
30 rp_scope ::= rp_scope_start | rp_scope_end | rp
31 rp_scope_start ::= rp '{'
32 rp_scope_end ::= '@rp' '}'
33 rp ::= rp_simple | rp_type_specific | rp_ref
34 rp_ref ::= '@RetainmentPolicy' ref IDENTIFIER
35 rp_simple ::= '@RetainmentPolicy' IDENTIFIER ':' retainment_kind
36    'synchronizeChildren'? reordering_strategy?
37 rp_type_specific ::=
38    '@TSRetainmentPolicy' IDENTIFIER ':' retainment_kind
39    (type_specific_retainment ':' retainment_kind )* {separator = ','}
40    'synchronizeChildren'? reordering_strategy?
41 type_specific_retainment ::= 'retainAdded' | 'retainDeleted' |
42    'retainOrdering'
43 retainment_kind ::= 'NEVER' | 'TARGET_EX' | 'SOURCE_EX' |
44    'SOURCE_AND_TARGET' | 'SOURCE_XOR_TARGET' | 'SOURCE' |
45    'TARGET' | 'ALWAYS'
46 reordering_strategy ::= 'STRICT' | 'NON_STRICT'
```

Listing 3.2: EBNF grammar for parsing the RetainmentPolicy annotation syntax.

opening curly brace "{" (ro_scope_start). Starting from such a definition all rules up to a scope end definition using "@rp }" are included in a rule retainment scope of the given *RetainmentPolicy*.

2. If the order of the transformation rules is not fitted, so that a positional retainment scope can be declared by surrounding scope definitions, an alternative approach can be used. Instead of defining a new *RetainmentPolicy*, it is also possible to refer to an existing one via its identifier (rp_ref). All areas that refer to a *Retainment-Policy* are also included in its rule retainment scope.

Furthermore, different possibilities exist how the *RetainmentPolicies* are applied in the final transformation.

- One possibility is to hold the *RetainmentPolicies* in a separate model that decorates the actual transformation. Then, a special interpreter that knows of QVT-R as well as *RetainmentPolicies* can be used to execute the transformation while paying respect to the retainment policies. However, this would require a special implementation of a QVT-R engine that includes extensions for *RetainmentPolicies*.

- A different approach includes the application of a higher order transformation (HOT). This hot is used to transform the given transformations plus the attached

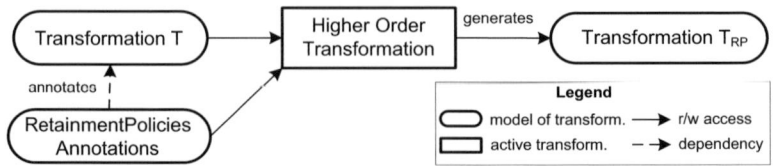

Figure 3.21.: Generation of the RetainmentPolicy transformation using a higher order transformation.

RetainmentPolicy-model to a second transformation as it is depicted in Figure 3.21. Ideally this transformation is again standard QVT-R and can be executed using an existing QVT-engine. This approach has the advantage over the previous one, that it independent from the used QVT-engine. The QVT engine can be easily exchanged.

The latter approach seems to be the more flexible one. Assuming a complete mapping of the *RetainmentPolicy* approach to standard QVT-R is possible it yields its full potential of not needing to extend the QVT-R engine. Therefore, in the approach presented in this thesis, the HOT approach is used. Roughly speaking, the presented approach takes a transformation that is annotated with retainment policies as input and creates an equivalent transformation that can be executed by the transformation engine. Therefore the engine needs no knowledge about the original transformation rules with the retainment annotations. All retainment policies have been translated into standard QVT-R constructs.

3.11.2. Weaving Retainment Policies into QVT-R Transformations

Based on the augmented abstract syntax representation of the transformation it is now possible to generate a new transformation that realises the retainment policies. This is done using a higher-order transformation. The target of this transformation is standard QVT-R code which allows for the execution of the generated transformation using any standard compliant QVT-R engine.

There are different patterns how a specific retainment policy is mapped to the generated transformation T_{RP}. Some policies can be mapped to the transformation by only changing the annotated rule or adding queries to the transformation that are then used in those rules. However, for some policies it might be necessary to use the information of

	Attribute		Model Element		Link	
	Retain	!Retain	Retain	!Retain	Retain	!Retain
RetainChanged	1, 2	0	2, 3, 5	0	1	1
RetainAdded	1	0	3, 5	0	1	2
RetainRemoved	2	0	2, 5	0	2	1
RetainOrderingChanged	0	4	0	4	0	4

Table 3.4.: Pattern usage in realisation of RetainmentPolicies.

how the transformation was executed in the previous transformation run, which is stored as the trace model.

Table 3.4 shows which combination of change type – attribute change ($\delta_{o,a,v}^{s,u}$, δ_{o,a,v_1,v_2}^{o}), model element change ($\delta_o^{+,-}$) and link change ($\delta_{l,o_1,o_2}^{+,-}$, δ_{l_1,l_2}^{o}) – and attribute of *(TypeSpecific)RetainmentPolicy* maps to which type of pattern. The possible pattern types are:

Pattern 0 - **Default Behaviour**: If the semantics of a *RetainmentPolicy* match the default behaviour of the QVT engine, there is no need to add any additional constructs. The transformation rule to the corresponding rule in T_{RP} is an identity transformation.

Pattern 1 - **Property by Query**: The value that should be assigned to a property that is protected by a *RetainmentPolicy* is determined by checking the currently set value in the target model. This check can be expressed by formulating a query on the target model and comparing that value with the one determined from the current source model. This pattern can be expressed by using only information from the source and target model. No trace links are needed. This can, for instance, be used whenever the applied *RetainmentPolicy* can be expressed without requiring the information from the trace model. It then can be checked if the target value has been set and if so it can be retained. For primitive valued properties this pattern can be produced by modifying the assignment of a feature with a query method that handles this check. See example 1 (Listings 3.3 and 3.4 for an example application of this pattern.

Pattern 2 - **When-based Trace Check Rule**: As the application of a rule in QVT-R can be controlled using its when-pattern it is possible to add additional logic to the when pattern that checks for a certain combination in the trace model and, based on this, decides whether the rule is executed at all. This pattern is implemented by an additional rule that gets called in the when clause of the annotated rule. This additional rule is then used to check whether a trace link existed before for the given elements or not. Depending on the involved *RetainmentKind* a decision can then be made on whether the annotated rule is executed or not. Listings 3.5 and 3.6 show an example application of this pattern.

Pattern 3 - **Virtual Rule**: According to the QVT specification all elements within an enforce domain for which no transformation rule holds will get deleted upon execution of the transformation (see enforcement semantics in [Obj11] Section 7.10.2). However, it is not necessary that the same rule that once created the element holds. It just needs to be any rule due QVT's "avoid delete followed by an immediate create" semantics ([Obj11] Section 7.10.2 Enforcement Semantics). To be able to retain manually created elements a "virtual" transformation rule will be created for each rule to which this pattern is applied. This virtual rule contains an empty original source domain and the same target domain and pattern as the original rule. Additionally it checks if there exists a trace for the target element and the original rule. Furthermore all *when* conditions from the original rule have to be satisfied to ensure that the element might indeed have been created by the original rule. During execution this rule will match any manually created target model elements as they could have been produced by the original rule. This avoids deletion of these elements. Listing 3.7 shows an example application of this pattern.

Pattern 4 - **Handling of Ordering**: Ordering in QVT-R is handled by so called *CollectionTemplates*. Using these constructs it is possible to handle ordering within the transformation rules explicitly. However, if no explicit ordering is defined, ordering of elements in the target model, especially if elements are created by different rules, one can not even rely on that the ordering as it was in the corresponding source model elements is kept. One solution to ensure a certain order is to call the rules, that are responsible for putting the elements in the target model, within an `iterate` expression in the where clause of the parent element's rule. Another possibility to do this is to check in the when clause whether the current relation already holds for the predecessor of the current element in the collection. However, this only ensures that the ordering is kept the first time of the execution. If a reordering has to be made because elements in the source domain swapped places or a manual ordering in the target model should be undone due to a *RetainmentPolicy* an in-place transformation has to be executed that does this re-ordering.

Pattern 5 - Explicit Modification of Trace Model: To realise some kinds of retainment, it is necessary to explicitly modify the otherwise implicitly created trace model created by the transformation. For example, if the deletion of elements should be retained, also the, partly inconsistent trace link (because of the reference to the deleted element), needs to be retained. This is realised by an additional *trace conservation* relation, that explicitly creates a trace of the respective type is created and triggered by the relation for which the respective *RetainmentPolicy* is specified. An overview on the execution that results from this pattern is given in Figure 3.22. In addition to the creation of explicit trace model elements, these elements also needs to be added to the actual trace model that was created implicitly during runtime of the transformation. Furthermore, traces that were created due to the trace handling rules should not be part of the final trace model as they would interfere with the trace handling. A deletion of these traces is therefore required. Figure 3.22 also shows that, this merging and deletion is done by an additional transformation that takes the explicit as well as the implicit trace model as input and merges them to a final trace model. This final trace model will then serve as input trace model for the next transformation execution.

Pattern 6 - Including ModelElementRetainmentScopes: Patterns 1 to 5 operate on the whole scope that is defined by a transformation rule. Therefore, also they can only be used for *RetainmentPolicies* that define a rule retainment scope. To incorporate the definition of model retainment scopes these patterns can be extended by an additional pattern that filters the set of matched elements of a transformation rule with the set of elements defined in a model element retainment scope. To achieve this, the application of the *RetainmentPolicy* code is combined with a check whether the elements under consideration are in this scope. Listing 3.4 shows an example application of this pattern.

Figure 3.23 depicts the detailed process on how an annotated transformation T is transformed into an executable transformation that implements the annotated retainment rules T_{RP}.

1. First (1) a higher order transformation (HOT) is used to create a copy of the original transformation. In this step all retainment rules are incorporated which do not rely on information from the trace model (patterns 1, 3 and 4) as extensions to the actual transformation rules called T_{RP}.

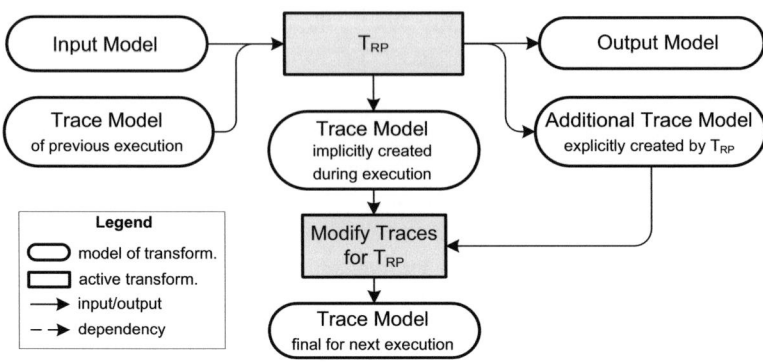

Figure 3.22.: Trace modification during runtime of a RetainmentPolicy-modified transformation.

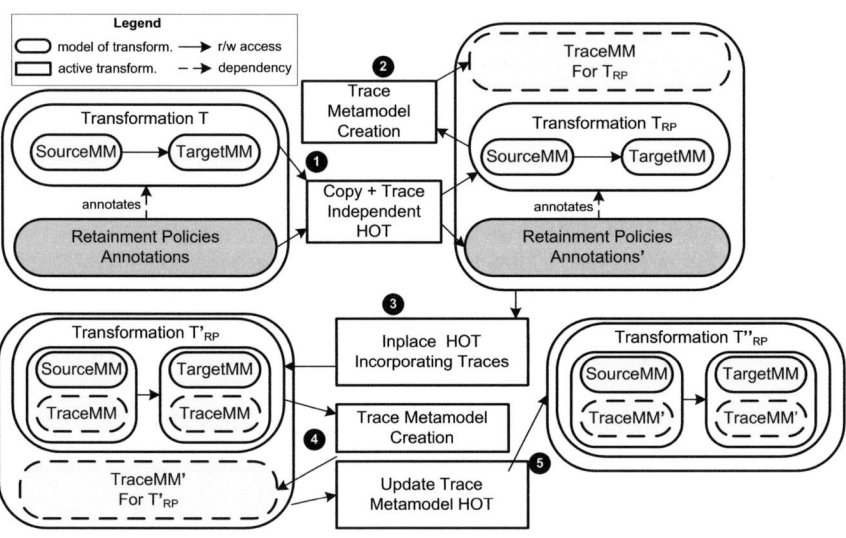

Figure 3.23.: Detailed process for the generation of the RetainmentPolicy transformation using higher order transformation.

2. In the case of QVT-R, traces are instances of a strongly typed metamodel that is created before a transformation can be executed. This metamodel consists of one class per transformation rule that has properties for each element that is matched or enforces in one of the rules' domains. However, this implies that after a change to the transformation this metamodel needs to be updated as well. The trace metamodel is generated from the T_{RP} in step (2).

3. As we want to use the trace information directly within the actual transformation, for example to check which elements in the target model were externally modified, we need to use the generated trace metamodel as an additional domain of the newly generated transformation. Therefore, in the next step (3), an in-place HOT from T_{RP} to T'_{RP} is performed to add this additional domain and transformation code that incorporates the semantics of the corresponding retainment policies according to pattern 2. All remaining retainment policies are now translated into rules that use such trace domains.

4. Due to these changes all affected transformation rules now have additional parameters. The additional domain needs to be reflected in the trace classes so that the traces creation during the runtime of the transformation can be performed correctly. This, in turn, requires an update of the trace metamodel (4).

5. Finally (5), the new trace metamodel is used as third domain replacing the old trace metamodel, resulting in the final version of the transformation T''_{RP}. As no more modifications to the actual transformation have been performed a further regeneration of the trace metamodel is unnecessary.

3.11.3. Examples

Listing 3.3 shows an example in which pattern 1 is applied. The property that should be retained is a single, optional, primitive valued attribute which gets annotated with a *TypeSpecificRetainmentPolicy* specifying a `never` *RetainmentKind* in combination with an `always` *RetainmentKind* for `retainAdded`.

The retainment policy annotation in Listing 3.3 is transformed into an additional query that decides that an already existing "name" from the target model or the "name" coming from the source model should be used. If the name in the target is undefined, which would be the case if the transformation is executed initially where the element in the target model does not yet exist, it is set according to the transformation. Unsetting the value

125

```
1  transformation Bo2Db (bo : BO, rdms : RDBMS) {
2    top relation BO2Table {
3      varName : String;
4      checkonly domain bo myBo : BO::BusinessObject {
5        umlName = varName };
6      enforce domain rdbms table : RDBMS::Table {
7        tableName = varName
8          --@TSRetainmentPolicy MyTSRP: NEVER retainAdded: ALWAYS
9      };
10   }
11   ...
12 }
```

Listing 3.3: Example 1: Example transformation rule with a *TypeSpecificRetainmentPolicy* specifying a never *RetainmentKind* in combination with an always *RetainmentKind*
for retainAdded - **annotated**

externally will not be retained (as this would have required setting retainDeleted
to a target retaining *RetainmentKind*), it will be then again set according to the transformation. The generated transformation that incorporates this *RetainmentPolicy* can be
seen in 3.4. Furthermore, this example uses a model element retainment scope which is
indicated by the additional domain providing the set of elements within this scope.

Listing 3.5 depicts an example where a *TypeSpecificRetainmentPolicy* with Retain-
Removed = TARGET is used. Again the BOToDB example is used. In this case
there are two transformation rules. The first rule creates a table for each business object
in the BO model, whereas the second adds a column for each association end of the
business object. In this example we want to specify that all manually deleted columns
should not be re-created by the transformation. Therefore an annotation is added to the
ClassToTable rule specifying RetainRemoved=TARGET.

The rules from Listing 3.5 are then translated into the rules depicted in Listing 3.6. As
it can be seen an additional rule IdentifyTracesForAssociation2Foreign-
KeyColumn has been added which is used for the conservation of the traces for the
deleted element. This relation ensures that the trace for the deleted element is not deleted during re-execution of the transformation. This is achieved by matching the trace
element itself which Furthermore, a helper query was added that is used to resolve the
traces belonging to the ClassToTable transformation.

Example 3 is also based on the rules from Listing 3.5 where only the *RetainmentKind*
is not RetainRemoved=TARGET but Retain**Added**=TARGET. The annotated rules
are then translated into the rules depicted in Listing 3.7. For the ClassToTable trans-

126

```
1  transformation Bo2Db (bo : BO, scopes : RDBMS, rdbms : RDBMS) {
2    top relation BO2Table {
3      varName : String;
4      checkonly domain bo myBo : SimpleUML::UmlClass {
5        umlName = varName };
6      enforce domain rdbms table : RDBMS::Table {
7        rdbmsName = varName };
8      when { not IsInScopeOf_MyTSRP(table); }
9    }
10   top relation BO2Table {
11     varName : String;
12     checkonly domain bo myBo : SimpleUML::UmlClass {
13       umlName = varName };
14     enforce domain rdbms table : RDBMS::Table {
15       rdbmsName = getNameRetainAddedALWAYS(table.rdbmsName,varName)};
16     when { IsInScopeOf_MyTSRP(table); }
17   }
18   top relation IsInScopeOf_MyTSRP {
19     checkonly domain rdbms table : RDBMS::Table { }
20     when {
21       retainmentPolicies::RetainmentPolicy {
22         id = 'MyTSRP',
23         scope = retainmentPolicies::ModelElementRetainmentScope {
24           modelElements = table
25         }
26       }
27     }
28   }
29   query getNameRetainAddedALWAYS(targetName : String,
30              default : String) : String {
31     if targetName.oclIsUndefined() then
32       default
33     else targetName endif
34   }
35   ...
36 }
```

Listing 3.4: Example 1: Example transformation rule with retainment policy using a `target` changed *RetainmentKind*- **transformed**

```
1   top relation BusinessObject2Table {
2     checkonly domain bo myBo : businessObjects::BusinessObject{
3       elementsOfType = td : businessObjects::TypeDefinition {
4       }
5     };
6     enforce domain db table : rdbms::Table {
7       tableName = myBo.name
8     };
9   };
10  top relation Association2ForeignKeyColumn {
11    checkonly domain bo assoc : businessObjects::Association{
12      ends = end : businessObjects::AssociationEnd {
13        type = td : businessObjects::TypeDefinition {
14          entity = bo : businessObjects::BusinessObject{}
15        }
16      }
17    };
18    --@TSRetainmentPolicy RetainDeletedColumns:NEVER
19    -- RetainRemoved: TARGET
20    enforce domain db keyColumn : rdbms::Column {
21      table = tab;
22      ...
23    }
24    when { BusinessObject2Table(myBo, tab); }
25  }
```

Listing 3.5: Example 2: Example transformation rule with a *TypeSpecificRetainmentPolicy* with RetainRemoved=TARGET - **annotated**

formation an additional transformation that only matches the target domain and also checks for the existence of traces for this target element is generated.

3.12. Limitations

The *RetainmentPolicies* approach presented in this chapter works for a vast range of model transformation approaches. Furthermore, the presented realisation allows to map the retainment policies to standard QVT-R relations allowing to use standard compliant engines to execute an *RetainmentPolicy*-enhanced transformation. However, the approach also has some limitations:

- Changes to the target model can only be retained if they lie inside the image of the transformation (cf. Section 3.5.1). If modifications to the target model are applied, that lie outside of the transformation's image no *RetainmentPolicies* can be defined for their retainment. However, in most transformation approaches it is possible to

```
1   top relation BusinessObject2Table { [...] }
2   top relation Association2ForeignKeyColumn { [...]
3   when {
4   BusinessObject2Table(myBo, tab);
5   --RetainmentRule trace handling start
6     if getTraceForAssociation2ForeignKeyColumn(end).oclIsUndefined()
7     then
8       true
9     else
10      --Call relation that always matches
11      --to ensure trace is not deleted
12      ConserveTracesForAssociation2ForeignKeyColumn(end,
13              getTraceForAssociation2ForeignKeyColumn(end))
14    endif;
15  --RetainmentRule trace handling end
16  }
17 }
18 --RetainmentRule trace handling start
19 query getTraceForAssociation2ForeignKeyColumn(
20     e : BO::AssociationEnd)
21     : Traces::Association2ForeignKeyColumn {
22  Traces::Association2ForeignKeyColumn.allInstances()->select(
23    a2fk | a2fk.end = e)->asSequence()->first()
24 }
25 top relation ConserveTracesForAssociation2ForeignKeyColumn {
26   checkonly domain bo endInTrace : BO::AssociationEnd { };
27   checkonly domain traces trace :
28     Traces::Association2ForeignKeyColumn{
29   end = endInTrace };
30 }
31 --RetainmentRule trace handling end
```

Listing 3.6: Example 2: Example transformation rule with retainment policy RetainRe-
⋄ moved=ALWAYS - **transformed**

define that these kinds of elements should ignored anyway, by the transformation. This possibility, at least allows to distinguish that either all outside changes should be reverted or all of them should be ignored.

- Changing of the *RetainmentPolicies* that are attached to a transformation requires the re-generation of the derived transformation. This implies that a full round-trip concerning the generation of the final transformation has to be made whenever a change is made to the retainment policies. However, as the HOTs are not that complex concerning their execution time, this limitation can be alleviated.

```
1  top relation BusinessObject2Table { [...] }
2  top relation Association2ForeignKeyColumn { [...] }
3
4  top relation IdentifyTracesForAssociation2ForeignKeyColumn {
5    checkonly domain bo endInTrace : BO::AssociationEnd { };
6    checkonly domain traces trace :
7      Traces::Association2ForeignKeyColumn{
8    end = endInTrace };
9  }
10 top relation Association2ForeignKeyColumnRetainAdded{
11   cn : String;
12   enforce domain rdbms c : RDBMS::Column {
13     table = t : RDBMS::Table {},
14     columnName = cn
15   };
16   when {
17   not IdentifyTraces(t, getTraceForClassToTable(t));
18   BO2Table(
19       getTraceForBO2Table(end.otherEnd().type.businessObject).p,
20       c.table); }
21   where { cn = c.columnName; }
22 }
23 query getTraceForAssociation2ForeignKeyColumn(
24                   e : BO::AssociationEnd)
25                 : Traces::Association2ForeignKeyColumn {
26   Traces::Association2ForeignKeyColumn.allInstances()
27     ->select(a2fk | a2fk.end = e)->asSequence()->first() }
28 query getTraceForBO2Table(bo : BO::BusinessObject)
29                 : Traces::BO2Table {
30   Traces::BO2Table.allInstances()->select(bo2tab | bo2tab.myBo = bo)
31     ->asSequence()->first() }
```

Listing 3.7: Example 3: Example transformation rule with *RetainmentKind* RetainAdded=TARGET - **transformed**

- Some transformation approaches, such as QVT Relations allow to create transformations that work bidirectional. As mentioned in Section 3.4, the approach presented in this thesis can, in general, also be applied to bidirectional transformations. As the annotations for the *RetainmentPolicies* can also be attached at domain, or even template expression (see QVT example 1 on page 126) level. Therefore, it is also possible to define different *RetainmentPolicies* depending on the direction of the transformation. In turn, this enables the *RetainmentPolicy* approach to be applicable to bidirectional transformations.

Chapter 4.

Views on Models

In order to identify challenges which view-based modelling poses on textual modelling languages, this chapter presents an analysis of different classes and properties of view points, view types and views.

4.1. Scientific Challenges

The notion of having different views on underlying data is wide spread in different areas of software engineering. Starting from views in (object-oriented) data bases, over views on models in MDE up to the different views that are used in software architectures. However, especially in the area of MDE there are still challenges that have not been solved yet:

- What are the exact relations between views-points, views and types of views? MDE literature mentions a lot of work that has to do with views on models. However, apart from a very broad definition, given by the IEEE 1471-2000 standard [IEE00], no common understanding of these terms has been given, yet.

- Defining the semantics of views does have a lot to do with understanding which parts of the underlying models are part of the view and which are not. A further property of importance is the type of synchronisation that is performed between the views and the model. Also, the way a view deals with inconsistencies during editing is an important aspect of view-based modelling Is it, for example, possible to create incomplete modifications in one view, then switching to a second view and completing the work there? Finkelstein et al. [FKN+92] found this support for temporary inconsistency an important aspect of view-based modelling. A clear determination of these properties is still lacking. However, in order to define a view based modelling approach solid foundations have to be provided. This avoids incompleteness and errors stemming from ad-hoc decisions.

- To allow for reasoning over these defined properties, formal definitions should be provided. These formal definitions can then later-on be used to check whether a view-based approach conforms to certain properties or not. This, in turn, allows to reason about the completeness or validity of the approach in general.

4.2. Contributions

In this chapter, the presented scientific contributions are tackled in the following way:

- This chapter first presents a clear distinction between the terms that are used in the area of views in MDE. Three well defined layers, i.e., view point, view type and view (instance), including their relations are introduced. This clear distinction helps to guide discussions on view based approaches and resolves ambiguous usage of the different terms.

- For each of these layers properties, such as partiality, completeness or editability are presented and discussed. The complete listing of these properties gives an overview on which aspects need to be accounted for in the definition of a view-based modelling approach.

- To give a solid basis for view-based modelling approaches, each of these properties is enhanced with a formal definition. The definitions are based on set logic and some basic definitions published by Amelunxen et al. [AS07]. These definitions can be used to validate any view-based approach and identify areas that are weakly supported and where no clear definition is made on how the views are defined or used.

- Furthermore, this chapter discusses issues that need to be taken into account when defining synchronisation transformations between views and models. Reasoning on the requirements for these transformations is conducted in the course of this chapter. For example, a theorem is introduced that says that partial views can only be synchronised with partial, non-injective transformations. Approaches realising these transformations are therefore required to fulfil these requirements.

- At last, an overview own patterns of view types is presented, as they appear in practice. For example, the master / detail pattern is analysed concerning the previously defined view type properties. This classification helps to understand the meaning of the defined properties as well as giving hints to when they are useful.

4.3. Determination of View-Points, View-Types and Views

It can be distinguished between different flavours of the term *view*. The definition given here is based on the IEEE 1471-2000 standard [IEE00]: A *view* is "a representation of a whole system from the perspective of a related set of concerns". Additionally, the standard defines a *view point* as "a specification of the conventions for constructing and using a view. A pattern or template from which to develop individual views by establishing the purposes and audience for a view and the techniques for its creation and analysis." The standard does, not restrict the terms to more specific definitions, which allows for the application of the standard in different areas of software engineering.

However, for a more specific view-based modelling approach it is not enough to rely on the broad definition of the standard. A more detailed and well-defined basis needs to be given. Thus, in order to give a formal basis a more precise definition is presented here. An overview on the three different concepts related to views is given in Figure 4.1.

View Point: A *view point* represents a conceptual point of view that is used to define a certain concern. Often this is also specific to a certain stakeholder. A view point includes both, the concern, and also a certain methodology on how the concern is treated. A viewpoint may include one or more *view types*. For example, the static architecture of a system would be a view point whereas the dynamic aspects of a system would form a different view point.

View Type: The definition of which types of elements are displayed in a certain type of view is also called *view type*. This description takes place at the metamodel level and provides rules that can comprise of a definition of a concrete syntax and its mapping to the abstract syntax. It defines how elements from the concrete syntax are mapped to the abstract syntax, which is in this case the meta-model. For example, a view type could be defined to only show deployment nodes for a deployment view type. In UML a view type would be called a diagram. UML, for example, defines view types such as the class diagram view type, the sequence diagram view type or the activity diagram view type.

View: Also called *view instance*. A view is defined as the actual set of elements and their relations displayed using a certain representation and layout. The set of elements that is represented within a view can either be automatically or manually selected. The automatic selection can, for example, be defined using a query given in the corresponding view type. A view resembles the application of a view type on a

Figure 4.1.: Overview on the different view concepts.

specific set of model elements. A view can therefore be considered an instance of a view type. For example, a developer could configure a view showing deployment nodes that are used for a certain part of the system. In UML, a view is for example a specific class diagram showing classes A, B and C.

A well known example for view-based modelling is the UML [Obj10b]. A view points in UML are characterised by the aspect that is modelled using them. The UML provides, for instance, a static and a dynamic view point. The static view point defines a view types as well as a methodology of how static aspects are modelled and expressed using this view point. Furthermore, several types of diagrams belong to a view point. For example, class or component diagrams belong to the static view point. Figure 4.2 depicts an example for the threefold view hierarchy in UML.

4.3.1. Advantages and Disadvantages of Multiple Models as Views

A general question, when it comes to the definition of a view-based modelling approach is whether to use a single underlying model and define each view to be based on it or to have multiple models, i.e., each view having its own model, and defining transformations between these models. The answer to this question, mostly depends on how many different view types are going to be employed as well as how big their overlap between each other is. In the following advantages and disadvantages of either approach is discussed.

One advantage of this approach is that the views types are more or less independent from each other. Each view then posses its own underlying model and can operate on it without having to interact (and thus possibly interfere) with other views. This independence is an advantage if the models on which the views operate do not have too much in common. Therefore, the transformations that synchronise the models with each only need to consider these few common constructs only need to be extended whenever a new common construct is introduced. Additionally, concerning metamodel evolution,

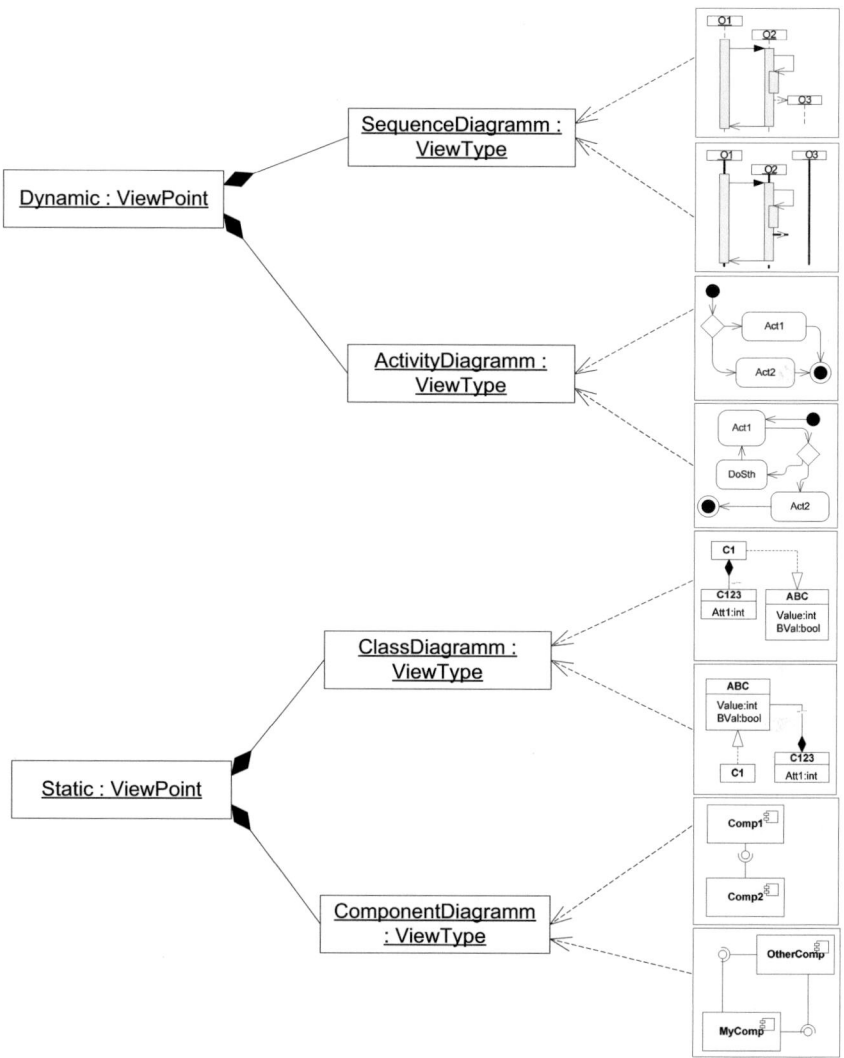

Figure 4.2.: Examples for view points, view types and views in UML.

having multiple metamodels may be an advantage as they can evolve independent from each other.

However, being an advantage in this scenario, the same arguments turn into counter-arguments when such an approach is employed having many views types and/or a larger overlap between the views. For each view, a transformation to each other view type with which it overlaps needs to be provided. Thus, having a large number of overlapping view types results in an even greater number of transformations that need to maintained. Furthermore, not having to define all constructs in a single metamodel also increases the probability of defining the same semantic entity multiple times.

4.3.2. Advantages and Disadvantages of a Central Model with Transformations for Synchronisation

A single underlying model is useful when the number and/or the overlap between the views exceed a certain threshold. Especially the synchronisation effort between the views is affected to a large extend. For each view only one transformation needs to be provided that synchronises the view with the central model. Furthermore, having a single metamodel for the central model forces to think about conciseness and expressiveness of that metamodel. This reduces the probability of defining the same things multiple times.

On the other hand, only having one central model can also cause problems concerning flexibility of the modelling approach. Evolution tasks have to be considered more centrally and cannot be handled in a more or less independent way. Additionally, having a single metamodel may also lead to artificial links between elements of the metamodel that would otherwise be defined in a more abstract and less interconnected way.

4.4. View Type

View types can have different properties in relation to the underlying metamodel as well as other view types. Figure 4.3 gives an overview on the different properties of view types expressed as a feature diagram. To be able to validate view-based approaches w.r.t. their fulfilment of these properties, an explicit, formal definition is given for each of the properties. Given a mapping of a certain view-based approach to the generic constructs that this chapter uses, it is possible to formally validate the properties of the given approach. For example, the FURCAS approach presented in this thesis will be evaluated against these formal definitions in Chapter 7. The following sections and subsections will deal with the explanation and definition of these properties.

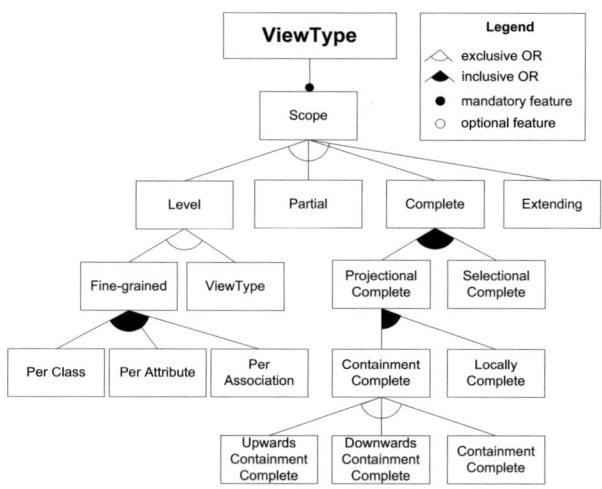

Figure 4.3.: Properties of view types.

A view type defines rules according to which views of the respective type are created. A view type always refers to one or more metamodels. The rules, that are defined by a view type, can be considered as a combination of projectional as well as selectional predicates. The main features of a view type include its scope, i.e., which general types and which specific instances a view type includes as well as the rules on how these elements are represented within a view type's instance.

Note that, depending on whether a view type is editable or read-only, these rules have to be considered in a bidirectional way: I) the direction which specifies how a view is created for an underlying model. And II) defines how a model is created and/or updated based on changes that are performed in a view.

Definition 4.1. *A view type VT is a tuple*

$$VT = (MM, \Phi) \tag{4.1}$$

where

MM is the referenced metamodel for which the view type is defined and

Φ *is a finite set of predicates which denote the rules according to which the view is constructed and the underlying model is updated.*

Views creation in databases distinguishes between projections, i.e. columns of a table are omitted in a view, and selections, i.e., rows of a table are omitted due to some criteria that is based on the actual values of a row. This distinction can also be transferred to views on models. Therefore, the application of a predicate p to an element $e \in M$ of a model $M \in Models_{MM}$ is also defined on these two levels. First a function ϕ_p that decides on metamodel level if the view type can represent a certain class, association or attribute. The function ϕ_p is responsible for the projectional part of the view construction. This function is defined as:

$$\phi_p : Models_{MM} \to \mathbb{B} \text{ where}$$

$$\phi_p(e) = \begin{cases} true & \text{if } e \text{ lies within the projection of the view type} \\ false & \text{else} \end{cases}$$

The second function for each p called σ_p is responsible for the selectional part of the view creation. It decides based upon actual attribute values and association links whether a model element is included in the view or not. This function is defined as:

$$\sigma_p : Models_{MM} \to \mathbb{B} \text{ where}$$

$$\sigma_p(e) = \begin{cases} true & \text{if } e \text{ is in the selection of the view type} \\ false & \text{else} \end{cases}$$

The combination of both functions is denoted as ∂_p where ∂ is a function that is defined as:

$$\partial_p : Models_{MM} \to \mathbb{B} \text{ where}$$

$$\partial_p(e) = \begin{cases} true & \text{if } \phi_p(e) = true \wedge \sigma_p(e) = true \\ false & \text{else} \end{cases}$$

In its decision ∂ may not only include the type of e but also traverse links between objects or values of attributes of objects.

Additionally, each predicate p includes rules that are responsible for defining the layout of the element within a respective view. The application of the layout rules for p to an element $e \in M$ is denoted as $\Lambda_e = \lambda_p(e)$ where λ is defined as $\lambda : Models_{MM} \to \mathcal{P}(Models_\Lambda)$ and $Models_\Lambda$ is the infinite set of all possible layout information. This information includes the actual elements of the concrete syntax which represent an element e as well as additional information that make up the format of the displayed view. For a graphical view the latter is, for example, the exact position of the view's elements or their size. The former would be, for example, that a certain element e_1 is represented by a rectangular shape with its name attribute as label.

Considering the example metamodel presented in Section 2.1.1.1 on page 18, a graphical view type Φ_{bo} could be defined that shows elements of type `BusinessObject`, their `name` property as well as an indicator if the property `valueType` is set to `true`. The set Φ for this view type would then include three predicates resulting in the following functions (c_{bo} is the `BusinessObject` class):

$$\Phi_{bo} = \{p_1, p_2, p_3\}$$

$$\phi_{p_1}(e \in M) = \begin{cases} true, \text{ if } class(e) = c_{BusinessObject} \\ false, \text{else} \end{cases}$$

$$\phi_{p_2}(v \in V_M) = \begin{cases} true, \text{ if } attribute(v) = a_{name} \wedge attribute(v) \in attributes(c_{bo}) \\ false, \text{else} \end{cases}$$

$$\phi_{p_3}(v \in V_M) = \begin{cases} true, \text{ if } attribute(v) = a_{valueType} \wedge attribute(v) \in attributes(c_{bo}) \\ false, \text{else} \end{cases}$$

The predicates may not only do projections on type level, but also provide selection patterns on on instance level, referring to special attribute or link values. For example, if only value types should be included in a new view type $VT_{valueTypes}$, $p_1 \in VT_{bo}$ could be extended such that:

$$\partial_{p_1}(e \in M) = \phi_{p_1}(e) \wedge \sigma_{p_1}(e) \text{ where}$$

$$\sigma_{p_1}(e) = \begin{cases} true, \text{ if } \exists v \in M \mid v = \text{``}true\text{''} \wedge attribute(v) = a_{valueType} \\ false, \text{else} \end{cases}$$

Figure 4.4.: Example view instance for the BusinessObject view type showing business objects (Customer and Address) and their names. The "v" denotes that Address is a value-type.

The layout information rules $\Lambda_e = \lambda_{p_i}(e)$ for an element e provided by a view type, for this example, could look as follows:

$$\lambda_{p_1}(e) = \{ \text{ create rectangular box }, position = (0,0)\}$$
$$\lambda_{p_2}(e) = \{ \text{ create label with value: } value(e, a_{name}), position = (5,5)\}$$
$$\lambda_{p_3}(e) = \{ \text{ create small rectangular box }, position = (0,0),$$
$$\text{create label with value: "v"}, position = (1,1)\}$$

An example, instance of this view type for the example model given on page 22 would look as depicted in Figure 4.4.

4.4.1. Composite Metamodel

Definition 4.1, which is given above, restricts a view type to be based on only one metamodel. However, one could always define a metamodel being a composite of several sub-metamodels using the following definition.

Definition 4.2. *A* composite *metamodel CMM is defined as a sequence CMM =* $MM_1...MM_n$ *where*

$$C_{CMM} \quad = C_{MM_1} \cup ... \cup C_{MM_n} \text{ and}$$
$$A_{CMM} \quad = A_{MM_1} \cup ... \cup A_{MM_n} \cup A_{crossMM} \text{ and}$$
$$P_{CMM} \quad = P_{MM_1} \cup ... \cup P_{MM_n} \text{and}$$
$$A_{crossMM} \quad \text{is a finite set of links where}$$
$$\forall a \in A_{crossMM} \mid (first(a) \in MM_i \leftrightarrow second(a) \notin MM_i).$$

In the following, metamodel and composite metamodel will be used as synonyms. Wherever a metamodel is referenced it may also be a composite metamodel. Only for cases where the composition of metamodels actually makes a difference the formulas will explicitly use the term *composite metamodel* or *CMM*.

4.4.2. Partial View Type Scope

The scope of a view type is considered *partial* concerning a metamodel, if it only covers a certain part of the element types that are defined within the metamodel. This means for example that certain properties or relations are not shown in this view. The example view type VT_{bo}, given above, is partial concerning the BusinessObjects metamodel as model elements such as associations or association ends are not included.

Definition 4.3 (Partial View Type Concerning Metamodel). *A view type VT is partial concerning a metamodel MM iff*

$$\exists M \in Models_{MM}, e \in M \mid (\forall p \in \Phi \mid (\partial_p(e) = false))$$

On a more fine grained level the definition of partiality declares whether a view type is partial concerning a specific class c of a metamodel. If a view type does not include all possible instances of c it is considered *partial* concerning c. Analogously, a view type may also be partial concerning associations or attributes. For example, view type $VT_{viewType}$ is partial concerning class BusinessObject, as it does not include instances which have set the valueType attribute to "false".

Definition 4.4 (Partial View Type Concerning Classes). *A view type VT is partial concerning a specific class $c \in C$ iff*

$$\exists M \in Models_{MM}, e \in M \mid (\forall p \in \Phi \mid (class(e) = c \wedge \partial_p(e) = false))$$

Partiality concerning associations or attributes is defined analogously.

4.4.3. Complete View Type Scopes

As opposite to *partial* a view type may be *complete* which means that it considers all properties and relations of a metamodel that are reachable from the part of the metamodel for which the view type is defined. Hence, this means that if an element is not shown within a *complete* view (which accords to a *complete* type view) there can be no direct or transitive reference from elements that are shown in the view to this specific element.

Definition 4.5 (Complete View Type Concerning Metamodel). *A view type VT is complete concerning a metamodel MM iff*

$$\forall M \in Models_{MM}, e \in M \mid (\exists p \in \Phi \mid (\partial_p(e) = true)).$$

141

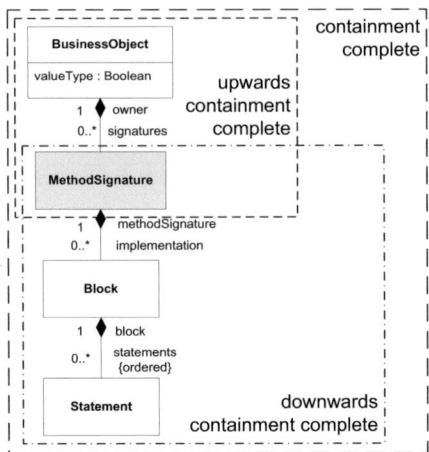

Figure 4.5.: Excerpt of the containment hierarchy of the BusinessObjects metamodel showing the different notions of containment completeness.

Analogously to Definition 4.4, the *complete* property can be defined on a per class, association or attribute level. For example, the VT_{bo} view type is complete concerning the BusinessObject class as it shows every instance of it without restrictions.

Views creation databases distinguish between projections, i.e. columns of a table are omitted in a view, and selections, i.e., rows of a table are omitted due to some selection criterion. This distinction can also be transferred to views on models. Thus, it can be distinguished between *projectional* completeness (which includes the *containment* and *local completenes*) and *selectional* completeness (see the definition of *instance completeness* below).

4.4.3.1. Projectional Complete View Type Scope

Projectional completeness of views based on the MOF meta-metamodel can be defined on several levels. *Containment-complete* concerning a specific element o means that all elements that are related to it via containment associations are shown in the view. For example imagine excerpt of the containment hierarchy of the BusinessObjects metamodel as depicted in Figure 4.5. Three different notions of containment complete can be defined.

- Downwards containment-complete means that all elements that are transitively connected to o are part of the view if o is their transitive parent.

- Upwards containment-complete means that all elements that are transitively connected to o are part of the view if they are a transitive parent of o.

- The third notion specifies that all transitive parents and children of o are part of the view.

Definition 4.6 (Downwards Containment-complete View Type Concerning Metamodel). *A view type VT is* downwards containment-complete *concerning a metamodel MM and a given class $c \in C$ iff*

$$\forall M_i \in Models_{MM}, o \in O_{M_i} \mid ($$
$$class(o) = c \rightarrow (\exists p \in \Phi \mid (\forall o_i \in childObjects^*(o) \cup \{o\} \mid$$
$$\phi_p(o_i) = true)))$$

Definition 4.7 (Upwards Containment-complete View Type Concerning Metamodel). *A view type VT is* upwards containment-complete *concerning a metamodel MM and a given class $c \in C$ iff*

$$\forall M_i \in Models_{MM}, o \in O_{M_i} \mid ($$
$$class(o) = c \rightarrow (\exists p \in \Phi \mid (\forall o_i \in compositeParent^*(o) \cup \{o\} \mid$$
$$\phi_p(o_i) = true)))$$

Definition 4.8 (Containment-complete View Type Concerning Metamodel). *A view type VT is* containment-complete *concerning a metamodel MM and a given class $c \in C$ iff VT is* downwards containment-complete *concerning MM and c as well as* upwards containment-complete *concerning MM and c.*

Another dimension of view types completeness is the level of *local completeness* concerning properties. Local completeness is fulfilled if a view type can display all possible combinations of attribute assignments. A view type is locally complete concerning a class c if every possible combination of attribute values can be displayed for each attribute of c and furthermore every class that is directly referenced by c can be displayed by the view. Considering the BusinessObject class from the running example metamodel local completeness would include the following associations and attributes: name, valueType, elementsOfType as well as signatures.

Definition 4.9 (Local-complete View Type Concerning Metamodel). *A view type VT is locally complete concerning a metamodel MM and a given class $c \in C$ iff*

$$\forall M_i \in Models_{MM}, o \in O_{M_i} \,|\, (\exists p \in \Phi \,|\, ($$
$$class(o) = c \wedge$$
$$(\forall a_i \in attributes(class(o)) \,|\, \phi_p(a_i) = true) \wedge$$
$$(\forall l_i \in \{l \in L_{M_i} \,|\, fistObject(l) = o \vee secondObject(l) = o\} \,|$$
$$\phi_p(l_i) = true)))$$

Analogously to Definition 4.4 the all projectional completeness properties can be defined on a per class, association or attribute level.

4.4.3.2. Selectional or Instance Completeness

Selectional completeness, or *instance* completeness means that the selection of the view type includes all model instances that appear in the underlying model as long as the projection of the view type also includes them. However, the projection does not need to be *complete* in order to fulfil the *instance* completeness property. For example, a view type can have a projection of a class A which does not include a property $propA$. As long as the view type includes all possible instances of A it is still *instance complete*. In contrast to that, if a view type defines a selection criterion for A, such that only As having a $propA$ value of let's say "selected", are included the template for A is not *instance complete* anymore.

Definition 4.10 (Instance-complete View Type). *A view type VT is* instance complete *concerning a metamodel MM iff*

$$\forall M \in Models_{MM}, e \in M \,|\, (\exists p \in \Phi \,|\, (\sigma_p(e) = true)).$$

4.4.4. Extending View Type Scope

Partial views are used to hide details of an underlying model, whereas the various types of *complete* views are used to provide more vast representations of this model. In contrast to these two options, there also exist views that combine elements from the underlying model with additional information from outside, i.e., another model M_{ex}. The extended information is defined as such by the fact that it is not directly reachable by model navigation from the extended view type. Often, the information that should be

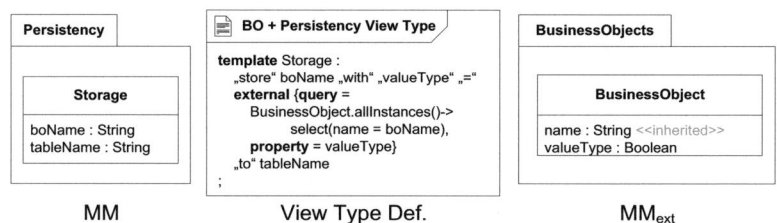

Figure 4.6.: Using an external metamodel *Annotations* that is connected via a query in the view type to an existing metamodel *BusinessObjects*.

added in such a view type is additionally defined using a different metamodel MM_{ex}. This external information is then merged with elements from the actual model. This merging can, for example, be done by specifying a query that relates the elements to each other.

A concrete example that shows how such an extension view type could be defined is depicted in Figure 4.6, based on the example business object metamodel. The example shows that there is an external *persistency* annotation metamodel that does not have any connection with the business object metamodel. The storage annotation only contains a hint to the name of the business object that should be persisted in its *boName* attribute. However, it might be a requirement that a language engineer needs to define a view type not only showing elements of the persistency metamodel but also presenting information from the business object metamodel, i.e., if the mentioned business object is a value type or not. Therefore, a query is given in the view type that retrieves the corresponding business object with the specified name and from which the *valueType* property is then shown in the view, as illustrated in Figure 4.7.

Formally, the *extending* view type property can be expressed based on whether the view type refers to elements that are not directly reachable from the model elements of the actual model that is viewed. The reachability of a target model element t from a model element f is given by a function $e = reachable_n(t)$ where n is the number of navigation steps required to get from f to t.

145

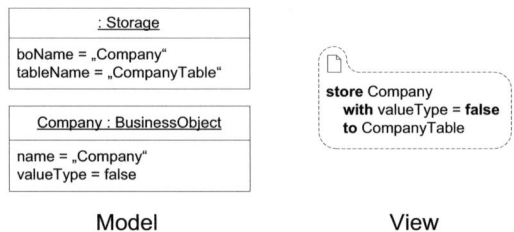

Model   View

Figure 4.7.: Example view instance of the view type specified in Figure 4.6.

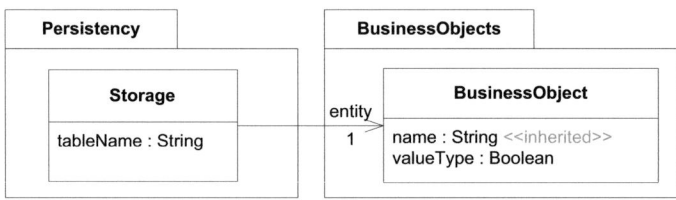

Figure 4.8.: Using an external metamodel *Annotations* to non-intrusively add persistency annotations to an existing metamodel *BusinessObjects*.

Definition 4.11 (Extending View Type). *A view type VT is extending with n the information contained in a model M with n steps, where $n \in \mathbb{N}^+ \cup \{\bot\}$ where $\bot$ is the undefined value, iff:*

$$
n = \begin{cases} i & \textit{if } \exists i \in \mathbb{N}^+; p_1, p_2 \in \Phi_{VT}; e \in \mathit{Models}_{MM_{VT}}; e_{ext} \in \mathit{Models}_{MM_{ext}} \mid \\ & \partial_{p_1}(e) = \mathit{true} \wedge \partial_{p_2}(e_{ext}) = \mathit{true} \wedge e = \mathit{reachable}_i(e_{ext}) \\ \bot & \textit{else} \end{cases}
$$

If $i \neq \bot$ the extending information is still directly connected to the used metamodel MM for which the view type is responsible, for example via (non-intrusively, by exposing the property only in the annotating metamodel leaving the annotated metamodel untouched) attached associations that reference elements of MM. However, in this scenario the differentiation to a non-extending view type VT_{comp} with considering a composite metamodel $MM_{comp} = (MM, MM_{ex})$ is quite blurry. Depending on how closely related both metamodels are to each other, one or the other property fits best.

146

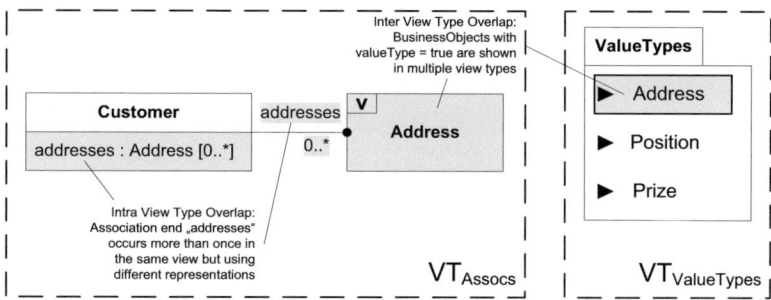

Figure 4.9.: Two different view types, showing the two different flavours of overlaps.

For example, the business objects view type VT_{bo} considered as example in previous sections, could be extended to display annotations that are added as shown in Figure 4.8

If $i = \bot$ arbitrary information, not necessarily having any connection to the viewed model can be blended into the view. This *extending with $i = \bot$* case is much more difficult to realise in a view based approach, as additional query rules need to be allowed in the view type definition that can find the corresponding blended information without using direct model navigation.

4.4.5. Overlapping View Type Scope

View types may also cover scenarios where there is more than one view type that is able to represent the same element. On the other hand it is also possible that the same view type can handle one unique element in different places but e.g., from different view types each having a different focus. This is not a property that is directly expressed within a view type but is rather a derived properties from a set of view types or different parts of the same view type. Both types are explained in detail as *inter-* and *intra view type overlaps*. Figure 4.9 shows an examples for both types of overlaps.

4.4.5.1. Inter View Type Overlaps

An *inter view type overlap* occurs whenever one or more view type is able to represent the same element. A prerequisite for this property is, of course, that the involved view types are based on the same metamodel. A view type VT_a is inter view type overlapping

147

with respect to a view type VT_b iff

$$MM_a = MM_b \wedge \exists c \in MM_a \mid (\exists o \in Models_{MM_a} \mid (class(o) = e \wedge$$
$$\exists p_a \in proj_2(VT_a), p_b \in proj_2(VT_b) \mid (\partial_{p_a}(o) = true \wedge \partial_{p_b}(o) = true)))$$

where $MM_a = proj_1(VT_a)$ and $MM_b = proj_1(VT_b)$.

To get those tuples (e, p_a, p_b) where $e \in MM$ and $p_a \in VT_a, p_b \in VT_b$ that are responsible for the overlapping of the view types the following shorthand notation will be used throughout the rest of this thesis: $\{(e_1, p_{a,1}, p_{b,1}), ..., (e_n, p_{a,n}, p_{b,n})\} = VT_a \sqcap VT_b$.

4.4.5.2. Intra View Type Overlaps

If the same view type can represent the same element in different ways an *intra view type overlap* is present. This means that there is more that one predicate in the view type that includes the same element. Thus, a view type VT has intra view type overlaps iff

$$\exists p_1, p_2 \in \Phi_{VT} \mid (p_1 \neq p_2 \wedge \exists e \in Models_{MM} \mid (\partial_{p_1}(e) = true \wedge \partial_{p_2}(e) = true))$$

4.5. Views

Views, as instances of view types can also have different properties which are depicted in Figure 4.10 using a feature diagram. Using these properties, views can be classified and related to each other concerning the extent of information they show of the underlying model(s). Similar terms as those specifying the types and properties of view types could have been used here to define these properties (such as partial or complete). However, to avoid confusion between properties of views and those of view types different terms are used here (e.g., selective or holistic).

If a view is able to fulfil these properties may also depend on the definition of its view type. So, whether a view is selective can be specified by its corresponding view type.

Definition 4.12 (View). *A view is defined as a tuple*

$$V = (M_V, VT, S, \Lambda, layout) \tag{4.2}$$

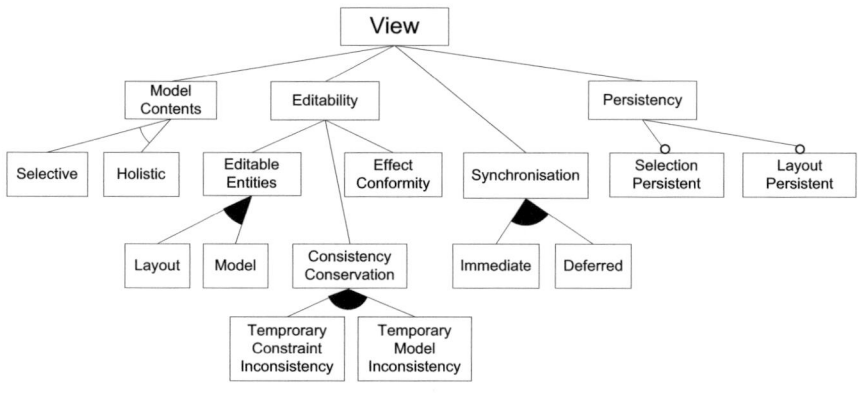

Figure 4.10.: Properties of view types.

where

M_V	*is a model that is represented in the view,*
VT	*is the VT view type that defines the rules for the view construction,*
$S \subseteq M_V$	*is a finite set of model elements (objects, links and attribute values) that represent the current selection of elements from the model M_V that is shown in V.*
Λ	*is the finite set of layout information used to display the view contents.*
$layout \subseteq S \times \Lambda$	*is a binary relation relating the model elements of the view with their layout information*

4.5.1. View Scope

A view shows a specific selection of elements from its underlying model. If the model is changed, i.e. elements are added or deleted, the view needs to be updated according to this change. Whether this is done automatically or only if a user explicitly requests the update is a property of the employed view type.

To support further formalisations of view properties the definitions of atomic and complex changes on models 2.4 and 2.5 given in 2 published by Hettel et al. [HLR08], formalise atomic and complex changes to models. These definitions are now used in order to define the impact of arbitrary modifications that occur in the model to it's views.

4.5.1.1. Selective View Scope

A view is considered *selective* if it can show only a selected part of the model. Only specific elements are shown in such a view. The selection may either be done automatically or manually, by a user of the view. This type of view is mostly used to highlight a special aspect of a model. It provides focused information, while restricting the set of displayable elements to those that are necessary to understand this specific aspect.

A view can be selective concerning different types of changes:

Addition Selective Additions of elements to the model that fall into the scope of a view's view type are only added to the view's selection, if added manually. Furthermore, this property can be applied to the addition of links. Then it means: The addition of links between two elements of the model that fall into the scope of a view's view type are only added to the view's selection, if added manually. An example, where selective views are used to a large extent is the modelling within UML diagrams. For example, class diagrams for a certain package mostly do not show all classes at once. The user can select whether a newly added class should appear in a certain diagram or not.

Deletion Selective Deletions of elements from the model that fall into the scope of a view's view type are propagated to the view's selection, if deleted manually. The same property applies for links between two model elements. This results in elements or links that are displayed in a view that are not part of the model anymore. Several tools for UML modelling also use this notion of deletion in selective views. Elements that are deleted from the underlying model do not necessarily result in deletions of their view representations. For example, in many graphical modelling tools (such as Rational Rose or GMF), view elements where the underlying model partition is not available anymore, are not automatically removed from the diagrams but are rather annotated indicating that the underlying model element is missing.

The possibility to explicitly define that a view should be *selective* allows for a more flexible model modelling experience. Practice shows that view-based modelling approaches already make use of this distinction and even let modellers decide their preferences for selectiveness of certain parts of a view type.

Definition 4.13 (Addition Selective). *A view* V *is called* addition selective *if after the addition of objects, links or attribute values* $M' = \delta_e^+ M$, *where* e *is the added element the following holds:* $S' = S$. *Analogously,* deletion selective *is defined for changes* δ_e^-.

4.5.1.2. Holistic

In contrast to addition selective views, a view may be *addition holistic*. This means that it always presents the whole set of possible elements that can be displayed by the view. If elements are added and/or removed this is immediately reflected view. This type of view is mostly used to present the user an overview on the underlying model. Often an important property of such a view is its actuality.

Definition 4.14 (Addition Holistic View Scope). *A view* V *is called* addition holistic *if after the addition of objects, links or attribute values* $M' = \delta_e^+ M$, *where* e *is the added element, this change is immediately shown in the view and the following holds:*

$$
S' = \begin{cases} S \cup \{e\}, & \text{if } \exists p \in \Phi \mid \partial_p(e) = true \\ S, & else \end{cases}
$$

Analogously, deletion holistic *is defined for deletion changes* δ_e^- *but with* $S \cup \{e\}$ *being replaced by* $S \setminus \{e\}$.

4.5.1.3. Partially Selective/Holistic

The properties *selective* and *holistic* must be applied both to a whole view but it is also possible to limit them to certain predicates of the associated view type. Then, the holistic/selective property only holds, i.e., for a adding elements to a certain association. For example, a UML class diagram may be addition holistic concerning the attributes of the displayed classes, showing them whenever they are added to the classes that are displayed. At the same time it may be addition selective concerning classes that are added to packages displayed by the view. This means that classes are not automatically added to class diagrams for the respective package when they are added to that package.

Definition 4.15 (Predicate Selection). *A predicate selection* $S_{p_0} \subseteq S$ *of a predicate* $p_0 \in \Phi$ *is defined as:* $S_{p_0} = \{ s \in S \mid \partial_{p_0}(s) = true \}$

Definition 4.16 (Partially Selective). *A view V is selective concerning a predicate $p_0 \in \Phi$ if after additions of objects or links changing a given M to M' where $M' = \delta_e^+ M$ it holds that $S'_{p_0} = S_{p_0}$.*

Definition 4.17 (Partially Holistic). *A view V is holistic w.r.t. a predicate $p_0 \in \Phi$ iff*

$$S'_{p_0} = \begin{cases} S_{p_0} \cup \{e\}, & \text{if } \partial_{p_0}(e) = true \\ S_{p_0}, & \text{else} \end{cases}$$

Definitions for partial addition and deletion selective/holistic are defined analogously.

4.5.1.4. Overlapping

A third property of views w.r.t. their scope is whether it is *overlapping* with another view. In this case elements may occur in more than one view at once. This may be a view of the same view type but also a different one.

Definition 4.18 (Overlapping). *A view V_1 is overlapping concerning another view V_2 iff*

$$S_{V_1} \cap S_{V_2} \neq \varnothing$$

In contrast to the other properties, which are defined on a single view, overlapping *of views is a "derived" property given for a set of views.*

4.5.2. Editability

Views in which the user can not only view elements but also conduct changes to the model is an *editable* view. In addition to displaying model elements in a defined way, an editable view needs to provide means to interact with the model. Actions such as create, update and delete need to be performable to make a view editable. Editability of views can also be subdivided into two different degrees of editability. First, if only the layout information can be changed but not the actual model content the view is only *layout editable*. Second, if the model content is editable through the view it is considered *content editable*.

Special attention needs to be taken if an editable view is also partial. In this case editing actions may indirectly affect elements that are not represented in the current view. If such changes are possible it might be important to make possible repercussions on elements outside the current view. For example, if a link to an element that was outside of a view is added to an element within the view, the element might need to be added to the current view as well. Within overlapping views editing becomes even more challenging. In this case changes need to by synchronised between the views. If it is possible to edit elements in parallel using different views it might furthermore be necessary to provide means for conflict resolution.

Furthermore, editability may be allowed only on certain parts of the same view type. This may either be a restriction directly specified in the definition of the view type or it may be a result of the model partition being the container of displayed model elements and that partition is read-only. This will result in a *partial editability* of the view.

From the area of relational and object databases there are, according to [Cod91], several preconditions known that are required to make a view editable:

- **Effect conformity**: After a user made a change to the data through a view the view needs to be updated according to the change. This requires a consistent bidirectional transformation, or two corresponding transformations that are inverse to each other, between the view and the underlying data.

- **Minimality**: Views only perform minimal changes to the underlying data.

- **Consistency conservation**: Changes that are made through a view shall not lead to the violation of integrity constraints.

- **Respect to access control**: Views that are created for reasons of access control shall not allow changes that affect areas that lie outside of the view.

Those properties mostly apply to views in modelling as well. However, minimality is a property that should be disregarded in the context of a view-based modelling approach. Considering that a model, in such an approach, is always edited through a view, the minimality of changes would constrain the editability of the model in general. Furthermore, we will omit a formal definition of the access control aspect as this would exceed the scope of this work.

To be able to express what editability of view actually means, the definitions of morphisms between model (cf. Definition 2.6 on page 25) and transformations (cf. Definition 2.7) by Amelunxen and Schürr [AS07] are referenced. The relation between a view and its underlying model can be considered a model morphism and based on this transformations for synchronising them can be defined.

$$M \xrightarrow{T_v} V$$

$$\downarrow \Delta \qquad \downarrow \Delta'$$

$$M' \xleftarrow{\quad} V'$$
$$T_m$$

Figure 4.11.: T_v and T_m are effect conform with respect to M and V if the application of Δ to M results in the same M' as if the chain of T_v, Δ' and T_m is applied. Where Δ' is an equivalent change on view level to Δ.

Definition 4.19. *The view type definition of a view type* VT *implies the existence of transformations* T_v *and* T_m. *Both transformations are used to realise the functionality of the* ϕ, σ *and* λ *functions in the original definition of view type. So definition 4.1 is extended in the following way:*

$$VT = (MM_{VT}, VMM, T_v, T_m) \tag{4.3}$$

where
T_v *is the transformation defined from* MM_{VT} *to the view metamodel* VMM *so that* $\rightsquigarrow_{T_v} \subseteq$ $Models_{MM_{VT}} \times Models_{VMM}$ *and*
T_m *is the transformation defined from* VMM *to* MM_{VT} *so that* $\rightsquigarrow_{T_m} \subseteq Models_{VMM} \times$ $Models_{MM_{VT}}$ *and*
$T_v \cup T_m \equiv \Phi$ *where*

$$\partial_p(e) = true \iff \exists V_e \in Models_{VMM} \mid (\{e\}, V_e) \in \rightsquigarrow_{T_v} \wedge (V_e, \{e\}) \in \rightsquigarrow_{T_m} \tag{4.4}$$

4.5.2.1. Effect Conformity

For an editable view, the morphism defined for the view type needs to be bidirectional and comply with the *effect conformity* requirement. As depicted in Figure 4.11, to be effect conform, changes made directly to the model should leave it in the same state as an equal change on the view level and then propagated by the update transformation back to the model would do. Furthermore, vice-versa, changes made through the view to the model should leave the view in the same state as an equal change on the model level which is propagated by the update transformation would do.

Definition 4.20 (Effect Conformity). *Effect conformity of a view type VT holds iff*

$$\forall V \in Models_{VMM} \mid (\quad proj_2(V) = VT \wedge (\forall M \in Models_{MM} \mid$$
$$\forall V' \in Models_{VMM} \mid (\quad proj_2(V') = VT \wedge (\forall M' \in Models_{MM} \mid$$
$$((M,V) \in \leadsto_{T_v} \wedge (V',M') \in \leadsto_{T_m}) \rightarrow$$
$$((M',V') \in \leadsto_{T_v} \wedge (V,M) \in \leadsto_{T_m})))))$$

where $M' = \Delta_M M$, which means that M' is the same as model M but after an arbitrary set of changes Δ_M was performed and $V' = \Delta_V V$ meaning that V' is the same as view V but after an arbitrary set of changes Δ_V was performed.

4.5.2.2. Consistency Conservation

Considering the rules of a view type a transformation, the creation of models through this view should only produce valid models. As modelling is a creative process models are mostly created step-by-step. In order to support this creative process by editable views this this process should be supported to foster the usability and productivity of a view. One possibility to allow this is if a view supports for the creation *temporarily inconsistent* states [Fow05]. If this is the case, an editable view might contain valuable information that was created during modelling but that is not yet transformable into a valid model.

Imagine a UML model under development. There are two classes connected through an association. Now the developer decides to delete one of these classes. An association which refers to only one class would be inconsistent according to the UML metamodel. Hence, making the model consistent again, the association would also need to be deleted. However, a view might still allow to keep an intermediate state. This would allow the developer to create a new class and attach the dangling association to it.

There are different classes of inconsistency: (I) violation of metamodel constraints that lead to what is called *constraint inconsistency* and (II) *model inconsistency* if a model that is not valid in itself without taking constraints into account. For example, the latter would be the case of a link referring to only one element or an element which has a different type than is specified in the link's association exists. A more detailed description of what a valid model is is given in [AS07].

Metamodel constraints constrain the validity of models that would theoretically be constructible obeying only the rules defined in the metamodel without constraints. Multiplicity definitions for associations and attributes are also included here. For example,

155

considering the business object example metamodel, an invariant may be defined so that every business object needs to have its name attribute set (expressed as OCL invariant: `inv:    not self.name.oclIsUndefined()`). If there exists a business object instance with no name set, this constraint is violated. Using the view type VT_{bo}, which allows to model business objects and allows to edit their names constraint inconsistency is supported if during any stage of the usage of this view, constraints such as the name constraint can be violated.

If metamodel constraints are violated (including multiplicity constraints) a model is in the state of *constraint inconsistency*.

Definition 4.21 (Constraint Inconsistency). *A view type VT supports* constraint inconsistency *iff:*

$$\exists V \in Models_{VMM}, M \in Models_{MM} \mid ((V, M) \in \leadsto_{T_m}) \land$$
$$\exists \xi \in \Xi, o \in O_M, \xi \in constraints(class(o)) \land \xi \text{ is violated for } o$$

In case (II) a greater degree of freedom in modelling can be reached if a view even supports to hold content that cannot be translated into a model at all. This allows a developer to work with the view like a "scratch pad". This type of inconsistency is denoted *model inconsistency*.

For example, allowing in a view-based editor for the view type VT_{Assocs} (cf. Figure 4.9) to draw the associations end by end could result in having an association that has only one end connected to a class, leaving a dangling link on one end of the association. However, especially if an element was deleted using another view, still conserving this inconsistent state may improve the usability of the view type.

Definition 4.22 (View with Support for Model Inconsistency). *A view V that supports* model inconsistency *is defined as follows. Definition 4.12 remains unchanged except for formula 4.2 which is replaced by:*

$$V = (M_V, VT, S, \Lambda, I) \tag{4.5}$$

where
I is a set of view elements $I \subseteq Models_{VMM}$ so that $\forall i \in I, e \in M_V \mid (i, e) \notin \leadsto_{T_m}$.

This means that in addition to the view elements that are a combination of the model elements from M_V in combination with the layout information given by Λ there is a place for additional view elements I which are currently not translatable to valid elements in

M_V. These elements allow to represent and store view elements of nearly arbitrary shape and allow to work with the view like a "scratch pad".

4.5.3. Storage and Synchronization of Views

Apart from the static properties of view types and views another important aspect of view-based modelling is the synchronisation between model and view as well as storage of views.

4.5.3.1. Synchronisation

A synchronisation process between a model and its views is needed to keep both up-to-date. Especially within partial views synchronisation between model and views can become difficult. Transformations that are partial and non-injective are hard to keep bidirectionaly valid. Hettel et al. (cf. [HLR08]) analyse this problem in the context of model round-trip engineering and present two different approaches that alleviate this problem. In order to apply these approaches also for transformations in the context of view-based modelling we first need to see if the problems can be mapped. Therefore, Lemma 4.1 formulates that transformations for the synchronisation of partial views are always partial and non-injective.

Lemma 4.1. *In a partial view type the synchronisation transformations are always partial and non-injective:*

A partial and non-injective transformation T is characterised as follows: There is at least one model M_s with an element e_1 for which the transformation T to M_t can never produce an element e_2. Formally, this can be expressed as:

$$\exists M_s \in Models_{MM_1}, M_t \in Models_{MM_2}, e_1 \in M_1 \mid (\forall e_2 \in M_2 \mid ((e_1, e_2) \notin \leadsto_T))$$

Proof. Through Definition 4.19:

$$\exists M \in Models_{MM}, e \in M \mid (\forall p \in \Phi \mid (\partial_p(e) = false))$$
$$\iff \exists M \in Models_{MM}, e \in M \mid (\forall p \in \Phi \mid \neg(\partial_p(e) = true))$$
$$\overset{\text{Def. 4.19}}{\iff} \exists M \in Models_{MM}, e \in M \mid \neg(\exists V_e \in Models_{VMM} \mid (\{e\}, V_e) \in \leadsto_{T_v} \wedge (V_e, \{e\}) \in \leadsto_{T_m})$$
$$\iff \exists M \in Models_{MM}, e \in M \mid (\forall V_e \in Models_{VMM} \mid (\{e\}, V_e) \notin \leadsto_{T_v} \vee (V_e, \{e\}) \notin \leadsto_{T_m})$$

Which is stronger than what would be required by a partial, non-injective transformation, which would be:

$$\exists M \in Models_{MM}, e \in M \mid (\exists V_e \in Models_{VMM} \mid (\{e\}, V_e) \not\leadsto_{T_v} \vee (V_e, \{e\}) \not\leadsto_{T_m})$$

$$\square$$

According to Hettel [Het10], a bidirectional transformation that is partial and non-injective needs to fulfil certain properties in order to be considered a valid *round-trip transformation*:

- Target model changes can be classified into two disjoint sets of changes: relevant and irrelevant changes Δ_R and Δ_I. Relevant changes modify a part of the target model which is in the image of the respective transformation whereas irrelevant changes lie outside of this image.

- To be able to synchronise relevant target changes back to the source model a corresponding source change must exist for each of them. The resulting set of source changes for a set of relevant target changes is denoted Δ_S.

- Furthermore, each $\delta \in \Delta_S$ must exactly perform the original change in Δ_R when the transformation is applied again.

Bidirectionality To keep models and views on them in sync, the transformations that do this synchronisation to be bidirectional (or there need to be two transformations where one resembled the inversion of the other). Matsuda et al. [MHN+07] define three *bidirectional properties* that need to be fulfilled in order to create consistent view definitions:

- If a view is unmodified the result of the a backwards transformation to the model is the same as the original source of the view (no additional information is introduced by):

$$\begin{pmatrix} V = T_V(M) \wedge \\ V' = \Delta V \wedge \\ \Delta = \varnothing \wedge \\ M' =\leadsto_{T_M} (V') \end{pmatrix} \rightarrow (M' = M)$$

- A user needs to have the possibility to cancel updates to a view that are a result from a modification to the view's underlying model. The a view-based approach requires means to restore a version of the underlying model (or a part of it according to the views partiality) just through the interaction of the user with the view. This is the case if there exists a transformation T_M^{-1} that restores a modified model M' to the the version M which was the original source for the view V.

$$\exists T_M^{-1} \in Transformations_{MM} \mid (V = \leadsto_{T_V} (M)) \wedge (M' = \Delta M) \wedge$$
$$(V' = \leadsto_{T_V^{\bullet}} (M')) \to (\leadsto_{T_M^{-1}} (V, M') = M)$$

- The transformation that does the backward synchronisation to the model should be agnostic to the order in which the changes to the view were made. Only the state in which the view is just before the transformation is executed determines the result of the transformation.

$$\begin{pmatrix} V = T_V(M) \wedge \\ V_1' = (\Delta_1 \circ \Delta_2)V \wedge \\ V_2' = (\Delta_2 \circ \Delta_1)V \wedge \\ M_1' = \leadsto_{T_M} (V_1') \wedge \\ M_2' = \leadsto_{T_M} (V_2') \wedge \end{pmatrix} \to (M_1' = M_2')$$

Point in Time   The actual transformation and updating process can be classified into two different types.

- An update can be performed at the very moment a change is made to one of the sides, either model or view. This kind of update is denoted an *immediate* update strategy.

- An update may occur at a point in time decoupled from the actual change event. This kind of update is denoted *deferred* update strategy.

This point in time implies the cardinality of changes that are performed between two subsequent runs of the synchronisation transformations. In the *immediate* update strategy the transformations are executed as soon as an atomic change was performed to either the view or its model. This strategy allows a tighter coupling between view and model and avoids conflicts that may occur if an arbitrary number of changes is performed before the next synchronisation. On the other hand, the *deferred* update strategy allows to have an arbitrary number of changes in this time span. This allows to work with views in a more flexible way, as they can be changed offline, i.e., if the underlying model is currently not available. However, having an arbitrarily large number of changes, that need to be synchronised, dramatically increases the probability of conflicts.

Definition 4.23 (Immediate Update). *When an* immediate *update strategy is employed the cardinality of changes that occur between a model in version i, M_i and a model in version $i + 1$, M_{i+1} has to be exactly 1:*

$$M_{i+1} = \Delta M_i \rightarrow \#(\Delta) = 1$$

Definition 4.24 (Deferred Update). *In an* deferred *update scenario the cardinality of a set of changes Δ can be arbitrarily large.*

$$M_{i+1} = \Delta M_i \rightarrow \#(\Delta) = n$$

Mergeability   Synchronisation always gets a lot more difficult if concurrent updates on both sides are made. Especially in a deferred update strategy, where a delay between the actual change and the transformation to the respective other side may occur, concurrent, incompatible changes can happen. So for example, a developer changes something in one view and no synchronisation with the model is done, yet. Then, he uses a second view on the same model to apply some changes to the model which affect parts of the model shown in the first view. If the changes are irreconcilable with each other they have to be merged.

Merge problems may only occur if at least one of the involved views employs a deferred update strategy. The transformation from model to view and from view to model need to be aware of changes in their respective target model in order to support *mergeability*.

Definition 4.25 (Mergeable). *A view and a model are considered mergeable iff the intersection of the change sets Δ_V and Δ_M that result from the re-applying the synchronisation transformations T_V and T_M does not contain changes that were applied to the same element but are* inverse *(cf. Section 3.9.1 on pages 91ff) to each other:*

$$\forall \delta_1, \delta_2 \in (\Delta_V \underset{element(\delta)}{\cap} \Delta_M) \mid \delta_1 \neq invert(\delta_2)$$

In combination with the different types of consistency conservation the type of synchronisation becomes even more important. A view may allow temporary inconsistency and contain content that is not (yet) transformable to a valid model. Depending on the synchronisation strategy either the view or the model have to support the corresponding type of inconsistency. If synchronisation is done in an *immediate* fashion, to support temporary inconsistency, the model itself needs to allow inconsistency. On the other hand, if synchronisation is done in a deferred way, only the view needs means to represent inconsistent states.

4.5.3.2. Respect to Access Control

Respect to access control means that only those elements can be changed through a view that are represented by it. Elements are not directly represented in a view, i.e., they are only treated by the synchronisation transformation to retain consistency within the model, they can be considered also part of a view.

Definition 4.26 (Respect to Access Control). *A view respects aspect control if it only allows to modify elements that are, directly or indirectly, part of the view:*

$$\forall V \in Models_{VMM}, M \in Models_{MM} \mid ((v \in V), (m \in M)) \in \leadsto_{T_V} \cup \leadsto_{T_M} \to m \in S_V$$

4.5.3.3. Persistency

A view may be *persistent*. A persistent view is stored in addition to the rough model data that is shown in the view. Having a stored view enables faster access, as it does not need to be created newly every time it is accessed. Additionally, if a *persistent* view it is at the same time *editable* enables for customisation of a view's layout. A user may customize the view by manually changing certain parts, such as explicit ordering of the elements occurring in the view or adding additional information. This information may be simply used to add additional layout information such as custom structuring, or, for textual views, white-spaces or indentations. On the other hand, it may add additional content, such as comments or annotations. This content may not directly have impact on the viewed elements themselves, but may still be worth being persisted. A huge challenge is, if views are being persisted, keeping them synchronized with the underlying model data. Non-persistent views can be simply re-computed every time they are used. Persistent views need to be synchronized when the underlying data changes.

4.6. Classification of View-Types in Practice

There exist several special patterns where views are applied in practical model driven engineering. In this section an overview on several view patterns is given, which are characterised by the set of properties they support. The examples given below are only considered to represent a typical setting of these properties. Still, depending on the realisation of the actual view, other setting might also be possible.

4.6.1. Master / Detail

This view pattern [Tid05] actually consists of two different views – master and detail – that are connected with each other. The master view is used for navigation over a model. If a selection is made in the master, the second view – detail – presents more detailed information of the selected elements. The master view therefore mostly supports navigation over the containment hierarchy of the model, i.e., being at least *downwards containment-complete*, sometimes even *containment-complete*. The master then displays at most one property which is used for the identification of the element which makes it *partial*. The master view is also mostly the same for all classes of the metamodel. Thus, it can be considered as being defined on *view-type level*.

In contrast to the master view, the detail view completely omits the containment hierarchy (at least after the first level), therefore, it is also mostly *partial*. Concerning the element that is displayed by the detail view, mostly all directly accessibly elements as well as attributes are shown (*locally complete*). Apart from generic implementations of the detail view, as each detail view type is only responsible for a certain type of model element it can be considered to be defined on a *per-class level*.

4.6.2. Inclusion of Annotations

This kind of view is used to show and edit annotations to a basic model, that is instance of a certain metamodel MM. Annotations are mostly based on a separate metamodel AMM that non-intrusively associates annotation elements to elements of MM. To view all annotations of a certain model element m, the view needs to be *locally complete* w.r.t. the associations that annotate this element.

4.6.3. Overview

An overview is used to give an outline on the structure of a certain model element. The structure is mostly represented by the elements that are directly contained by the element. Therefore, the overview is often *(downwards) containment complete* for at least one level of containment. As the intention of an overview is to hide details of the viewed element, an overview can be considered to be *partial*.

4.6.4. Navigation

A navigation view is mostly the same as the master view in the master / detail view pattern. Therefore it is *(downwards) containment complete*. As an extension to this definition, it is also possible to have a navigation view that is furthermore *locally complete* w.r.t. associations. Similar to overview details are hidden in this view, therefore it is *partial*.

Chapter 5.

Textual Views

Textual views, as opposed to graphical or tabular views, present data in a purely textual way. However, inherited from the view-based paradigm the displayed text can not always be considered as being the whole "universe", a textual view may also be partial hiding details or giving an outline of a larger underlying model. This implies a lot of new effects on the way how to interact with a textual editor. Normally, developers are used to, whenever they see text, the text is physically stored as it is shown in the editor. When using text as means to provide a view on an underlying model, this fact is not valid anymore. Especially selective views, or views resulting from partial view types hide information resulting in the existence of a richer underlying model as it might be displayed in a single view.

For example, there are two different notions of what happens if text is deleted from a textual view. One meaning could be that the underlying elements should also be deleted by this action. On the other hand, a different notion is the "remove from view" action. This action does not delete the underlying model elements but only removes their textual representation from the current view. The same applies for adding elements to a selective view. In this case it is up to the user to decide which elements are represented in the view an which are not. Thus, there are also two different ways of adding already existent elements to a view. First, they can be added by the use textual editing means only and once the text is finished, the reference to the existing model elements "snaps in", resulting in the element being part of the view. On the other hand, by enabling a textual view to accept commands such as *drag and drop*, from an outside editor, reveals a second possibility of adding existing elements to a selective view. An element can be dragged into the textual view, and at positions where the view type allows the element to be displayed, a drop is possible; showing, if performed, the adding the element in its textual representation to the view.

The novelty of the type of interaction with text also requires support for specifying view properties such as partiality or selectivity (as introduced in Chapter 4) in the definition language/view type that allows language engineers create textual views. Furthermore, an approach is required that allows for the representation of elements from an underlying domain model as a textual view that may be overlapping or partial. This chapter deals with both of these areas, i.e., the specification of view types as well as the actual representation of view for a model.

5.1. Scientific Challenges

While generating models from text or text from models has already been researched from different communities, the view aspects have never been transferred to textual representations of models. Therefore, the following challenges need to be tackled in order to provide a textual, view-based modelling approach.

- View types are not meant to be explicitly encoded in the metamodel for which a view type is created. Therefore, an approach needs to be introduced that allows to describe view types independent from the structure of its underlying metamodel.

- As views are mostly projections or selections of an underlying model, a way to represent textual views as such projectional or selectional representations, needs to be found. This is an approach for creating, modifying and storing textual representations of a domain model separately to the actual model.

- As presented in the previous chapter, several properties of views (selective, holistic, etc.) and view types (partial, complete, etc.) can be defined that make up the features of a view-based modelling approach. In order to be as general and as flexible as possible, the developed approach needs to take these properties into account and present solutions for their implied challenges for the textual modelling domain. This includes the following major features:

  - Support for the definition of complete as well as partial view types, including the possibility of selecting members of a view type's instance not only on metamodel but also on model level (i.e., by providing support for querying specific elements).

  - Support for handling inter- as well as intra-view type overlaps.

  - The textual view approach, furthermore, needs support for providing selective as well as holistic views. Support for different types of actions to add or remove elements to and from the view need to be provided.

Textual views in the context of this thesis always refer to textual views on models, not on data in databases or anything different.

5.2. Contributions

In this chapter, a view-based textual modelling approach called FURCAS is introduced. FURCAS stands for **F**ramework for **UUID**-**R**etaining **C**oncrete to **A**bstract **S**yntax mappings. The name stems from the a specific part of the motivation of the approach that should allow to define textual concrete syntaxes with a projectional editor that allows to hide the UUID of model elements while retaining this ID during subsequent transformations from and to the textual representation of a model. However, the capabilities of FURCAS are not limited to just hiding and retaining this special attribute, it is rather possible to define projectional textual views on models in general.

The following contributions are part of the FURCAS approach:

- FURCAS allows to define arbitrary textual views, that are specified in a template based language. As basis for this approach serves the Textual Concrete Syntax (TCS) approach published by Jouault et al. [JBK06, JB06b]. This approach is extended by FURCAS to allow for the definition of textual views.

- As part of this extension FURCAS contributes an approach that allows to define class as well as instance scoped queries on the underlying models. This allows to define partial as well as complete view types independently from the domain metamodel.

- FURCAS explicitly takes into account the properties of views that where defined in the previous chapter. Especially the notion of holistic and selective views is supported. The representation of a model in a textual view is achieved by employing a decorator pattern based approach. A metamodel called TextBlocks metamodel is introduced for this purpose. Instances of this metamodel allow to non-intrusively build textual views on underlying models. The TextBlocks models are constructed according to the rules and templates defined in the concrete to abstract syntax mappings that can be developed with FURCAS. With help of these decorator models partial textual views can be represented.

- The synchronisation of textual views with its model in a bidirectional way is also a central part of the FURCAS approach. This means that the view type definition approach employed in FURCAS also needs support bidirectionality. Solutions for this challenge are presented in more detail in the next chapter (cf. Chapter 6, page 239), which explicitly deals with this topic.

- In order to provide a formal basis that allows to reason on the synchronisation algorithms introduced in the next chapter, the TextBlocks decorator approach is formalised in this chapter. The formalisation is closely connected to the generic view definition given in Chapter 4. Thus, the properties given there can easily be translated into specific ones for the TextBlocks models.

Excursion: Origin of the Name FURCAS

The name "Furcas" is not only an acronym for **F**ramework for **U**UID-**R**etaining **C**oncrete to **A**bstract **S**yntax mappings but also has itself a meaning as a name. Mathers describes Furcas, in his book "The Goetia: The Lesser Key of Solomon the King" [MCnt] as:

"In demonology, Furcas or Forcas is a Knight of Hell, and rules 20 legions of demons. He teaches Philosophy, Astronomy (Astrology to some authors), Rhetoric, Logic, Chiromancy and Pyromancy. Furcas is depicted as a strong old man with white hair and long white beard, who rides a horse while holding a sharp weapon (pitch fork). He knows the virtues of all herbs and precious stones, can make a man witty, eloquent, invisible [..], and **live long**, and can discover treasures and **recover lost things**. ".

This actually fits pretty well with the purpose of the approach, meaning the long living model elements that are retained over modifications from different views and the recovering. Also his ability to make things invisible fits the purpose of FURCAS to support partial view exceedingly well.

The combination of the FURCAS rune [MCnt] and the Eclipse platform [Ecl10c] on which the implementation of FURCAS is based, resembles the icon that is used for the FURCAS framework and is depicted below.

5.3. Definition of Textual View Types

To be able to define textual view types, a mechanism is required that allows to map elements from the model world – i.e., the abstract syntax – to elements from the grammar world – i.e., the textual concrete syntax. The way this is usually done for textual modelling languages is by the definition of a, often template-based, mapping language. From such a mapping definition, parser components as well as transformations that instantiate the corresponding metamodel elements can be generated. In the following sections, an approach will be introduced that allows to define textual view types based on a template based mapping language.

5.3.1. Mapping Definition

A multitude of approaches for textual concrete syntaxes for models have been developed in recent years. The focus of this work is not to invent a new CTS mapping approach but rather concentrate on giving support for the definition of views for a textual modelling language. Therefore, the existing approaches have been analysed w.r.t. to the properties given in Chapter 4 as well as other challenges that are posed on a textual view-based approach (cf. Section 5.1). Especially template-based approaches that can be defined externally to the metamodel can serve as a good foundation that can be extended to support textual views, since they define the textual syntax in a declarative and fine-grained way.

5.3.1.1. TCS

After the thorough analysis of existing CTS approaches (cf. Section 2.5 on page 44), that are able to define concrete textual syntaxes for existing metamodels, the Textual Concrete Syntax (TCS) [JBK06, JB06b] approach was chosen as base language for the definition of the mapping between text and model. The reasons for this choice and remaining limitations of TCS which need to be solved for FURCAS are the following:

- TCS supports externally defined metamodels by default. This is important for being able to provide the possibility to define views. The mapping definitions need to be non-intrusive to the metamodel, thus, other approaches that define a metamodel implicitly are not possible to be used as basis for FURCAS.

- Templates in TCS are defined declaratively and are therefore easily modularisable. This enables for language composition. Thus, multiple views types may reuse common language constructs by importing them. Language composition is not supported by default in TCS but the structure of the mapping definitions can serve as a solid basis for this. Furthermore, the declarative nature of the templates enables to reason about partiality of the templates: Each template, can be seen as a model pattern that can be matched against the model. For example, a template that defines that a certain property appears in the concrete syntax will also only match elements which have this property set. Partiality can then be determined based on these patterns (cf. Section 5.3.2.1).

- Through the *mode* property it is possible to define alternative syntaxes for the same class of a metamodel. This allows for the definition of view types that have *intra view type overlaps* (cf. Section 4.4.5.2 on page 148), i.e., representing the same element differently within the same view type. This fits well with the view concept of FURCAS even though it was not originally designed for that purpose.

- TCS templates are bidirectional. If only a unidirectional mapping from text to model could be specified, an update of the textual views would not be possible. Therefore, this property can be seen as a basic requirement for any view-based textual modelling approach.

- The TCS mapping language already has some support for resolving references by specifying queries for model elements by a certain property value. It is possible to specify by-name references to existing model elements. However, the query capabilities of TCS are still very limited. In order to enable the query capabilities that are needed to support the creation of powerful textual views, this feature needs to be extended significantly. Special attention needs to be paid in order to keep the query approach bidirectionally.

- A concept of partiality is, however, not present within TCS and needs to be newly defined and developed. Templates in TCS are, by definition, unaware of every element that does not fit one of the mappings's templates. Elements that are outside of these definitions cannot be handled by TCS. Therefore, in order to support partial view types, an extension needs to be provided that allows for the explicit definition of the scope of a template. Additionally, this includes explicit support for defining that a view that is instance of the specified view type can be *selective* or *holistic*.

5.3.2. Extending TCS to Handle Textual View Types

To allow for the specification of textual view types FURCAS extends TCS in several aspects. The extensions add the view concepts to the TCS metamodel as well as provide support for them in the TCS generator and framework. The following sections will therefore describe each extension in terms of the concepts that it adds to the TCS metamodel, accompanied by the extensions for the concrete syntax of TCS. The concrete syntax is described, again using TCS.

One part of these extensions deals with the partiality of view types. These extension reside in two different areas, first the *text to model partiality* – i.e., which elements can be included into a view that is instance of a certain view type and how is its scope defined. Section 5.3.2.1 covers this area. Second, the *model to text partiality* – i.e., how can partial textual information be used to construct model elements. This part of the problem is dealt with in Section 5.3.2.2.

5.3.2.1. Support for Partial View Types in Model to Text Direction

There needs to be support for the selection of elements that are included within a *partial* view. As defined in Chapter 4, a view type definition needs to define predicates Φ that decide on the inclusion of a models elements within a view type's instance. The structure of a template as it can be defined by standard TCS means is one component of these predicates. However, due to the "local" character of TCS templates, elements that are part of the view and therefore reachable due to the transitive navigation over a sequence of templates decide on the inclusion of an element into the view.

Given the example metamodel depicted in Figure 5.1 and given three templates for the classes $A, B,$ and C, where A refers to B via a property toB and B refers to C via a property toC. If the properties toB and toC are mandatory features and no further template restrictions (such as *isDefined*-clauses, as presented in the corresponding paragraph of Section 2.5.2.11) apply, a view will only include such instances of A which refer to an instance of B, which again refers to an instance of C (forming a chain: $A \to B \to C$). For standard TCS, an element A that does not fit this pattern would produce an error when the model to text transformation tries to create its textual representation. Due to the explicit focus on partiality where such cases are rather the rule than an exception, this is not acceptable for FURCAS. Thus, support for explicit template scopes is required.

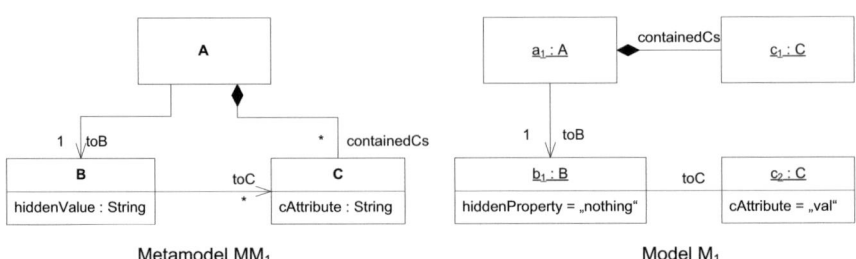

Figure 5.1.: Metamodel MM_1 defines three classes A, B and C. Model M is an instance of MM_1.

Extended Support for Partial Template Patterns   As a first extension towards a view based creation of textual concrete syntaxes, FURCAS weakens this rule by explicitly supporting elements that are not in the scope of a sequence of templates. FURCAS allows to distinguish between the different types of completeness that need to be fulfilled in order to let a model be valid according to a view type. These types will be explained based on the example depicted in Figure 5.1. The example metamodel MM_1 consists of three classes A, B, and C, where A has a containment association to C as well as a non-containment association to B. B refers to C via another containment reference. The corresponding view type definition given in Listing 5.1 defines how a view on an instance of MM_1 is created. However, the example model instance depicted in Figure 5.1 would cause an error upon view building. According to the metamodel, each A has to refer to exactly one B via its toB reference. For the referenced B-instance b_1 of a_1, however, the value of its `hiddenProperty` attribute is set to "nothing". The template for B explicitly defines a *PropertyInit* (cf. the corresponding paragraph in Section 2.5.2.11) that defines the value of `hiddenProperty` as "hiddenValue". Because the values do not match b_1, the view creation will fail with an error.

To aid a language developer in defining complete and partial view types, FURCAS provides means to explicitly declare whether a a template or a property within a template should fulfil a certain degree of completeness or be partial. To achieve this, the TCS metamodel is extended by the so-called *ScopeArg* which allows to define a certain element of *ScopeTypeKind*, as defined in Figure 5.2. The different possible settings for the *ScopeArg* are the following: *InstanceComplete, DownwardsContainmentComplete,*

```
1  template A {
2    "A" toB "containedCs:" containedCs
3  }
4  template B {
5    "B" toC {{hiddenProperty = "hiddenValue"}}
6  }
7  template C {
8    "C" {{cAttribute = "someValue"}}
9  }
```

Listing 5.1: An example mapping definition defining three different templates A, B and C which form a pattern against the metamodel given in Figure 5.1.

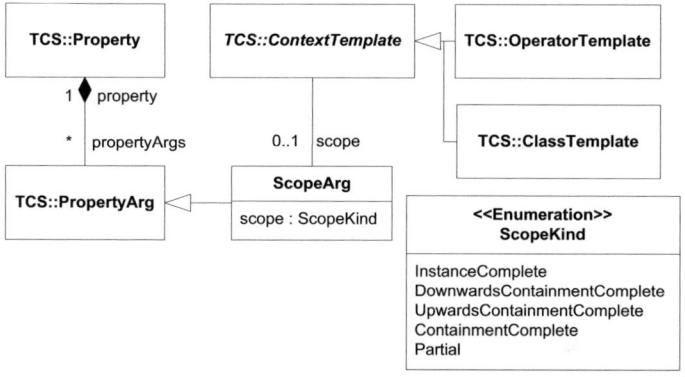

Figure 5.2.: FURCAS's extension to the TCS metamodel providing the *ScopeArg* class.

UpwardsContainmentComplete, *ContainmentComplete* and *Partial*. The semantics of each of these settings are:

- **Instance Complete:** This is the default behaviour, as TCS would react without FURCAS's extensions. In this setting, the template is considered to be able to create a representation of all possible instances of its referred class. Note that this only applies to selections and not projections, as projections do not limit the scope of elements that are included. Any element that is of the respective type but that is not matched by the (transitive) template(s) will raise an error. To help a language developer in creating a complete template, warnings will be shown whenever, a template construct is defined that makes it possible that a model element is not

```
1  context Template inv(Warning):
2    self.scopeArg.scope = ScopeKind::InstanceComplete implies
3      self.isPropertyInitComplete()
```

Listing 5.2: OCL expression defining consistency of templates for the *scope = instanceComplete* option.

```
1  context Template::isPropertyInitComplete() : Boolean body:
2    self.allSequenceElements()->forAll(
3      s | (s.oclIsTypeOf(TCS::InjectorActionsBlock) implies (
4  let iaBlock : TCS::InjectorActionsBlock =
5    s.oclAsType(TCS::InjectorActionsBlock) in
6    iaBlock.injectorActions->forAll(ia |
7      ia.oclIsTypeOf(TCS::PropertyInit) implies
8        ia.oclAsType(TCS::PropertyInit).isDefault or
9        ia.oclAsType(TCS::PropertyInit).isDomainComplete() or
10   )
11  ))
12  )
```

Listing 5.3: OCL body definition of the isPropertyInitComplete operation.

matched by it. Therefore, FURCAS provides an OCL invariant, presented in Listing 5.2, that checks if the *instance complete* property is fulfilled for a given template.

The isPropertyInitComplete operation, shown in Listing 5.3, will return true if the template has either only *PropertyInits* that are used as default values (line 6) or if the value range is completely covered using alternatives of the template, which is covered by the isDomainComplete operation. For example, considering a template that has one alternative a_1 with a *PropertyInit* that sets a boolean property *boolProp* to true. To be complete w.r.t. the domain of the property, the template needs to have a different alternative where the value is set to false. Otherwise, the template could not represent model elements that have set *boolProp* to false, which would contradict the specified *complete* property.

If an alternative defines more than one *PropertyInit*, also the domain coverage of the referenced properties needs to be checked. The algorithm that handles this check is included in the definition of the isDomainComplete operation. The subsequent paragraph, **Determining Domain Completeness**, will give more detail on the algorithm.

```
1  context Template inv(Warning):
2    self.scopeArg.scope = ScopeKind::DownwardsContainmentComplete
3      implies self.isDownwardsContainmentComplete()
4
5  context Template::isDownwardsContainmentComplete() : Boolean body:
6    self.alternativePropertySets->forAll( p : Property |
7      self.metaReference.allContent()->select(c |
8      if c.oclIsTypeOf(Reference) then
9        c.oclAsType(Reference).aggregationKind =
10         AggregationKind::Composite
11     else
12       false
13     endif
14     )->includes(p.strucfeature)
15     or p.isPartial()
16   )
```

Listing 5.4: OCL invariant definition for the *downwards containment complete* constraint.

- **(Upwards/Downwards) Containment Complete:** According to the previous chapter (cf. page 142), another type of completeness is the *containment* completeness. FURCAS also allows to define a template to be *containment complete*. This option requires that the template covers all containment references to other elements. If a template does not include a containment reference, the *containment complete* constraint, as defined in Listing 5.6 will raise an error. FURCAS furthermore allows to define a more fine-grained specification of containment completeness for templates. A Template can be *downwards* containment compete (cf. Listing 5.4) or *upwards* containment complete (cf. Listing 5.5). Both check the template w.r.t. the properties as they were defined in the previous chapter.

To be able to check whether a template fulfils the downwards or upwards containment complete property FURCAS defines two operations on the template class: These operations isDownwardsContainmentComplete() and isUpwardsContainmentComplete() determine the completeness property by checking whether the containment references are included in the template definition. An exception is made for properties which are explicitly marked as *partial* (p.isPartial()). For the definition of explicit partial properties see the below at paragraph **Partial**.

```
 1 context Template inv(Warning):
 2   self.scopeArg.scope = ScopeKind::UpwardsContainmentComplete
 3     implies self.isUpwardsContainmentComplete()
 4
 5 context Template::isUpwardsContainmentComplete() : Boolean body:
 6   Template.allInstances()->exists( t |
 7     self.metaReference.allContent()->select(c : ModelElement |
 8     if c.oclIsTypeOf(Reference) then
 9       c.oclAsType(Reference).otherEnd().aggregationKind =
10         AggregationKind::COMPOSITE
11     else
12       false
13     endif
14     ).namespace->includes(t.metaReference) or
15     t.alternativePropertySets()->forAll(p: Property | p.isPartial())
16   )
```

Listing 5.5: OCL invariant definition for the *upwards containment complete* constraint.

```
 1 context Template inv(Warning):
 2   self.scopeArg.scope = ScopeKind::ContainmentComplete implies
 3     self.isUpwardsContainmentComplete() and
 4       self.isDownwardsContainmentComplete()
```

Listing 5.6: OCL invariant definition for the *containment complete* constraint.

```
1 template A {
2   "A" b {partial} "containedCs:" c
3 }
4 template B {
5   "B" c {{hiddenProperty = "hiddenValue"}}
6 }
7 template C (partial) {
8   "C" {{cAttribute = "someValue"}}
9 }
```

Listing 5.7: Example templates from Listing 5.1 extended with explicit *partial* declarations.

For example, template A, defined in Listing 5.1, is containment complete (i.e., downwards *and* upwards) as it includes its only containment reference $containedCs$.

- **Partial:** Finally, specifying a template to be partial explicitly allows model elements to be excluded from the view without raising errors during the view creation. For the example defined in Listing 5.1, a valid application of the *partial* property would be as given in Listing 5.7 where an element with hiddenProperty ≠ "hiddenValue" would not be part of the view. Note, that it is possible to define the partial property either for a whole template or for single properties where a language developer wants to define that elements referenced by the template are not all to be included in the view.

Determining Domain Completeness Whether a template completely covers all possible instances of a metamodel class depends on how much the template constrains the value of the class's properties. For example, a template that defines a PropertyInit for a boolean property, setting its value to true removes all instances from its scope that have set this property to false. However, if the template has two different alternatives where the first one defines a PropertyInit with true and the second one defines false, the scope of the template is still complete w.r.t. the domain of possible instances of the class. Therefore, the idea behind the algorithm that determines wither a template is domain complete or not, is to combine the properties of each possible alternatives path of a template an check whether there is a path for each possible combination of values. Note that if an alternative completely omits a property in one of its alternatives, the algorithm will complete the scope of this property for this specific path.

```
1  context Alternative::propertySet(initSet : Set(
2  Tuple( property : StructuralFeature, values : Bag(OclAny) ) ) ) :
3  --this is the property set structure, consisting of
4  --the property which is initialised and all values that
5  --are used initialise it in the current alternative
6  Set( Tuple( property : StructuralFeature, values : Bag(OclAny) ) )
7  body:
8  --iterate over all directly contained (not in sub alternatives)
9  --injector actions add them to the resulting set
10  self.sequenceElements->select(se |
11  se.oclIsTypeOf(InjectorActionsBlock)).injectorActions->iterate(
12  ia ; result : Set( Tuple( property : StructuralFeature,
13  values : Bag ( OclAny ) ) ) = initSet |
14  if result.property->includes( ia.strucfeature ) then
15  --property already in the set, just add the value
16  let currentProperty =
17  result->select( e | e.property = ia.strucfeature ) in
18  result->excluding(property)->including(
19  Tuple (
20  property = currentProperty.property,
21  values = currentProperty.values->including(ia.value)
22  )
23  )
24  else
25  result->including(
26  Tuple (
27  property = ia.strucfeature
28  values = Bag { ia.value }
29  )
30  )
31  endif
```

Listing 5.8: OCL body of the `propertySet()` operation which is also defined analogously on `Template`.

```
1  context AlternativeSequence::propertySetsTree(initSet :
2    Set(Tuple(property : StructuralFeature, values : Bag(OclAny)))) :
3    Set(Set(Tuple(property: StructuralFeature, values: Bag(OclAny))))
4  body:
5    self.alternatives->iterate(alt;
6      result = Set(Set(Tuple(
7        property : StructuralFeature, values : Bag ( OclAny )))) =
8        Set{} | let subAlts = alt.sequenceElements->select(se |
9        se.oclIsTypeOf(AlternativeSequence)) in
10       if subalts->size() = 0 then
11         result->including( Set { alt.propertySet(initSet) } )
12       else
13         result->union( subalts->collect(subAlt |
14           subAlt..propertySet(initSet)) )
15       endif
16   )
```

Listing 5.9: OCL body of the `propertySetsTree()` operation.

The algorithm shown in Listing 5.10 consists of two phases, first, for each leaf in the tree of alternatives a set of init values is determined. Figure 5.3 illustrates an example for this tree. Second, the algorithm checks if there exists a value for any of the involved properties that is not covered by any of the tree's leafs. Finally, the algorithm clusters the leafs per range of the property values. Within these clusters, all other property inits need to cover the whole domain of their properties. For the example depicted in Figure 5.3, the first phase computes the three property sets at the leafs of the tree. The second phase then clusters these sets according to the values of each property one after another. Starting from $valueType = false$ which results in a cluster set $Cluster_{valueType=false} = \{visibility = \{public, private\}\}$. As all possible values of the visibility property attribute are contained in this set, $domainComplete(Cluster_{valueType=false})$ will return $true$. The cluster $Cluster_{valueType=true} = \varnothing$ is the empty set and therefore also results in $true$. Thus, the template for business object *is domain complete*.

Figure 5.4 depicts another example for the computation of the domain completeness. In this case, however, the result is $false$ as will be argued below. The property sets in this example consist of three different attributes. The first cluster is $Cluster_{lower=0}$, for which the resulting clustered set is $Cluster_{lower=0} = \{upper = \{1, \bot\}, ordered = \{true, false\}\}$, where $\bot$ denotes that there is an alternative specifying no explicit value for the property. As $ordered$ is a boolean property, the domain of $ordered$ is completely covered in this case. As the values for $upper$ includes the undefined value $\bot$, all values are also covered in this case. The next step is to proceed in this $lower = 0$ branch, which

```
 1 context Template::isDomainComplete() : Boolean
 2 body:
 3   let startPropertySet = self.propertySet() in
 4   let propertyTree =
 5     self->select(se | se.oclIsTypeOf(AlternativeSequence))
 6   ->collectNested(alts | alts.propertySetsTree(startPropertySet)) in
 7   propertyTree->forAll( leaf :
 8   Set(Tuple(property : StructuralFeature,values : Bag(OclAny)))|
 9     --build a cluster for each literal value of a property and check
10     --whether the other properties form their complete domain
11     leaf->values->forAll( v |
12       --first select those property sets that include
13       --this property/value combination
14       let cluster = propertyTree->select(propertySet |
15         propertySet->exists(
16           ps | ps.propery = leaf.property and ps.values->includes(v)))
17       --now ensure that every property occurs in its complete domain
18       in cluster->collect(pset | pset.property)->asSet()->forAll( p |
19         let clusterValues = cluster->collectNested(pset |
20           if pset->includes(ps | ps.property = p) then
21             --add the values to the collected set
22             p.values
23           else
24             --add the undefined value ⊥
25             OclUndefined
26           endif
27         ) in
28         --domain completeness for this property is fulfilled
29         --if the ⊥ is contained or if the domain for the
30         --property's type is covered
31         clusterValues->contains(OclUndefined) or
32           domain(p.type) = clusterValues
33       )
34   )
35 )
```

Listing 5.10: OCL body of the isDomainComplete() operation.

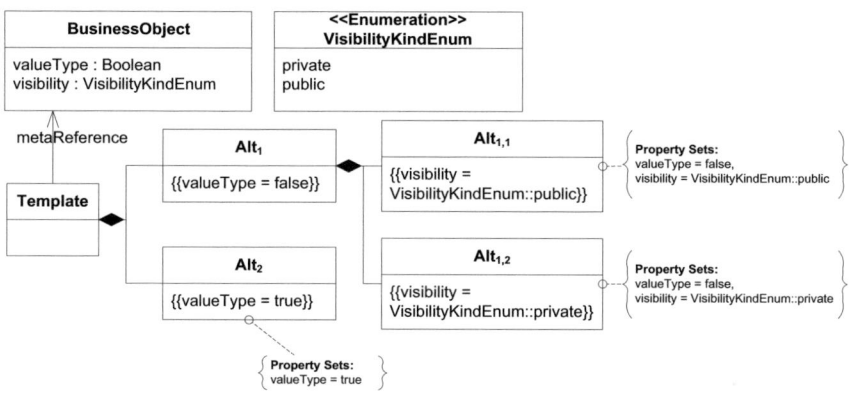

Figure 5.3.: An example for the computation of the domain completeness of a template resulting in $true$.

is the clustering according to the *upper* property. Clustering for *upper* $= 1$ results in $Cluster_{lower=0,upper=1} = \{ordered = \{true, false\}\}$. Being a complete domain, this branch is marked as domain complete. The second branch *lower* $= \perp$ results in the cluster set $Cluster_{lower=0,upper=\perp} = \{ordered = \{true, false\}\}$ and is also marked as domain complete.

Then, according to the second phase of the algorithm, the second root branch is analysed: $Cluster_{lower=1} = \{ordered = \{true, \perp\}, upper = \{1, \perp\}\}$. As both sub branches contain the undefined value $\perp$, they can be marked domain complete. Also, as their clustered sets, $Cluster_{lower=1,ordered=true}$ and $Cluster_{lower=1,upper=1}$ are the empty set, they are domain complete.

However, as the values for *lower* are not domain complete – *lower* $= \{0, 1\}$ – which does not cover the domain of its type Integer (which would be complete $\mathbb{N}_0^+$), the template *is not domain complete*.

Extended Selection Support Using Reference Only Templates and OCL

Using the extended scope specifications for templates and properties, FURCAS allows to define projections and selections in its templates. However, using the constructs defined in paragraph **Extended Support for Partial Template Patterns** on page 173, the selection criterion and the representation of elements are tightly coupled. If a language

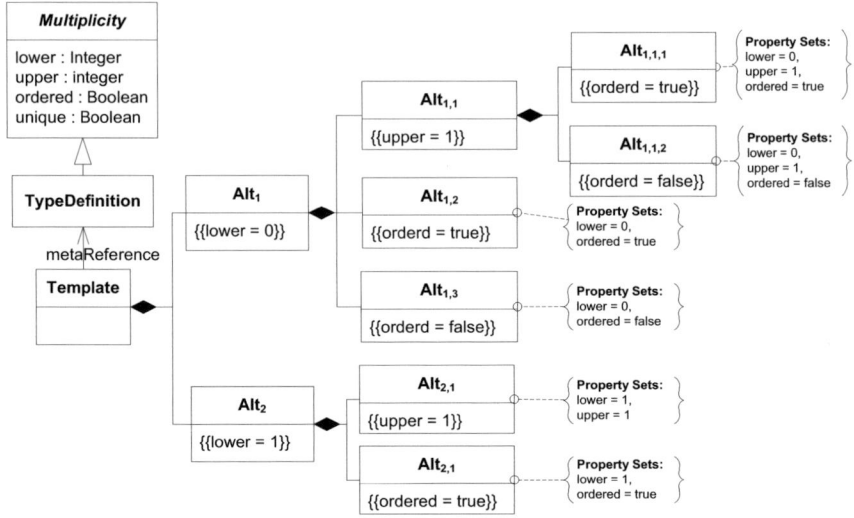

Figure 5.4.: An example for the computation of the domain completeness of a template resulting in *false*.

developer wants to define for a template for a class A that should only be included in the view if an attached class B has an attribute *selectioncriterion* set to a certain value "selected". The developer could specify this scenario by creating a template for B and adding a *PropertyInit* to B declaring that *selectionCriterion* should always equal "selected" in the following way: `{{ selectioncriterion = "selected"}}`. However, this would imply that whenever an element A is created according to the template, an instance of B is created and its *selectionCriterion* value is set to "selected". This might not match the intention of the language developer, as he or she might not want to have Bs created but rather have them looked up in an existing pool of instances of B.

FURCAS provides a solution to this problem by allowing to define a template as a so-called *referenceOnly* template. If a template is defined as *referenceOnly* it can be used in model to text direction to select only model elements that match the specified pattern. For example, if B would be *referenceOnly* only As would be part of the view for which the pattern *A.b.selectionCriterion = "selected"* holds. For the text to model direction, a *referenceOnly* template is used to find an existing model element of type B that matches the sub-pattern *B.selectionCriterion = "selected"*.

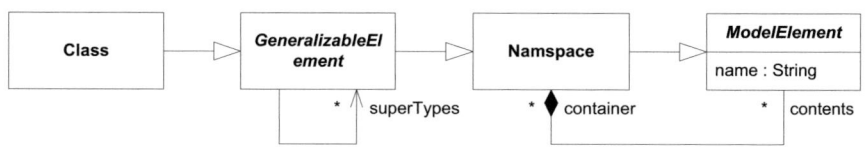

Figure 5.5.: Excerpt of the MOF Metamodel showing the relevant parts for the *referenceOnly* example.

Listing 5.11 shows an example application of *referenceOnly* templates taken from the MofClass case study (cf. Section 7.3.4.2). The metamodel structure used in this scenario is recalled in Figure 5.5. An example text that would be a representation of such a *referenceOnly* classifier template would then be: `class classA extends packB::subPackC::classD {}`. The qualified name `packB::subPackC::classD` would then resolve to a namespace `packB` containing a namespace `subPackC` which itself contains a `GeneralizableElement` `classD`.

Templates defined as *referenceOnly* allow to define a view type's selection with template means. For complex patterns, however, a language developer might need to define a lot of different templates to map the selection pattern. Especially for long navigation paths (e.g., `self.container.type.name`) or if more complex expressions, such as if-then-else, need to be specified, using templates to represent these patterns becomes infeasible. Therefore, FURCAS provides an additional concept for model element selection: OCL queries.

OCL queries can be used in *PropertyInits* to define a complex computation of the initialisation value of a property in text to model direction. For the model to text direction, an OCL query specifies a selection criterion for the template. The extension FURCAS provides to the TCS metamodel is depicted in Figure 5.6.

As these queries narrow the scope of a template, the computation if a template is *instance complete* (cf. Section 5.3.2.1) also needs to take this query into account. However, determining the semantic equivalence of two OCL expressions is a complex problem. For example, the Higher-Order-Logic (HOL) - OCL approach [BW02], deals with the problem of formalising the semantics of OCL expressions. However, there are still unsolved problems in this area [BDW06], mainly due to the fact that the OCL specification [Obj10a] is "based on naive set theory and an informal notion of *model*" and "it

```
 1  template Class main context(class)
 2    : $annotation
 3      $visibility
 4      (isAbstract?"abstract")
 5      "class" name
 6      (isDefined(supertypes) ? "extends"
 7        supertypes{mode = supertypes, separator=","}
 8    --refers to the GeneralizableElement template in mode #supertypes
 9      )
10      <space> "{" [
11          contents
12          (isDefined(invariants) ? "invariants" "{"
13            contents{mode=invariants} "}")
14      ] "}"
15    ;
16
17  -- A GeneralizableElement is either its container followed by ::
18  -- and a name, or just a name
19  template Model::GeneralizableElement #supertypes referenceOnly
20    : ( isDefined(container) ? container -- is of type Namespace in MM
21    "::" name : name)
22  ;
23
24  -- Namespace gets operatored using the :: operator to resolve
25  -- left recursion
26  template Model::Namespace abstract operatored("::");
27
28  -- any following elements in a package path are resolved using this
29  -- this applies for Namespaces as well as its contained elements
30  operatorTemplate Model::ModelElement(operators = "::",
31    source = 'container')
32  referenceOnly : name ;
```

Listing 5.11: Example templates which declare *referenceOnly* templates.

```
1  template ocl::CollectionItem (partial)
2    : item {{ type=self.item.type }}
3    ;
```

Listing 5.12: Example for the use of OCL within a *ProperyInit*

assumes a universe for values and objects and algebras over it without any concern of existence and consistency". A stronger semantic definition for OCL is required for this. As this definition is currently lacking, reasoning over the domain completeness of OCL property inits is out of the scope of this thesis. This issue is also discussed in the the concluding chapter in Section 8.2.1.

However, in many cases the OCL property inits are used to define computation rules of default values that are assigned during the construction of a model element from its concrete syntax. To cover this purpose, FURCAS introduces three different notions of property inits – *defaultValue*, *constraint* and *bidirectional*. These notions are distinguished by a newly introduced attribute `direction`. In the view type definition value of *defaultValue* for this property is represented by using the "< −" symbol (see for example Listing 6.3 in the next chapter). A property init which is defined as *defaultValue* will not prevent a template from creating the textual representation of a model elemenet where the property's value does not comply to the specified OCL expression. If the `direction` attribute is set to `constraint`, which is represented in the view type definition using the "==" symbol (see for example Listing 6.1 in the next chapter), the scope computation of a template will compare the value of the property to the result of the property init's expression. As stated before, FURCAS will not analyse the expression statically. Instead, FURCAS will do this comparison at runtime, during the creation or update of the textual representation of the model. Still, in the *constraint* case, no value will be assigned to the property upon the creation of the model element from the textual representation. Finally, the *bidirectional* case involves both notions, checking upon view creation and setting of a default value upon model creation. This case is represented using the standard notation for property inits using the = symbol.

An example for the application of OCL queries within *PropertyInits* is given in Listing 5.12, which is also taken from the MofClass case study. Here, the type of a `CollectionItem` is determined by an OCL query (line 2) that navigates to the item property of the `CollectionItem` and retrieves the type value from there. During the view creation this query will result in a selection so that only `CollectionItems` which have their type set equal to the item's type are represented by that template.

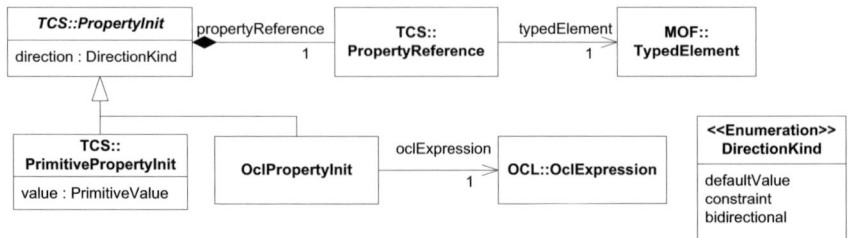

Figure 5.6.: OCL PropertyInit extension to the TCS metamodel.

```
1 template A {
2   "A" b "containedCs:" c
3 }
4 template B (partial) {
5   "B" c {{hiddenProperty = self.c.cAttribute}}
6 }
7 template C {
8   "C" cAttribute
9 }
```

Listing 5.13: Example view type definition illustrating a query overlap.

Overlapping Queries   Specifying queries and templates over the same elements of a metamodel may lead to difficult scenarios: A change in the textual representation given by one template might lead to the removal of a different element that specified a selection criterion for the very same element. Such a scenario may occur whenever there is an *intra view type overlap*, as defined in Section 4.5.1.4, where more than one predicate is specified for the same element in a metamodel.

Given the example metamodel with classes A, B, and C as defined in Figure 5.1 and a slightly different view type definition, given in Listing 5.13, the *PropertyInit* defined in B overlaps with the *Property* defined in C over C's *cAttribute*. An example instance that is represented by this view type could then, assuming B's instance to have its hiddenProperty set to "cAttValue", be:

   A B C cAttValue containedCs: C cAttValue.

If now the latter occurence of C is changed so that its cAttribute is set to, for example "anotherValue", B will be removed from the view as the values of B's hiddenProperty and C's cAttribute differ. The result would be:

   A containedCs: C anotherValue.

Such repercussion effects might be irritating for the user of the view type. In order to reduce the possible irritation, FURCAS provides features within its editor to notify the user about the reason of such changes. Furthermore, visual highlighting is used to indicate areas where such removals (or additions, as the same effects apply for inclusions into a view) occurred. Section 6.4 in the subsequent chapter describes an approach, called *OCL Impact Analysis* [CT05, CT09, AHK06], that allows to identify whenever the resulting value of an OCL expression changes. If the impact analysis detects that a selection restricting OCL based *PropertyInit* changes its value, e.g., from true to false, the textual representation of the underlying element will be removed from the view.

5.3.2.2. Support for Partial View Types in Text to Model Direction

Creating references to existing elements by constructs of a concrete syntax is a key feature for CTS approaches. TCS provides support for lookups by allowing to declare that the value for a property within a template is looked up within a certain scope – called context. Using this lookup, it is possible to resolve elements that are bound e.g., by using their name. An example for this would be a method call expression a() that refers to its corresponding method a by the name written in an expression, for example, return someA.a(). However, to find the referred element, a rather complex resolution mechanism might be necessary. As, for example, the type of the source expression someA of the method call a() has to be evaluated and from there on the corresponding method needs to be found. This is comparable to static type analysis in compiler construction techniques.

Though having some support for building contexts and defining lookups over these contexts (cf. Section 2.5.2.11 on page 55), TCS alone does not provide support for this kind of complex lookup. TCS, as many other CTS approaches, assumes that all referable elements are known to it and therefore, the lookup mechanisms for elements can be based on TCSs internal constructs (see the *context* mechanism in Section 2.5.2.11). However, in view-based environments, this assumption does not hold anymore. A view designer might need to include elements to a view that are reachable by navigating over a domain model but that are not visible for the current concrete syntactical representation of the model. FURCAS, extends TCS's capabilities by adding model query support by the use of OCL expressions.

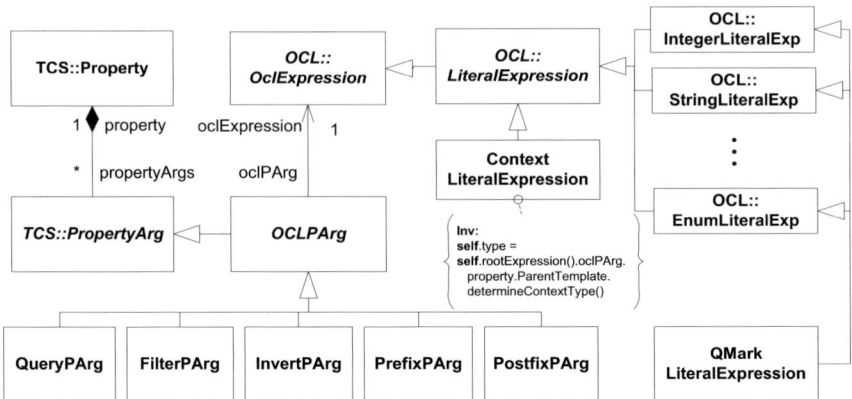

Figure 5.7.: OCL Query Mechanism Metamodel.

Model Element Lookup Support via OCL Queries

FURCAS already incorporates support for OCL in its extension for *PropertyInits*. Looking up elements by their textual representation, i.e., their names or other identifiers is also a task that can be supported by the use of OCL queries. This allows for the definition of complex model element lookups that are furthermore not limited to the scope of the current view type. Moreover, such queries can be expressed using the whole expressiveness of the underlying metamodel.

For evaluating the OCL query, the element that is currently processed by the template is set to `self`. Additionally, it is possible to specify that the current context is used within the query. Figure 5.7 depicts how this integrates into the metamodel. The syntax specification of the query element is presented in Listing 5.14.

To be able to use the currently parsed token in the scope of the OCL query, a special expression subtype is used, called `QMarkLiteralExpression`. This expression is represented within the concrete syntax of an OCL query by the "?" symbol as placeholder. The "?" place-holder will be replaced by the value of a token written at the location where the `Property` element is located within the template. The rule used to parse the bit of textual representation that is substituted for the "?" is determined by the place of the `QMarkLiteralExpression` within the OCL expression. For example, for the OCL query `self.elements->select(e | e.name = ?)`, the type of "?" has to be equal to the type of the property `name` of the element *e*. If the `name`

188

```
 1  template FURCAS::QueryPArg
 2    : "query" "=" oclExpression
 3    ;
 4
 5  template FURCAS::FilterPArg
 6    : "filter" "=" oclExpression
 7    ;
 8
 9  template FURCAS::InvertPArg
10    : "invert" "=" oclExpression
11    ;
12
13  template FURCAS::PrefixPArg
14    : "prefix" "=" oclExpression
15    ;
16
17  template FURCAS::PostfixPArg
18    : "postfix" "=" oclExpression
19    ;
20
21  template FURCAS:QMarkLiteralExpression
22    : "?" {{type = inferTypeFromSurroundingExpressions(self)}}
23    ;
24
25  template FURCAS:ContextLiteralExpression
26    : "#context"
27      {{type = commonSuperType(
28          rootExpression(self).queryPArg.property.
29            parentTemplate.determineCommonContextType())
30      }}
31    ;
```

Listing 5.14: Syntax specification of the Query Property Argument.

property is of type `String`, then the primitive template for this type is used in the generation of the parse rules.

Listing 5.15 shows how an OCL query can be specified in a FURCAS mapping definition. Whenever an element of type `ReferencingElement` is created via this view, it can get its `reference` set if the user writes its name after the constant token "references:". For example, in the textual representation `RefEl references: A`, the query would be, after the substitution: `self.elements->select(e | e.name='A')`.

If more than one `QMarkLiteralExpressions` occurs within a query, they may have different types, leading to ambiguities in the determination of the template used for

```
 1  viewtype OclQuery {
 2    primitiveTemplate string for PrimitiveTypes:STRING;
 3    template ReferencingElement :
 4      "RefEl" "references:"
 5      reference{query=self.elements->select(e | e.name=?)}
 6    ;
 7    template ReferenceableElement :
 8      name
 9    ;
10  }
```

Listing 5.15: Example mapping using an OCL query.

the parsing of the textual representation. For expressions of the form `<Exp1>.prop1` = ? ...`<Exp2>.prop2` = ?, where `prop1` has not the same type as `prop2`, the determination of a common type of all `QMarkLiteralExpressions` is not possible. If the type determination is ambiguous, the language developer has to provide either an additional argument directly referring to the correct template (e.g., `as=StringLiteralTemplate`), or a *refers to*-argument which specifies which property in the referenced model element should be used to determine the type of the parse rule (e.g., `refersTo=name`).

Occurences and Type of the "?"-Expression   To be able to correctly parse the OCL query that contains a `QMarkLiteralExpression`, such an expression needs to have a defined type. If the parser cannot determine the type unambiguously, the query cannot be evaluated. Depending on the place in the query where the `QMarkLiteralExpression` occurs, this context determines the type of the `QMarkLiteralExpression`.

As the `QMarkLiteralExpression` derives from all `LiteralExp` (cf. Figure 5.7), it may only occur in places within an OCL expression where a `LiteralExp` can occur. As shown in the expressions part of the OCL metamodel in Figure 5.8, a `LiteralExp` is an `OclExpression` that may occur as body of `LoopExp`, as init expression for a `Variable`, or source of a `CallExp`. Additionally, such an expression may be the parameter of an `OperationCallExp`. This limits the context in which a `QMarkLiteralExpression` can occur in the following way:

LoopExp: A `QMarkLiteralExpression` may only occur directly within a loop expression if its type is `Boolean`, thus the value of a `QMarkLiteralExpression` is limited to `[true|false]`. This holds for all

190

predefined `IterateExps` such as `select`, `reject`, `any` and so on, except for `IteratorExp`. For example, such an expression may look as follows: `elements->any(?)` where the "?" is of type `Boolean`, i.e., its value is then `true` or `false`. The only exception is the *generic* `IteratorExp` which can have expressions of arbitrary type as its body.

Variable: If a `QMarkLiteralExpression` occurs as init expression for a `Variable`, the variable's type determines the type of the `QMarkLiteralExpression`. For example, in an expression `let a : String = ?` the type of "?" would be `String`.

CallExp: As primitive types do not define any associations or attributes, their corresponding literal expression may not be the source of a `PropertyCallExp`, which is one of two subclasses of the `CallExp`. The second subclass is the `OperationCallExp`, for this type the OCL specification defines a fixed set of operations. Depending on the actual type of the `QMarkLiteralExpression`, the respective set of operations may have the `QMarkLiteralExpression` as their source. For example, assuming the following expression': `? or self.a`, the `or` operation from the primitive type `Boolean` uses the "?" as its source and thus implicitly defines its type to be `Boolean`. Furthermore, in contrast to the `QMarkLiteralExpression` as source of an operation call, it may also be used as parameter within an operation call. This implies the same type constraints as for the former case. For example, the expression `self.a or ?` implies the "?" to be of type `Boolean`.

Furthermore, a `QMarkLiteralExpression` may also occur in the `condition`, `then` or `else` part of an `IfExp` as well as an item within a `CollectionLiteralExp`:

IfExp: There are three different possible occurrences of a `QMarkLiteralExpression` within an `IfExp`. Used as condition, the `QMarkLiteralExpression` has to be of type `Boolean`. If it is used as `then` or `else` part, is has to have the same type as the respective other part. For example, the `QMarkLiteralExpression` within the expression `if true then ? else 'Something' endif` implies that the "?" is of type `String`. Having the "?" occurring in both parts would not make any sense as the `IfExp` would then always evaluate to the same value, that is "?".

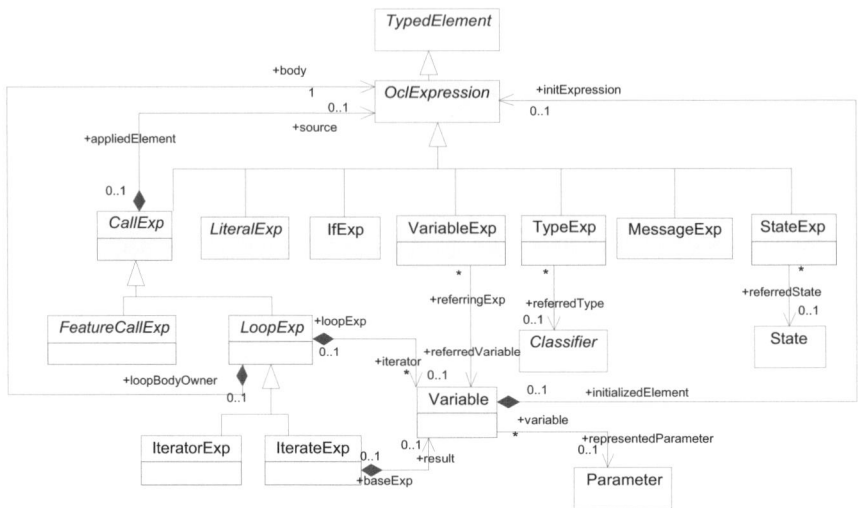

Figure 5.8.: The expressions part of the OCL metamodel, taken from [Obj10a].

CollectionLiteralExp: A `QMarkLiteralExpression` can occur within a `CollectionLiteralExp`. The type of the `QMarkLiteralExpression` is then determined by the type of the collection in which it occurs, which, in turn, is given by the types of its elements. For example, the type of the "?" in expression `OrderedSet{1, 2, ?}` the type of the "?" is `Integer`.

5.3.3. Inversion of OCL queries

Keeping the bidirectionality of the view type definitions, which is needed to support editable views, requires to keep all kinds of mapping constructs bidirectional. To ensure the bidirectionality of the OCL query concept, FURCAS allows the automatic inversion of all OCL queries that are used in arguments of the *Property* construct. To achieve this inversion, FURCAS needs to determine the inverse query of the defined one, to be able to produce the value which was used as query parameter "?" in the original query.

5.3.3.1. An Automatic Approach for OCL Query Inversion

An OCL query that contains at least one "?" place-holder can be considered as an equation with one variable. To determine the value of this variable, the equation needs to be solved. The "?" place-holder always represents the same value, i.e., there is only one token that can be used for the query at a time. This reduces the complexity to an equation having one variable with one or more occurrences.

Assuming an OCL query of the following form:

$$< Exp > \rightarrow\ select(var | var.prop =<? - Exp >)$$

where $<? - Exp >$ is an OCL expression where the "?" place-holder occurs at least once. The goal is to solve the equation to get the following resulting equation:

$$< Exp' >:=<? - Exp' >$$

where $<? - Exp' >$ only contains only one QMarkLiteralExpression. The OCL solving approach employed in FURCAS tries to solve the expression by a fixed set of rules starting from the root expression on the right-hand side. For each context in which a QMarkLiteralExpression can occur (as defined previously) one of the following rules defines a transformation that will finally lead to the solving of the given equation.

For an OCL query to be invertible, it needs to fulfil certain assumptions. First, the value for the replacement of the "?"-expression needs to be completely covered by the combination of data from the model, such as attribute values, and the literals contained in the OCL query itself. For example, an expression

```
self.contents->select(e | e.name.concat('_name') = ?)
```

fulfils this assumption, as the value for the "?"-expression can be completely expressed using the name attribute of an e in combination with the '_name' literal. In contrast to this example, the expression

```
self.contents->select(e | e.magicNumber = ?.size())
```

is not invertible as the "?"'s value does neither appear in the model over which the query is executed nor does it appear in the OCL expression itself. The following formula determines whether an OCL query fulfils the invertibility assumption:

$$\{(1,i),\dots,(j,j+m),\dots,(n,?.size())\} \wedge$$
$$\forall 1 < x <?.size() \mid \exists (r_1, r_2) \in Coverage \mid r_1 \le x \le r_2$$

This formula expresses that for each sub-string of the "?"-expression an element in the *Coverage* set needs to exist that covers the respective sub-string. The *Coverage* set is determined by a combination of model and expression data:

$$Coverage = expdata(< exp >) \cup modeldata(< model >)$$

where the sets determined using the *data* function are:

expdata($< exp >$): For each literal expression which is part of an operation call expression to the equals ("=") operation where the other side of the expression is a "?"-expression, the corresponding range is added to the resulting set. For example, for the expression `< exp >= self.contents->select(e | e.name.concat('Name') = ?)`, the range (?.size() - 4, ?.size()) results from *expdata*($< exp >$).

modeldata($< model >$): For each expression in which a property of the model is compared to a sub-string of a "?"-expression the corresponding sub-string range is added to the resulting set. For example, for the (sub-) expression `< exp >= self.contents->select(e | e.name = ?.substring(1, 3))`, the range (1, 3) results from *data*($< exp >$). The *modeldata*($< model >$) function operates on every sub-expression that can be transformed into an expression of the form $< exp_1 > .prop = \{substring/concatops\}(<? - exp >)$.

If the above assumption is fulfilled, the following rule set describes the transformation rules that are responsible for inverting an OCL query to determine the value of the "?"-expression. The decision which of the rules is applied depends on the root expression of the right hand side of the equation. For example, Figure 5.9 depicts the model representation of an expression `self->select(e | e.name = ?)`, showing that the root expression is the `select` expression, thus the according rule will be applied for transforming the expression in order to solve an equation of the form: `ModelElement(name = "M") = self->select(e | e.name = ?)`.

The following rules show how the remaining expression types of OCL can be inverted:

Collection-rules: Collections based expressions (such as `select` or `reject`) using a "?"-expression in their body also require rules how to solve the expression to find out the value of the "?"-expression.

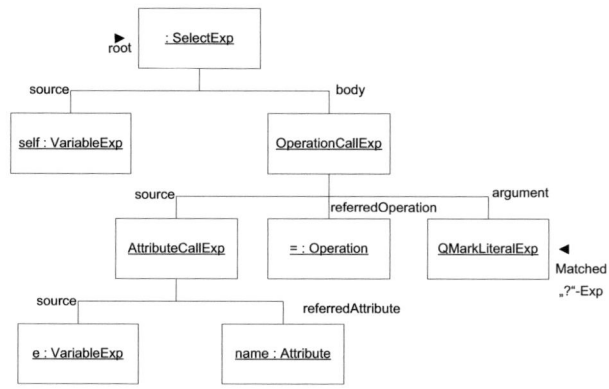

Figure 5.9.: Model representation of `self->select(e | e.name = ?)` showing the root node and the matched "?"-expression used for the decision of the rule application.

select() The `select(<?-Exp>)` operation is the most frequently used operation when it comes to looking up an element within a model. As only elements for which $<? - Exp >$ is `true` result from this operation, the inverse operation is the `any()` operation on the respective other side of the equation. The following equation show the inversion of the `select()`-expression:

$$< Exp_r >:= < Exp_1 > .select(e|e.prop_1 = (<? - Exp_1 >)\ldots e.prop_n = (<? - Exp_1 >))$$
$$\Longleftrightarrow \begin{pmatrix} (1) < Exp_r > .prop_1 =<? - Exp_1 > \\ \vdots \\ (n) < Exp_r > .prop_n =<? - Exp_n > \end{pmatrix}$$

The results of the expressions $1..n$ are then concatenated based on the indices in the $<? - Exp_i >$-expressions. For example:

$$Person(name = `A`, surname = `B`) := \{Person_1, Person_2\}- > select(p|$$
$$p.name =?.substring(1,1) and p.surname =?.substring(2,2)) \Longleftrightarrow$$
$$\begin{pmatrix} (1)p.name =?.substring(1,1) \\ (2)p.surname =?.substring(2,2) \end{pmatrix} \Longleftrightarrow$$
$$? = `A`.concat(`B`)$$

reject() As the `reject` operation produces the difference set of the `select` operation, building the difference set from the result is the inverse operation for it:

$$< Exp_r >:=< Exp_1 > .reject(<? - Exp >) \iff$$
$$< Exp_1 > -> select(e| < Exp_r > -> excludes(e)) -> any(true) :=<? - Exp >$$

For example:

$$\{1,2,6\} := \{1,2,5,6\} -> reject(e|e =?) \iff$$
$$\{1,2,5,6\} -> select(e|\{1,2,6\} -> excludes(e)) -> any(true) := e =? \iff$$
$$5 := e =?$$

The same applies for negated (using the `not`-operation) terms within a `select()`-expression.

append()/prepend()/including() Each ordered collection type defines this operation. The operation adds its argument at the last position of its collection (self).[1] The OCL specification defines that the last element of the collection is the argument of the operation: `post: result->at(result->size() ) = object.` Due to this constraint, the following inversion will return this added element:

$$< Exp_r >:=< Exp_1 > .append(<? - Exp >) \iff$$
$$< Exp_r > -> last() :=<? - Exp >$$

The same applies, at least for `Sequences` also for the `including()` operation. This works because, as the OCL specification defines, the semantics of `Sequence::including()` is the same as for `append()`. The following constraint ensures these semantics: `post:result=self.append(object)`. Furthermore, the same rule applies analogously for the `prepend()` operation.

iterate() The result of an `iterate` expression is an accumulator expression that is specified in addition to the iterator. For example, using the expression `col->iterate(item : Type; acc : Set(Type) = Set |`

---

[1] The OCL specification [Obj10a] seems to be incomplete as it defines the semantics of the append() operation on `OrderedSet` without taken the set semantics into account. I.e., there is a constraint that defines: `post: result->size() = self->size() + 1`. However, if the argmunt is already contained in the set this will not hold!

196

`acc.including(item)`), after each iteration step the body's value is assigned to `acc`. The result of the whole iteration process is the accumulator. Therefore, to be able to invert an `iterate` expression, the inversion rule for this type of expression needs to go back from the resulting accumulator to the initial set over which the iterate expression loops.

Depending on the position of the "?"-expression within the iterate, one of two different rules defines the inversion of the iterate expression:

Case 1: ?-Exp in body In this case the body expression contains the "?"-expression. The inversion will create a section-wise parted array or expressions until the init expression of the accumulator is reached. By substituting the determined values back in the array the values of the segments can be determined.

$$< Exp_r >:=< Exp_1 > - > iterate(i; < acc >=< init > \,|\, <? - Exp >) \iff$$

$$\left(\begin{aligned} &<? - Exp >_{last_i} = invert(< Exp_r >=<? - Exp with acc =<? - Exp >_{last_i-1}>)) \\ &\vdots \\ &<? - Exp >_1 = invert(< Exp_r >=<? - Exp with acc =< init >>)) \end{aligned} \right)$$

An example for this case is the following:

$$'asdfasdf' = Sequence\{1, 2\} - > iterate(i; acc : String = \text{"}|acc.concat(?)) \iff$$

$$(1)\ <? - Exp >_2 = 'asdfasdf'.substring(<? - Exp >_1 .size(), <? - Exp > .size())$$

$$(2)\ <? - Exp >_1 = 'asdfasdf'.substring(1, <? - Exp > .size()) \overset{(2)in(1)}{\iff}$$

$$<? - Exp >_2 = 'asdfasdf'.substring('asdfasdf'.substring(1, <? - Exp > .size())$$
$$.size(), <? - Exp > .size()) \iff$$

$$<? - Exp >= 'asdf'$$

Case 2: ?-Exp in source If the "?"-expression occurs as source of an iterate expression, the inversion of the iterate as shown in case 1 is performed. The main difference is that there are only so many occurrences how often a "?" occurs in the source collection:

$$< Exp_r >:=<? - Exp > - > iterate(i; < acc >=< init > | < Exp_1 >) \iff$$

$$\left(\begin{array}{l} <? - Exp >_{last_i} = invert(< Exp_r >=<? - Exp \text{ with } acc =<? - Exp >_{last_i-1}>)) \\ \vdots \\ <? - Exp >_1 = invert(< Exp_r >=<? - Exp \text{ with } acc =< init >>)) \end{array} \right)$$

An example for this case is the following:

$$'12' = Sequence\{?, '2'\} - > iterate(i; acc : String = ``|acc.concat(i)) \iff$$

$(1) <? - Exp >_2 = '12'.substring('12'.size() - '2'.size(), '2'.size())$

$(2) <? - Exp >_1 = <? - Exp >_2 .substring('2'.size() - <? - Exp >_1 .size(),$

$\qquad\qquad\qquad <? - Exp >_1 .size()) \iff$

$(1) <? - Exp >_2 = '1'$

$(2) <? - Exp >_1 = '1'.substring('2'.size() - <? - Exp >_1 .size(),$

$\qquad\qquad\qquad <? - Exp >_1 .size()) \iff$

$\qquad <? - Exp >= '1'$

String rules

concat(): A `concat` operation on the right-hand side of the equation will be replaced by a `substring` operation on the left-hand side. Depending on whether the ?-expression occurs as source or as argument of the `concat` operation different inversion rules apply:

Case 1 (?-Expr. in source):

$$< Exp_r >:=<? - Exp > .concat(< Exp_1 >) \iff$$

$$< Exp_r > .substring(< Exp_r > .size() - < Exp_1 > .size(), < Exp_r > .size()) :=$$

$$<? - Exp >$$

Case 2 (?-Expr. as argument):

$$< Exp_r >:=< Exp_1 > .concat(<? - Exp >) \iff$$
$$< Exp_r > .substring(1, < Exp_1 > .size()) :=<? - Exp >$$

If the ?-expression appears as source and as argument at the same time, the expression will result in two parallel expressions that can be inverted further. A special rule applies for cases such as `'TT'` `=` `?.concat(?)` where the resulting string is `?.substring(1,` `'TT'.size()` `/` `2`.

substring(): A `substring` operation on the right-hand side of the equation will be replaced by a `concat` operation on the left-hand side. Note that this substitution is only possible if all parts of the original string are used somewhere in the expression. For example, `a.b` `=` `?.substring(1,3)` and `a.c` `=` `?.substring(3,?.size())` would be solvable, where the same expression without the second part would not. Furthermore, no implicit knowledge about the length of "?" shall be used. Therefore, somewhere in the expression the term `?.substring(<Exp>,` `?.size())` has to occur, otherwise this part is irrecoverably lost and therefore not reconstructible by the inversion approach. We define the following substitution rules for the `substring` operation:

$$\begin{pmatrix} < Exp_1 > := & <? - Exp > .substring(< Exp_{1,1} >, < Exp_{1,2} >) \\ \vdots \\ < Exp_n > := & <? - Exp > .substring(< Exp_{n,1} >, < Exp_{n,2} >) \end{pmatrix} \iff$$
$$< Exp_1 > .concat(< Exp_2 >).....concat(< Exp_n >) =<? - Exp >$$

Assuming the equations for $< Exp_i >$ are independent from each other and sorted ascendingly according to the value of $< Exp_{i,1} >$ a further requirement for the application of this rule is that $< Exp_{1,1} >$ evaluates to 1and $< Exp_{n,2} >$ has to evaluate to $<? - Exp > .size()$. Additionally, note that this substitution rule only works in the defined way if the sequence of pairs $(< Exp_{1,1} >, < Exp_{1,2} >), \ldots (< Exp_{n,1} >, <? - Exp > .size())$ is formed so that $< Exp_{i,2} >=< Exp_{i+1,1} > +1$. Intuitively speaking: the string chain must be entirely complete. If $< Exp_{i,2} > >= < Exp_{i+1,1} >$, the overlapping parts of each pair $(< Exp_i >, < Exp_{i+1} >)$ need to be omitted in the concatenation (as they represent redundant information). This refines the above defined rule to:

$$
\begin{pmatrix}
< Exp_1 > := & <? - Exp > .substring(< Exp_{1,1} >, < Exp_{1,2} >) \\
\vdots & \\
< Exp_n > := & <? - Exp > .substring(< Exp_{n,1} >, <? - Exp > .size())
\end{pmatrix} \Longleftrightarrow
$$

$$< ? - Exp > \quad :=$$

$$< Exp_1 > .substring(< Exp_{1,1} >, < Exp_{1,2} > - < Exp_{2,1} >).concat(< Exp_2 >)$$

$$.substring \ldots$$

$$.substring(< Exp_{1,1} >, < Exp_{n-1,2} > - < Exp_{n,1} >).concat(< Exp_n >)$$

The following is an example for a case in which the string parts overlap:

$$resultElements = elements-> select(e|e.firstName =$$

$$?.substring(1, ?.indexOf(':'))$$

$$and \ e.lastName =?.substring(?.indexOf(':') + 1, ?.size()) \overset{selectrule, substringrule}{\Longleftrightarrow}$$

$$resultElements-> any(true).firstName.concat($$

$$resultElements-> any(true).lastName) =?$$

toInteger(), toReal(), toBoolean(), toReal(): The replacement for this kind of operation on the right hand side is the $toString()$ operation on the respective other primitive type.

$$< Exp_r >:=<? - Exp > .to < PrimitiveType > () \Longleftrightarrow$$

$$< Exp_r > .toString() :=<? - Exp >$$

If the source of the `toInteger()` operation is a real, the expression is not invertible as the decimals are lost and connot be reconstructed.

toLowerCase(), toUpperCase(): As both of these operations are not bijective they cannot be inverted.

Number and Boolean-rules: Operations on numbers or boolean values that perform a bijective operation can be inverted as every mathematical expression. For example, the expression $< Exp_1 >=< Exp_2 > / <? - Exp >$ has the inverse function $< Exp_2 > / < Exp_1 >=<? - Exp >$.

$$< Exp_r >:=<? - Exp >< op >< Exp_1 > \Longleftrightarrow$$
$$< Exp_r >< inverseop_{op} >< Exp_1 >:=<? - Exp >$$

IfExp-rules: If the `QMarkLiteralExpression` occurs within the condition or either the `then` or `else` part of an `IfExp`, the inversion rules to determine the value of the "?" are the following:

condition: Occurrences of a `QMarkLiteralExpression` within the condition of an `IfExp` can be solved by the following rule:

$$< Exp_r >:= if(<? - Exp >)then < Exp_{then} > else < Exp_{else} > endif \Longleftrightarrow$$
$$if(< Exp_r >=< Exp_{then} >)then <? - Exp > elsenot <? - Exp > endif$$

This might lead to a partially defined equation depending on the domain of the `QMarkLiteralExpression`'s type. For example, if the $<? - Exp >$ is ? = 2 the inversion of a corresponding `IfExp` would result in the unambiguous `then` part where ? = 2 and a not completely solvable `else` part with ? <> 2.

then,else: An `QMarkLiteralExpression` can also occur in the `then` or `else` part of an `IfExp`.

$$< Exp_r >:= if(< Cond >)then <? - Exp > else < Exp_{else} > endif \Longleftrightarrow$$
$$\left(\begin{array}{c} if(< Exp_r >=< Exp_{else} >)then \\ <? - Exp >:=< dom(<? - Exp > -typew.o. < Exp_r >) \\ else <? - Exp >:=< Exp_r > endif \end{array} \right)$$

An example for the solution of this expression type, for the expression `5 :=` `if(a = 1) then ? else 2 endif` is then the following expression: `if(5 = 2) then ? = Sequence{0..*}.excluding(5) else ? = 5 endif`.

LetExp: A `let` expression binds a variable to an expression and makes it available to the expression in its scope (expression after `in`). To be able to invert an expression where the `QMarkLiteralExpression` occurs in the init expression of the let expression, this expression needs to be inlined into the `in` part of the expression.

$$let < var >:= \left(<? - Exp >\right)in < Exp_{in}withvar > \Longleftrightarrow$$
$$< Exp_{in}withvarreplacedby <? - Exp >>$$

For example, given an expression `let var=?.concat('Var')` in `'My'.con-cat(var)` results in `'My'.concat(?.concat('Var'))` after the application of this inversion rule.

Combined Example   Given the following expression, which is applied in a view type definition for the metamodel of the running example (cf. page 18), queries for a signature that where the value in the concrete syntax is prefixed by the '+=' string:

$$result : MethodSignature := self.signatures->select(s|s.name =' + =' .concat(?))$$

First, we can easily determine the type of "?"-expression by using the `name` attribute's type: `String`. In the following the ^{R} will denote the root expression which is used to determine which rule will be applied next:

$$result :$$
$$MethodSignature := \quad self.signatures->^Rselect(s|s.name =' + =' .concat(?)) \overset{\text{select rule}}{\Longleftrightarrow}$$
$$result.name := \quad ' + =' .^Rconcat(?) \overset{\text{concat rule}}{\Longleftrightarrow}$$
$$? := \quad result.name.substring(' + =' .size(), result.name.size())$$

A more complex example where the OCL inversion is applied to can be found in Appendix B.

Realisation   FURCAS realises the OCL inversion approach by applying QVT transformations to the OCL expression tree which match the initial patterns described in the rules presented in the previous section. If the rule matches, an in-place transformation is performed on the left and the right hand side of the OCL expression model. As an OCL expression may only have one root expression (cf. Section 12.2.1 "ExpressionInOcl" in [Obj10a]), and for every possible type of expression one distinct rule exists, there cannot be a case where more than one rule can be applied at once. If no rule can be applied

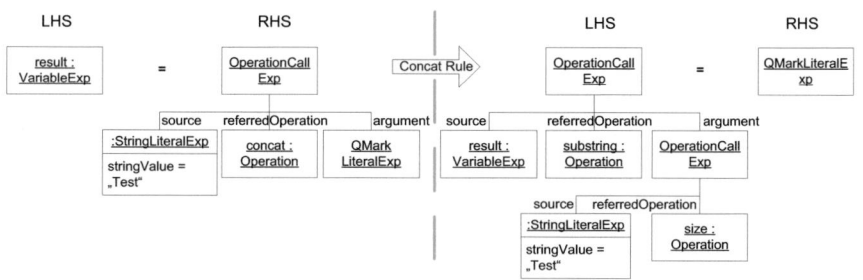

Figure 5.10.: Model representation of the equation `var = "Test".concat(?)` with application of the concat transformation rule.

anymore and the right hand side of the equation is the "?"-expression (or if there is more than one right hand side, as for example produced by the substring rule) the equation is solved. If no rule can be applied anymore and (any of) the right hand side(s) is still not the "?"-expression (or a sub part of it, due to the substring rule), the equation is considered unsolvable.

Listing 5.16 shows an example QVT rule which realises the `concat` transformation rule. Figure 5.10 depicts an example application of the concat transformation rule to an OCL model equation.

5.3.3.2. Deriving Code-Completion Proposals for OCL Queries

So called "code-completion" or "auto-completion" proposals can help the developer by presenting a choice of referencable elements from a pop-up dialogue. Those points within a textual representation with lookups for elements by a certain query are the places where a developer that uses the language would most probably want to be supported in creating a reference to one of the proposed elements. The queries in the view type definition of FURCAS define how elements are resolved based on a textual representation of a reference to them. Based on these expressions also proposals based on incomplete textual reference representations can be determined. This improves the productivity of the developer, as he or she does not have to think about the correct reference name but gets a complete list of possible identifiers to choose from. Furthermore, this feature lowers the probability of errors, as only valid identifiers are proposed. Research in this area has come up with a multitude of solutions for this problem [JP08]. How-

```
 1  transformation InvertOclQuery (sourceOcl : oclEquation,
 2         targetOcl : oclEquation, stdLib : ecore) {
 3   top relation ConcatRule {
 4    checkonly domain stdLib string_class : EClass {
 5     eOperations = concatOp : ecore::EOperation {
 6       name = 'concat' },
 7     eOperations = substringOp : ecore::EOperation {
 8       name = 'substring' },
 9     eOperations = sizeOp : ecore::EOperation {
10       name = 'size' }
11    };
12    checkonly domain sourceOcl source: oclEquation::Equation {
13     left = leftSource : ocl::ecore::OCLExpression {},
14     right = rightSource : ocl::ecore::OperationCallExp {
15      referredOperation = concatOp.oclAsType(ecore::EObject),
16      source = rightSource_opCallSrc:ocl::ecore::OCLExpression{},
17      argument = rightTarget: furcas::QMarkLiteralExp { }
18     }
19    };
20    enforce domain targetOcl target: oclEquation::Equation {
21     left = leftTarget: ocl::ecore::OperationCallExp {
22      source = leftSource,
23      referredOperation = substringOp.oclAsType(ecore::EObject),
24      argument = from : ocl::ecore::IntegerLiteralExp {
25       integerSymbol = 1
26      },
27      argument = to : ocl::ecore::OperationCallExp {
28       referredOperation = sizeOp.oclAsType(ecore::EObject),
29       source = rightSource_opCallSrc
30      }
31     },
32     right = rightTarget: furcas::QMarkLiteralExp { }
33    };
34    [...]
35   }
36  }
```

Listing 5.16: Example inversion rule in QVT for the concat rule.

ever, for the specific problem of deriving auto-completion proposals from templates in combination with OCL queries, no generic solution is available, yet.

FURCAS tackles this problem by applying a similar approach as for the computation of QMarkLiteralExpressions in OCL queries. The solution uses the same rules as for the inversion of "?"-expressions but the result is different. The goal of the auto-completion feature is to reduce a set of candidate elements, which are initially defined by their type by filtering them according to a certain query and a certain prefix, which the user might already have typed.

Assuming an OCL query of the following form:

$$E = <Exp> \rightarrow select(var | var.prop = <? - Exp>)$$

where $<? - Exp>$ is an OCL expression where the "?" place-holder occurs at least once and is of type String and a given prefix that has been typed by a developer using the language, $< prefix >$. The goal is to get a set of elements E for which the following holds:

$$\forall e \in E \,|\, e \in result(<Exp>) \wedge e.prop.startsWith(< prefix >)$$

In fact, we want to reduce a set of candidate elements C resulting from the evaluation of $< Exp >$ for a specific self to a subset $E \subseteq C$. We will call the set C the set of *candidate model elements*.

The process of computing E works also similar to the previously defined solving of the QMarkLiteralExpressions equations. However, the auto-completion case always operates on a concrete set of model elements and therefore consists of two major steps that are uses some additional rules for this:

Step 1 Evaluate $< Exp >$ with a specific value for self to obtain the candidate set C.

Step 2 For each element $e \in C$, try to solve the equation: $e.prop := < prefix > <? - Exp >$. If the equation is solvable so that it results in $? = < resultstring >$, add e to the result set E.

Prefix rule: This rule operates on a string based equation and checks whether the left-hand side is actually prefixed by the $< prefix >$ that is specified on the right-hand side.

$$< String >:=< prefix ><? - Exp > \quad \overset{\text{<}prefix\text{> is prefix of <}String-Exp\text{>}}{\Longleftrightarrow}$$

$$< String >:=<? - Exp >$$

If the rule cannot be applied when this initial situation occurs the equation is considered unsolvable.

Concat rule: The concat rule as defined in the OCL inversion rule-set is slightly modified to only be applicable if the left-hand side actually contains the given prefix/postfix. This modification is due to the fact that in the auto-completion case one cannot guarantee that the concat rule is always solvable:

Case 1:

$$< Exp_r >:=<? - Exp > .concat(< Exp_1 >) \quad \overset{<Exp_r> \text{ has } <Exp_1> \text{ as postfix}}{\Longleftrightarrow}$$

$$< Exp_r > .substring(< Exp_r > .size()- < Exp_1 > .size(), < Exp_r > .size()) :=$$

$$<? - Exp >$$

Case 2:

$$< Exp_r >:=< Exp_1 > .concat(<? - Exp >) \quad \overset{<Exp_r> \text{ has } <Exp_1> \text{ as postfix}}{\Longleftrightarrow}$$

$$< Exp_r > .substring(r, < Exp_1 > .size()) :=<? - Exp >$$

In the following example, the presented process determines the elements that are valid identifiers for completing a token that started with a given prefix. Given the example query-pattern:

$$self.object.getType().getAllSignatures()- > select(s|s.name =?.concat('+ ='))$$

and a prefix that was already typed by a developer: prefix= "b+" the following rules apply:

$$\{self.object.getType().getAllSignatures()\} =$$

$$\{MethodSignature(name : "b+ = "), MethodSignature(name : "b+ +")\}$$

First the object $MethodSignature(name : "b+ = ")$ will be checked:

$$MethodSignature(name : "b+ = ").name := "b + "?.concat(`+ = `) \qquad \overset{\text{property}}{\Longleftrightarrow}$$

$$`b+ = ` := "b + "?.concat(`+ = `) \qquad \overset{\text{prefix}}{\Longleftrightarrow}$$

$$`b+ = ` :=?.concat(`+ = `) \qquad \overset{\text{concat 1}}{\Longleftrightarrow}$$

$$? := `b+ = `.substring(1, `b+ = `.size() - `+ = `.size()) \qquad \Longleftrightarrow$$

$$? := `b+ = `.substring(1, 3 - 2) \qquad \Longleftrightarrow$$

$$? := `b+ = `.substring(1, 1) \qquad \Longleftrightarrow$$

$$? := `b`$$

Thus, we add the $MethodSignature(name : "b+ = ")$ to the result E. Now we try to apply the rules to the second object $MethodSignature(name : "b + +")$:

$$MethodSignature(name : "b + +").name := "b + "?.concat(`+ = `) \qquad \overset{\text{property}}{\Longleftrightarrow}$$

$$`b + +` := "b + "?.concat(`+ = `) \qquad \overset{\text{prefix}}{\Longleftrightarrow}$$

$$`b + +` :=?.concat(`+ = `)$$

This time, since we can not apply the concat rule, the equation is unsolvable. The result set is therefore $E = \{MethodSignature(name : "b+ = ")\}$

5.3.3.3. An Alternative to the Automatic Inversion: The Invert Argument

For cases that are not automatically invertible, FURCAS provides the additional *Invert* argument for the *Property* construct. The *Invert* argument again uses an OCL expression to determine the value which was originally used to lookup the element that is held in the annotated property. Listing 5.17 shows an example usage for the *Invert* argument. In combination with the invert argument, FURCAS also allows to define the optional filter argument which is combined with the *Query* argument to build a complete selection expression. In this case this combined expression is the one to be inverted.

5.3.3.4. A Pragmatic Simplification of the Invert Argument: Usage of prefix/postfix

With the use of the *Invert* argument for OCL queries, FURCAS is able to express arbitrarily complex inversion rules for these queries. However, in practice, many queries

```
 1  viewtype OclQueryWithInvert {
 2    primitiveTemplate string for PrimitiveTypes:STRING;
 3    template ReferencingElement :
 4      "RefEl" "references:"
 5      reference{query = self.elements,
 6        filter = e | e.name = 'reference'.concat(?),
 7        invert = self.name.substring(
 8          'reference'.size(),self.name.length)} ;
 9    template ReferenceableElement :
10      name ;
11  }
```

Listing 5.17: Example mapping using an OCL query with invert.

```
 1  viewtype BusinessObjectsMethodImpl {
 2    ...
 3    primitiveTemplate string for PrimitiveTypes:STRING;
 4    ...
 5    template MethodCallExpression :
 6      source "."
 7      referredMethodSignature{query = self.source.methodSignatures,
 8          prefix = 'method_', postfix = '_in_' + self.name}
 9      ;
10    ...
11  }
```

Listing 5.18: Example mapping using an OCL query with prefix/postfix.

do only additions to the beginning or the end of the "?"-argument and use it as predicate within a `select` operation. Thus, to further improve the usability of the FURCAS
mapping language, a third possibility for the definition of inversions exists. Instead of
defining an *Invert* argument, a view developer may also specify the base selection string
and two optional arguments, *prefix* and *postfix* that are attached to the "?"-expression
and used to filter elements from the basic selection. Figures 5.7 and Listing 5.14 show
the integration of these arguments into the FURCAS metamodel as well as the mapping
syntax. Listing 5.18 shows an example application of the prefix/postfix notation.

5.3.4. Advanced Model Construction Rules

With the extensions that FURCAS provides with respect to the computation and lookup
of model elements, a view type definition in FURCAS forms a special kind of attribute
grammar [DJL88]. The nodes in this case are the model elements of the model and the

attributes are the properties of these model elements, i.e., model attributes and association links.

Attribute grammars consist of two different types of rules for determining the value of attributes, *inherited* attributes, and *synthesised* attributes. *Inherited* attributes are values that are propagated through the syntax tree. *Synthesised* attribute rules compute and create new values. The attribute rules in FURCAS are defined using the property inits as well as the OCL queries that a view type definition provides. However, using this kind of rule, only inherited attributes can be expressed as no new model elements are created. Which, per definition of the side effect freeness of OCL, would not be possible by only using OCL expressions. Synthesised, on the other hand, can therefore not be expressed by this means.

However, for the same reasons as traditional attribute grammars include synthesised attribute rules, also textual view type definitions require means to provide this kind of rule. FURCAS therefore, provides two different flavours of model construction rules. First, by defining templates without syntax contribution (or syntax-contribution-less (SCL) templates), it is possible to define element creation rules that a template can trigger explicitly. Second, a view type developer may specify a so called *foreach* rule that is used to create multiple elements based on the result of an OCL expression. Both possibilities will be explained in the subsequent Sections 5.3.4.1 and 5.3.4.2.

5.3.4.1. SCL Templates: Templates without Syntax Contribution

The first possibility to define model construction rules uses standard TCS constructs with special constraints. Listing 5.19 shows an example for this kind of template which is responsible for creating a method signature for each exposed association end (cf. excerpt of the relevant metamodel elements in Figure 5.11). The template for an association end explicitly call template `MethodSignature` in mode `#propertyGetter`. This template does not contain any element which has a syntax contribution it only consists of property inits. Therefore, no parse rules are created that have to match elements in the textual representation. Hence, the template is always "executed" whenever its calling template is. This leads to the creation of a method signature for each association end including the setting of its properties according to the defined property inits.

If not only a single element but a certain statically defined number of elements should be produced the *Property* may define additional arguments. More specifically, to control how often the SCL template is invoked, a view type developer may specify additional

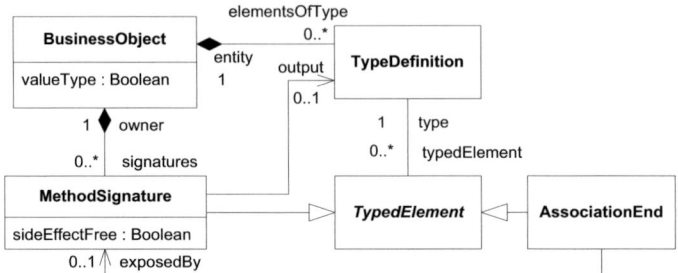

Figure 5.11.: Excerpt of the BusinessObjects metamodel showing the relevant elements for the creation of a getter method.

```
1  syntax GetterForAssiciationEnd {
2    ...
3    template AssociationEnd context
4      : ... exposedBy{mode = propertyGetter} ...
5      ;
6    template MethodSignature #propertyGetter
7      : {{ name = 'get'.concat(#context.name)),
8         output = #context.type),
9         sideEffectFree ='true',
10        owner = #context.otherEnd().type.entity }}
11     ;
12     ...
13 }
```

Listing 5.19: Example view type definition defining model creation rules with templates without syntax contribution. In this case the template creates a getter method for each association end of the business object.

forcedLower and *forcedUpper* arguments. Note, however, that the values for these arguments have to be exactly the same, i.e., *forcedLower* = *2* and *forcedUpper* = *2*, as there is no syntax contribution part in which a parser could decide based on the occurrences in the textual representation how often it should exactly trigger the template.

5.3.4.2. The *Foreach*-Rule: Creating Additional Model Elements Based on Existing Ones

The *foreach* rule is an extension to the TCS language, which allows to define more flexible model construction rules. One disadvantage of the previously mentioned flavour of constructing model elements using SCL templates is that the multiplicity of the called template has to be known in advance, i.e., during template definition time using the *forcedLower* and *forcedUpper* arguments. Templates can only be called from other templates at places where the result of the called templates is added to a property of the template's referred class. Thus, the decision of when to create an element and where to store it in the parent element is strongly coupled.

The *foreach* rule aims at providing support for the definition of which and how often a SCL template is executed. The basic idea behind the *foreach* rule is to first, determine a set of context elements for which new elements should be instantiated and then give rules that describe which SCL template should be called for which resulting element. For example (again using the business object running example), a *foreach* rule can define that it triggers sub-SCL templates for each association end that is connected to a business object. Furthermore, for an association end with an upper multiplicity of > 1, template `MethodSignature #multi` should be called, whereas for an upper multiplicity of 1 the `MethodSignature #single` should be called.

To implement this functionality, the *foreach* rule again makes extensive use of OCL queries to determine the set of context elements for the execution of the SCL templates. For the above example, one would define the *foreach* rule as shown in Listing 5.20.

Figure 5.12 shows the extensions of the TCS metamodel for the *foreach* rule. The *foreach* rule itself defines the context expression, which is an OCL expression used for determining the context objects Ctx. In the above example, this is the `self.elementsOfType` expression. Furthermore, the *foreach* rule itself also has a reference to an `as` template. This template is used whenever no detailed `WhenAs` elements are given. The `defaultMode`, which can be specified for each *foreach*, is also used in this case. To be able to specify conditional SCL template calls, a *foreach*

```
1  syntax SetterForAssiciationEnd {
2    [...]
3    template BusinessObject
4      : [...] methodSignatures {
5         foreach( self.elementsOfType,
6         when = self.upperMultplicity > 1 or self.upperMultplicity = -1,
7                 as = MethodSignature, mode = setterMulti),
8         when = self.upperMultplicity = 1,
9                 as = MethodSignature, mode = setterSingle),
10      } [...]
11   ;
12   template MethodSignature #setterMulti
13     : {{ name = 'set'.concat(#foreach.name)),
14        output = #foreach.type) }}
15   ;
16   template MethodSignature #setterSingle
17     : {{ name = 'addTo'.concat(#foreach.name)),
18        output = #foreach.type) }}
19   ;
20   ...
21 }
```

Listing 5.20: Example for the *foreach* rule creating method signatures.

may contain several WhenAs elements. These elements consist of a combination of an OCL expression as condition when and a template reference as. Additionally a (non-default) mode can be specified. If the OCL expression evaluates to true for an element $c \in Ctx$, the template that is referenced as as is called. If no mode is specified the defaultMode of the *foreach* rule is used.

There are several constraints on the *foreach* metamodel elements. First, the OCL expressions that are used in the WhenAs elements need to return a boolean, as this is the decision on whether to use a certain WhenAs for a certain element. Second, the templates that are called from a *foreach* rule shall not have a syntax contribution, they shall be SCL templates. Finally, the templates that are called from a *foreach* rule have to refer to classes that are assignable to the property to which the *foreach* rule assigns the created elements.

5.3.4.3. Semantic Predicates

Comparable to traditional compiler construction, during the construction of models from textual views, a developer may want to specify a textual view for a given metamodel where the concrete syntax is ambiguous w.r.t. to its abstract syntax. For example,

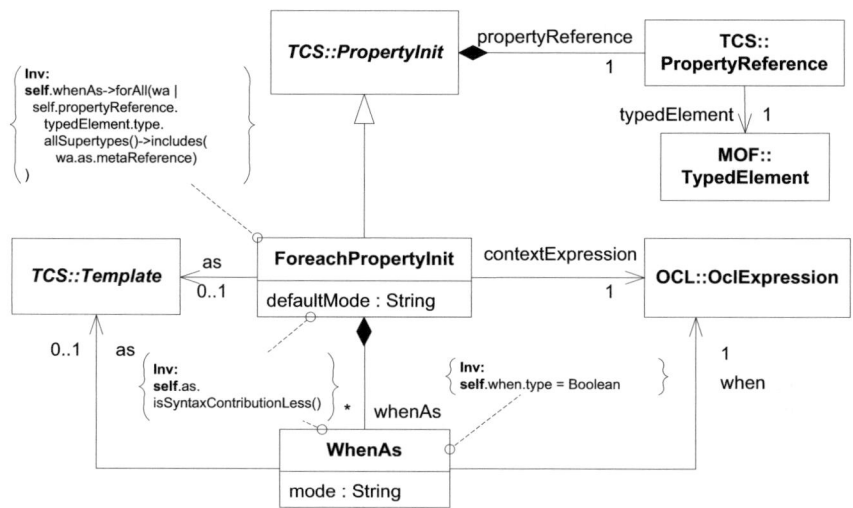

Figure 5.12.: The *foreach*-rule extensions in the FURCAS metamodel.

in a view that provides textual support for the Object Constraint Language (OCL), two constructs from the abstract synax, namely the `AttributeCallExp` and the `AssociationEndCallExp` have the same textual representation. Given two expression `self.name` and `self.reference`, the parser cannot distinguish which of the expressions is a `AttributeCallExp` and which is a `AssociationEndCallExp`, both are represented by a dot followed by an identifier. However, taking the class of the model element into account on which these expressions are called, i.e., the `self` expression, one would find that `name` is an attributes, whereas `reference` is an association end.

To solve this kind of problem, FURCAS provides the possibility to define semantic disambiguation expressions for templates. FURCAS evaluates these expressions during parse time and decides upon their results which template of those that have to be disambiguated is used to instantiate the appropriate model elements. Consequently, as for all other model-based expressions, FURCAS uses OCL to express them. Figure 5.13 shows the integration of these expressions into the FURCAS metamodel. The expression used for disambiguation has to be of type `Boolean` as only `true`, which means "use

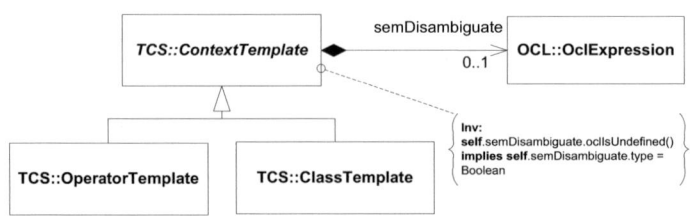

Figure 5.13.: The *semantic disambiguation* extensions in the FURCAS metamodel.

this template", or `false`, meaning "don't use this template" may be returned by these expressions.

Another important constraint for the application of a *semantic predicate* is that, the templates that are disambiguated need to have the exactly same syntax contribution. Otherwise a disambiguation would not make sense, as the parser could already decide which template to use. On the other hand, this also implies that whenever, two templates for an element in the same inheritance hierarchy, i.e., being subclasses of the same superclass, have the same syntax contribution, they need to be disambiguated. Listing 5.21 shows this constraint, which uses the same basic functionality as the computation of property init trees as introduced in Section 5.3.2.1. Just instead of gathering all kinds of SCL sequence elements, in this case all elements that *have* a syntax contribution are gathered. Based on the resulting tree, FURCAS checks if all subtemplates of an abstract template have the same syntax contribution. If they do, and the developer did not specify a semantic disambiguation, the constraint is violated.

The `syntaxContributions()` operation works as follows. First, it collects all sequence elements that are either a literal or a property. Then, it iterates over the alternatives of the template and creates a new entry in the result collection for each alternative that it finds and populates it with the previous contents of the result collection including the literals and properties found in the current alternative. An additional helper operation `alternativeSyntaxContributions()` (cf. Listing 5.23) is responsible for the collection of the alternatives' syntax contribution. This operation calls itself recursively to gather all sub-alternatives. Finally, the resulting sets are sorted according to the occurence of the sequence elements in the list of all sequence elements of the template.

The syntax contribution algorithm would work for the example templates shown in Listing 5.24 as follows. First, the algorithm determines a set of directly con-

```
1 context ContextTemplate inv:
2 let allSubTemplates = self.concreteSyntax.templates->select(t |
3   t.metaReference.allSuperTypes()->includes(self.metaReference) and
4   t.mode = self.mode) in
5 allSubTemplates->forAll(t |
6  if t.syntaxContribution()->forAll(
7    sc | allSubTemplates->one( st |
8    st.syntaxContribution()->includes(sc) ) ) then
9      not t.semDisambiguate.oclIsUndefined()
10  else
11   t.semDisambiguate.oclIsUndefined()
12  endif
13 )
```

Listing 5.21: Constraint on ContextTemplate, specifying that syntactically equal templates need to be disambiguated.

```
1 context ContextTemplate::syntaxContributions()
2   : Sequence(OrderedSet(TCS::SequenceElement))
3 body:
4 let seqs = self.templateSequence.elements->select(e |
5   e.oclIsTypeOf(TCS::LiteralRef )
6  or e.oclIsTypeOf(TCS::Property )) in
7  let alts : Sequence(TCS::Alternative) =
8   self.templateSequence.elements->select(
9    e | e.oclIsTypeOf(TCS::Alternative))
10  if alts->isEmpty() then
11   Sequence{seqs}
12  else
13   self->alternativesSyntaxContributions(alts, Sequence{seqs})
14  endif
15  ->collect(seq | seq->sortedBy(se |
16   self.allSequenceElements()->indexOf(se)))
```

Listing 5.22: The semantics of the syntaxContributions() operation.

```
1  context ContextTemplate::alternativeSyntaxContributions(
2      alts : Sequence(TCS::Alternative), result :
3        Sequence(OrderedSet(TCS::SequenceElement)))
4      : Sequence(OrderedSet(TCS::SequenceElement))
5  body:
6  let altSeqs = alts.sequences->asSequence() in
7  let localResult = altSeqs->iterate(
8    seq; result:Sequence(OrderedSet(TCS::SequenceElement)) =
9    Sequence{startSequence} |
10   Sequence{1..result->size() - altSeqs->indexOf(seq)+1}->iterate(
11     i; subResult : Sequence(OrderedSet(TCS::SequenceElement)) =
12     result | subResult->append(
13       seq.elements->select(e | e.oclIsTypeOf(TCS::LiteralRef ) or
14       e.oclIsTypeOf(TCS::Property ))->iterate(
15         sss; subsubResult : OrderedSet(TCS::SequenceElement) =
16           subResult->at(i) |
17       subsubResult ->append(seq)
18     )
19   )
20   )
21   ) ->excluding(startSequence)
22 let localAlts = alts.elements->select(
23     e | e.oclIsTypeOf(TCS::Alternative)) in
24 if localResult.isEmpty() then
25   self.alternativeSyntaxContributions(startSequence, localAlts)
26 else
27   self.alternativeSyntaxContributions(localResult, localAlts)
28 endif
```

Listing 5.23: The semantics of the helper operation `alternativeSyntaxContributions()` operation.

```
1  template AssociationEnd context:
2     [[ --variant 1 with named local end
3        name "<-" {{ navigable = true, isStorage = true }}
4        |
5        --variant 2 with unnamed/non-navigable local end
6        "unnamed" {{ navigable = false, isStorage = false }} ]]
7
8     association
9  ;
```

Listing 5.24: Example for the application of the `alternativeSyntaxContributions()` operation.

tained sequence elements resulting in the orderd set $Seqs = \{Property(association)\}$. Next, it analyses the alternatives and creates a set of sequence elements for each alternative and joins each of them with the initial set $Seqs$. This joining results in the nested ordered sets $syntaxContributions = \{\{Property(name), LiteralRef("<-"), Property(association)\}, \{LiteralRef("unnamed"), Property(association)\}\}$. If one of the subsets of this result occurs within another sibling template of the current template it will require a semantic disambiguation.

Listing 5.25 shows an example usage of the semantic disambiguation. The subtemplates for `AttributeCallExp` and `AssociationEndCallExp` both have the same syntax contribution, i.e., both are operator templates with the dot-operator and define a string identifier as their right-hand side. The disambiguation expressions look up the given identifier and decide if the found model element is an attribute or an association.

Formal Representation of a FURCAS view type definition   To validate the textual view type approach of FURCAS against the generic view type properties presented in Chapter 4, a formal representation of the FURCAS view type definition approach is required.

Definition 5.1 (Containment-Property). *The containment-property is a formal definition of the composite association concept in MOF [Obj06]. For our special case we further define that the multiplicity of the containment end should be 1..1. Formally, the containment-property is fulfilled for a tuple (A, B, rel) where A and B are disjoint sets of model elements of a different type and rel is a bijective relation $rel \subseteq A \times B$. That means rel is fulfilled when $(a \in A, b \in B) \in rel \iff b$ is contained in a.*

```
1 template PropertyCallExp abstract operatored(dotOps);
2 operatorTemplate AssociationEndCallExp (
3   operators = dotOp, source = source,
4   semDisambiguate = not AssociationEnd.allInstances()->select(e |
5     self.source.type.allSupertypes()->includes(e.type))
6     .otherEnd()->select(e |
7       e.name = ${referredAssociationEnd})->isEmpty())
8   : referredAssociationEnd (
9     query = AssociationEnd.allInstances()->select(e |
10      self.source.type.allSupertypes()->includes(e.type))
11        .otherEnd()->select(e | e.name = ?))
12  ;
13 operatorTemplate AttributeCallExp (operators = dotOp,
14   source = source, semDisambiguate =
15 not self.lookUpElementExtended(${refferedAttribute}).oclIsInvalid())
16   : referredAssociationEnd (query = self.lookUpElementExtended(?))
17  ;
```

Listing 5.25: Example for the semantic disambiguation.

For the sake of readability, we define $B_a = rel(a) \iff \forall b \in B_a \mid (a,b) \in rel \wedge a \in A \wedge B_a \subseteq B$.

Definition 5.2 (FURCAS View Type Definition). *Formally, the mapping definition is a tuple*

$$VT = \left(T, Alts, Seq, MM_{VT}, tempalts, tempseqels, altseqels, orderS\right) \qquad (5.1)$$

where

T is a finite set of templates and

Alts is a finite set of alternatives and

Seq is a finite set of sequence elements and

$MM_{VT} \subseteq MM$ *is defined as a set of model elements within the metamodel MM for which VT is responsible.*

orderS is a strict partial order $orderS \subseteq Seq \times Seq$ *where* $(s_1, s_2) \in orderS \iff s_1$ *occurs before* s_2 *within its composite parent. "Occurs before" holds if the elements occur in sequence within their parent alternatives and templates.*

218

tempalts, tempseqels and altseqels are relations that are defined so that tuples $(T, Alts, tempalts)$, $(T, Seq, tempseqels)$ and $(Alts, Seq, altseqels)$ fulfil the containment-property.

The set of alternatives $Alts_t$ that belong to a template t are given by $Alts_t = \{a \in Alts \mid (t, a) \in tempalts\}$. [2]

The set of Sequence elements Seq_t that belong to a template t are given by the following relation: $Seq_t = \{s \in Seq \mid (t, s) \in tempseqels\}$.

The set of Sequence elements Seq_a that belong to an alternative a are given by the following relation: $Seq_t = \{s \in Seq \mid (a, s) \in altseqels\}$.

Definition 5.3. *The* complete-containment-property *of a tuple $(A, B, func)$ where A and B are disjoint sets and rel is a relation, is fulfilled iff rel partitions B so that each element of B is contained in a partition B_i:*

(1) $A \cap B = \emptyset$

(2) $(A, B, func)$ *fulfills the containment-property (cf. Definition 5.1)* $\land$

(3) $\forall b \in B \mid \exists! B_i \subseteq B \mid b \in B_i$

The corresponding meta-model element $m_c \in MM$ for a given $t \in T$ can be queried through the function $mmelem : T \rightarrow C$.

Definition 5.4 (Types of Sequence Elements). *Different types of sequence elements of a template t that are of relevance in the later-on presented definitions and algorithms are:*

Property Sequence Elements: Property referring elements are denoted as set $Seq^{prop} \subseteq Seq$. The corresponding property p_s has to be an element that is either an attribute or an association end navigable from the corresponding metamodel element of t which is defined as the set

$$P_t = attributes(mmelem(t)) \cup \{a \in associations(mmelem(t))$$
$$\mid first(a) = mmelem(t) \lor second(a) = mmelem(t)\}$$

for a given $s \in Seq$ can be queried through the function $mmprop : Seq^{prop} \rightarrow P_t$. Those sequence elements are responsible for defining where and how a specific property of a model element is rendered as text.

---

[2] According to the metamodel each $a_i \in Alts_t$ might actually be nested within another alternative $a_j \in Alts_t$ where $a_i \neq a_j$. However, this relation is not important in this context and therefore omitted in this formalization.

Literal elements: $Seq^{lit} \subseteq Seq$, *where a* $s \in Seq^{lit}$ *is responsible for representing a static literal within the text. The literal value is yield through:*

$$literal : Seq^{lit} \rightarrow [String]$$

5.4. Representing Textual Views

Having the possibility to define textual view types using the FURCAS mapping language, enables for the construction of textual representations of a model. The representation of textual views in the context of model driven engineering requires to bridge an abstract model and its textual representation, which is ultimately a stream of characters. However, having two different types of representations would also require to separately manage models and their textual representations, i.e., a model repository and a store for text files. To bridge this gap, FURCAS raises the textual representation to the model level. This enables to transform, store, version and merge the textual representation as a model.

However, this decision raises new challenges. For example, how can a developer interact with a textual view model using traditional ways of interacting with text? Cut, copy, paste and straight on typing as well as deletion of arbitrary characters at arbitrary positions are some of the key factors of textual editing. How can a textual model editor "feel" like editing a conventional text editor whilst providing enhanced view features such as removing and adding elements from and to the view without modifying the underlying model. To be able to deal with these challenges as well as being applicable in practice, several factors have to be taken into account:

1. The solution shall support all different kinds of views, as defined in Chapter 4, which are for example, partial, extending or selective views.

2. In order to blend with the interaction with standard text editors within Integrated Development Environments (IDEs), the user should be able to interact with the solution as if he or she would interact with a standard text editor.

3. The solution should be integrateable with the underlying modelling infrastructure. This especially concerns the way views are made persistent. Persistent views should be versioned and stored in the same way as the models themselves are.

5.4.1. Views in Graphical Modelling

Within graphical modelling several approaches have been developed that allow to define explicitly holistic, partial or combined graphical views for models. The Graphical Modelling Framework (GMF)[Ecl10b], as part of the Eclipse Modelling Framework (EMF) provides means to define view types and create views for nearly arbitrary metamodels. Furthermore, these views are not view-only but rather provide functionality to edit the underlying models through its views. The information on how a specific model element is displayed in the graphical representation is given using a decorator pattern [GHJV95] based approach. The original decorator pattern is used to non-intrusively, dynamically add functionality to a class that is wrapped by the decorator while still fulfilling the same interface. In the context of views on models, the functionality consists of information that is added to a model element that describes how it is represented in a certain view.

Many graphical approaches handle their diagrams as models, too. This means that there is a generic meta-model for diagrams which could be called a "diagram metamodel". Instances of this metamodel are then graphical elements such as rectangles or arrows. The decorator pattern comes into play as these instances decorate (non-intrusively reference) elements from the domain model. Hence, what a diagram model actually does is to describe how a specific domain model is represented as a diagram.

The usage of the decorator approach means that the graphical information is clearly separated from the actual model content, allowing to define different views on the same model elements. Many graphical UML modelling tools even show this separation to the user. If a diagram element referred to a model element that is not accessible anymore, due to whatever reason, the diagram element may still be shown. The absence of the underlying model element will be indicated by an annotation that is attached to the diagram element. This way, the graphical view model is relatively independent from the underlying domain model.

5.4.2. Limitations for Textual Views

In contrast to graphical views, which can display nearly arbitrary information, textual views incur some limitations, mostly due to their sequential nature – a stream of characters.

- Not everything that could appear in a model can be represented by a textual view. For example, identifiers with white spaces can appear in models but are hard to implement using parser technologies. As textual views need means for lexing and parsing character streams, this constrains the expressiveness of textual views.

- As opposed to graphical view models, which may be any type of graph, a textual concrete syntax that is represented as a textual view model is more likely a tree structure. Therefore, interdependencies between elements are limited to a parent - child relationship. This relationship can mapped to a textual representation by using structural elements such as parenthesis or indentations with whitespaces. Additional links have to be mapped to references by some kind of identifier.

- The way of interacting with text is much different than the way of interacting with graphical views. In graphical views, a developer interacts with the editor using discrete, predefined, atomic actions. For example, an action for creating a graphical representation of a UML class would be such an action. In contrast to such actions, the way of naturally interacting with text is by typing and deleting characters. Typing of a single character can not necessarily be seen as an atomic editing action. Mostly such an atomic editing event consists of a series of character insertions and/or deletions. Thus, intermediate states with incomplete editing actions may occur. This difference in the way of interactions needs to be accounted for in a view-based textual modelling approach.

5.4.3. The TextBlocks Model Decorator Approach

The basic idea of FURCAS is to use decorator models to specify how a certain domain model element should be presented as text. This decorator model is called *TextBlocks model*. A textual view is then represented by the specific structure of a TextBlocks model that references the model to be viewed. View types defined in a mapping definition then tell how a TextBlocks model is constructed to represent a certain domain model.

However, just having the TextBlocks decorator model is not enough to be able to edit a model in a textual way. Thus, the FURCAS approach includes a textual editor that is able to directly work with a TextBlocks model as if it was a real text document. This editor knows how to interpret, on the one hand, a TextBlocks model in combination with the underlying domain model and represent it as text and, and on the other hand, how commands that are executed by a developer are mapped to changes within the Text-Blocks model. The FURCAS editor looks and feels like a full-featured (cf. [Fow05]) code editor including all usability enhancing features such as auto-completion, syntax highlighting, etc. Since the TextBlock model is a pure decorator model the overhead concerning redundant information concerning the domain model is kept to a minimum.

To keep the textual view model and the underlying model in sync FURCAS employs a model-view-controller (MVC) ([KP88]) approach. Some existing approaches for textual modelling, such as TEF [Sch07] already proposed to employ MVC for textual modelling but came away from doing it because of the many unsolved challenges that are present in this area. A discussion of advantages and challenges of the MVC approach in combination with textual modelling can be found in [Sch07].

Also in the compiler construction literature there are similar approaches that are called *Syntax Directed Programming Environments*[TR81, RT84]. In these approaches, commands are derived from the (attributed) grammar of a programming language that can be used to interact with the code document. Thus, ensuring the document is always syntactically correct. However, in these environments, the editing process is limited to executing only these predefined commands. Freely typing code in direct combination with MVC based updates of the underlying model is not possible. Additionally, the challenges posed by allowing partial, selective and overlapping textual views are not tackled by the work in this area.

FURCAS now picks up the idea of MVC based textual modelling and employs an approach for this three-way-factored architecture. The three components of MVC, mapped to FURCAS, are:

The model: This is, the underlying domain model that should be represented in the view.

The view: A view in FURCAS is the textual representation that is produced by the combination of the information from the domain model and the decorating TextBlock model. The metamodel for such views is presented in Section 5.4.3.1.

The controller: The controller in the context of the FURCAS approach consists of several equally important components. First, there is the FURCAS editor which is responsible for the interaction between the textual view and the modeller. The editor captures the commands (such as *Insert("New Text", 25 /* offset */, 10 /* length to overwrite*/)*) that are produced by a modeller modifying the textual representation and translating it into events that modify the underlying TextBlock model. During this editing process, a TextBlock model may be in several states. These states as well as the transitions between them will be presented in Section 5.4.3.3.

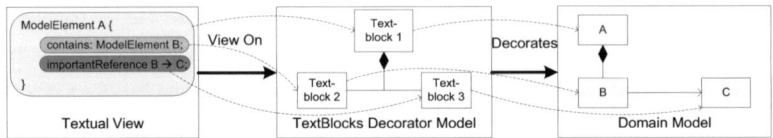

Figure 5.14.: Overview on the TextBlocks-decorator approach.

Second, FURCAS employs a stack of incremental parsing tools (lexer, parser, etc.) that allow to incrementally analyse a TextBlock model and bring it to a consistent state after its textual representation was modified. Based on a consistent state, an incremental model transformation approach updates the domain model from the changed TextBlock model. Third, for updating a TextBlock model upon changes to the underlying domain model, this transformation is bidirectional. For each view type, a bidirectional transformation, that is responsible for these updates, is generated from the view type definition. The actual synchronisation process between textual view model and domain model is presented in Chapter 6.

5.4.3.1. The TextBlocks Meta-Model

The basic idea of this TextBlocks metamodel is based on the decorator pattern[GHJV95]. The elements that the TextBlocks model decorates are the model elements of the domain model. To be able to decorate an arbitrary model as a textual view, FURCAS incorporates a metamodel that can represent generic text structures. As shown in figure 5.14, the textual view is then in fact a view on the decorated domain model. The developer still types text as in any other development environment but what actually happens within the FURCAS editor is that this text is mapped to changes in the TextBlocks and transitively the domain model.

Figure 5.15 depicts an overview on the TextBlocks metamodel. As the structure of text is rather simple, the metamodel only contains a few different constructs. The main class of this metamodel is, as the metamodel's name, the TextBlock class. A TextBlock represents one or more domain model elements having a defined textual representation. For example, this could, for a Java like language, be a declaration of a member variable within a class. These TextBlocks can then have nested TextBlocks as their children (cf. subNodes and getSubBlocks() in the Text-

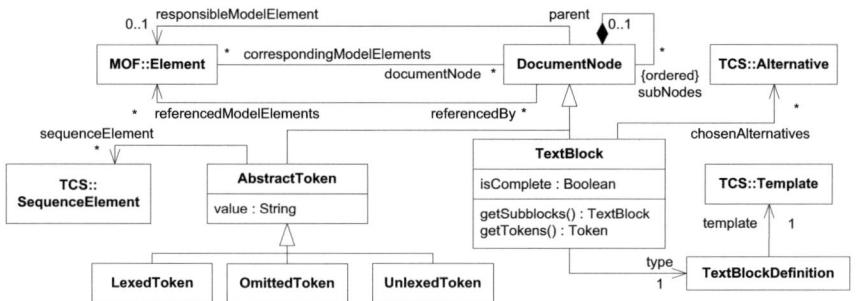

Figure 5.15.: Simplified version of the TextBlocks-Metamodel.

Blocks metamodel). In the Java example, this could be, for example, the initialisation expression of the member variable.

As it can be seen in the metamodel each `TextBlock` element may reference corresponding model elements (cf. `correspondingModelElements`) for which it is used as decorator for the textual view. However, only one of them, the one also referenced as `responsibleModelElement` is the model element for which the TextBlock actually provides a syntax contribution. Further elements are included in the corresponding elements if they where created together with the leading model element but do not have an own syntax contribution. For example, elements that are created by subsequent calls to SCL templates (see Section 5.3.4.1) are included here. The semantics of this set is, that elements that are corresponding elements will get deleted when their corresponding TextBlock is deleted.

Elements that are represented by document nodes but are not coupled to the life-cycle of the node, such as elements that were resolved using an OCL query for a property are referenced by the `referencedModelElements` association. These elements will not be deleted once the node is deleted.

The `TextBlockDefinition` is responsible for defining the correspondence between the `TextBlock` and a template from the view type definition. A `Text-BlockDefinition` refers to a `Template` element from the TCS metamodel. This correspondence defines the *type* of a `TextBlock`. Thus, it is possible to see which rule from the view type was used to create a particular `TextBlock`. Furthermore, there might have been a series of alternative choices within the template during the instantiation of the `TextBlock`. To be able to completely reconstruct the exact textual representation from the `TextBlock`   these choices are also stored by referencing the `Alternative` elements from the TCS metamodel.

A similar concept is used for the tokens that a TextBlock contains. To be able to identify what the meaning of a certain token is, it needs a reference to its corresponding `SequenceElement` from the template of its parent TextBlock. However, it is not necessary to store the actual value of the token redundantly. This is either done by the referred attribute from the domain model (when the `SequenceElement` is a `Property`) or by a literal that the mapping model defines (when the `SequenceElement` is a `LiteralRef`). However, if a more loosely coupled view representation is required, FURCAS also supports to keep token values stored in the TextBlock model. This option is useful if it is known that certain elements that a TextBlock model decorates are not always available during usage of the view. Then the values stored in the tokens can still be presented to the developer. However, then the FURCAS editor will indicate by applying a certain highlighting function to it, that these elements are currently not available and only the last existing synced version is shown. A developer then has three different options:

1. Leave these parts as they are. The developer may decide that FURCAS should keep these areas as they are, perhaps knowing that the referenced elements will be available again at some later time.

2. If a developer knows that the referenced elements were deleted somewhere, but he or she requires them to exist again in the current model, he or she can tell FURCAS to re-create the elements from their textual representation.

3. The last option is to remove also the textual representation of the missing elements from the TextBlock model.

Format information such as indentation or additional decorating information that is not part of the domain model is represented by the use of `OmittedTokens`. These tokens are included in a TextBlock tree but do not contribute to the domain model once the incremental update transformation updates the domain model.

Thus, a TextBlock model only contains elements that are responsible for the structure and the layout of the textual representation of a model. No redundant information is stored. This allows to quickly update a view once its underlying model changes. The values from the model that are part of a certain view are directly taken from the underlying model. Not only the updateability w.r.t. to the underlying model and views

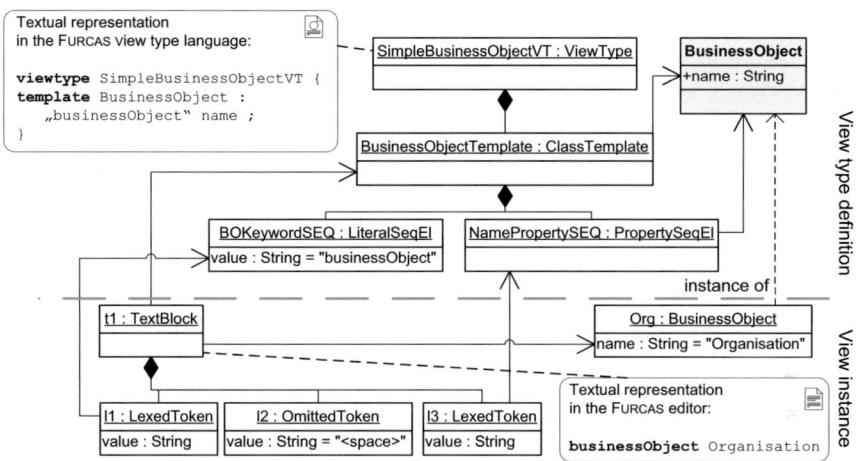

Figure 5.16.: Example for a TextBlock including the references to the mapping model of the view type. The `TextBlockDefinition` is omitted in this example.

on it is realised in this way, This redundancy also allows to change e.g., the name of a keyword in the mapping and automatically changing all representations of it within textual models.

Figure 5.16 depicts an example for a TextBlock instance including its references to the view type definition model and the domain metamodel. The textual representation in the lower right corner shows how the FURCAS editor would render this TextBlock model as text. The TextBlock t_1 represents the business object *Organisation* in the textual view; t_1 references the *Organisation* using its `correspondingModelElements` association. As it can be seen in the Figure, the two `LexedToken` do not hold any value but directly reference the attribute within the metamodel that they represent. The FURCAS editor will interpret this construct and show the value at the appropriate place within the textual view.

For tokens that are neither valid tokens according to the lexical rules of textual view type definition nor `OmittedTokens` used for formatting purposes, they will be represented as `UnlexedTokens`. For example, given a lexical rule for an identifier token defining a regular expression $[a - zA - Z]([a - zA - Z0 - 9])*$ which means that an identifier may not start with a digit. Assuming, in the example given in Figure 5.16, this

227

rule is used for the name property of the business object, changing the name the business object from "Organisation" to "0815Organisation" would result in a change from the lexed token representing the name property to an unlexed token that holds the new value. How the incremental update approach deals with this kind of inconsistencies is presented in Chapter 6.

5.4.3.2. Formal Definition of a Decorating Textual View

In order to check the TextBlock decorator approach against the generic definitions of views from Section 4.5 a a formal representation if the TextBlock approach is required. In this section we provide a formal definition of the relations between domain models and their views. Furthermore, the formalisation is basis for the description of the transitions between the different states of a TextBlock model throughout the process of displaying and editing a textual view.

A Textual View V_t is defined as a transient representation of a Domain Model M. V_t is therefore an ordered set of characters that can be displayed in a textual editor. Additionally V_t can be augmented with visual enhancements such as syntax highlighting, annotations, error markers and so on.

Definition 5.5 (TextBlocks Model)**.** *A persistent model that describes the exact presentation of M as text, according to the view type definition VT, is defined as a TextBlocks model*

$$B = (N, VT, M, ID_{sec}, subblocks, toks, orderNodes) \tag{5.2}$$

where

- *N is the set of document nodes within a TextBlocks model,*

- *ID_{sec} is a set of secondary identifiers that are used to resolve "refers to" relationships from within the text,*

- *$subblocks$, $toks$ and $orderNodes$ are relations (see exact definitions below).*

- *The set of document nodes N, can be split into 2 disjoint subsets $N = \Pi \cup \Omega$ where*

  - *Π is a set of TextBlocks $b \in \Pi$ and Ω is a set of tokens.*

  - *Ω can be split into 3 disjoint sets $\Omega = L \cup O \cup U$ where L is a set of lexed tokens $l \in L$, O is a set of omitted tokens $o \in O$ and U is a set of unlexed tokens $u \in U$.*

Such TextBlocks models can non-intrusively annotate (or decorate) a given M.

$ID_{sec} = L \cap M$ defined as secondary IDs are the only elements that are redundantly stored in the TextBlocks model. Those secondary IDs are fallback identifiers which can be used to re-resolve a reference that was based on a identifier stored as token value to resolve another model element. However, due to FURCAS being a fully incremental approach this information would only be necessary of coarse grained changes from outside are made to either B or M.

The subblocks within a TextBlock $B_b \in \Pi$ for a given TextBlock b are identified through the *subblocks* relation. The relation $subblocks : \Pi \times \Pi$ is a *strict partial order* and $subblocks^+$ is the transitive closure of *subblocks*. For the sake of readability we define $B_b = subblocks^+(b) \iff \{b_i \in B_b \mid (b, b_i) \in subblocks^+\}$.

Relation *toks* yields the tokens within a TextBlock b: $\Omega^b \in \Omega$ where $(\Pi, \Omega, toks)$ fulfils the *complete-containment-property*.

Relation $orderNodes) : N \times N$ is a total order that defines the ordering in which the document nodes occur when traversing the TextBlock tree in a left-<u>root</u>-right manner:

$$(n_1, n_2) \in orderNodes \iff n_1 \text{ occurs before } n_2$$

The concatenation of relations $subblocks^+$ and *toks* yields all tokens of a TextBlock including those of its transitive sub-blocks. This concatenation is denoted as

$$toks^+ \subseteq \Pi \times \Omega = \{\omega \in \Omega, \pi \in \Pi \mid (\pi, \omega) \in subblocks^+ \circ toks\}$$

where there is a transitive relation over the sub-blocks and tokens from a given π:

$$subblocks^+ \circ toks = \left\{(\pi, \omega) \mid \exists_{\pi' \in \Pi} \left(\begin{array}{c} (\pi, \pi') \in subblocks^+ \wedge \\ (\pi', \omega) \in toks \\ \vee (\pi = \pi') \end{array} \right) \right\}$$

The referred template $t^b \in T$ for a given TextBlock b is defined as: $reftempl : \Pi \to T$. $refalts : \Pi \to \mathcal{P}(A)$ yields the referred alternatives $A^b \subseteq A$ for a given TextBlock b. $corelem : N \to \mathcal{P}(M)$ retrieves the corresponding model element $e^n \in M$ for a given document node n whereas $refelem : N \to \mathcal{P}(M)$ retrieves the referenced model elements $Referred^n \subseteq M$ for a given document node n. $refseq : L \to S$ yields the referred sequence element $s^b \in S$ for a given lexed token l. The value contained in a token ω can be retrieved by a function $v : \Omega \to V_t$.

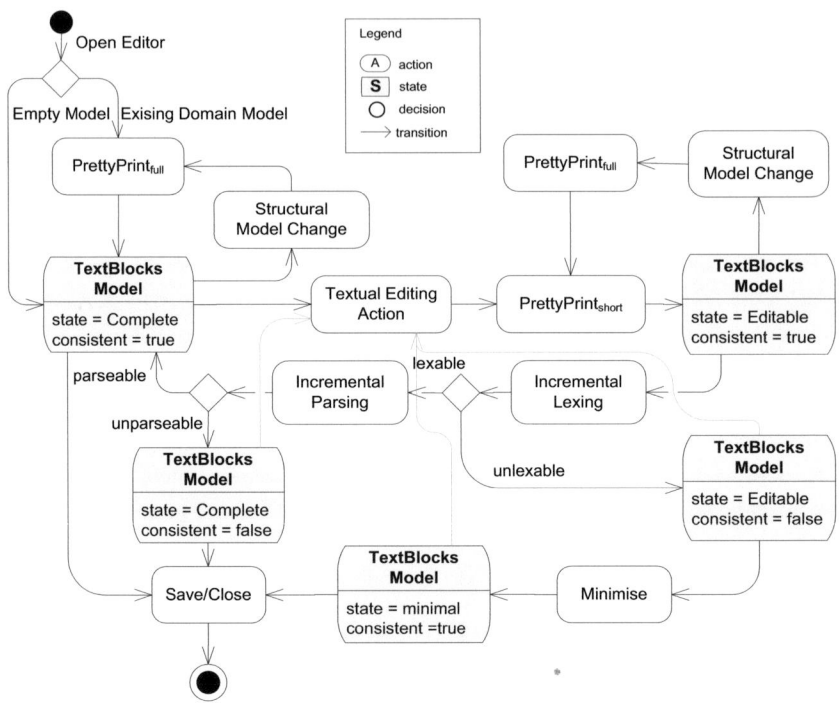

Figure 5.17.: Activity Chart for the different TextBlock States.

5.4.3.3. States of a TextBlock-Model

During its lifetime a TextBlock-Model may be in different states. There are different states for different purposes. For example, there is one state that allows to represent a textual representation that a developer edited but that is not yet in consistent state. Still FURCAS allows to represent and also persist such a TextBlock model. To illustrate the different states of the TextBlock model Figure 5.17 depicts the states including the actions that trigger state transitions and bring a TextBlock model into a different state.

As Figure 5.17 shows, there are five different states a TextBlock can have:

1. A TextBlock may be *complete* (cf. Definition 5.7) and *consistent*. In this state a TextBlock model purely decorates a domain model and does not contain re-

230

dundant information in its token values. Furthermore, no `UnlexedTokens` exist in the model. Being *consistent*, in addition, means that the structure of the TextBlock model is in a shape so that the rules defined in the view type definition can transform it into a valid domain model. Initially, either after opening a new empty FURCAS editor or opening it with a different view type on an existing model, the TextBlock model will be in this state. If opened on an existing model the $PrettyPrint_{long}$ transformation creates a new TextBlock model according to the mapping rules of the current view type. Structural changes to the underlying domain model lead to a re-application of the $PrettyPrint_{long}$ transformation and an updated TextBlock model, which is still in the same state.

2. To be able to receive textual change events a TextBlock model needs to undergo a transition to the *editable* state. The $PrettyPrint_{short}$ transformation is responsible for doing this. The values from the domain model are then synced into the TextBlock model so that textual editing events can modify it the TextBlock model is in *editable* state (cf. Definition 5.8). Initially, for example after a transition from *complete and consistent*, the TextBlock model is also still *consistent*. For example, if a developer wants to modify the name attribute in the above example, turning the respective part of the TextBlock model in editable state would allow to perform a change to for example **businessObject** NewOrganisation. In this state the value from the domain model and those that are present in the TextBlock model may be out of sync. Upon structural changes to the underlying domain model, the $PrettyPrint_{long}$ followed by the $PrettyPrint_{short}$ transformations keep the TextBlock model in the same state with updated content.

3. After a textual change event updated the TextBlock model, FURCAS tries to apply this change through the incremental update transformations to the underlying domain model, however, a prerequisite for this transformation is that the TextBlock model is in *complete* and *consistent* state. Thus, the incremental lexing and parsing steps follow from the current state. If the lexing process results in errors, `UnlexedTokens` result from the process leading to a transition into the *editable* and *inconsistent* state. From this state it is still possible to *minimise* the TextBlock model to come to a redundancy free view representation in *minimal* but *inconsistent* state (5.).

On the other hand, if lexing succeeds FURCAS runs the parser to update the structure of the TextBlock model. If the parsing process fails, this leaves the TextBlock model in the *complete* and *inconsistent* state (see 4.). If this process succeeds the resulting state is again *complete* and *consistent* (1.).

4. A TextBlock may be *complete* (cf. Definition 5.7) and *inconsistent*. In this state a TextBlock model is still synchronised with the values of the domain model but its structure contains elements that restrain it from being transformable into a valid domain model. For example, adding into the following textual representation: **businessObject** Organisation an additional token so that it looks this way: **businessObject businessObject** Organisation. This change will still keep the TextBlock models values (e.g., the name property of the business object) in *complete* state. However, the this representation is not valid anymore w.r.t. the view type definition and is therefore marked as *inconsistent*. From this state the TextBlock model can be saved even though it is inconsistent.

5. The *minimal* (cf. Definition 5.6) but *inconsistent* state also allows to save the Text-Block model. In this state all redundant values are removed from the TextBlock model except for those that stored in the `UnlexedTokens`.

Based on the formal representation of a TextBlock model, the states in which a TextBlock model can occur the following definitions give a formal description of these states.

Definition 5.6 (Minimal State). *A TextBlock model B is in* minimal state $\iff$

$$(1) \forall b \in \Pi \, \left| \, \begin{pmatrix} (toks(b) \neq \emptyset \vee subblocks(b) \neq \emptyset) & \wedge \\ (tempref(b) \neq \emptyset) & \end{pmatrix} \wedge \right.$$

$$(2) \forall l \in L \, \left| \, \begin{pmatrix} (v(l) \neq \emptyset \leftrightarrow v(l) \in ID_{sec}) & \wedge \\ (refseq(l) \neq \emptyset) & \end{pmatrix} \wedge \right.$$

$$(3) \forall b \in \Pi \, \left| \, \begin{pmatrix} tempalts(reftempl(b)) \neq \emptyset & \leftrightarrow \\ \bigvee_{a \in tempalts(reftempl(b))} (a \in refalts(b)) \end{pmatrix} \right.$$

Which informally means that (1) each TextBlock contains at least one token or Text-Block and refers to a template, (2) each lexed token in the TextBlock contains only then a value iff it is used as a secondary id and each lexed token refers to a valid sequence element. Additionally, (3) if there are alternatives within the template, one of it (or a

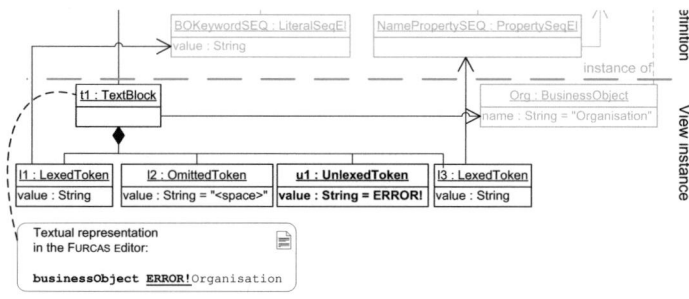

Figure 5.18.: Example for a TextBlock in minimal State.

sequence in case of nested alternatives) has to be chosen.[3] An example for a TextBlock model in *minimal* state is depicted in Figure 5.18.

Definition 5.7 (Complete State). *A TextBlock model B is in* complete state $\Leftrightarrow$

$$(1)\,B\ is\ in\ \text{minimal state} \quad \wedge$$
$$(2)\,U = \varnothing$$

Which informally means that it has to be minimal but in addition there are no erroneous (unlexed) tokens contained anymore. An example for a TextBlock in complete state is depicted in Figure 5.19. Note that the TextBlock metamodel (cf. Figure 5.15 on page 225) explicitly supports the marking of complete and incomplete TextBlocks through the `isComplete` attribute which is defined on the TextBlock metaclass. For TextBlocks that are not complete, this attribute will be false. This allows the FURCAS editor to annotate incomplete TextBlocks and thus indicate to the developer that this part of the textual representation may be out of sync with the underlying domain model.

Definition 5.8 (Editable State). *A TextBlock $b_{root} \in B$ is considered a TextBlock (sub-)model B^* in* editable state $\Longleftrightarrow$

$$\forall l \in L \cap toks(b_{root}) \mid \left(\begin{array}{l} refseq(l) \neq \varnothing \quad \wedge \\[6pt] v(l) = PrettyPrint_{short}\left(\begin{array}{l} corelem(b_{root}), \\ mmprop(refseq(l)) \end{array} \right) \end{array} \right)$$

---

[3]Furthermore, this minimising could be extended: if there are no omitted or unlexed tokens and there is no collection of elements that need to be rendered even the lexed tokens themselves could be omitted and produced upon transition to the editable state

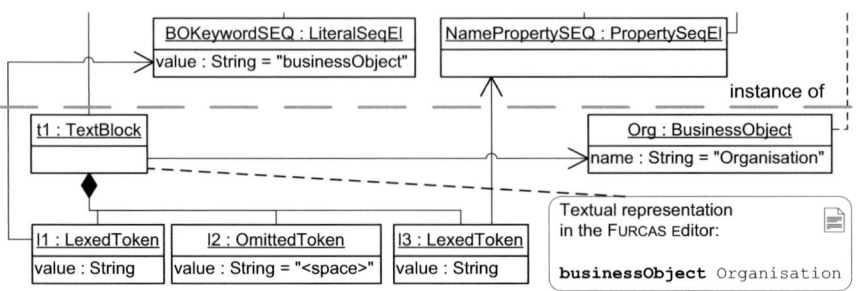

Figure 5.19.: Example for a TextBlock in complete State.

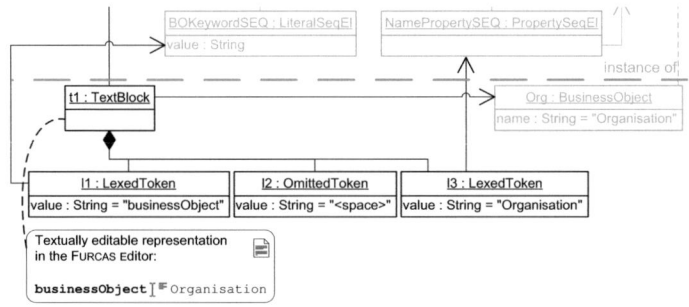

Figure 5.20.: Example for a TextBlock in editable State.

where $PrettyPrint_{short} : M \times P \rightarrow ([String])$ *is called* Pretty Print shorthand *and produces the textually representative value of a property* $p \in P$ *for a given domain model element* $e \in M$ *according to the view type definition* VT.

Which means that all lexed tokens need to have a referenced sequence element defined and their values are equal to those that would have been computed from the domain model and therefore given by function $PrettyPrint_{short}$. Figure 5.20 shows an example for a TextBlock model in *editable* state.

5.4.4. Support for Temporary Inconsistency

As mentioned in the *scientific challenges* section (5.1), supporting temporarily inconsistent views, improves the flexibility of a textual modelling approach. FURCAS tackles this problem by supporting the different states of the TextBlock model. Thus, being in a *editable* and *inconsistent* state allows to store arbitrary text within a TextBlock model. This flexibility gives developers the feeling that they are really editing just text hiding the model nature of the textual view. Section 4.5.2.2, introduced a generic notion of view consistency having two different levels, *constraint inconsistency* and *model inconsistency*. *Constraint inconsistency* is supported by FURCAS on two different levels. Due to the flexibility of the TextBlock model, views displaying models which violate their metamodel constraint can still be represented. On the other hand, the violation itself is recognised and presented to the developer using annotations in the displayed text. However, if the constraint inconsistency leads to the exclusion of a model element due to mismatched view construction rules (cf. Section 5.3.2.1), the element will be removed from the view. This is due to the fact that it is indistinguishable if a certain model element is not intended for the inclusion into a view or if the view construction rules do not match due to an inconsistent model.

Model inconsistency means that a model itself is inconsistent. For example, there may be links where the only one end is connected to a model element, or, the current representation within a view cannot be translated to a model as it contains erroneous content. FURCAS recognises the former case and displays error markers at the corresponding elements within the textual representation. The latter case is also not problematic as FURCAS can represent arbitrary text even if it is not translatable to a model.

5.4.5. Representing Selective Views with a TextBlocks Model

As presented in Section 4.5.1 whether a view includes a certain element or not may not only be dependent on the element itself but also on whether the employed view is *holistic* or *selective* w.r.t. the set of elements in which this element resides. For example, there may be a view that shows method signatures of a certain business object. However, the decision which of the method signatures are *actually* shown in a concrete view should be decided by the developer using the view.

The TextBlock model is not only responsible for controlling the format in which FURCAS presents elements of the domain model but also which of the elements are included in a textual view. I.e., a view only displays an element if a TextBlock is available for it that references the domain model element in its correspondingModelElements. Thus, by controlling the creation of TextBlocks for domain model elements, it becomes possible to realise also a *selective* behaviour.

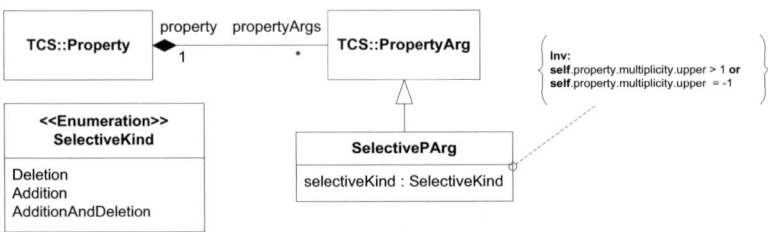

Figure 5.21.: Metamodel excerpt responsible for the *selective* feature.

```
1 viewtype Selective { ...
2    template BusinessObject
3        : ... methodSignatures { selective = Addition } ... ;
4    template MethodSignature
5        : output name implementation ;
6 }
```

Listing 5.26: Example mapping using an *selective feature*. In this case the method signatures shown within a business object should be added selectively.

For specifying which behaviour – selective or holistic – FURCAS should use for a given part of a view type the FURCAS view type definition language provides dedicated support for this feature. A selection of elements is only possible if there is a collection of elements to choose from. Therefore, FURCAS allows to specify the `selective` keyword for optional or multi-valued references at the corresponding property definition in a template. Figure 5.21 depicts the extensions for the *selective* feature within the FURCAS metamodel. Listing 5.26 shows an example which utilises the `selective` keyword. In this example, it specifies that the inclusion of a method signature into the textual view has to be triggered explicitly by a developer.

The *selective* feature supports three different modes:

Addition: The setting constitutes the *addition selective* property as specified in Section 4.5.1. TextBlocks for elements in this property will only be created upon explicit commands by a developer. Still, if the element is deleted from the model, the textual representation will be removed automatically. As showing only a selection of elements within the textual representation is rather uncommon for a textual language, FURCAS will indicate the presence of more elements than those that

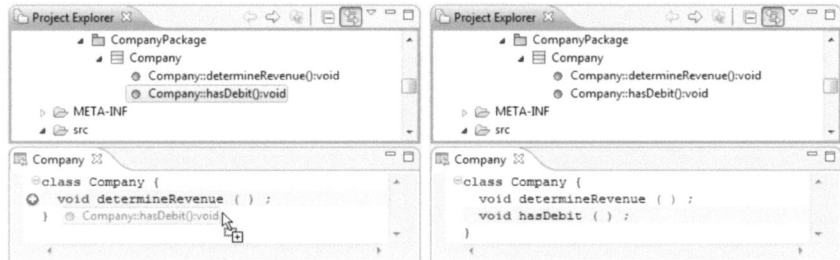

Figure 5.22.: The plus symbol in the left image indicates that there are more elements that could be displayed at this position. Using drag-and-drop the second method is added to the view resulting in the the view being updated as shown in the right image.

are displayed using a special icon. Figure 5.22 shows how this can be done using simple drag-and-drop comamnds.

Deletion: Using this setting, FURCAS will only delete the textual representation of domain model elements upon explicit request by the developer. However, an indicator is presented showing that the referenced element is not present in the underlying model anymore. Still, additions to the model will be instantly reflected in the view.

AdditionAndDeletion: Both, additions and deletions are only performed upon explicit commands given by a developer.

Chapter 6.

Synchronisation of Textual Views

Modelling software is a creative and long enduring task. Throughout this process a modeller needs to tackle a certain problem from different angles. Thus, having different views on a model helps to analytically work on a problem and model its solution using different views [FKN+92]. During this process these different views need to be kept in sync with the underlying model and, in the case of overlapping views, with the other views on the same model.

Special attention needs to be taken when partially viewed elements are modified in a textual view. If larger, structural modifications are made in such a view, a traditional update process may need to completely re-create model elements from their current representation as text. For partially viewed elements this, however, is a problem. A re-creation of a model element can only use the information that is currently present in the view. However, in the case of a partial view there is more information in the model element. This information that is outside the view's scope will then be lost. Therefore, a synchronisation process for views needs to avoid this step.

Also, depending on the degree of freedom that is allowed in a certain modelling environment, view synchronisation becomes a tough problem. For example, in a textual modelling view, a modeller wants to be able to write not necessarily consistent (with respect to the parser grammar) text in order to scratch some initial ideas. The usage of a textual model editor or any kind of model editor as a kind of "scratch book" may support the creativity of a modeller [LS93, DC01] as he or she can make his or her ideas tangible, even if they are not yet as structured as it would be required by a parser to be able to create real model elements from it. This temporary inconsistency exacerbates the synchronisation as, upon external changes the view itself may require an update that will overwrite the "scratched" parts. In order to conserve this work, the synchronisation transformation needs to be aware of areas that should be treated specially during the update process.

The UUIDs of model elements as well as the retainment of format information pose additional challenges to the view synchronisation transformations. These scientific challenges as well as solutions for them are tackled within this chapter.

6.1. Scientific Challenges

The degree of freedom of editing actions that are allowed during the creation and modification of a model poses a challenge to the modelling environment when it comes to synchronisations between a model and its views. Especially if the underlying model elements are only partially represented by a view, this challenge becomes even more difficult. A trade-off has to be found allowing to freely edit the view whereas still keeping the viewed model elements as consistent as possible and not loosing the information that is outside of the scope of the view.

Especially in textual modelling these challenges are hard to tackle, as the synchronisation has to be made through several levels, i.e., lexing, parsing, model update. Thus, FURCAS, the textual modelling approach presented in this thesis needs to cope with the following challenges:

- A model that is subject to modification from multiple but partial views needs to be treated warily than a model that is completely covered by a textual representations. This is due to the fact that not all parts of a model element may be represented in a view. Therefore, it is not possible to reconstruct a model element completely from its partial representations. For example, if a view type omits an attribute a, it is not possible to reconstruct a's value from an instance of that view type. This problem implies that a naive approach for parsing the textual representation and deriving the model from a parse tree of that representation is not sufficient. In fact, an approach is required that updates a partially viewed model incrementally and fine grained while not re-instantiating model elements that are in fact only meant to be updated. Current approaches for textual modelling (cf. Section 2.5.2), do not support this retainment.

- Having a model changed through different *partial* views may also lead to unwanted effects, if a model is changed through one view such that it leaves the scope of another view. For example, imagine two different views from the running example of the previous chapters, one showing business objects in general and a different one only those that are marked as value type. Changing an element a that was a value

240

type and therefore shown in the latter view, to a non-value type trough the first view, will result in the exclusion of a from the value type view. This kind of repercussions may be irritating for a modeller. Thus, a solution is required to attenuate these effects and therefore help the modellers to identify such occurrences.

- Support for creating *temporarily inconsistent* states of a view. Furthermore, storage of intermediate inconsistency is also required if "scratched" work shall be preserved over a longer period of time.

- *Partial synchronisation* is especially important if a view covers larger or distributed parts of a model. Areas which are in an inconsistent state or covered by probably inconsistent modifications should be excluded from updates to the view. Areas that view other parts of the model should be synchronised with it. Another area where partial synchronisation is required is the support for selective views. Elements in these views may or may not be automatically added to an existing view once they fulfil the constraints of its view type. Therefore, the synchronisation transformation needs to be aware of which elements to add or delete automatically and which should be handled by the manual selection of the user.

- If retainment of model element identifiers (UUIDs) is required, this requirement further exacerbates the synchronisation. Allowing for inconsistent states and at the same time retaining the elements' IDs is a grave challenge.

6.2. Contributions

In general the challenges mentioned above can be applied to all kinds of view types. However, most of them require specialised solutions when *textual view types* are employed. The contributions presented in this chapter present solutions for the synchronisation of textual views based on an underlying UUID-based model.

- To support the synchronisation transformations from and to the textual view model, i.e., the TextBlocks model, an incremental parsing approach [Wag98] is utilized and adapted so it can be employed in this special scenario. This approach allows to represent a textual representation in the form of a self-versioning document. Having these multiple versions, including a fine-grained change history, allows to base incremental synchronisation transformations on them and support the transformation with the necessary versioned information.

- The synchronisation transformations are specific to the underlying view types. This thesis shows a schema which defines a way how view to model as well as model to view transformations can be generated from the view type definitions that were introduced in Chapter 5. These synchronisation transformations handle modifications made by editing the TextBlock-Model and update the underlying domain model incrementally and fine grained. This is realised by a set of algorithms that are based on self-versioned TextBlocks and allows to retain the so called *umbilical cord* that represents the connection of a TextBlock with its corresponding model element.

- Furthermore, FURCAS contributes an approach that allows for the incremental update of a TextBlock-Model upon changes made to the underlying model. For this approach, the retainment policies approach introduced in Chapter 3 is utilised in the definition of transformation rules that incrementally update a TextBlock-Model. Special attention is paid in the validation of views when elements are co-modified in overlapping views in a way that they leave the scope of the current view. This direction of the incremental update process is described in Section 6.6.

- Support for selective views is a further contribution of this thesis. The selectiveness of a view depends on the definition of this property in its corresponding view type. From this view type definition the synchronisation transformation is generated. This is the point where special rules are inserted into the transformation that deal with this selectiveness. Therefore, the synchronisation transformation is augmented with retainment policies that define which elements should be added or deleted automatically and which are handled manually by a developer.

- In order to solve the UUID retainment problem, this thesis introduces an approach to reduce the UUID retainment problem to a more generic partial view problem. This is achieved by providing implicit extensions to the standard view type definitions that declare every view type to be partial concerning a synthetic UUID attribute. Furthermore, the synchronisation transformations need to deal with retaining the UUID attribute upon changes to the textual view. Special instances of *RetainmentPolicies* are introduced that serve this purpose.

6.3. Synchronisation from Textual View to Model

FURCAS includes an approach for synchronising the textual view model (i.e., the Text-Block model) with its underlying domain model. The main difference to existing synchronisation approaches lies in the fact that the TextBlocks model is a *decorator* w.r.t. its underling domain model, which is updated step-wise depending on a classification that is done for the incoming change events.

The incremental update process, that allows for the synchronisation from textual views to their model, including its driving components is depicted in Figure 6.1. The following text will first provide an overview on the incremental update process. Later sections will then detail on the exact conditions and sub-processes.

All textual editing that is done by the user is first captured as event by the event manager of the IDE. A central component within the presented approach is the *Event Classification* component (bottom left). This component, which is described in more detail in Section 6.3.1, decides what to do with a sequence of user events (in this case these events are textual editing events, meaning inserting or deleting characters). The classification component then triggers the incremental update components accordingly. For instance, upon a modification of an identifier in the text the classification component triggers the incremental lexer to check whether the change results only in a lexical value change of the token itself or if the modification resulted in the creation or deletion of tokens. Depending on the outcome of the incremental lexing process the incremental parser may be triggered to check if the structure of the TextBlock-Model has to be changed due to the changed token types. Change in this case means the change of the token type, as those are the relevant changes for the parser. Depending on these changes, as a next step, a model-to-model (M2M) transformation is triggered that updates the model correspondingly. Model elements which are deleted in the textual representation are for example deleted in the domain model representation.

6.3.1. Classification of Changes to the Textual Representation of a Model

The decision on which component of the incremental parsing process is triggered after which kind of change during editing of a textual view is based on the classification of the events that occur during this process.

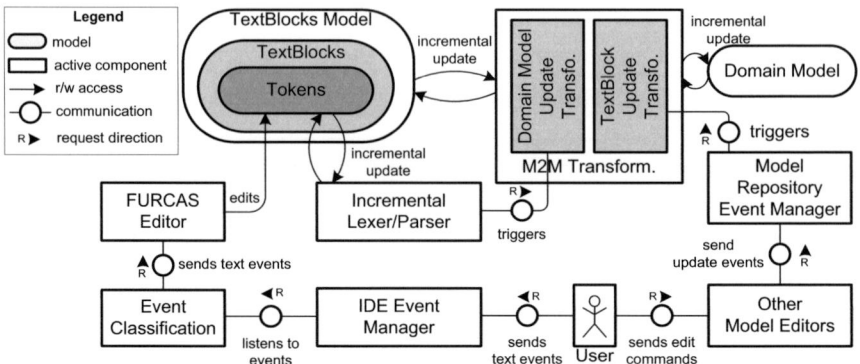

Figure 6.1.: Incremental Process - Overview

6.3.1.1. The Scope of Textual Changes

For a detailed analysis of the possible changes FURCAS distinguishes between *tokens*, *blocks* and *regions*. *Token* refers to the concept of terminals as it is known from compiler construction. A token is the smallest entity which can be affected by a change. For example, given a token with the value "MyBusinessObject", a change on token level may affect the value to be changed to "YourBusinessObject". Still, depending on the rules for the lexical analysis such a change may also lead to the creation of a new token, resulting in the tokens "Your" and "BusinessObject". Mapped to the TextBlocks decorator model for textual views, changes on token level map to changes of values of subclasses of AbstractToken. Also the creation and deletion of AbstractTokens falls under this category.

Changes on *block* level always include modifications of *whole* consistent blocks representing a non-terminal, as known from compiler construction. A block may include subblocks as well as tokens. However, a change on block level must always include *all* subblocks and tokens of a given block. For example the deletion of the text "bool hasDiscount { return false; }" which conforms to one complete block of our running example would be considered a change on block level. Mapped to the TextBlocks decorator model for textual views, changes on block level map to the creation/deletion/move of TextBlocks.

Changes that occur on *region* level can span over more than one block but do not include the whole block. For example, the cutting of the last three of four tokens of one block including the first token and the first subblock of the subsequent block would be a modification on region level. Changes that occur on region level but are not at the same time only on block level or only on token level are changes to an *inconsistent region*.

6.3.1.2. Types of Textual Changes

Basically, FURCAS distinguishes two different types of changes: (A) changes that are either an insertion or deletion of a sequence of characters at a specific position or a replacement of a sequence of characters on token or block level. The standard and probably most often occurring case during textual editing is the insertion or deletion of exactly one or more characters at a time. Type (B) describes copy & paste replacements on the granularity of an *inconsistent region*.

The following changes are handled by the incremental update process presented in the next Section 6.3.2.

1. Insertion of a sequence of characters or by pasting whole blocks or tokens at specific position which are changes on token or block level.

2. Deletion of a sequence of characters at a specific position on token level.

3. Deletion of whole blocks (on block level).

4. Replacement of a sequence of characters on token level.

6.3.2. Incremental Updates of the Textual Model after Type (A) Changes

The basis for all incremental update steps is the existence of a TextBlock including its links to the domain model. In FURCAS these links represent *umbilical cords* as they are vital for the *survival* of the domain model elements that are decorated by a corresponding TextBlock. As presented in Section 5.4.3 on page 222ff, the function that is used to yield this relation is called *corelem*. This link becomes essential during the incremental parsing process.

An update approach that translates text into any kind of structure requires some kind of compiler technique. As FURCAS is based on TCS which also internally uses compiler technology to translate its mapping definitions into parser generator compatible grammars, FURCAS also uses this technique. In general, the parser grammar that is generated

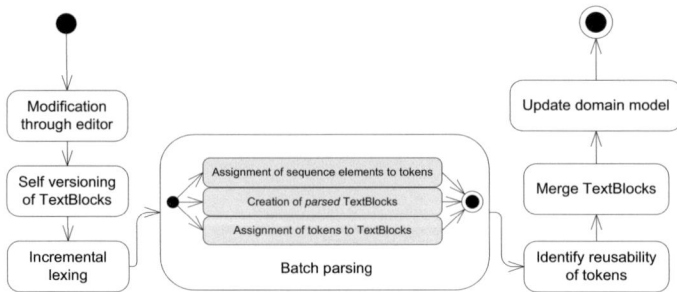

Figure 6.2.: Overview on the phases of the incremental textual view to domain model update process.

by FURCAS is quite similar to the one generated by TCS. An overview on this generation is given in Section 2.1.3.2. The biggest difference, in the generated artefact are the constructs for the OCL based features as presented in the previous chapter. However, when it comes to the usage of the generated parser components FURCAS behaves completely different.

The FURCAS parsing process is, after reacting to a modification event through the editor (0), divided into the following phases: (I) *self-versioning of TextBlocks* , (II) *incremental lexing*, (III) *incremental parsing*, (IV) *textblock merging* and (V) *domain model update*. An overview on the phases of the incremental update process is given in Figure 6.2. Phase (II) and (III) rely on techniques known from compiler construction, namely lexing and parsing. The basic techniques are taken from literature, however, this thesis introduces a novel approach on how the special links, called *umbilical cords*, are maintained throughout these steps. Using this approach phases (0) to (III) prepare a TextBlock-Model that makes the changes accessible to phases (IV) and (V) which update the TextBlock-Model and the domain model respectively. In the final phase FURCAS employs a model transformation that applies the changes in the prepared TextBlock-Model to the previously existent model. To be able to retain the umbilical cords and thus the information of partially viewed elements from the domain model a reuse and merge approach is employed based on the different version of the TextBlock-Model. Finally, FURCAS triggers a model transformation for updating the underlying domain model with the modifications made to the view. The following section will explain the subsequent phases step by step in detail.

246

```
 1  viewtype BusinessEntityWithRefs {
 2    primitiveTemplate string for PrimitiveTypes:STRING;
 3    template BusinessEntity :
 4      (isValueType ? "valueType" ) "bo" name
 5      (isDefined(elementyOfType) ? "{" elementyOfType "}")
 6    ;
 7    template TypeDefinition :
 8      typedElement ";"
 9    ;
10    template AssociationEnd context:
11      [[ --variant 1 with named/navigable local end
12        name "<-" (isOrdered ? "ordered") (isStorage ? "store")
13          association {{ navigable = true }}
14        --isStored only set if the end is the end is also navigable
15        |
16        --variant 2 with unnamed/non-navigable local end
17        (isOrdered ? "ordered")
18          association {{ navigable = false, isStorage <- false }} ]]
19    ;
20    template Association :
21      name "->" ends{forcedMult = 1..1, mode=otherEnd}
22
23    ;
24    template AssociationEnd #otherEnd :
25      (isStorage ? "store") name
26      {{ navigable = true,
27        type == association.ends->reject(#context.type) }}
28      --the constraint property init (==) is responsible for choosing
29      --the association end that is not the same as the one the
30      --Association template was called from
31    ;
32  }
```

Listing 6.1: Example view type "BusinessEntityWithRefs" for BusinessEntities

6.3.2.1. Running Example

The syntax definition given in Listing 6.1 will serve as running example to explain the update approach. It defines a view type for the representation a part of the example metamodel given in Section 2.1.1.1 on page 18 that represents business entities and their relationships.

The given syntax allows to specify Associations between *BusinessEntities*. Remember from the definition of TCS language (Section 2.5.2.11) that the isDefined clause specifies that the part of the syntax written in parentheses will only be required if there is at least one element in elementsOfType to be matched. These

```
1  --variant 1
2  bo Customer {
3    --vartiant 1
4    customer <- CustomerHasInvoices -> invoices;
5  }
6
7  --variant 2
8  bo Customer {
9    --vartiant 1
10   ordered CustomerHasAddress -> address;
11 }
```

Listing 6.2: Example views for a BusinessEntities using the "BusinessEntityWithRefs" view type

`Associations` may be navigable in both directions thus variant 1 is used where the name of the local `AssociationEnd`, the name of the association and transitively through the template for `AssociationEnd` with mode #otherEnd the name of the other `AssociationEnd` is specified. This variant will set the `navigable` property of the local `AssociationEnd` to `true`. Furthermore, it is possible to define whether the a link is stored at the local and/or the other end by declaring it a "`store`". Using variant 2 the local `AssociationEnd` will be not navigable (`navigable` set to `false`) and only the name of the `Association` and the other end will be specified. If an end is not navigable it cannot be stored at this side. Therefore variant 2 does not allow to define "`store`". Listing 6.2 shows an example using both variants.

The TextBlock-Model representing the example given here looks as depicted in Figure 6.3. This example shows the relation of the TextBlock-Model to the underlying domain model. As the `TypeDefinition` does not have a syntax contribution of its own, the element is included in the corresponding model elements of the respective `AssociationEnd`.

6.3.2.2. Modification Through Editor

The FURCAS text editor projects its underlying TextBlock-Model to a textual view using the approach presented in Chapter 5. Thus, the editor can be used as every other text editor. By typing or deleting characters, the editor produces events that are passed to the appropriated places in the TextBlock-Model. A change event is formed using the following schema: $ChangeEvent(< position >, < length >, < value >)$ where position is the offset in the document where to insert the value and length defines how many characters will be overwritten by an event. Depending on the range of characters that

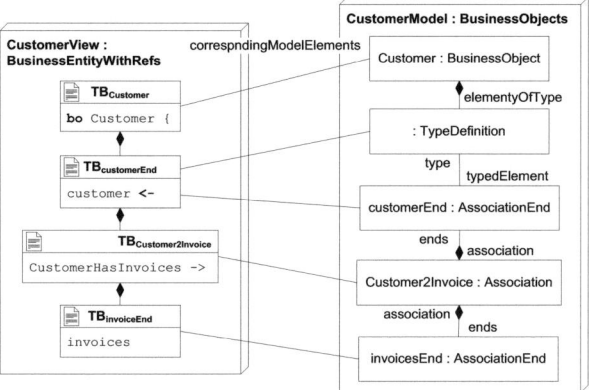

Figure 6.3.: TextBlock-Model for the running example.

are overwritten, FURCAS determines the scope of the change according to the classification presented in Section 6.3.1.1. For the elements in the determined scope, the
self-versioning process is triggered and subsequently all following processes.

6.3.2.3. Deletion of Elements versus Removal of Elements from a View

In the case of *selective* views, deleting elements from the textual representation needs to
come in two different flavours. One, for deleting elements from the view as well as from
the underlying domain model (*deletion*) and one where only the textual representation is
removed from the view while the underlying element is retained (*removal*). As deletion
is also an interaction with the editor that will be propagated to the corresponding $B$the
latter case also needs to be represented in the TextBlock-Model.

Standard deletion actions will delete the tokens representing the deleted text. From
these TextBlock deletions the incremental update algorithm will, as will be shown in
later sections, detect that a deletion action was performed and that the underlying model
elements have to be removed as well. Thus, to be able to distinguish the *removal* action
form the *deletion* action it is not sufficient to just delete the TextBlocks. The incremental
update algorithm will decide upon the deletion of an element based on the existence of
its corresponding TextBlock in a specific version (see Section 6.3.2.4 for details on the
versioning of TextBlocks). If a TextBlock of an element existed in a previous version

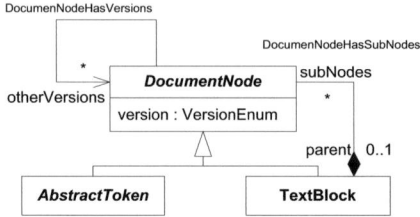

Figure 6.4.: Versioning represented in the TextBlocks metamodel.

and is deleted in a later version, FURCAS will delete its corresponding model element. In contrast to this *deletion* action, the *removal* action will therefore remove the complete history of a TextBlock. In this case, FURCAS will detect that the element wasn't even represented in the view in a previous version and will not delete it.

6.3.2.4. Self Versioning of the TextBlock-Model

The identification of changes to the textual view model relies on the analysis of its change history. To be able to represent a change history versioning of the view model is required. The versioning needs to be fine grained enough to allow for the representation of small changes including their exact ancestors. The incremental view synchronisation transformation (cf. Section 6.3.2.10) later-on relies on this history.

To be able to incrementally analyse the modifications that occur during the editing of a textual view FURCAS employs the concept of self-versioning documents as introduced by Wagner in [Wag98]. A self-versioned document consists of a tree of nodes that may exist in different versions. Every textual change operation that is applied to the document is directly reflected in the document's nodes. No text file or buffer is edited in this approach but rather every modification is made on the contents of an underlying node. Every such modification creates a new version of the modified node. Therefore, a node may exist in several versions at the same time. At specific points in time (such as save of the document, or the run of a parser) the document can be restructured by transforming or merging of versions back into one consistent basis.

The FURCAS meta-model (Figure 6.4) also incorporates the capabilities of these self-versioning documents. Here, `DocumentNodeHasVersions` association is used for representing different versions of a TextBlock or a token. Each `DocumentNode` fur-

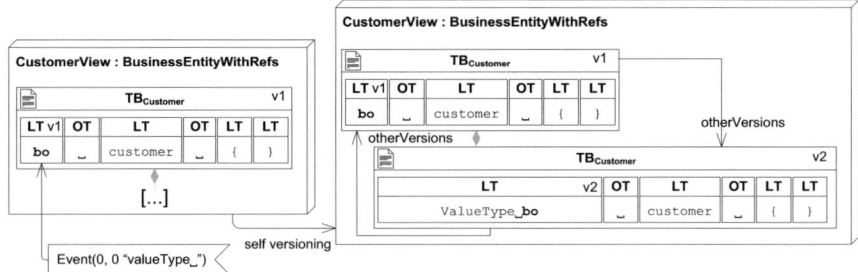

Figure 6.5.: TextBlock-Model for the running example showing the self versioning after an editing event $Event(0, 0, \text{valueType}_\sqcup)$.

thermore includes an attribute `version` that determines the version of the node. Other versions of a node can be retrieved by traversing the `DocumentNodeHasVersions` association transitively until the desired version of a node is reached.

Assuming the running example from Listing 6.2 and Figure 6.3 is represented using a self-versioned document, every token or symbol represents a node within this document. So for example, the first terminal token `bo` would be such a node. On the occurrence of a change event, for example the insertion of the text "value$_\sqcup$" in front of `bo` would create a new version of this token. This change is illustrated in Figure 6.5. The original token could be denoted as bo_{v1} and after the change a new version `value`$_\sqcup\text{bo}_{v2}$ would be present. After analysing the change, according to transformation rules (such as a lexical analysis being performed) a third version bo_{v3} would be created incorporating the results of this step. As the example change introduces new lexical constructs , this transformation would then also create new nodes representing the newly inserted values. Thus two new nodes `value`$_{v3}$ and $_\sqcup{}_{v3}$ would be created. Note that, the decision whether the original version of the three nodes in version $v3$ would be connected as ancestor of all of the three nodes or just bo_{v3} depends on the transformation that is applied to the document.

6.3.2.5. Incremental Lexing

The incremental lexing process is based on the algorithm presented by Wagner in [Wag98]. Basically, this approach works as follows: In Wagner's approach the self versioned documents support the incremental lexing and parsing process. The information of the newer versions that where produced by a textual modification event are compared to the already lexed and parsed reference version that is always kept. This comparison is then used to decide how the incremental lexing needs to be done. Wagner proofs that the lexing process is always optimal with respect to complexity. In FURCAS, this approach is reused and extended for the purpose of synchronising models with their textual views.

Wagner's [Wag98] Approach to Incremental Lexing Based on the existence of a self versioning document, Wagner introduced an incremental lexing algorithm that preserves as much tokens from the previous version as possible after a change has been performed. This section will shortly explain the lexing algorithm based on a running example.

The lexing algorithm consists of three major phases: *marking*, *lexing* and *lookback update*. To understand these phases, first the basic idea of the lexing approach needs to be understood which is the storage of the dynamic lookahead used to decide upon token types directly in the tokens. This way it becomes possible to compute which other tokens are affected by a change in one of the token's values. Figure 6.6 illustrates an example for the computation of the lookback counts. Assuming there are are lexer rules which support integer as well as float numbers and furthermore a construct like <number>..<number> that represents a range a lookahead of more than one is needed to distinguish between a string "1.2" which is a float number and a range "1..2" which is a range consisting of two integer numbers. Because the lexer needed to look at both "." characters to decide which token should be produced starting from the "1" character. The amount of tokens that reached to a specific token's position during their creation determines the lookback count of the token. The second "." token has a lookback count of 2 as two characters reached it in their lookahead, thus both previous tokens will be invalidated if its value changes.

Based on this idea the three phases work as follows:

1. In the *marking* phase all tokens that were target to modifications will be marked as to be *re-lexed*. Furthermore, the incremental lexer takes the lookback counts stored in the tokens into account to decide which other tokens are invalidated. All tokens in the lookback of a changed token will also be marked. For example, assuming the second "." in the above example is replaced by the number "3". The "1" token as well as the first "." tokens will also be marked.

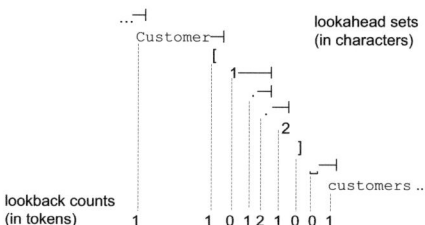

Figure 6.6.: Relation between character lookahead and token lookback counts. The T-lines show how many characters were needed to decide upon the token creation. The numbers at the foot of the dashed lines indicate how many tokens backward will be invalidated when the value of the current token changes.

2. The incremental lexer then triggers the *lexing* phase starting from the first invalidated area and produces new tokens from the values of the changed tokens. This process proceeds until it reaches the first token that is not marked anymore. Then the next area of marked tokens is processed. In the above example, the lexing phase would produce one new token from the three changed ones: the float token with the value "1.32".

3. Finally, the *lookback update phase* is responsible for updating the lookback counts of the newly created tokens. For example the new float token will get the lookback count of 0 assigned as the previous token "[" does not require a lookahead.

Using this approach it is possible to determine those tokens that are affected by an editing event. Wagner proves that his algorithm affect the minimal set of changed tokens (cf. [Wag98] page 47ff.) and thus enables for optimal token reuse.

Applying Wagner's Approach to FURCAS   Another advantage of Wagners approach is that it can be applied to nearly arbitrary existing lexers and thus, even though Wagner published his approach in 1998, enables for the use of contemporary parser generators. Figure 6.7 depicts the architecture of this approach and its application within FURCAS. Note that the classes and interfaces marked by the `external` package could be provided by an arbitrary lexing approach. The incremental lexer itself provides the functionality described above, which is given by the three phases of the incremental lexing.

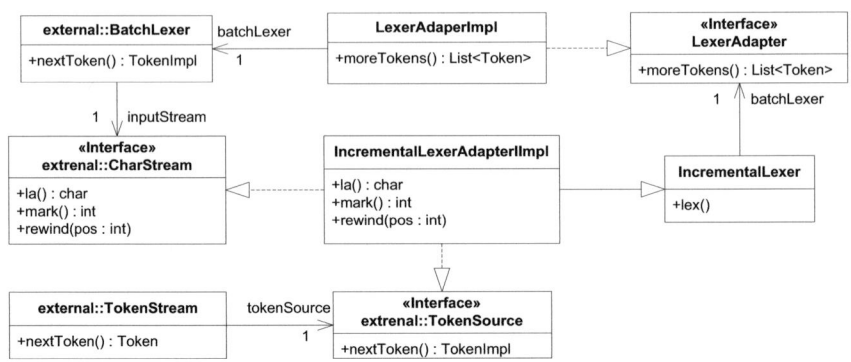

Figure 6.7.: The architecture of the lexing mechanism.

For tokenisation of the values that exist in a previous version, the interface called LexerAdapter provides the moreTokens() method. This method is implemented by a class implementing the LexerAdapter interface for a specific lexer implementation (such as the one from ANTLR [PQ95] which is used in the current implementation of FURCAS). This class acts as an adapter to the specific lexer implementation translating the moreTokens() method to the specific implementation. In the case of the ANTLR lexer, this is the nextToken() method. This specific lexer implementation can also be called *batch lexer*.

As the *batch lexer* normally would read from a character stream of a file this mechanism also requires adaptation. In the incremental lexing environment the *batch lexer* will not read from a file but rather from the previous version of the token model, which may contain changes from the last editing events. Therefore, a subclass of the incremental lexer is responsible for providing methods to that implement a character stream that can be read by the *batch lexer* component. Such methods are for example in the case of the ANTLR approach, la() : char which gives the next character in the lookahead, mark() or rewind() for implementing the *LL(*)* dynamic lookahead functionality of ANTLR (see [PQ95] for details on the LL(*) parsing approach of ANTLR). This lexer specific subclass also provides the functionality that passes the newly lexed tokens to subsequent components in the parsing process, such as token stream or parser component.

Versions Used During Incremental Lexing and Their Relation to a TextBlock-Model According to Wagner, the input of the incremental lexing algorithm consists of a three-versioned document model (the versions are named *reference*, *edited*[1] and *lexed*) where, applied to the FURCAS taxonomy, to a TextBlock b:

Reference: $b^{reference}$ is the version of the TextBlock in its last consistent state. This means that all TextBlocks are *complete* and form a consistent view on the current domain model. The exact conditions for a TextBlock to be complete are defined in Section 5.4.3.3. There is always at least one consistent state. The minimal consistent state that is always present for TextBlock-Model consists of one TextBlock having two tokens which represent the start (the *BOS* token) and the end (the *EOS* token) of a textual view model.

Edited: b^{edited} is the version of the TextBlock in its last complete state but after one or more editing actions (type (A) changes) have been performed. The FURCAS editor makes sure that an editing event of the form $edit(offset, length, value)$ is directed to the corresponding elements within the TextBlocks model. These are always the tokens over which the region of the edit event spans. Starting from the token at the given *offset* to the token at *offset* + *length* all subsequent tokens are considered as affected. For these tokens an *edited* version is created and their values are changed according to the *value* given in the edit event. For each affected token the parent TextBlock of the token is turned into its *edited* version. Furthermore each affected token is turned into *editable state* by applying the $prettyprint_{short}$ function to it (cf. Section 5.4.3.3.

Lexed: b^{lexed} is the version of b that is produced by the incremental lexer during the incremental lexing process. This version includes potentially new or deleted tokens that result from the edit event. To create this version the incremental lexing approach tries to make the TextBlock *complete* again. However, if the incremental lexer recognises elements that are not lexable the *lexed* version will still be created but it will be marked as *incomplete*. This marking will be used in later phases (parsing and TextBlock merging) to indicate that the element that is represented by this TextBlock has to be treated differently.

---

[1]Wagner called this "previous" and "current" but for the sake of better understandability we use "edited" and "lexed" here, respectively.

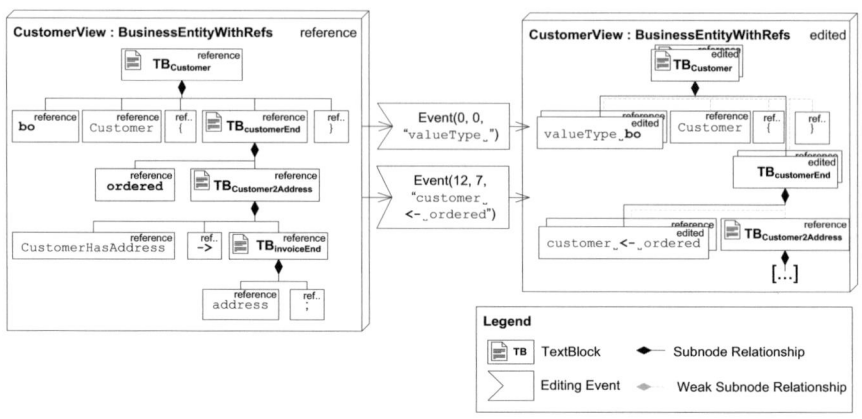

Figure 6.8.: TextBlock-Model for the running example after the self versioning phase.

Definition 6.1. *The finite set V denotes the possible version definitions $V = \{reference,$ edited, lexed\}. The function version : $N \times V \rightarrow N$ yields the corresponding element having a given version v from V of a* DocumentNode $n \in N$.

$$
version(n \in N, v \in V) = \begin{cases} n \text{ in version } v & \text{if } n \text{ exists in version } v \\ \varnothing & \text{else} \end{cases}
$$

So for example the *lexed* version of a given document node $n_1^{reference}$ would be returned by $n_1^{lexed} = version(n_1^{reference}, lexed)$.

Figure 6.8 shows the running example after editing events $Event(0, 0, \text{"valueType}_\sqcup\text{"})$ and $Event(12, 7, \text{"customer}_\sqcup\text{<-}_\sqcup\text{ordered"})$. The tokens at the positions to where the editing events point are self-versioned into their *edited* version. The self-versioning mechanism also creates *edited* versions for the TextBlocks that contain the modified tokens. These TextBlock then contain the *edited* tokens. The remaining sub-nodes of the *reference* TextBlock are also referenced using the WeakSubNodes association (cf. Figure 6.10).

Extending Wagner's Incremental Lexing Approach to Deal With View Synchronisation The primary focus of incrementality in FURCAS is not to provide a high performance parsing approach but rather to use incremental parsing techniques to ensure the correct update of an underlying domain model from a changed view. Therefore, the incremental lexer approach is used in FURCAS with the goal to detect which domain model elements should be changed due to changes in their textual representation. To achieve this task, FURCAS observes the incremental lexing process performed by Wagner's algorithms and plugs itself into the process where tokens of the *lexed* version of the document are created from those of the *reference* and *edited* version.

During this phase first decisive actions take place that are later-on responsible for the decision whether a (set of) token(s) is considered to represent a new domain model element or adding further information to an existing one. Recall that the *umbilical cord* of the model element (see association end `correspondingModelElements` in the TextBlocks metamodel) is attached to a TextBlock of the *reference* version. As the existence or removal of this link may decide on the retainment or deletion of the underlying domain model element the it is an important step to decide whether a TextBlock is considered to be reusable or not. A TextBlock itself is not directly represented within the textual representation. The only part of a TextBlock that is represented and is therefore modifiable by a developer, are its contained tokens. Therefore, the decision whether a TextBlock is for example deleted depends primarily on the fact whether its contained tokens where deleted. If token will be retained or in after the lexing process depends on whether there exists a *lexed* version for it or not. Therefore, it needs to be decided which tokens in the *lexed* version will be linked to the *reference* and *edited* version. A preparation for this step is made during the incremental lexing phase.

Therefore, FURCAS includes all tokens in *lexed* version into the `otherVersions` of the *reference* and *edited* versions from which they where created. This connection is made based on the text that was lexed from the *edited* version. For example, in the running example (depicted in Figure 6.9) a token "ordered"$_{reference}$ (line 5) is modified to "customer <- ordered"$_{edited}$ by the insertion of new text "customer <-". The incremental lexer then creates three tokens "customer"$_{lexed}$, "<-"$_{lexed}$ and "ordered"$_{lexed}$ from that token. All three *lexed* tokens will then refer to the "ordered"$_{reference}$ as their *reference* and "customer <- ordered"$_{edited}$ as their *edited* version.

However, FURCAS now needs to decide which token, if at all, in *lexed* version will eventually reuse the *reference* version. This is an important step, because, as mentioned above, based on the reused tokens the *umbilical cord* of their parent TextBlocks will be taken over by the *lexed* version of the TextBlock in the final phases (cf. Section 6.3.2.10 and 6.3.2.13).

257

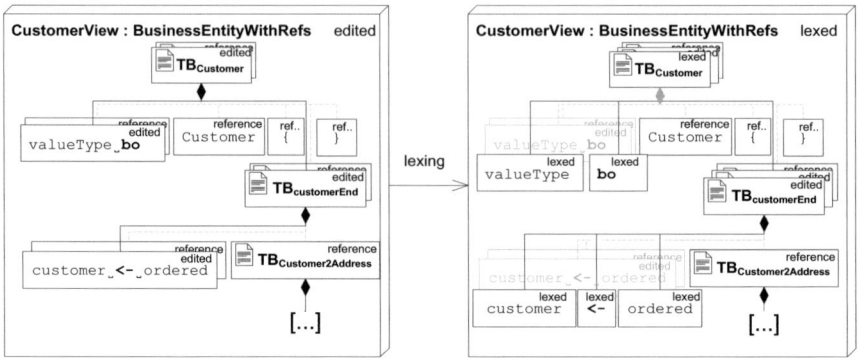

Figure 6.9.: TextBlock-Model for the running example after the incremental lexing phase.

The resulting TextBlock-Model contains only tokens in their *reference* or *lexed* state, otherwise TextBlocks that still contain tokens that were not lexable and are marked as *incomplete* (by setting their `complete` property to false). Handling of incomplete Text-Blocks during parsing and lexing is described in the respective Sections 6.3.2.9 and 6.3.2.12.

6.3.2.6. Incremental Parsing

The incremental parsing process is, opposed to conventional incremental parsing algorithms like [Li95], [Shi93] or [CW01], not based on pruning and grafting subtrees of the abstract syntax tree. Instead, a conventional LL parser is used to instantiate an intermediate new version of changed subtrees of the TextBlocks model. Algorithm 1 outlines the main steps of the parsing phase.

Algorithm 1 creates a TextBlock in *parsed* version for each changed region of the TextBlocks model. A changed region that is returned by `findNextRegion` (*findLeftBoundary* : $\Omega \rightarrow \Omega$) was marked before, during the incremental lexing phase (line 1). Each token that was turned into its edited and then lexed version can be the start of such a region. Function `findLeftBoundary` therefore finds the next token, starting from the given token that is present in *lexed* version (line 2). This loop is done in a left-to-right manner until the end of the token stream (EOS) is reached. For each of these regions the left and the right boundary are identified by traversing the leafs of the TextBlock tree. Where `findLeftBoundary()` gets the left-most token t_{left} for which the parsers lookahead reached the current token t. The lookahead is computed into a lookback from each TextBlock that denotes from how many preceding TextBlocks the left boundary or further right tokens of the current TextBlock was reached within the last parsing phase. The lookback is stored as a property in each TextBlocks model element if it differs from the default of 1. The right boundary is found by function `findRightBoundary()` (line 3).

Using the left to the right boundary the least common ancestor (LCA) of a region of changed tokens is determined. The result of this computation is then used to re-trigger the batch parsing process from that specific point on. Afterwards the corresponding parser production $prod$ for the template referenced by b_{ca} is called with b_{ca} as input (line 5-6). The batch parsing process (as described in paragraph **The Batch Parsing Process**) is performed, by calling `invokeParser`$(prod, b_{ca})$, based on the underlying *lexed* version of the TextBlocks model.

Input: TextBlock b having passed the lex phase.
Output: A TextBlock in *parsed* version b_i^{parsed} for each changed subtree b_i of b
1 **for** $t = findNextRegion(b), i = 0;\ t == EOS;\ t = findNextRegion(t), i = i + 1$ **do**
2 $\quad$ t_{left} = findLeftBoundary(t)
3 $\quad$ t_{right} = findRightBoundary(t)
4 $\quad$ b_{ca} = findCommonAncestorWithLookback(b, t_{left}, t_{right})
5 $\quad$ $prod$ = getProduction(b_{ca})
6 $\quad$ b_i^{parsed} = invokeParser$(prod, b_{ca})$
7 $\quad$ mergeTextBlocks(b_{ca}, b_i^{parsed})
8 **end**
9 **return** $\bigcup_i (b_i^{parsed})$

Algorithm 1: Outline of the incremental parsing phase.

Definition 6.2 (findRightBoundary). *Function $findRightBoundary$ is defined as*

$$findRightBoundary : \Omega \to \Omega\ such\ that\ (t, t_{right}) \in orderNodes^*$$

Starting from the given token t traverse the leafs of the TextBlock tree in a left-to-right manner and return the token that is the last one in this sequence of tokens that is still present in lexed *version.*

The Batch Parsing Process   The batch parsing process uses the the tokens as they result from the *lexed* version of the B. The batch parser (such as for example ANTLR [PQ95] which is used in the current implementation of FURCAS) does not require knowledge about its embedding into the incremental parsing process. The only requirements that need to be fulfilled are:

- The batch parser needs to be observable during or after its parsing. From the result of the parse run it needs to be reconstructible which tokens were consumed while a certain production rule of the parser matched. This information is required to link the newly created TextBlock in *parsed* version to the tokens from its previous version. ANTLR, for example, allows to define action code within its grammar definitions that is executed during the parsing process. Additionally, due to the modularity of parser, token stream and lexer, it is possible to recognise which tokens were consumed during the matching of a production rule by sub-classing the token stream class and combining it with the actions defined in the grammar definition.

- As the incremental parsing approach of FURCAS calls production rules of the batch parser explicitly for sub trees of the document tree public access to single production rules is required. This reduces the set of usable parser approaches to top-down parsers. ANTLR, for example, is an LL(*) top-down parser which exposes its generated production rule methods publicly.

- The type of language that can be built with FURCAS also depends on the type of the employed parser. For example, it is obvious that employing a LL(1) parser instead of a LL(k) or LL(*) parser reduces the set of mappable languages.

During the *batch parsing* phase FURCAS establishes the connection between the consumed tokens (cf. **Assignment of Sequence Elements to Tokens**) and based on the rules that matched during the parsing process creates the *parsed* versions of the TextBlocks (cf. Creation of the *Parsed* Version of a TextBlock-Model).

Assignment of Sequence Elements to Tokens   To be able to make detailed decisions on the changes in the textual representation, FURCAS requires the information which consumed token corresponds to which sequence element in the mapping declaration. For example, assuming a template that has two different alternatives as shown

```
1  template AssociationEnd context:
2    [[
3      name "<-" (isOrdered ? "ordered") (isStorage ? "store")
4        association {{ navigable = true }}
5      |
6      (isAssociationOrdered ? "ordered")
7        association {{ navigable = false, isStorage <- false }}
8    ]]
9  ;
```

Listing 6.3: Example view type definition defining two alternatives which use the same literals.

in Listing 6.3. Just from analysing the consumed token values it is e.g., not distinguishable which attribute should be update if a certain alternative matches. Assuming a TextBlock which was created according to the first alternative using the textual representation `localEnd <- ordered TheAssociation` .... According to the template rule, due to the occurrence of the `"ordered"` token the `isOrdered` attribute was set to `true`. However, for the same bit of text (`"ordered"`) the second alternative will be responsible for setting the `isAssociationOrdered` attribute. Therefore, FURCAS needs to assign the corresponding sequence element to the tokens upon consumption. This will lead to the assignment of the corresponding property sequence elements to the consumed tokens. From this information FURCAS can then infer which alternative was chosen and which properties need to be set in the underlying domain model.

Creation of the *Parsed* Version of a TextBlock-Model During the parsing process the parser instantiates TextBlock in their *parsed* version according to the rules in the mapping definition. Basis for the creation of this blocks is the selection of production rules the generated batch parser decides to take. Each generated parse rule contains a parse action that identifies the template from which the rule was generated. This action is responsible for attaching the corresponding `TextBlockDefinition` for that template to the newly instantiated TextBlock. The same applies for the alternatives that the parse rule chose during its execution. The chosen alternatives are stored using the `chosenAlternatives` association of the TextBlock.

The set of textblock stubs Π^{parsed} contains all TextBlocks in *parsed* version that were the result of the incremental parsing phase. For each changed region the next major phase (cf. Section 6.3.2.7 is invoked using the current b_{ca} and b_i^{parsed} (line 7).

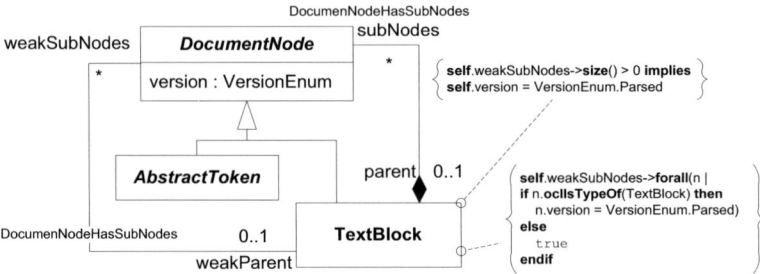

Figure 6.10.: Weak assignment constructs for representing the *parsed* version in the TextBlocks metamodel.

Assignment of Tokens to *Parsed* TextBlocks Just as the assignment of sequence elements to the consumed tokens, during the parsing the *lexed* token elements are assigned to new intermediate TextBlocks in a new version called *parsed*. This assignment is only done weakly, therefore, these tokens still keep their original TextBlock (*lexed* version) as composite parent. The combination of this assignment and the original assignment of tokens to their parent TextBlocks then serves as basis for the TextBlock merging phase.

The constructs in the TextBlock metamodel that are necessary to represent this weak, temporary assignment are depicted in Figure 6.10. The first constraint shown in this figure ensures that only TextBlocks in *parsed* version are allowed to reference other nodes through the `weakSubNodes` association. The second constraint ensures that a TextBlock in *parsed* version only contains either tokens or TextBlocks that are also in *parsed* version.

A formal definition of the weak assignment relation that is created between the *parsed* TextBlocks and the assigned tokens is given in the following Definition 6.3.

Definition 6.3 (tokenAssignment). *Relation $tokenAssignment^{parsed}$, is defined as $toks^{parsed} \subseteq \Pi^{parsed} \times \Omega$ and a pair $\left(b^{parsed}, \omega\right) \in tokenAssignment^{parsed} \iff \omega$ was assigned to b^{parsed} according to the parser in the incremental parsing phase.*

Result of the Batch Parsing Phase After the batch parsing phase is finished without error, such as parse errors in a changed region, for the changed region it holds that all tokens that exist in *lexed* version are assigned to a TextBlock in *parsed* version. Furthermore, each of the LexedTokens refers to a sequence element from the mapping. Formally it then holds, that:

$$\forall l \in L \mid \qquad\qquad version(l, lexed) \neq$$
$$refseq(version(l, lexed)) \neq \varnothing$$
$$\varnothing \rightarrow \exists b \in \Pi \mid version(l, lexed) \in toks(b)$$

6.3.2.7. Postprocessing of the Resulting TextBlock-Model after the Batch Parsing Phase

After the incremental lexing algorithm created new versions of tokens the next step does a post-processing to decide which *reference* token will be reused for for which *lexed* token. Now the process will decide if a token in reference version is suitable for being reused for a newly lexed token. The first candidates for taking over the reuse of existing *reference* versions of tokens are those *lexed* tokens that originated transitively through the *edited* version from it.

Reusability of Tokens   A precondition for the correct assignment of *lexed* tokens to their *reference* version correspondents is that for each token the corresponding sequence element was already assigned. As presented in Sections 2.5.2.11 and 5.4.3 the sequence element represents the location of an element within the syntax. Therefore, these are the smallest atomic parts on which it is possible to decide the actual meaning of an element written in a TextBlock-Model. The assignment of the correct sequence element was achieved in the batch parsing phase described in Section 9. Furthermore, recall that all the newly created tokens in *lexed* version still reference their *edited* and *reference* version from which their values were derived during during the incremental lexing phase (cf. Section 6.3.2.5). In this phase FURCAS now needs to decide which (if at all) tokens are actually represented by their lexed version. At most one *lexed* token may retain this this link. This link is important for the decision if the token's TextBlock represents a newly created model element or if an existing one that should be modified.

Formally, this *reusability* decision is given by:

Definition 6.4. *A token* $t^{reference} \in \Omega$ *where* $S_l = refseq(t^{lexed})$ *and* $S_r = refseq(t^{reference})$ *will be be considered* reusable *by view type definition for a token* $t^{lexed} \in \Omega$ *iff*

$$(1)\, S_l = S_r \quad \vee$$

$$(2)\, \exists a_1, a_2 \in A; t \in T \left| \begin{pmatrix} (2.1) & S_l \in altseqels(a_1) \wedge \\ (2.2) & S_r \in altseqels(a_2) \wedge \\ (2.3) & a_1 \neq a_2 \wedge a_1 \in tempalts(t) \wedge a_2 \in tempalts(t) \wedge \\ (2.4) & \begin{pmatrix} (2.4.1) & \begin{pmatrix} S_l \in S^{prop} \to mmprop(S_l) = \\ mmprop(S_r) \end{pmatrix} \wedge \\ (2.4.2) & \begin{pmatrix} S_l \in S^{lit} \to literal(S_l) = \\ literal(S_r) \end{pmatrix} \end{pmatrix} \end{pmatrix} \right.$$

Informally (1) means that the sequence elements attached to both tokens are identical. Having the same sequence element means that the token appears at the same position with respect to the mapping definition. For most changes this check is sufficient for the decision of a token being reusable for another one.

However, if the batch parser matched a different alternative when analysing the new *lexed* version, a different sequence element may have been assigned to it. Still, the token may represent the same conceptional element. For example, it may refer to the same constant literal (such as "class") or the same property of the corresponding model element that is represented by the token's parent TextBlock. To account for these cases (2) is true iff the sequence elements that are contained in different alternatives a_1 and a_2 (2.1 and 2.2), which are not the same ($a_1 \neq a_2$) and are both of the same parent template (2.3) but either refer to the same property from the metamodel (2.4.1) or have the same literal value (2.4.2).

This way the the incremental update approach ensures that all possibly reusable tokens will be linked to a token in *lexed* version. Case (2) also accounts for the change of a representation of the same domain model element as long as it is the same template that is responsible for the representation. The change from one alternative to another will still lead to the reuse of the tokens that represented the version that was represented by the old alternative. In the running example (cf. Section 6.2) a change from variant 1 of the local association template to variant 2 would be handled by case (2). Given this example is modified in the following way by setting a name to the local association end of the

```
1  bo Customer {
2    --variant 1
3    customer <- CustomerHasInvoices -> invoices;
4    --variant 2
5    customer <- ordered CustomerHasAddress -> address;
6  }
```

Listing 6.4: Running example: reusing tokens after alternatives changed.

`CustomerHasAddress` association by inserting "customer <-" at the beginning of line 5. Listing 6.4 shows the result of this modification.

Suppose the modification is not done by simply inserting "customer <-" before "ordered" but "ordered" is first overwritten completely by the newly entered text "customer <- ordered". Eventually, this modification leads to the a different choice in the alternatives of the template that is responsible for the local association end (see template `AssociationEnd` in Listing 6.1). The incremental update process now needs to decide if "ordered"$_{lexed}$ will reuse "ordered"$_{reference}$ token. Case (1) of Definition 6.4 will result in `false` as different sequence elements are used to match the "ordered" token. The original one comes from the first alternative and the one which is used now from the second alternative. However, case (2) will result in `true`, as the same literal value "ordered" (which is defined as a constant in the view type definition) is used. Furthermore, both sequence elements refer to the same property in the metamodel, namely `isOrdered`. Note that one of both cases would have been enough for the "ordered"$_{reference}$ being reused for "ordered"$_{lexed}$.

If no token can be identified for reusing a token in *reference* version using the *reusable by view type definition* definition there are still other criteria that possibly qualify for token reuse.

One of these criteria is the value of the token. If the value of the *lexed* token does occur within the *edited* token, the update process first checks whether the value changed concerning the *reference* version at all. If that is the case the *reusable by content* criterion is fulfilled.

Definition 6.5. *A token* $t^{reference} \in \Omega$ *will be be considered* reusable by content *for a token* $t^{lexed} \in \Omega$ *iff*

$$(1)\ value(t^{reference}) = value(t^{lexed}) \vee$$
$$(2)\ value(version(t^{reference}, edited))$$

265

Else, FURCAS will check whether the current value v^{lexed} of t^{lexed} is still contained in the originating token t^{edited}. If that is the case the current token will only be reused if it is the one which has the value v^{lexed} (lines 9-11). If the value does not occur any more in the *edited* version the "contentEquals" criterion is also set to `true`, considering the change as a complete rename of the tokens value (line 8).

The last check that is done is the check for multiple occurrences of the original value within the *edited* version of the token (`multipleReusePossibilityCheck`, lines 17-21). To decide upon the token reuse in that case, it is checked at which position the event that caused the change was performed. If there was a pre-existing token having this value this one will be used instead of a newly inserted one. This is checked by calling `checkMultipleOccurences` (line 20).

Finally all computed criteria are combined and compared for all possible candidate tokens and the result tells whether $t^{reference}$ can be reused for t^{lexed} (line 22). If $t^{reference}$ is re-usable for t^{lexed} both tokens will be linked together to finally be each others corresponding tokens in the respective version.

Table 6.1 gives an overview on the different cases that qualify for token reuse. The abbreviations used in the table stand for the corresponding criterion as follows: *sse* : same sequence element, *alt* : corresponding sequence element in different alternative but represents same property/literal, *val* : token value comparison and *mult* : multiple token value occurrences. It indicates under which condition the given criteria evaluate to true, given a single change in one of the column heads properties. For example, if the template to which a sequence element belongs for two reuse candidate tokens differs, the *same sequence element* property will evaluate to false. On the other hand, for the same change, assuming it is the only (single) change in this token, the *token value comparison* criterion would evaluate to true.

If there are multiple candidate tokens that match these criteria FURCAS takes the priority of the properties into account as they are shown in Table 6.1. The token which matches the property with the highest priority wins. If there are multiple tokens matching the same property, the overall amount of matching properties weighted by their priorities is used. The token with the highest reuse factor is determined by:

$$reuseFactor(tok) = \sum_{p \in ReuseProperties} \begin{cases} 10^{priority(p)} & \text{if } matches_p(tok) \\ 0 & \text{else} \end{cases}$$

Criterion	Priority	True if single change				
		Literal Sequence Element	Property Sequence Element	Template	Property	Value
sse	1	n	n	n	n	y
alt	2	y	y	n	n	n
val	3	n	y	y	y	y
mult	4	n	y	y	y	y

Table 6.1.: Overview on which token reuse criteria will return true due to which change. The abbreviations of the criteria mean the folling: *sse* : same sequence element, *alt* : corresponding sequence element in different alternative but represents same property/literal, *val* : token value comparison and *mult* : multiple token value occurrences.

For example, a token matching the *sse* as well as the *val* property would have a reuse factor of $10^{-1} + 0 + 10^{-3} + 0 = 0.101$. A property matching the *sse* as well as the *mult* property would, in turn, have a reuse factor of $10^{-1} + 0 + 0 + 10^{-4} = 0.1001$ which would lead to the reuse of the former token as it has the higher reuse factor.

6.3.2.8. Running Example

In the running example, the reusability of the tokens results in the assignment depicted in Figure 6.11. For the first changed region two candidates for token reusability exist. Both tokens `valueType` as well as `bo` stem from the same *reference* version which originally was `bo`. For the latter token several criteria for token reuse are fulfilled where for the former non is true:

The sequence element for $bo^{reference}$ is the same as bo^{lexed} because during the batch parsing phase, the sequence element for the literal `bo` was assigned to the *lexed* version of the token. Additionally the value of the token is the same as before. Therefore the reuse factor of bo^{lexed} w.r.t. $bo^{reference}$ is 0.101. Whereas the reuse factor for the `valueType` token is 0. Therefore, FURCAS will retain the versioning link for the bo^{lexed} token while removing it from the `valueType` token.

In the second region there are three tokens that are candidates for token reuse `customer`, `< –` and `ordered`. Obviously the last token is the one with the highest reuse factor as it matches *alt* and *val* which results in a factor of 0.011 which is higher than those of the other tokens, which is 0. Therefore, the versioning link of the `ordered` token is retained whereas the links of the other two tokens are removed.

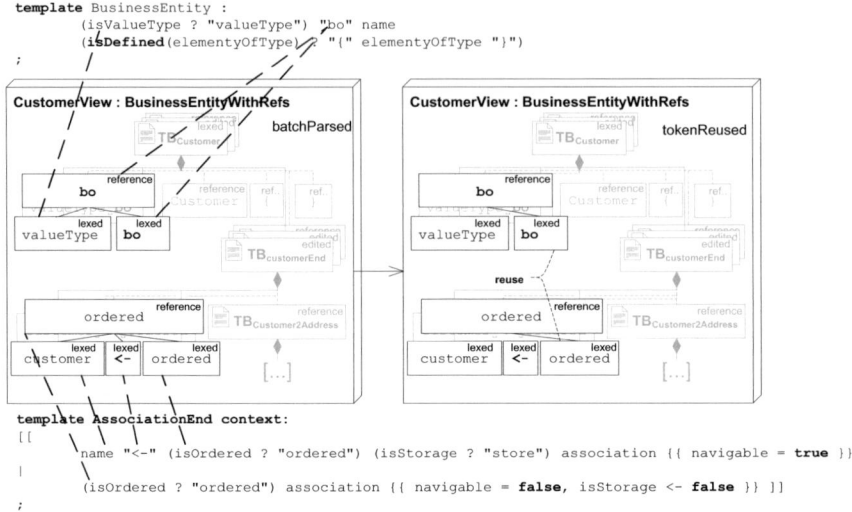

```
template BusinessEntity :
        (isValueType ? "valueType") "bo" name
        (isDefined(elementyOfType) ? "{" elementyOfType "}")
;
```

Figure 6.11.: Decision on token reuse made for the *parsed* version of the running example.

6.3.2.9. Handling of Errors and Inconsistencies in the Parsing Phase

If during the batch parsing phase a parse error occurs, for example because no matching template was found for a given modified stream of tokens, a TextBlock will be marked as *incomplete*. Still, the state of the modified region will be persistable and if further modifications are made, another attempt for the incremental update process is conducted. To indicate that there is an inconsistent region, FURCAS will mark it with one or more error markers depending on the amount of errors recognised.

The modifications are persisted even when the underlying domain model is changed. This enables for later-on merging of conflicting regions. As soon as the textual representation of the inconsistent region is again in a parseable state a merge based on both versions can be performed. This merge is based directly on the underlying model, as there may be multiple representations overlapping on the model. And as these representations may be partial a text based merge is not possible. The actual model merging process is beyond the scope of this thesis. However, there are multiple publications that deal with that problem, such as [KPP06] or [Bar08].

268

6.3.2.10. Textblocks Merging

In this phase the original textblocks model gets merged with the stub model produced by the incremental parsing phase. Algorithm 2 shows how this process works. A *lexed* TextBlock b is considered *mergeable* for a *parsed* TextBlock b^{parsed} if both represent the same element in the domain model and only differ in changes that would still retain the identity of the element. There are several criteria upon which this is decided. Based on a computed *mergeability factor* textblocks that are candidates for merging FURCAS completes the final *parsed* version of a TextBlock.

Computation of the Mergeability Factor The following list represents also the hierarchy in which the candidate TextBlocks are checked for their mergeability.

1. getTemplate(b) = getTemplate(b^{parsed}), which means that b and b^{parsed} were produced according to the same template within the mapping definition.

2. Chosen alternatives within the same template. A TextBlock may be constructed using a different alternative than its previous version while still being mergeable. However, if there is more than one reuse candidate which only differ in the chosen alternative of the same template, FURCAS will choose the one where the chosen alternatives still match best. A best match of alternatives is determined starting from the top level alternatives going down the sub alternatives. In the following example `template Alts :` `[[top`$_{1,a}$` |` `top`$_{1,b}$`]] [[` `top`$_{2,a}$` |` `top`$_{2,b}$`]]` `;`, there are two top level alternative sequences `top`$_1$ and `top`$_2$. Note that in this case it is possible that for a b with alternatives `top`$_{1,a}$, `top`$_{2,a}$ there is TextBlock b_1^{parsed} that matches `top`$_{1,a}$, `top`$_{2,b}$ and one TextBlock b_2^{parsed} that matches `top`$_{1,b}$, `top`$_{2,a}$. In this case the mergeability depends on the next lower prioritised mergeability features.

3. It might by the case that through changes in the call hierarchy of the templates a differently moded template for the same class was triggered. However, the element might still be considered the same and therefore b mergeable with b^{parsed}.

4. The number of tokens that where *reused* within the TextBlock. The more, tokens are reused from a b to a b^{parsed} the higher is the mergeability factor for this combination. If up to this point in the decision hierarchy two b^{parsed} are still considered equally the one with the higher number of reusabel tokens will be preferred. Note

that at least one reusable token is required to keep a TextBlock "alive". If there are no tokens left that are considered to be reusable for tokens of the *reference* version from within the TextBlock, it is not mergeable. Furthermore, FURCAS will later-on detect that the TextBlock has no textual representation anymore which will lead to the deletion of the TextBlock including its corresponding model element. The reuse factor at this stage is multiplied with the amount of tokens that were reused.

5. An override rule may have been specified by the language developer that may override one or more of these criteria. If a language developer identifies cases where a specialised behaviour concerning reuse should be used it is possible to define a special `ReuseStrategy` for a `TextBlockDefinition`.

The index in the list of mergeability properties also represents their priority when it comes to the determination of the *mergeability factor* of TextBlocks. The computation works the same way as the *reusability factor* for tokens. The TextBlock with the highest *mergeabilityFactor* will be considered the *mergeable* one for a given b.

$$
mergeabilityFactor(b, b^{parsed}) = \sum_{p \in mergeabilityProperties}
$$

$$
\begin{cases}
\#(reusedTokens(b, b^{parsed})) * 10^{priority(p)} & \text{if } matches_p(b^{parsed}) \text{ and } p = 4 \\
10^{priority(p)} & \text{if } matches_p(b^{parsed}) \\
0 & \text{else}
\end{cases}
$$

Apart from the rules that indicate the factor of mergeability of a given TextBlock, there are also changes that explicitly do not contribute to the reuse factor:

1. Comparison of tokens that correspond to optional elements within the mapping definition can be removed/added without contributing to the *mergeability* of b^{parsed} and b.

2. Tokens that belong to a property with a to-n cardinality (such as separators) can be removed/added without contributing to the *mergeability* of b^{parsed} and b.

3. Furthermore, `OmittedTokens` meaning for example, whitespaces and comments also can be added/removed without contributing to the *mergeability* of b^{parsed} and b.

4. The actual editing action that was performed by the user. This is represented in the history of the self-versioning TextBlocks model that was tracked since the last completed editing action.

Algorithm for Merging TextBlocks Algorithm 2 iterates is called during the incremental update process for each pair of TextBlocks (b, b^{parsed}) where the *reference* version of a token l is contained in the subnodes of b and the *lexed* version of l is assigned to b^{parsed}. The algorithm decides whether b and b's corresponding model element is retained or not. The algorithm works based on the assignment of the reused tokens to the TextBlocks in *parsed* version. Thus, it can be ensured that all potentially reusable TextBlocks can be analysed using their previous versions and newly assigned/removed tokens.

For each candidate TextBlock that is *mergeable* (line 2), all contained tokens of b^{parsed} are analysed. If they were not reused or their value changed the corresponding property will be updated using this value. Furthermore, if the token was not originally contained in b it is now assigned to it (lines 3-11).

In the next step each sub-TextBlock of b^{parsed} is analysed and tried to be merged with a reuse candidate which is computed from the original parent TextBlocks of the tokens that are now assigned to b^{parsed}. If b'_{merged} was newly created or moved to a different parent the corresponding properties within the model element connected to b need to be updated (lines 12-23).

TextBlocks that now got all contained elements removed (because their tokens were assigned to different TextBlocks) are deleted and therefore also their connected model elements using `deleteRemovedSubblocksInclCorrespElements(b)` (line 24).

If a TextBlock b^{parsed} is not mergeable, it will be completed by the algorithm (line 27). During this process all tokens are finally assigned to b^{parsed} and it is integrated into the TextBlocks tree. Furthermore the transient model element referenced by it will be made explicit and integrated into the domain model.

ReuseStrategies for TextBlocks The ability to specify `ReuseStrategies` on a template based level enables further flexibility concerning the retainment of model elements. We use OCL as language to specify this behaviour. The OCL expression can access all versions of the current TextBlock as well as the attached model elements. Furthermore, predefined operations that allow to navigate the relations between the TextBlocks model and the domain model are available. A reuse strategy

Input: A pair of TextBlocks b, b^{parsed} for which holds:

$$\exists l \in L \mid version(l, reference) \in toks(b) \wedge (version(l, lexed), b^{parsed})$$
$$\in tokenAssignment$$

Output: An textblock b' that represents the merge version of b with b^{parsed}.

1   **Procedure** mergeTextBlocks(b, b^{parsed}) :
2   **if** (b, b^{parsed}) *is mergeable* **then**
3   **foreach** $t \in getTokensFrom(b^{parsed})$ **do**
4   **if** *not t was reused or t.value changed* **then**
5   setPropertyValue(getCorrespElement(b), t)
6   b_{parent} = getParentBlock(t)
7   **if** $b_{parent} \neq b$ **then**
8   relocateToken(t, b)
9   **end**
10   **end**
11   **end**
12   **foreach** $b'^{parsed} \in getSubBlocks(b^{parsed})$ **do**
13   b'_{org} = getReuseCandidate(b'^{parsed})
14   b'_{merged} = mergeTextBlocks(b'_{org}, b'^{parsed})
15   **if** b'_{merged} *was newly created or moved* **then**
16   addToBlock(b, b'_{merged})
17   **if** b'_{merged} *is considered to be removed* **then**
18   deleteElement(getCorrespElement(b'_{org}))
19   deleteBlock(b'_{org})
20   **end**
21   **end**
22   **end**
23   deleteRemovedSubblocksInclCorrespElements(b)
24   **return** b
25   **else**
26   completeTextBlock(b^{parsed})
27   consider b to be removed
28   **return** b^{parsed}
29   **end**

Algorithm 2: TextBlock merge phase.

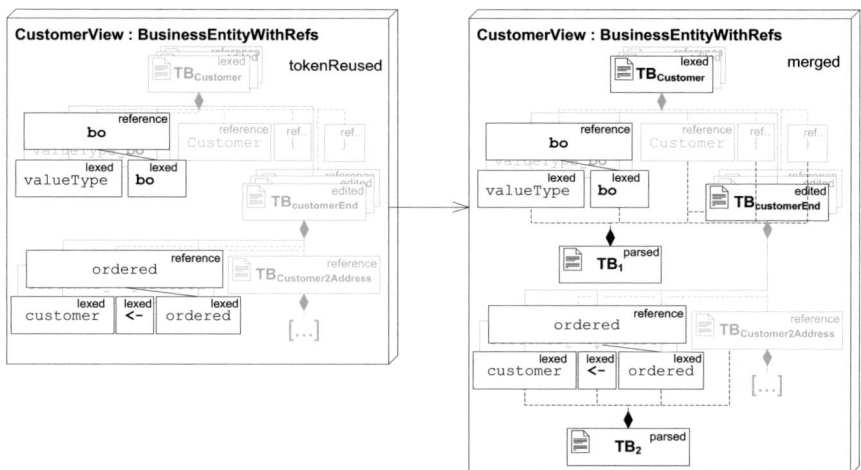

Figure 6.12.: Assignment of *lexed* and *rerference* tokens to the *parsed* version of TextBlocks.

uses an OCL statement like this: `tokenForProperty(reference.name).value = tokenForProperty(edited.name).value` which lets a TextBlock including its corresponding model element only then be reused if the tokens representing the "name" property of the element have still the same value.

6.3.2.11. Running Example

In the running example used throughout the previous Sections, the changes applied to the TextBlock model through the different previous phases would lead to the merging of two pairs of TextBlocks as illustrated in Figure 6.12. FURCAS creates TextBlock TB_1 and TB_2 according to the batch parser production rules and assigns the consumed tokens to as weak sub nodes to the newly created TextBlocks. Based on this information FURCAS computes the mergeability factor for all candidate TextBlocks. Thus, TB_1 will have a mergeability factor of $10^{-1} + 10^{-2} + 0 + (5 * 10^{-4}) + 0 = 0.1104$. As there is no other merge candidate for this TextBlock, TB_1 will be merged with $TB_{Customer}$. The same applies for TB_2 which has a mergeability factor of $10^{-1} + 0 + 0 + (2 * 10^{-4}) + 0 = 0.1002$ and the only candidate for merging is $TB_{customerEnd}$.

6.3.2.12. Handling of Errors and Inconsistencies in the Merging Phase

During merging of the different versions of a TextBlock-model errors may occur. For example the decision of whether a parsed TextBlock is mergeable with a TextBlock in reference version might be true for more than one TextBlock. According to the rules given in the previous section, this might be the case if the tokens of an old TextBlock are distributed over two new TextBlocks and all other merge factors are also true for both TextBlocks. A concrete example would be as follows: Starting from a textual representation `void a() { doSth(); }` of a business object declaring a method a, a change to its textual representation is made such that the first part of the method's text is reused by text representing a method a_1': `void a() { noOp(); }`. However, by inserting a closing brace within a, a_1' is finished and a second method a_2' can be recognised: `void b() { doSth(); }`. As tokens of a are reused within a_1' as well as a_2' it cannot be generically decided whether the TextBlocks of a_1' or a_2' should be merged with a.

For such cases, there is a default behaviour which prefers the first mergeable TextBlock over latter ones. Additionally it is, again, possible to consult the *ReuseStrategies*, in order to decide which of the tokens are responsible for making up the identity of an element. For the previous example, it could be specified that the name of a method, i.e., a, always represents the identity of a method element. Then the decision above would result in a_1' being reused for a, as this is the TextBlock which includes the name token.

6.3.2.13. Model Update Transformation

After the mergeable TextBlocks have been prepared in the TextBlock merging phase, it is now possible to update the domain model according to the mergeable and new TextBlocks. This is done by a model to model transformation T_{tb2dom} (see Figure 6.13) which uses as input both the reference TextBlock-model as well as the parsed version of the TextBlock-model. Based on the mergeability of the TextBlocks in the parsed TextBlock-model, new elements are created or existing elements are updated in the domain model.

Higher-Order Transformation for Generating the Update Transformation
The model update transformation is automatically derived from the mapping by a higher-order transformation (HOT). This $T_{map2qvt}$ HOT uses as input the mapping for a specific view type in combination with the referenced metamodel and produces the model update

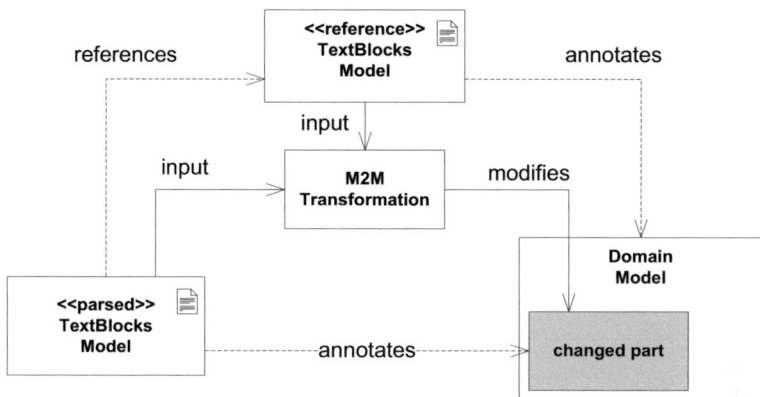

Figure 6.13.: Transformation T_{tb2dom} updates the corresponding part of the domain model based on the changes represented in the two different TextBlock-models.

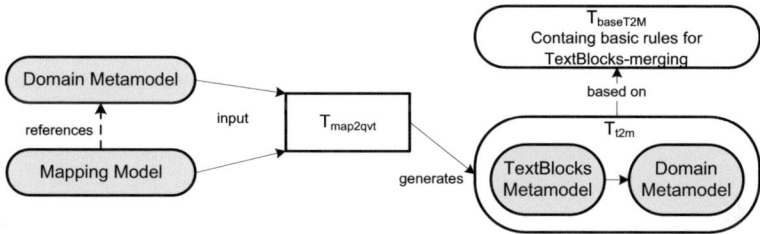

Figure 6.14.: The higher-order transformation $T_{map2qvt}$ genererates the synchronisation transformation T_{t2m}.

transformation T_{t2m} that then transforms from a TextBlock-model into a corresponding instance of the domain metamodel. An overview on this process is given in Figure 6.14.

The generated T_{t2m} is based on a special transformation $T_{baseT2M}$ that serves as library for the complex decisions that are done when deciding how TextBlocks are merged. These basic transformation rules are consulted by the generated transformation in order to decide if new elements should be created or if existing ones should be reused. Basically, $T_{baseT2M}$ encodes the reusability and mergeability computations as presented in the previous Sections. Thus, one part of $T_{baseT2M}$ is the determination whether one TextBlock is mergeable with a certain other one. Listing 6.5 gives an impression on this specific part of the transformation.

```
47 top relation Mergeable {
48   checkonly domain referenceTB reference : textblocks::TextBlock {
49     version = Version::REFERENCE };
50   checkonly domain parsedTB parsed : textblocks::TextBlock {
51     version = Version::PARSED };
52   when {
53     let candidates = referenceTB.allTokens()->collect(tok |
54       tok.getOtherVersion(VersionEnum::PARSED).parentBlock) in
55     parsedTb = candidates->sortedBy(
56        candidate | mergeabilityFactor(candidate))->last() }
57 }
```

Listing 6.5: Excerpt of the base transformation $T_{baseT2M}$ for text to model synchronisation showing the *Mergeable* relation.

A generated transformation T_{t2m} then refers to $T_{baseT2M}$ in its *when* clauses in order to decide upon the reuse of an existing domain model element or the creation of a new instance. Figure 6.6 gives an example for this usage. Notice that the transformation has four domains. The first domain for the view type model (viewtype) matches the template which is matched which defines the model construction rules. The structure of this match pattern resembles the structure of the template. For example, conditional elements, such as the declaration of the valueType property in the running example, shown Listing 6.1, also the surrounding elements will be matched. The second and third domain match the reference and parsed TextBlocks, respectively. For the parsed TextBlock the template should be the same as the one from the first domain. Futhermore, in this domain, the tokens of the parsed TextBlock are matched. Tokens for mandatory elements will be directly matched using a collection template (cf. [Obj11]). In the running example, this is the token for the name property. Finally, the fourth domain matches the domain model element. Token values responsible for attributes of an element will be set here. In the running example, the value of the name attribute is set to the value coming from the corresponding token.

The when clause is responsible for selecting the correct pair of reference and parsed TextBlocks. The Tb2Bo relation therefore calls the Mergeable relation in its when clause. This will decide upon the actual combination of TextBlock pairs that the relation matches.

Optional attributes will have their own relations which will be called in the where clause of their main relations. Whether the relation holds or not depends on whether the corresponding token is present. In the example given in Listing 6.6 the

`BusinessObject_ValueType` is called to check for a token that corresponds to the `valueType` property.

Properties of model elements that are not primitive valued attributes but refer to other model elements are handled by separate relations. These relations are responsible for the creation of the corresponding model element, just as the example in Listing 6.6 shows but in addition they will establish the link to the corresponding model element of their parent TextBlock.

In addition to the merging relation an additional relation without the matching of the reference version will be generated by FURCAS. This relation has the exact inverse of the when clause for the merging relation. This relation is responsible for instantiating a new element if there is no existing element to merge with.

Mapping View Type Constructs to Transformation Constructs Depending on the used constructs (cf. Section 2.1.3.2) in the view type definition, FURCAS maps them to specific constructs in the generated transformation. As shown above, the basic relation created for a template is responsible for matching the template, the mergeable TextBlocks as well as the target model element. Mandatory features will be matched directly in this relation by matching the tokens with the corresponding sequence elements in the parsed TextBlock. Other constructs such as alternatives or conditionals are matched as follows:

Conditionals and Alternatives A conditional element, such as (`isDefined(` `valueType ) ?  "valueType"`) specified in a template will cause the generation of an additional relation. This relation will be called from the `where` clause of the template's main relation. The call generated in the `where` clause then has the form `RelationName(TextBlock, ModelElement,` `conditionalSequenceElement)` or `true`. The `or true` part is required because a where predicate in QVT may only return true. However, as in this case the relation will only hold if the token is present, the false value needs to be prevented. In this additional relation the source domain will check for the existence of a token that refers to the enclosed sequence element. If such a token could be found the transformation will update the property accordingly.

A conditional may be a ternary expression of the form $condition?alt_1 : alt_2$. This means depending on the condition different alternatives including different sequence elements may be chosen. For each alternative a separate

```
58 top relation Tb2Bo {
59   checkonly domain viewtype template : TCS::Template {
60     metaReference = mofClass : mof::Class {
61       name = 'BusinessObject'
62     }
63     sequence : TCS::Sequence {
64       elements = namePropSE : TCS::Property{
65         metaReference = nameMetaProp : mof::Attribute {
66           name = 'name'
67         }
68       }
69       [...]--match conditional containing the value type property
70       valueTypePropSE : TCS::Property{
71         metaReference = valueTypeMetaProp : mof::Attribute {
72           name = 'valueType'
73         }
74       [...]
75     }
76   };
77   checkonly domain TB tbReference : textblocks::TextBlock {
78     correspondingModelElements = boRef : BusinessObject {}
79   }
80   checkonly domain TB tbParsed : textblocks::TextBlock {
81     correspondingModelElements = bo : BusinessObject {}
82     textBlockDefinition = tbDefRef: textblocks::TextBlockDefinition{
83       template = template : TCS::Template {}
84     },
85     subNodes = sNodes : OrderedSet(DocumentNode) {
86       _ ++
87       --match all tokens for mandatory features
88       nameTok : textBlocks::LexedToken{
89         sequenceElement = namePropSE,
90         value = nameVal
91       }
92       ++ _
93   };
94   enforce domain BO bo : businessObjects::BusinessObject {
95     name = nameVal
96   }
97   when {
98     Mergeable(tbParsed, tbReference) implies boRef = bo
99   }
100  where {
101    --each optional feature will have its own relation e.g., the
102    --value type relation will check if there exists a corresponding
103    -- token for the property and set the value on bo accordingly.
104    -- As there also may be no such token, we need to add "or true".
105    BusinessObject_ValueType(tbParsed, bo, valueTypePropSE) or true;
106  }
107 }
```

Listing 6.6: Excerpt of the generated model synchronisation transformation T_{t2m}.

relation will be generated containing the respective patterns for matching the alternative's tokens and the corresponding properties of the model element. As only one of the alternatives may match the calling predicate in the `where` clause of the template's main relation will have the following form: `RelationAlt1(TextBlock, ModelElement, conditionalSequenceElement)` or `RelationAlt2(TextBlock, ModelElement, conditionalSequenceElement)`

Alternatives are handled similar to conditionals. For each alternative as well as the its sub-alternatives a separate relation will be generated which are then called from the template's main relation and parent alternative's relation respectively.

Property Inits and Queries As propery inits in FURCAS are already present as OCL expressions, they can simply be included into the generated transformation. The assignment of these expressions to the domain elements property is performed in the `where` clause of the relation. For example, a property init `{{ name = parent.name.concat('C')}}` defined in the view type definition will result in the following predicate: `where { elem.name = parent.name.concat('C') }`.

The same applies for queries that a view type includes. The "?"-expressions defined in a query are replaced with the values of the corresponding tokens. For example, a query `ref {query = self.elements->select(name = ?)}` will result in the following predicate: `where { ref = self.elements ->select(name = tokForRef.value)}`.

6.3.2.14. Running Example

According to the mergeability computation of the previous phase, all TextBlocks of the running example could be reused by their parsed version correspondents. Thus, the update transformations will match the mergeable rules for the modified elements. The main relation for the business object `Tb2Bo` will match the existing business object *customer*. As now also a `valueType` token is present, the `BusinessObject_ValueType` relation, called from the top relations `where` clause, will set the `valueType` attribute of *customer* to `true`. As the alternative of the $TB_{customerEnd}$ changed from variant 2 to variant 1(see the view type definition in Listing 6.1) where the name of the local association end is explicitly stated the update transformation will also need to update this name. The property init of variant 2 set the name of the association end to "unnamed". As this this value is now explicitly represented by the a token the transformation will set the name to the token's value, which is "customer".

6.3.3. Incremental Updates of the Textual Model After Type (B) Changes

Whenever a cut/copy/paste is done within the FURCAS editor, not only the text is stored in the clipboard but also the underlying TB-model. Depending on the part of the text that is cut and the position where it is pasted again different updates are performed.

If the TextBlock-type of the pasted block is the same as the one over which it is pasted: A deletion of the overwritten part and move of the pasted part to its (potentially) new parent block is performed. Afterwards the incremental update transformation for the domain model is triggered based upon the the the (re-)moved TextBlocks. This also works if more than one TextBlock is pasted and one or a tuple of them matches the original TextBlock type, plus the surrounding newly pasted TextBlocks are allowed to appear at this position according to the mapping definition.

If the TextBlock-types do not match the result of the paste would be inconsistent according to the mapping. Therefore, the reference version of the overwritten will be kept and the pasted TextBlock will be appended into the edited version of the parent TextBlock. As soon as a consistent state is reached to further editing actions the class A update transformation can be used again to update the domain model accordingly.

6.4. Efficient Attribute Evaluation for OCL Based Attribute Grammars

As presented in Chapter 5 the FURCAS approach for specifying textual views heavily relies on the specification of OCL based attribute for the evaluation of non-syntactically specified properties within the domain model. These OCL expressions are used for the creation of views as well as the construction as well as updating of domain model elements upon changes through a view. However, especially due to the fact that a model can be edited through multiple views, these expressions have to be reevaluated whenever their result value may have changed. Thus, the same constructs of a model may have been created using different views types, it needs to be determined which parts of a model are under *maintenance* of which view type, and therefore needs to fulfil the construction and property rules defined in that view.

For the decision *when* an OCL expression needs to be evaluated in *general* FURCAS employs an approach called OCL Impact Analysis [AHK06]. OCL Impact Analysis

(IA) is used to solve the problem of, does an OCL expression o defined on a context type c change its value given a change event e. Therefore, the IA first performs a step called *Class Scope Analysis* which computes the set of event filters (such as "filter for `AttributeChangeEvent` of a specific attribute a of a (meta-)class m") which filter all events that, by looking statically at them, could possibly invalidate the current value of the expression. This step can be performed at design or build time of the repressions. Later on, during the runtime of an expression a second phase called *Instance Scope Analysis* can be performed. This step finds, for an expression o and a change event e all context elements c for which the value of o may have changed. This is achieved by navigating backwards over the OCL expression to all possible context elements.

The *Class Scope Analysis* has been thoroughly researched in different publications such as [CT05, CT09, AHK06]. However, the *Instance Scope Analysis* has only been described incompletely, omitting difficult structures such as operation calls and loops. Furthermore, there is a multitude of additional optimisations that reduce the effort of computing the possible contexts elements. An improved IA approach was developed in the broader scope of the creation of the FURCAS approach. However, the presentation of the details of this approach lies beyond the scope of this thesis.

Only to give an indication on the performance impact of the IA in comparison to a naive approach that reevaluates all constraints upon a change the validation results for this approach are summarised here. Figure 6.15 shows a comparison of OCL query reevaluation times with and without impact analysis for a given set of OCL queries taken from the Runlet case study (cf. Section 7.3.2). The delta propagation, also shown in the diagram is a further optimisation of the IA approach. With all optimisations the revevaluation time remains nearly constant with the size of the model on which the query is performed. In contrast, the reevaluation time for a naive approach which requires the reevaluation of all queries grows linearly.

In conclusion, the IA approach allows FURCAS to incrementally and efficiently re-evaluate the OCL expressions that are used in the *query* (cf. Section 5.3.2.2) as well as the OCL property init expressions (cf. Section 5.3.2.1) used in the FURCAS view type definitions. As the IA works on a predefined scope, which may include the whole work-space a developer works on and FURCAS registers all of these expressions in this scope, it is possible to iteratively satisfy all these expressions by reevaluating them according to the IA.

As there may be an arbitrary number of overlapping view types where each of them defines such OCL rules that are reevalutated by the IA cycles may occur. For example,

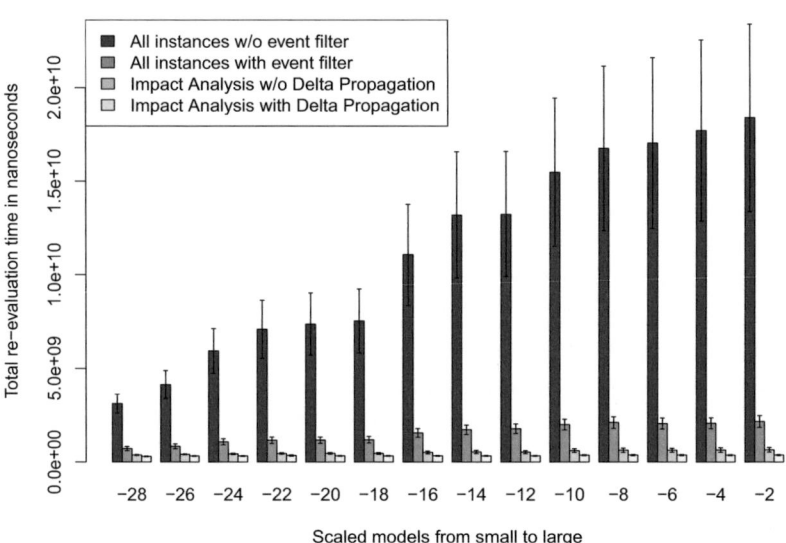

Figure 6.15.: Comparison of performance for reevaluating a given set of OCL queries with and without impact analysis. The x-axis shows different model sizes where -28 is the smallest model (meaning 28 metamodel packages where cropped out of the test model) and -2 is the largest model. The y-axis shows the evaluation time of around 250 different OCL queries from within the view type definition, meaned with a 90% confidence interval (CI). The darkest and left-most bar is the reference time with no impact analysis activated. The next bars show the re-evaluation times with subsequently activated optimisations and impact analysis.

an OCL property init may define the expression `{{ x = self.aToB.y + 1 }}` which computes the value of the attribute x to equal the value of the attribute y of an element b that is reachable through the association `aToB`. Whenever, y changes its value x will be updated accordingly. Assuming a second view type that defines a different property init on a template for b as `{{ y = self.bToA.x + 1 }}` the reevaluation of both property inits will result in a cycle. To avoid this kind of problem a cycle detection mechanism, such as [Niv04], is required. However, this problem is more in the focus of the IA approach in general and is therefore beyond the scope of this thesis.

6.5. UUIDs and Views

The fact that an element has an internal ID or UUID that is not shown in any user view and should never be changed needs to be tackled in order to be able to provide editor support on top of UUID-based model repositories. However, taking a closer look on the problem reveals that the problems occurring in this context are of a much more general nature. Hiding information that is contained within a model but still allowing to edit the non-hidden parts while keeping the hidden parts consistent is a significant problem when talking about editable views.

Consequently, this means that is is possible to tackle the UUID problem from the angle of *partial* view types. No view type definition should include this special property and therefore every view type should be considered partial. Therefore, the UUID problem can be reduced to the partial view type problem. Every view type on a UUID-based model will mask the UUID. This makes all view type partial concerning the metamodel.

Partial view types need special synchronization actions to allow the specification of how to handle hidden parts of the model when other parts are changed. It is not possible to re-create an element only using the textual representation of one of its views as the information might not be complete when it is a partial view type. The attribute values and links that are not visible in the textual representation can not be recreated by using the information from a single view as they are simply not present in the view. Therefore, the UUID retainment problem is not different from the problem that view based textual modelling faces anyway when it comes to partial views types. With some theoretical extensions to the employed metamodels of a textual view based modelling environment it becomes clear that FURCAS will retain the UUID of underlying model elements just as it would retain any partially viewed element.

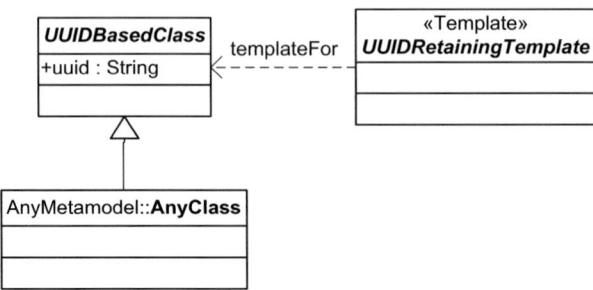

Figure 6.16.: Artificial extension of meta-classes by UUIDBasedClass.

In order to map the UUID-retainment problem to a partial view type problem we need to apply some implicit extensions to each metamodel. What needs to be done is to represent the UUID of a model element using standard meta-modelling means. Figure 6.16 shows that this can be done. A meta-class UUIDBasedClass is implicitly added as base class for every manually modelled meta-class. UUIDBasedClass has exactly one property uuid. The most flexible primitive type to represent the value of the UUID is the String-type. Therefore the type of uuid is defined as String. By introducing an artificial super-class to each meta class of a metamodel the fact that model elements have UUIDs is made explicit. Furthermore, consider that the attribute is unchangeable and all instances will get a unique value assigned upon instantiation.

With these preconditions, one can say that an elements UUID is retained exactly when the element itself is not deleted and re-created. As this is the major purpose of the FURCAS incremental update approach presented in this chapter one can say, that if FURCAS is validated to serve the generic purpose of retaining partially viewed elements, it also meets the requirement of UUID retainment. Chapter 7 will show that this is the case.

6.6. Synchronisation from Model to Textual Views

As discussed in chapter 4 the synchronisation between a model and its views can be considered as two transformations (or one bidirectional transformation) defined on the metamodels of the (domain) model and the respective view model (thus called the *View Metamodel*). Then one requirement to the transformation is to allow for certain areas where manual modifications are retained even if the source model has eminent pending changes and thus require the transformation to be re-executed. This requirement is, for example, present for those parts of a view that do not directly represent parts of the model but rather are defaults generated by an initial pretty printing transformation. Such a transformation is mostly used to generate default layout information in a target view model.

Now, to be able to retain changes to that kind of format information without loosing them upon re-execution of the model-to-view transformation it is required to add knowledge about how to identify changes that have been applied to the target model to the transformations. Furthermore, based on the identification of target model changes it needs to be possible to specify how these changes should be handled by the transformation. I.e., if they should be overwritten, or certain types of changes such as additions or removals should be treated differently.

6.6.1. Running Example

The running example to explain all kinds of retainment scenarios employs as source model a domain model representing business entities, associations between them as well as methods declared on them as presented in Chapter 2 on Page 18. This model is transformed to a target model being a textual view on the domain model and expressed in the TextBlock decorator metamodel presented in Section 5.4.3 on Page 222.

The example model, as depicted in Figure 6.17 consists of a simple business entity "Customer" having two methods "hasDiscount" and "hasDebits". The textual view is generated using the transformation T_{bo2tb}. Furthermore T_{bo2tb} also generates default layout information (depicted as $\llcorner$, $\rightarrow$ and $\lrcorner$).

A transformation that realises the mapping within the given example is sketched in Listing 6.8. The transformation consists of different types of relations. First relations such as `BusinessObject2TextBlock` or `MethodSignature2TextBlock` are responsible for creating TextBlocks from elements of the domain model. Furthermore, relations like `AddTokensForBusinessObject2TextBlock` add tokens to the TextBlocks representing keywords as well as values from the domain model that should be visible in the view. Additionally, relations such as `AddLayoutTokens` add additional layout information to the TextBlock. In this case this is achieved by interleaving each pair of LexedTokens in a TextBlock with an additional OmittedToken

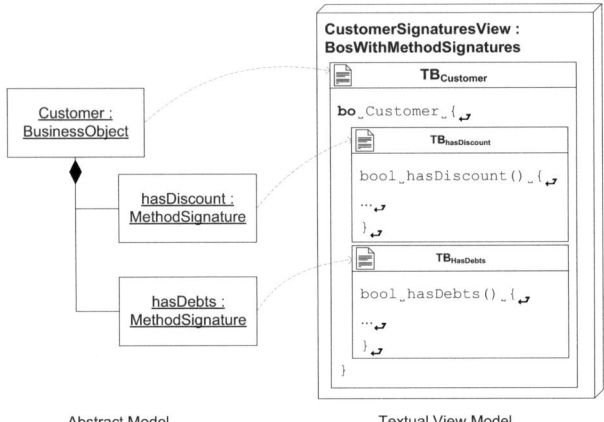

Figure 6.17.: Example model showing source and target model of a model to view transformation.

(See the collection template expression in AddLayoutTokens). Addition of further layout information such as → and ↵is omitted in here.

6.6.2. Incremental Pretty Printing

For a complete view based approach it is also necessary to update views upon changes to the model. In our case what we need is a backwards transformation from the domain model to the TextBlocks model that incrementally updates existing views, or if none

```
108  viewtype BosWithMethodSignatures {
109    template BusinessObject
110      : "bo" name "{"
111          methodSignatures
112      "}"
113    ;
114    template MethodSignature
115      : output name "(" implementation ")"
116    ;
117    ...
118  }
```

Listing 6.7: View type definition for business objects with method signatures.

```
119 top relation BusinessOject2TextBlock {
120   checkonly domain bo myBo : businessObjects::BusinessObject{ };
121   enforce domain tv textblock : furcas::textBlocks::TextBlock {
122     correspondingElement = myBo; };
123   where {
124     AddLayoutTokens(myBo, textblock);
125     AddTokensForBusinessObject2TextBlock(myBo, textblock);
126   }
127 }
128 relation AddTokensForBusinessObject2TextBlock {
129   checkonly domain bo myBo : businessObjects::BusinessObject{ };
130   enforce domain tv textblock : furcas::textBlocks::TextBlock {
131     tokens = classTok : furcas::textBlocks::LexedToken {
132       value = "bo"; };
133     tokens = nameTok : furcas::textBlocks::LexedToken {
134       value = myBo.name; };
135     [...]
136   };
137 }
138 relation AddLayoutTokens {
139   checkonly domain bo myBo : businessObjects::BusinessObject{ };
140   enforce domain tv textblock : furcas::textBlocks::TextBlock {
141     tokens = OrderedSet {
142       beforeTok : furcas::textBlocks::LexedToken,
143       formatTok : furcas::textBlocks::OmittedToken {
144         value = "␣"}
145       , afterTok : furcas::textBlocks::LexedToken }
146     };
147     [...]
148   };
149 }
150 top relation MethodSignature2TextBlock {
151   checkonly domain bo decl : businessObjects::MethodSignature{
152     businessObject = bo : businessObjects::BusinessObject {}
153   };
154   enforce domain tv textblock : furcas::textBlocks::TextBlock {
155     [...] };
156   where { [...] }
157   when { BusinessObject2TextBlock(bo, textblock);
158   }
159 }
```

Listing 6.8: Example Transformation: BusinessObjects to Textual View exists creates an initial version of it. FURCAS provides a pretty printer that implements this transformation. The pretty printer creates a *minimal* TextBlocks model from a given domain model according to the, bidirectionally specified, mapping definition.

TCS in its original form also provides a pretty printer that interpreted the mapping definition to create an initial textual representation of a given model. However, as FURCAS furthermore provides support for textual *views* a trivial version of the pretty printer that simply traverses a model and prints text is not enough. A view may also be a partial view on a model representing only a specific part of the actual domain model. Furthermore, a model might have been produced or modified by a different view (specified within a different mapping definition) and might therefore leave the producible image of another view.

To cope with this problem we introduced two concepts from the view type definition approach (cf. Chapter 5) are considered within the pretty printing approach:

1. FURCAS uses the pretty printing model transformation that tries to find a valid combination of template appliances that best suite the current combination of features of a given model element. Therefore, the two different kinds of `PropertyInit` definitions (cf. Section 5.3.2.1) that can be used in the mapping definition are considered . A *standard* `PropertyInit` has to be matched mandatorily for the template to be used as a pretty printing rule. Whereas a *default* `PropertyInit` is only used as additional hint for the pretty printer to favour one template over another in case both would be a match.

2. A `PropertyElement` defined within a template may be defined as being *partial*, which means that any subtree created down from this template is optional. If no matching template for the current view is found the whole subtree is omitted.

6.6.3. Detecting and Retaining Layout Modifications

The transformation from model to view does not only contain rules that are responsible for creating the textual representations of the model elements but also contains rules for default layout of the representing elements. There rules add `OmittedTokens` to a TextBlock. However, these rules should be handled differently to those creating the actual textual contribution of an element. It should be possible for a user that interacts with a view to freely adjust the layout of a view. This may result in addition, modification or removal of these `OmittedTokens`. To achieve the retainment of these changes to

```
160  top relation BusinessObject2TextBlock {
161    checkonly domain bo myBo : businessObjects::BusinessObject{ };
162    enforce domain tv textblock : furcas::textBlocks::TextBlock {
163      correspondingElement = myBo; };
164    where {
165      AddLayoutTokens(myBo, textblock);
166      AddTokensForBusinessOject2TextBlock(myBo, textblock);
167    }
168  }
169
170  -- @RP RetainLayoutModification:TARGET
171  relation AddLayoutTokens {
172    checkonly domain bo myBo : businessObjects::BusinessObject{ };
173    enforce domain tv textblock : furcas::textBlocks::TextBlock {
174      tokens = OrderedSet {
175        beforeTok : furcas::textBlocks::LexedToken,
176        formatTok : furcas::textBlocks::OmittedToken {
177          value = "␣"}
178        , afterTok : furcas::textBlocks::LexedToken }
179      };
180      [...]
181    };
182  }
183
184  [...]
```

Listing 6.9: Example Transformation: BusinessObjects to Textual View with *RetainmentPolicy* annotations

the view model, FURCAS employs a set of *RetainmentPolicies* (as introduced in Chapter 3).

Each rule that is considered a layout rule is annotated with a *target changed* ■▶ *RetainmentPolicy*. The *RetainmentPolicy* will make sure that the layout can be manually changed and these changes are retained across changes to the underlying model that are going to be propagated to the textual view.

The running example, including the *RetainmentPolicy* annotation is shown in Figure 6.9. An example change based on the running example given above would be the addition of a format element (OmittedToken) in the view model. The detection of this kind of change would work as follows. Suppose an addition of an additional OmittedToken ("␣") after the keyword bo. To be able to detect this addition, the change detection would analyse the traces of the transformation run $Trace_{Tbo2tv}$ and then identify that there is no tracelink that references the new OmittedToken ("␣") even though it could have been produced by the transformation (i.e., the

289

`AddLayoutTokens` relation). Thus, the result of the change identification would be $identifyTargetChanges(M_t, Trace_{T_{bo2tv}}) = \{\delta^+_{OmittedToken\langle "\_"\rangle}\}$. The added element is part of the target addition change set: $\delta^+_{OmittedToken\langle "\_"\rangle} \in \Delta_o^{+,targetChanges}$. As the *target changed RetainmentPolicy* retains elements that are in the target addition change set the omitted token will not be overwritten or removed upon an update from the domain model.

6.6.4. Supporting Selective Views

One of the key concepts of FURCAS is that it supports full featured selective or holistic textual views. Section 5.4.5 gave an introduction in how FURCAS supports selective textual views. As described in Section 4.5.1 on page 149, the selection scope of a view may either be *holistic*, *selective* or a mixture of both distinguished on a per template level. The sync transformation from domain model to textual view realises a *holistic approach* per default. This means, that whenever elements are added to the domain model, the views that cover that specific part of the model will update to include the element. For example, a view that shows business objects and their method signatures will show all added method signatures as soon as they are added to the domain model. In a *selective* view, the decision of whether to include an element into a view or not depends on the decision of the developer using the view. Thus, to realise *selective* views, the update transformation needs to be made aware of the selection of elements a developer made. FURCAS uses *RetainmentPolicies* (cf. Chapter 3) for this purpose.

6.6.4.1. *RetainmentPolicy* Annotations for the Model Update Transformation

Given a generated update transformation (using the approach introduced in Section 6.3.2.13) for a given view type that has properties that are declared as *selective* (using the `SelectivePArg` within the view type definition as presented in Section 5.4.5). In the transformation all those annotated transformation rules receive an additional *RetainmentPolicy* annotation. Depending on the type of selectiveness, i.e., *deletion*, *addition* or *addition and deletion* selective, different *RetainmentPolicy* are used:

Deletion Selective: Retaining a textual representation if if its underlying model element was removed is achieved by the "retain deleted if source changed exclusively" ($\blacktriangleleft^-$) *TypeSpecificRetainmentPolicy*. This will retain textual representations for removed

```
185  viewtype SelectiveMethodSignatures {
186    ...
187    template BusinessObject
188      : ... methodSignatures { selective = Addition } ...
189    ;
190    template MethodSignature
191      : output name implementation
192    ;
193  }
```

Listing 6.10: View type definition for business objects view with selected method signatures.

elements but will also allow to delete them manually. The latter case is supported due to the exclusiveness of the ◀⁻ *RetainmentPolicy* to source model changes. If the target model changed at the same time, this would indicate a manual deletion and thus the deletion is allowed to take place. If the "source changed" (◀■) *RetainmentPolicy* would have been used as basis also manual deletions, occurring as simultaneous changes to the target model would also have been undone.

Addition Selective: To achieve the behaviour not adding new elements to the view (target) model if new source elements occur but removing existing ones if they are removed from the (source) model FURCAS uses the type specific retainment policy "retain added if source changed exclusively" ◀⁺. The exclusiveness to the source model is required because if source at the same time a target model change occurred, this means that the element was added to the view from outside the transformation, i.e., by manually adding it to the view (cf. Section 6.6.4.2). In combination with with an additional policy "retain removed if target changed" ■▶⁻ also elements that were manually deleted from the view will not be added again.

Addition and Deletion Selective: If both types of selectiveness are defined, the higher order transformation that generates the model update transformation will create annotations for the respective transformation rules using the ◀⁺,⁻ *RetainmentPolicy*.

Listing 6.10 shows an example view type definition that is responsible for defining a textual view on business objects including a selection of their method signatures. The method signatures for a business object are defined to be handled selectively. Thus, the generated model update transformation, shown in Listing 6.11 incorporates the *RetainmentPolicies* that handle this selectiveness accordingly.

```
194  top relation BusinessOject2TextBlock {
195    checkonly domain bo myBo : businessObjects::BusinessObject{ };
196    enforce domain tv textblock : furcas::textBlocks::TextBlock {
197      correspondingElement = myBo; };
198    where {
199    AddLayoutTokens(myBo, textblock);
200    AddTokensForBusinessOject2TextBlock(myBo, textblock);
201    }
202  }
203  relation AddTokensForBusinessOject2TextBlock {
204    [...]
205  }
206  relation AddLayoutTokens {
207    [...]
208  }
209
210  /*
211  @TSRetainmentPolicy Addition_Selective_MethodSignatures1:
212    NEVER retainAdded: SOURCE_EX
213  @TSRetainmentPolicy Addition_Selective_MethodSignatures2:
214    NEVER retainDeleted: TARGET
215  */
216  top relation MethodSignatures2TextBlock {
217    checkonly domain bo decl : businessObjects::MethodSignatures{
218      businessObject = bo : businessObjects::BusinessObject {}
219    };
220    enforce domain tv textblock : furcas::textBlocks::TextBlock {
221    [...] };
222    where { [...] }
223    when { BusinessOject2TextBlock(bo, textblock);
224    }
225  }
```

Listing 6.11: Transformation business objects to textual view annotated with the generated *RetainmentPolicy* annotations.

6.6.4.2. Supporting Manual Additions to a Selective View

The dual operation for omitting the automatic addition of existing elements to a view once they are created is the explicit manual addition to a view. As this operation is an explicit command that is not part of the general model update transformation there need to be separate transformations for these commands. Therefore, to complement the selectiveness of templates in the view definition, FURCAS generates separate transformations for each of these commands. These transformation contain the rules for the creation of the textual representation of the selective element itself as well as all subtemplates that can possibly create child elements within the textual representation of the added element.

6.6.5. Handling Inconsistent Regions in an TextBlocks model

During the incremental parsing phase it is possible that a TextBlocks model is turned into an *inconsistent* or *incomplete* state. This state temporarily decouples the textual view from the underlying model and turns it out of sync. Until the errors in the textual representations are resolved and the synchronisation is re-established changes to the underlying model can not and should not be translated into the textual view. Otherwise, the inconsistent but presumably updated information would be lost. To avoid this loss of information FURCAS will protect this region from further updates from the underlying domain model.

The retainment policy approach presented in Chapter 3 not only supports the definition of *RetainmentPolicies* for transformation rules but also allows to define a scope within the target model for which certain *RetainmentPolicies* should apply. FURCAS uses this kind of *RetainmentPolicy* to protect the inconsistent region in the textual view model. Each TextBlock that is inconsistent is, at the same time FURCAS sets the `incomplete` flag to true, added to the *model element scope* of a *always* (◄■►) *RetainmentPolicy*. In this case not only a *target changed RetainmentPolicy* is used because also TextBlock that are themselves not directly modified but are not valid in their context anymore due to changed therein should be protected from being overwritten. The employed *always RetainmentPolicy* also includes protection for this kind of elements.

```
226 viewtype ConstMethodSignatures {
227   template BusinessObject
228     : "class" name "{" methodSignatures "}"
229     ;
230   template MethodSignature
231     : "const" output name "(" ")" implementation
232       {{ const = true }}
233     ;
234   ...
235 }
```

Listing 6.12: View type definition for business objects view with *const* method signatures.

6.6.6. Exclusion of Model Elements that Leave the Scope of a View

Having multiple partial view on the same underlying model also implies that there may occur situations where a model element leaves the scope of one view after a modification from another view. To always show the most recent version of the underlying model, a view is updated either directly when a change is performed to the underlying model, or upon re-opening it. When FURCAS performs this view update all elements that are not in the scope of the view type anymore are removed from the textual representation. However, in some situations this fact will be misleading or irritating for a developer that looks onto the modified view. He or she might think that the element was completely deleted and not just excluded from the view's scope.

To deal with this situation, FURCAS indicates such removals by a so called *change bar*, as it is also employed in pure text based IDEs such as the Eclipse Java Development Tools (JDT) [Ecl10a]. Figure 6.18 shows an example where this change bar indicates the removal of a method signature from a view where only method signatures that have their const flag set to true, are shown. The view type definition for this example is shown in Listing 6.12.

294

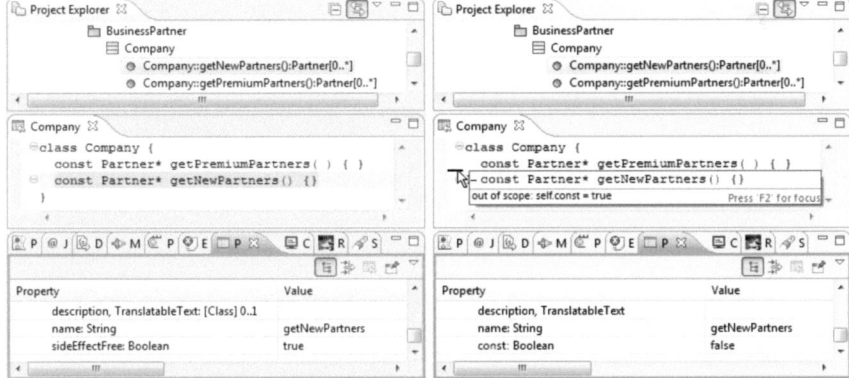

Figure 6.18.: Due to a change of the property value of `const` attribute of the method signature which decides upon its inclusion into the view the second method signature is removed from the view. In the image on the right hand side the editor shows the change bar which allows a developer to see what elements and why they were removed from the view.

Chapter 7.

Validation

The validation of the FURCAS approach is done on several levels. First, the view based properties of FURCAS are validated against the generic properties of view based modelling presented in Chapter 4. This validation is presented on a formal level in Section 7.1. This part validates the *adequacy* of FURCAS w.r.t. view based modelling in general. The view synchronisation process is a vital part of FURCAS. To validate the *applicability* and *usability* of this part of FURCAS, a validation against certain bidirectional view synchronisation properties, as presented by Matsuda et al. in [MHN⁺07] was conducted and is presented in Section 7.1.2.6.

The *correctness* of the incremental update approach is evaluated by means of a classification of possible change events that may occur in the textual view based editor. The argumentation for this part of the validation is presented in Section 7.2. Furthermore, some critical cases are analysed and discussed.

Finally, to evaluate the *applicability* in practice, as well as the *expressiveness* of FURCAS, several internal as well as industrial case studies were conducted. Having different foci, a selection of these case studies is presented in Section 7.3. To find out to which extent the view-based capabilities of FURCAS were exploited in these case studies, a Goal Question Metric (GQM) based metrics suite is used to gather metrics on different aspects of the view types that were defined in these case studies.

7.1. Validating the View Type and View Properties of FURCAS

Chapter 4 introduced formalisations of generic properties of views and view types in view-based modelling. As FURCAS was designed to contribute to the yet unsettled area of *textual* view-based modelling a validation against these properties will show to which extent FURCAS matches these criteria. The properties of views as well as view types are considered in the generic analysis in Chapter 4. Therefore, also both parts will be validated for FURCAS, the FURCAS view type definition approach against the view type properties (Section 7.1.1) and the TextBlock view approach against the view properties (Section 7.1.2).

7.1.1. Validation of the Generic View Type Properties of FURCAS

The generic components of a view type, according to Section 4.4, are defined by the tuple $VT = (MM, \Phi)$ where Φ defines the actual view construction rules. In the case of FURCAS, a view type definition incorporates all rules that are required by Φ. Both levels of a $p \in \Phi$ are included in this definition. The first level requires to define a projection function ϕ_p, that decides upon the inclusion of a model element into a view. This decision, in the case of FURCAS, is provided by the ability to define templates based on the type of an element. The second is the definition of a σ_p which lets a language engineer define certain selection patterns an element has to conform to. This selection function is supported by FURCAS by the definition of property sequence elements as well as property inits (cf. Section 5.3.2.1) within the templates of a view type.

Finally, for the construction of the layout of each $p \in \Phi$ FURCAS provides constructs inherited from TCS such as literal sequence elements as well as additional format control structures. The tighter definition of a view type given by Definition 4.3 which introduces the notion of a view metamodel, including transformations from (T_m) and to (T_v) this metamodel also fits the transformations employed in FURCAS. These transformations are given by the multi-phased incremental parsing and update mechanism (Section 6.3) as well as the pretty printing transformation (Section 6.6).

Based on these mappings, the view type properties of FURCAS are evaluated in the following sections.

7.1.1.1. Partiality and Completeness of View Types

The following lemmas will propose that FURCAS allows to define partiality and completeness properties as they were defined in Sections 4.4.2 to 4.4.3.1.

Lemma 7.1. FURCAS *allows to define partial view types.*

Proof. Assuming the combined selection and projection function ∂_p for each predicate p is expressed in FURCAS by the combination of a template t's meta-reference $type_t$ and the pattern described by the set of t's sequence elements Seq_t, there are several dimensions in which a view type definition can be partial:

The *partial concerning metamodel* property requires a view type to fulfil what is defined by Definition 4.3 on page 141. The projection based on the template type $type_t$ performed by FURCAS for a view type VT is formulated as a function ∂_{type}. ∂_{type} reduces the set of elements of a model M, representable by the view type, by those for which holds $\{e \in M \mid class(e) \in \bigcup_{t \in T_{VT}} mmelem(t)\}$. Therefore, it is always possible to define a view type $VT_{partial}$ for which a certain class $c_{omitted}$ is not part of this set. Thus, we can conclude that for such a $VT_{partial}$ the *partial* requirement is fulfilled by:

$$\exists M \in Models_{MM}, e \in M \mid \left(\forall p \in \Phi_{partial} \mid \left(\partial_p(e) = false\right)\right) \overset{class(e)=c_{omitted}}{\Longleftrightarrow}$$
$$\exists M \in Models_{MM}, e \in M \mid \left(\forall p \in \Phi_{partial} \mid \left(false = false\right)\right)$$

□

The proof for the fulfilment of all further partial and completeness properties works analogously.

7.1.1.2. Extending View Types

In an *extending* view type (cf. Section 4.4.4), information from more than one underlying model and/or metamodel can be jointly handled. This is, for example, useful for scenarios where a model is non-intrusively annotated with external information. This property can be fulfilled on different levels, depending on the elements which the view type may include. This level depends on the reachability of these included elements. The reachability of a target model element t from a model element f is given by a function $reachable_n(t)$ where n is the number of navigation steps required to get from f to t.

Lemma 7.2. FURCAS *supports view types which are extending with level $n = 1$.*

Proof. The templates of TCS and therefore also FURCAS are based on the classes from the metamodel referenced by the templates and their properties P_t, as given by Definition 5.4:

$$P_t = attributes(mmelem(t)) \cup \{a \in A \mid first(a) = mmelem(t) \vee second(a) = mmelem(t)\}$$

As both, $attributes()$ as well as the elements reachable through an association $a \in A$ are reached with $reachable_1(e)$ for a given element e we can say that $n = 1$ is also the maximum n for $reachable_n()$. □

7.1.1.3. Overlapping View Types

Chapter 4 defines two different notions of overlaps within view types. One is the *inter view type overlap* which denotes that there is more than one view type for a certain type of element. The other one is the *intra view type overlap* which denotes that an element may have multiple occurrences within the same view type. Both types are intended to be supported by FURCAS.

The former type, *inter view type overlap*, is not a problem w.r.t. to the mere definition of more than one view type for a certain element. This property can easily be supported as the definition of a view type in FURCAS is external to those of a metamodel. However, additionally the view instances need to support this option by allowing multiple view elements to refer to the same underlying model element. This property is validated in Section 7.1.2.2. The latter type, *intra view type overlap*, requires to define multiple templates for a single metamodel class within the *same* view type.

Lemma 7.3. FURCAS *supports overlapping view types.*

Proof. For the definition of view types, FURCAS uses template elements that refer to their corresponding class from the metamodel via the `metaReference` association. As there is no restriction on the multiplicity of the association end that points to a template, arbitrarily many templates for the same class of a metamodel may exist. This allows for *inter view type overlaps*.

A template t in FURCAS for a certain class of a metamodel may exist in different modes. Depending on the context, i.e., the possible parent templates which call t, a different mode for the template may exist (cf. Section 2.1.3.2 on modes for class templates). Therefore, the textual representation of an element e can be different and is representable multiple times within the same view.

(1) Assuming there is a template t with two modes $m1$ and $m2$ both being able to represent the same element e. (2) As each t_m may define its own sequence elements and therefore its own rules for the textual representation we can say that t_{m1} represents a single $p_{m1} \in \Phi$ and t_{m2} defines a single $p_{m2} \in \Phi$ where $p_{m1} \neq p_{m2}$. As per (1) we can conclude that $\partial_{p_{m1}}(e) = true \land \partial_{p_{m2}}(e) = true$. From this, we can finally proof that the *intra view type overlap* property is supported. Using the formula for the *intra view type overlap* from Section 4.4.5.2 this proof finalises as follows:

$$\exists p_1, p_2 \in \Phi \mid (p_1 \neq p_2 \wedge \exists e \in Models_{MM} \mid (\partial_{p_1}(e) = true \wedge \partial_{p_2}(e) = true)) \overset{p_1 = p_{m1} \wedge p_2 = p_{m2}}{\Longleftrightarrow}$$

$$\exists p_{m1}, p_{m2} \in \Phi \mid (p_{m1} \neq p_{m2} \wedge \exists e \in Models_{MM} \mid (\partial_{p_{m1}}(e) = true \wedge \partial_{p_{m2}}(e) = true)) \Longleftrightarrow$$

$$\exists p_{m1}, p_{m2} \in \Phi \mid (true \wedge \exists e \in Models_{MM} \mid true) \Longleftrightarrow$$

$$true$$

$\square$

7.1.2. Validation of the Generic View Properties of FURCAS

A view, according to Definition 4.12, is a tuple $V = (M_V, VT, S, \Lambda, layout)$. FURCAS's representation of a view is based on instances of the TextBlock metamodel (cf. Section 5.4.3.1) which, according to its formalisation in Definition 5.5, is a tuple $B = (N, VT, M, ID_{sec}, subblocks, toks, orderNodes)$. The *mappings* between the tuples' elements are given by:

1. M_V which is the view's underlying model is equal to the TextBlock model's model: $M_V \equiv M$.

2. Another direct equivalence is the reference of a view V and a TextBlock model B to their defining view type VT.

3. The selection of elements within a view S is given by the unification of all elements that are either referenced as `correspondingModelElements` by a TextBlock or as `referencedElements` by a TextBlock or a token. Thus we say that $S \equiv \bigcup_{n \in N} corelem(n) \cup refelem(n)$.

4. The layout Λ of a textual view is given by the structure of the B but primarily by the set of `OmittedTokens` that are part of the B. Thus we can say that $\Lambda \equiv O$.

5. Due to 4. we can define that the layout relation *layout* which connects the elements in a view with their layout information is given by:

$$(e \in M, \lambda \in \Lambda) \in layout \iff \lambda = \begin{cases} toks(e) \cap O & \text{if } e \in \Pi \\ \varnothing & \text{else} \end{cases}$$

7.1.2.1. Selective and Holistic Views

The holisticness of a view that is a textual view in FURCAS is achieved by the update transformation T_v which is part of the Φ of a view. In combination with *Retainment-Policies* FURCAS also supports selective views.

Lemma 7.4. FURCAS *supports addition holistic views. After an addition of an element e to a view V's model M where* $\exists p \in \Phi \mid \partial_p(e) = true$, *e appears in the selection S of V.*

Proof. For each rule in the view type specification FURCAS generates a transformation rule in T_v that maps a model element to its textual representation (cf. Section 6.6), This rule creates a TextBlock b for each new element e that matches its source. Therefore, we can say that $\leadsto_{T_v} (M', B) = B \cup b_e$ where $M' = \delta_e^+ M$ and B is the TextBlock model for M. As every such transformation rule in T_v also adds the element e to the corresponding model elements of b we can say that $corelem(b_e) = e$. Due to mapping 3. (as stated above) the selection S of a textual view is defined as $S \equiv \bigcup_{n \in N} corelem(n) \cup refelem(n)$. With $b_e \in N$ and $corelem(b_e) = e$ we conclude that the selection of the textual view is extended to include e as required by the definition of the *addition holistic* property given in Section 4.14. □

The proofs the fulfilment of addition holisticness. The proofs for the other types of holisticness and selectiveness work analogously.

7.1.2.2. Overlapping Views

Overlapping views allow to display the same model element from different view instances at the same time. A requirement for this property is that the views are, to a certain extent, independent from the underlying model. Section 4.5.1.4 defines this property to be fulfilled if intersection of the S of two different views is other than the empty set: $S_{V_1} \cap S_{V_2} \neq \emptyset$.

Lemma 7.5. FURCAS *supports the existence of overlapping view instances.*

Proof. (1) The S of a view in FURCAS is given, according to mapping 3., as the union of all elements that are referred to by the corresponding or referenced model elements association from the document nodes N of a textual view. As the TextBlocks follow the decorator pattern, they non-intrusively reference their model elements. This can be seen in the TextBlock metamodel presented in Section 5.4.3.1. The `correspondingModelElement` association has an upper multiplicity of *many* at the end of TextBlock.

(2) Thus, we may assume that there may be two TextBlock models B_1 and B_2 having the TextBlocks b_1 and b_2 respectively. Due two (1) we can say that both b_1 as well as b_2 may refer to the same model element e. Thus $corelem(b_1) = e$ and $corelem(b_2) = e$. Due to mapping 1. we can say that:

$$S_{B_1} \cap S_{B_2} \neq \emptyset \overset{\text{mapping 3.}}{\Longleftrightarrow}$$

$$\left(\bigcup_{n_i \in N_{B_1}} corelem(n_i) \cup refelem(n_i) \right) \cap \left(\bigcup_{n_j \in N_{B_2}} corelem(n_j) \cup refelem(n_j) \right) \neq \emptyset \Longleftrightarrow$$

$$\{corelem(b_1)\} \cap \{corelem(b_2)\} \neq \emptyset \Longleftrightarrow$$

$$\{e\} \cap \{e\} \neq \emptyset \Longleftrightarrow$$

$$\{e\} \neq \emptyset$$

$$\square$$

7.1.2.3. Partiality and Non-Injectiveness of Synchronisation Transformations

A challenge for the synchronisation of partial views in a bidirectional way with their underlying model, is that according to Lemma 4.1, also the employed synchronisation transformation is considered partial and non-injective. According to Hettel [Het10] this partiality poses additional requirements to the transformation, as presented in Section 4.5.3. The transformation needs to fulfil the following properties in order to correctly handle partial bidirectionality [Het10]:

1. Target model changes can be classified into two disjoint sets of changes: relevant and irrelevant changes Δ_R and Δ_I. Relevant changes modify a part of the target model which is in the image of the respective transformation whereas irrelevant changes lie outside of this image.

2. To be able to synchronise relevant target changes back to the source model a corresponding source change must exist for each of them. The resulting set of source changes for a set of relevant target changes is denoted Δ_S.

3. Furthermore, each $\delta \in \Delta_S$ must exactly perform the original change in Δ_R when the transformation is applied again.

Lemma 7.6. FURCAS *accounts for partiality and non-injectiveness of its view synchronisation transformations.*

Proof. The synchronisation transformations within FURCAS are given by two transformations T_M, syncing view to model, and T_V, syncing model to view. Both are generated from the respective view type specification of the view. For these transformations the properties given above are fulfilled as follows:

1. The set of relevant changes that can be handled by FURCAS's transformations is clearly defined by the scope of the view type as thoroughly explained in Section 5.3.2.1. In addition to simply leaving elements that leave this scope unattended, FURCAS additionally makes these changes visible to a view's user as described in Section 6.6.6.

2. The exact inverse change for a target model change in FURCAS is ensured by the bidirectional semantics of the constructs employed in the view type specification. All constructs in FURCAS's basis TCS [JBK06, JB06b] were initially designed to be bidirectional. The constructs for handling views in FURCAS, such as OCL property inits and OCL queries were also introduced in this thesis including an inversion function. However, one limitation is that for OCL queries that are not automatically invertible (see Section 5.3.3) an explicit *invert* statement has to be provided. If this holds, the inverse change, as required by property 2 can always uniquely be given.

3. Finally, the equality of the effect of the inverted change concerning the original target change is actually the same as proposed by Lemma 7.7 which will be proven in the next Section.

$\square$

7.1.2.4. Effect Conformity

Effect conformity (cf. Section 4.5.2.1) for a view-based approach is fulfilled if all constructs of a view type specification language have a deterministic bidirectional definition.

Lemma 7.7. *The textual views that are constructed using a* FURCAS *view type definition behave* effect conform.

Proof. FURCAS's view type specification language is based on TCS. All constructs of TCS are defined bidirectional [JBK06, JB06b], i.e., from model to text as well as from text to model. FURCAS adds several constructs to TCS to allow for the specification of views types. However, all added constructs, such as OCL queries (cf. Section 5.3.2.2) or OCL property inits are also defined bidirectionally. Especially, for the OCL query approach, an automatic inversion mechanism is provided which is backed up by the possibility to specify manual inversion expressions in the view type definition. Thus, we can say that FURCAS maintains the bidirectional character of TCS and behaves therefore *effect conform.* □

7.1.2.5. Consistency Conservation

Consistency conservation (see Section 4.5.2.2) of a view has mostly to do with the level of inconsistency that is allowed during the editing process. Two different types of inconsistency can be distinguished: *constraint inconsistency* and *model inconsistency*. While *constraint inconsistency* relates to the metamodel constraints that may be violated, *model inconsistency* deals with the aspect of really creating and storing temporarily inconsistent models.

Lemma 7.8. FURCAS *supports the modelling of views with* constraint inconsistency.

Proof. The model construction of FURCAS is based on model transformation rules that are formulated in QVT [Obj11]. As QVT is not restricted by the constraints of a metamodel, and neither are the view type definitions from which the transformations are generated, we can say that metamodel constraints are not considered when it comes to the model construction[1]. This allows for the creation of models for which metamodel constraints are unsatisfied. □

Lemma 7.9. FURCAS *supports the modelling of views with* model inconsistency.

Proof. Definition 4.22 specifies a view with explicit support for *model inconsistency* as: $V = (M_V, VT, S, \Lambda, I)$ where I is the set of view elements that are not translatable to elements in M_V. For FURCAS these are the tokens and TextBlocks from the *incomplete* or *inconsistent* as they may occur after certain editing events see Section 5.4.3.3.

In the simplest case, the whole textual representation of a model is contained in a single TextBlock having a single token which contains the complete text in its `value`

---

[1]However, to indicate their invalid state to the user, FURCAS presents them as error markers in its editors.

attribute. This value may be an arbitrary string that is independent from the view type definition (the TextBlocks metamodel is generic to all view type definitions). This allows FURCAS to store arbitrary text as a TextBlock model and therefore also text that is inconsistent according to the current view type definition of the TextBlock.

Assuming the universe of all possible textual representations is denoted as the set C_{Univ}. Furthermore, the set of textual representations that are translatable into a valid model instance of a given view type VT is denoted as C_{VT}. If we assume that the view type does not allow to represent all possible textual representations, we can say that the set of representations that are not translatable into a model according to VT is given by $\bar{C}_{VT} = C_{Univ} \setminus C_{VT}$. Due to the genericness of the TextBlock metamodel, we can still say that each $\bar{c}_{VT} \in \bar{C}_{VT}$ is representable as a TextBlock model or that $Models_{VMM} = C_{Univ}$ with VMM equals the TextBlock metamodel.

According to Definition 4.22 of *model inconsistency* the set I is defined as: $I \subseteq Models_{VMM}$ so that $(I, V) \not\leadsto_{T_m}$. If we set $I = \bar{C}_{VT}$ and $VMM = TextBlocks\ metamodel$ we can conclude that $\forall \bar{c}_{VT} \in \bar{C}_{VT}, e \in M_V \mid (\bar{c}_{VT}, e) \not\leadsto_{T_m}$, which proofs that FURCAS allows for the representation of arbitrary *model inconsistency*. □

7.1.2.6. Ensuring Bidirectionality for View Synchronisation

Having presented an approach, that allows to bidirectionally synchronise textual views with their underlying model, leaves the question if FURCAS also supports the requirements that are posed to bidirectional synchronisation transformations as they were introduced by Matsuda et al. To validate FURCAS with respect to Matsuda et al.'s [MHN+07] properties, this section presents proofs for the formalised properties as they have been presented in Section 4.5.3.1.

Backwards-Transformation From Unchanged View Keeps Identity of Model

This property ensures that the the fact that a model is just viewed does not imply changes to it once it is synchronised back without changes. The formal implication was defined as follows:

$$
\begin{pmatrix}
(1) V = T_V(M) \wedge \\
(2) V' = \Delta V \wedge \\
(3) \Delta = \varnothing \wedge \\
(4) M' = \leadsto_{T_M} (V')
\end{pmatrix} \rightarrow (M' = M)
$$

Lemma 7.10. *The* FURCAS *view synchronisation transformation ensures that the backwards transformation from an unchanged view keeps the identity of the underlying model.*

Proof. Starting from a domain model M (1), a TextBlocks model V (representing the view) is generated by the view synchronisation transformation in the direction of the view (representing T_V, cf. Section 6.6). In this scenario no changes are applied to the transformation ((2) and (3): $\Delta = \varnothing$). From this point on, the view synchronisation transformation is triggered in the opposite direction (cf. Section 6.3).

Having no changes at all within the textual representation, will result, due to the incremental character of the employed lexing and parsing approach (cf. Sections 6.3.2.5 and 6.3.2.6), in an empty set for the *parsed* version of the TextBlock model. Thus, the TextBlock merging process will also not be triggered and the underlying model remains unchanged as requested by this property: $[...] \rightarrow M' = M$. □

Model Updates do not Force Overwriting of Edited Views   To achieve this property, a transformation T_M^{-1} is required that restores a modified model M' to the version M which was the original source for the view V.

$$\exists T_M^{-1} \in Transformations_{MM} \mid (V =\leadsto_{T_V}(M)) \wedge (M' = \Delta M) \wedge (V' =\leadsto_{T_V}(M')) \rightarrow$$
$$\left(\leadsto_{T_M^{-1}}(V, M') = M\right)$$

Lemma 7.11. FURCAS *allows to retain unsaved modifications to a view even though the underlying model was updated and would require the view to update and loose these changes.*

Proof. Modifications to a textual view in FURCAS undergo a multi-phased, incremental update process (cf. Section 6.3). During this process FURCAS creates different versions of the textual view depending in which phase the update process currently is. Furthermore, if inconsistencies arise during the update process, the intermediate versions are retained and even persistable. The range of time in which such an intermediate version of the view exists is given by the point in time t_s which is the point of the first modification that triggered the first phase of the update process and t_e which denotes the point in time when the information of the view is consistently synchronised back to the underlying model. During the time $\Delta_t = t_e - t_s$ the view is temporarily out of sync with the underlying model. During Δ_t the view is vulnerable to changes that update the underlying model, as they cannot be synced to the view without loosing the temporarily inconsistent parts.

FURCAS, therefore, employs retainment policies (cf. Chapter 3 and Section 6.6.5) to alleviate this problem. During the time Δ_t the inconsistent parts of the textual view are protected by an *always RetainmentPolicy* (◄■►). Thus, we can say that that w.r.t. the protected region the *RetainmentPolicy* turns the view update transformation T_V into a modified transformation $T_V^{\bullet}$. According to the definition of the *always Retainment-Policy* the change set applied by a transformation that is combined with this *Retainment-Policy* is reduced to : $\overset{\bullet}{\Delta} = \varnothing$.

Thus, we can say that $V =\leadsto_{T_V^{\bullet}} (M) \iff V =\leadsto_{T_V^{\bullet}} (M')$. In this case the backwards transformation T_M^{-1} can be the standard transformation T_M and we get:

$$\exists T_M^{-1} \in Transformations_{MM} \mid (V =\leadsto_{T_V^{\bullet}} (M)) \wedge (M' = \Delta M) \wedge (V' =\leadsto_{T_V^{\bullet}} (M')) \rightarrow$$
$$(\leadsto_{T_M^{-1}} (V, M') = M) \overset{T_M^{-1}=T_M}{\iff}$$
$$\exists T_M \in Transformations_{MM} \mid (V =\leadsto_{T_V^{\bullet}} (M)) \wedge (M' = \Delta M) \wedge (V' =\leadsto_{T_V^{\bullet}} (M')) \rightarrow$$
$$(\leadsto_{T_M} (V', M') = M)$$

As we identified that $V =\leadsto_{T_V^{\bullet}} (M) \iff V =\leadsto_{T_V^{\bullet}} (M')$ we can go on with:

$$\exists T_M \in Transformations_{MM} \mid (V =\leadsto_{T_V^{\bullet}} (M)) \wedge (M' = \Delta M) \wedge (V =\leadsto_{T_V^{\bullet}} (M')) \rightarrow$$
$$(\leadsto_{T_M} (V, M') = M) \iff$$

By this, we can conclude that: $(\leadsto_{T_M} (V, M') = M) \wedge (V =\leadsto_{T_V^{\bullet}} (M))$ is always true.

However, as we assumed that during Δ_t, V is *never* modified by T_V this restricts the property that was proven here in a way that the user can *not* choose whether an update from the underlying model should be propagated to the view or not. This is a limitation of FURCAS. $\qquad\qquad\square$

Transformation is Agnostic to Order of Changes In order to provide a consistent behaviour, the backward transformation is required to be independent from the order of the changes that have been applied to the view. Section 4.5.3.1 stated that the following must hold in order to fulfil this property:

$$
\left(
\begin{array}{l}
V = T_V(M) \wedge \\
V_1' = (\Delta_1 \circ \Delta_2)V \wedge \\
V_2' = (\Delta_2 \circ \Delta_1)V \wedge \\
M_1' = \leadsto_{T_M} (V_1') \wedge \\
M_2' = \leadsto_{T_M} (V_2') \wedge
\end{array}
\right) \rightarrow (M_1' = M_2')
$$

Proof. (0) First we need to assume that Δ_1 and Δ_2 are not overlapping w.r.t. the view element they modify. Otherwise, if for example in Δ_1 an element a is moved under the containment hierarchy of an element b and in Δ_2 b and all its composite children are deleted an inverse application, i.e., Δ_1 after Δ_2 would not be possible anyway.

Two different cases need to be distinguished for this property. Depending on whether the first change Δ^{first}, be it Δ_1 or Δ_2, left the textual view V in a (1) consistent or (2) inconsistent state.

Case (1): If after the first change Δ^{first} the textual view V is in a *consistent* state (cf. Section 5.4.3.3) that means that the change has been propagated to the underlying model so that $M^{first} = \leadsto_{T_M} (\Delta^{first}V, M)$. For the application of the second change Δ^{second} we will then get

$$
\begin{array}{l}
M^{second} = \leadsto_{T_M} \left((\Delta^{second} \circ \Delta^{first})V, M^{first} \right) \iff \\
M^{second} = \leadsto_{T_M} \left((\Delta^{second} \circ \Delta^{first})V, \leadsto_{T_M} (\Delta^{first}V, M) \right)
\end{array}
$$

To proof this we need to make sure that the *effects* of the changes Δ^{first} and Δ^{second} propagated through the transformation do not overlap w.r.t. the elements in M. As FURCAS allows intra view type overlaps (cf. Lemma 7.3), this, however, cannot always be guaranteed. Thus, for case (1) it is required that the following restriction (3) holds: the view type VT_V does not have intra view type overlaps w.r.t. to the elements that may lie within $\Delta_1 \underset{element(\delta)}{\cap} \Delta_2$.

Case(2): If after the first change Δ^{first} the textual view V is in an *inconsistent* state (cf. Section 5.4.3.3) that means that the change has *not yet* been propagated to the underlying model so that $M^{first} = M$. Thus, according to assumption (0) we can say that $(\Delta_1 \circ \Delta_2)V = (\Delta_2 \circ \Delta_1)V = (\Delta_2 \cup \Delta_1)V$. With this and if $Delta^{second}$ made V consistent again, we can say that:

$$M_1' =\leadsto_{T_M} ((\Delta_1 \circ \Delta_2)V) \wedge M_2' =\leadsto_{T_M} ((\Delta_2 \circ \Delta_1)V) \iff$$
$$M_1' =\leadsto_{T_M} ((\Delta_1 \cup \Delta_2)V) \wedge M_2' =\leadsto_{T_M} ((\Delta_2 \cup \Delta_1)V) \iff$$
$$M_1' = M_2' =\leadsto_{T_M} ((\Delta_2 \cup \Delta_1)V)$$

If assumption (0) and restriction (3) holds FURCAS fulfils this property. □

7.1.2.7. Immediate vs. Deferred Update of Views

The update strategy with which modifications to a view are propagated to the underlying model can be distinguished by the amount of change events that may occur until the synchronisation between view and model is re-established: $M_{i+1} = \Delta M_i \to \#(\Delta) = n$. If $n = 1$ then the update process is *immediate*.

Lemma 7.12. *The update mechanism of* FURCAS *is a deferred update mechanism.*

Proof. Assuming a sequence of changes to a view $\Delta_v = (\delta_1, \delta_2, \ldots, \delta_n)$. Upon the first change δ_1 FURCAS will create a temporary version of the TextBlock model (cf. Section 6.3). This change may either lead to a full roundtrip bringing the model back to a consistent and updated state, but it might also be the case that the inconsistent and edited state is maintained as δ_1 may have made a token unlexable or a TextBlock unparseable (see Section 5.4.3.3). For the latter case, the underlying model M_i is still unmodified while the sequence of applied changes to the view is now $\Delta_v = (\delta_1)$. As FURCAS allows to make arbitrary textual modifications to its views this change may already include a part δ_1^p which would be translatable to an atomic change in M_i but is, for example, concatenated with a second change part δ_1^q which does not allow a translation to the underlying model. Upon the application of the second change δ_2, the same may apply, either the view reached a consistent state because the untranslatable remainder δ_1^q is now completed by δ_2 or δ_2 is itself again a part which may complete δ_1^q with a part δ_2^q but provide a further incomplete part δ_1^r. The set of pending changes that would be applicable to M_i is therefore enlarged each time another incomplete δ_i from Δ_v is applied. Therefore, by induction, we can conclude that the set of changes Δ that makes the difference between two subsequent versions of M may be as large as $\#(\Delta_v) = n$ where $n \geq 0$. □

7.1.2.8. Mergeability of Views

A model and a view are considered mergeable according to Definition 4.25 iff the change sets to the view Δ_V and to the model Δ_M do not intersect over the same elements with an inverse action. As FURCAS cannot not ensure this mergeability at any time, Lemma 7.13 will formulate that mergeability is *not* always fulfilled.

Lemma 7.13. FURCAS *does* not *ensure mergeability of views in arbitrary cases.*

Proof. As FURCAS employs a deferred update mechanism (cf. Lemma 7.12), arbitrarily many changes may occur between two synchronisation points between model and view. Therefore, it is also possible that during the time Δ_t in which the view is out of sync with the model arbitrarily many modifications can be made to the underlying model. Thus, it is also absolutely possible that there is a pair of changes $\delta_M \in \Delta_M$ and $\delta_V \in \Delta_V$ which are, mapped through the synchronisation transformations, inverse to each other. Therefore, we can conclude that views in FURCAS are *not* mergeable at arbitrary points in time. See also Section 8.2 for details in this limitation. $\qquad\square$

7.1.2.9. Respect to Access Control

According to Definition 4.26, a view fulfils respect to access control if it does not allow to modify elements that are not part of the view.

Lemma 7.14. *Views that are editable in* FURCAS *pay respect to access control.*

Proof. (0) We assume, for this proof, that transitive deletion through the composition hierarchy [Obj02, Obj06], which deletes all elements that are (transitive) composite children of an element e does not take place.

(1) The set of element types that can be modified through a view in FURCAS is limited to those that are part of the text to model update transformation T_M. This transformation is completely generated from the respective view type definition VT. All element types that are contained within VT are considered to be part of a view in general. This reduces the set of modifiable models to a subset $Models_{VT} \subseteq Models_{MM}$.

(2) Furthermore, only those models that are explicitly referenced by one or more Text-Blocks of a textual view of VT may serve as target model of T_M. This is denoted as $Models_{T_M} \subseteq Models_{MM}$. In combination with (1) we get $Models_{T_M} \cap Models_{VT}$ as elements that are potentially modifiable through a given view.

As a TextBlock may only reference elements that are typed according to the template a TextBlock references, we can say that $Models_{T_M} \cap Models_{VT} = S_V$ of a view V. This proofs that no element outside of S_V can be modified through a view which is the requirement for *respect to access control*.

However, according to assumption (0), this is only valid if we omit the concept of transitive deletion through the containment hierarchy of an element e. This is considered a limitation of FURCAS (see Section 8.2). □

7.2. Classification of Change Events

The incremental update process presented in this thesis (cf. Chapter 6) aims at retaining and updating elements in a fine-grained way that are (partially) represented in a textual syntax and edited with means of character insertion and deletion. In contrast to syntax directed editing [LP88], FURCAS allows to type or delete arbitrary characters in the textual representation. Form this, it is obvious that not every atomic operation performed on the view can directly be mapped to an atomic modification to the underlying model. Support for temporary inconsistency is also a key factor of a modern language workbench [Fow05] and allows to creatively work with the created languages (or view types in FURCAS). The combination of both poses challenges to the synchronisation mechanisms between view and model. It is not possible that after larger changes which require a complete reconstruction of a model element from the textual view, those sub-elements and properties of an element that are not part of the current view can be restored as they were.

FURCAS employs a multi-phased, incremental update process including different levels of reuse factors to alleviate this problem. This Section presents an analysis of critical change events and their impact on the underlying model.

7.2.1. Token Reuse

The reuse of tokens is based on the different previous versions on which the changes were performed. Table 6.1 on page 267 showed the criteria according to which a token may be reused after the lexing phase was performed. Due to the self-versioning of the tokens, this reuse is only possible if the modification was made near to the original position of the reusable token. Of course, a reuse of old tokens only makes sense if they are not still existent in the newer version. Then the existing ones will be kept and new elements will be created for the newly created tokens.

Thus, critical modifications are those where a token t is deleted from a position p_1 and the very same token is written at a different position p_2. If p_1 and p_2 are directly adjacent to each other the token reuse will still work as the change was still performed in the same *region* (cf. Section 6.3.1.1). In this case the token reuse algorithm will check all candidates within this region for their reuse capabilities. However, if the inserted token t' which, semantically should represent t, is inserted within a different region, token reuse is *not* possible.

For example, assume a textual representation of a business object with associations as follows: `bo Customer { Address a; PurchaseOrder* orders; }`. Deleting the tokens (`Address a;`) and typing the very same textual representation after the `orders` association will not allow for reuse of the old tokens `Address a;`.

Such cases will, in turn, lead to the problem, that the TextBlock merging phase will not recognise the two TextBlocks as being mergeable, as they have the same token content but do not have tokens in their version history in common.

This limitation impacts the way developers can work with textual views provided by FURCAS. Deletion of elements that are only partially viewed should be omitted if they are intended to be placed elsewhere. Note, however, that copy & paste in such cases is not problem for FURCAS, as in this case not only the textual representation, i.e., the character sequence, but also the TextBlocks of the respective region is copied and pasted. Furthermore, if the deleted and re-written region is *complete* according to its view type, this limitation also does not apply. In this case all information of the element can be re-constructed from the textual representation.

7.2.2. TextBlock and Model Element Mergeability

According to the TextBlock mergeability factor computation (cf. Section 6.3.2.10), several factors, such as the template, the chosen alternatives and mode of a template, the number of reusable tokens as well as the manually defined *reuse strategies* decide upon the mergeability of TextBlocks. As discussed in the classification of type A and type B changes in Section 6.3.1, changes that reach over more than one TextBlock while not completely enclosing a complete subtree of the TextBlock model are classified as type B. These changes cannot be directly treated by the default incremental update process of FURCAS. Still, FURCAS will try to stepwise integrate them using the type B update approach.

The whole synchronisation process depends on the fact that there are possible synchronisation points at which model and view are in sync again. FURCAS provides several mechanisms (for example, see Section 6.6.5 for the handling of inconsistencies) that try to alleviate the fact that, with the given high degree of freedom in interaction with the textual representation, it becomes unavoidable that view and model get temporarily out of sync. However, especially if multiple type B changes overlap with each other in between two synchronisation points the probability of loosing information from the partially viewed model increases.

7.2.3. Interaction Guidelines for Textual Modelling with FURCAS

The interaction with the textual editors in FURCAS is nearly as free as with using every "standard" textual editor. However, due to the reasons stated above, some textual interaction patterns may lead to unwanted effects w.r.t. the underlying model. Therefore, developers doing textual modelling with FURCAS should respect the following interaction guidelines to optimally work with FURCAS.

7.2.3.1. Awareness of Partiality

As view based modelling is in many ways different than interaction with, for example, text files, the user also has to be aware of these differences. Deletions of elements that are only partially viewed should only be made if explicitly intended. Developers deleting elements in a partial view should be aware that the element might represent more than what the view currently shows. A deletion of such elements will then not only delete the bits that a current, partial view shows, but also bits that are not directly visible in the current view. Especially undoing such a deletion is then problematic. Just re-typing the representation of the element within the current view is not enough to completely reconstruct it (see also Section 7.2.3.3). FURCAS provides several concepts, that allow language engineers to extend the generated FURCAS editors with functionality that can alleviate this problem.

- FURCAS easily allows to query all other views from which an element can be viewed and/or edited. This query is possible as all views are stored as (TextBlock-)models based on the same modelling infrastructure as the models themselves. FURCAS formulates this query based on the `correspondingModelElements` and `referencedModelElements` association of the TextBlock metamodel.

- Already during the creation of the view type, FURCAS gives hints on the partiality or completeness of a view type. As introduced in Section 5.3.2.1, either a language engineer has to explicitly state that a view type is partial w.r.t. a certain class of the metamodel or FURCAS will raise a warning that this is the case and it might not be intended.

- FURCAS editors explicitly mark regions where a view is *selective* (cf. Section 5.4.5). This informs the developer that there are more elements in a certain region than those that are currently shown in the view. These indications will make the developer even more aware of the partiality of a current view.

7.2.3.2. Deletion vs. Removal from View

As opposed to deleting characters from a text file, textual modelling incurs two different flavours of deletion. First, *removal from view* which only removes the textual representation from the view and does not delete the underlying element. And second, *deletion from model* which includes the fist case but furthermore also deletes the element from the model. Depending on the type of the view, i.e., selective or holistic, different types of deletion may be more intuitive than others. However, in contrast to traditional textual editing the mere existence of two different types of delete operations may seem unusual.

FURCAS supports both types of deletions and also lets the language engineer decide which one is the default behaviour for certain view types. In addition, each developer may configure his or her own precedences w.r.t. to this option.

7.2.3.3. Retyping vs. Undo

After accidentally deleting an element from a view there are two different options on how the element can be re-created. First, by using means of the editor to model the exact same element that once existed and second by using the undo functionality to let the editor rollback the deletion action. In traditional environments the former case is, of course depending on the size of the deleted text, as likely to occur as the latter. The larger the deleted text the more probable is that a developer would use the undo action instead of retyping the whole text again. However, the latter case is mostly restricted by the runtime of the editor as the undo stack is often cleared as soon as the editor is closed. Then this option cannot be used anymore.

315

However, with the use of partial views, retyping a deleted textual representation of a model element in just one editor is not enough. All editors that show an exclusive part of the deleted element need to be opened and the missing parts need to be completed. Therefore, the undo option should be preferred. For a textual editor this might seem uncommon but other editors, such as those for partial graphical modelling require the same actions. Developers just need to be aware of the partiality (cf. Section 7.2.3.1).

7.3. Case Studies

To validate the *applicability* of FURCAS in practice as well as the *automatability* of certain aspects, such as the automatic inversion of OCL query expressions, several academic as well as industrial case studies were conducted in cooperation with the SAP AG. SAP has many years of experience in developing platforms as well as applications for business information systems. In recent years also modelling became more and more attractive [AHK06] for the company. With their vast diversity of business domains SAP provides a large field of application for different domain specific languages. During the cooperation three different case studies were performed with FURCAS, each of which in a different domain and with a different focus.

The largest of the case studies aimed at creating a multi-purpose language for developing business applications called *Runlet*. *Runlet* covers many facets, such as, static and dynamic aspects of a system, analytic expressions and object queries as well as an integrated object persistence and versioning system. Furthermore, *Runlet* was designed to provide an extensible basis to build further languages on top. The main aspect that *Runlet* stresses w.r.t. to the capabilities of FURCAS is its *expressiveness*. *Runlet* provides a large set of different language constructs that all need to be expressed with the means of FURCAS's view type definition language. Section 7.3.2 describes the main aspects of *Runlet* as well as the results of the evaluation.

7.3.1. Metrics

To be able to measure certain properties of FURCAS in the course of the execution of the case studies a Goal/Question/Metric (GQM) based metric suite was applied. Section 7.3.1.1 gives an overview on the concepts of the GQM approach. The GQM approach has, for example, been applied successfully to evaluate the maintainability of model-driven approaches versus traditional approaches for the development of object-relational persistence adapters [GWR07, GRW08]. This thesis presents a set of metrics for answering specific questions w.r.t. the use of view-based textual modelling. Section 7.3.5 then analyses the values gathered for the metrics in the different case studies.

7.3.1.1. The Goal Question Metric Approach

The GQM approach [BCR94] is a systematic method to find and define tailored metrics for a particular environment. In contrast to the collection of metrics that are chosen just because they can be measured, the GQM approach helps to identify the reasons why particular metrics are chosen. It also helps to interpret the values resulting from the collection of these metrics. The GQM approach is a top-down methodology that consists of three steps:

1. Starting from the definition of *goals* that should be achieved by the conducted measurements. A goal is defined using a template which consists of the following parts:

   Purpose What should be achieved by the measurement?

   Issue Which characteristics should be measured?

   Object Which artefact will be assessed (this may be a product, a process or a resource)?

   Viewpoint From which perspective is the goal defined (e.g. the end user or the development team)?

2. The next step is to define *questions* that will, when answered, provide information that will help to find a solution to the goal.

3. To answer these questions quantitatively every question is associated with a set of metrics. It has to be considered that not only objective metrics can be collected here. Also metrics that are subjective to the viewpoint of the goal can be listed here.

Figure 7.1 depicts the three levels of the GQM approach. It can be seen that it is possible to reuse the same metrics for different goals.

7.3.1.2. Defining Metrics for The Evaluation of The Usage of View Based Textual Modelling

The main goal of the metrics that are defined in this Section is to give hints on the actual usage of view-based textual modelling. The goal deals with the usage of view specific

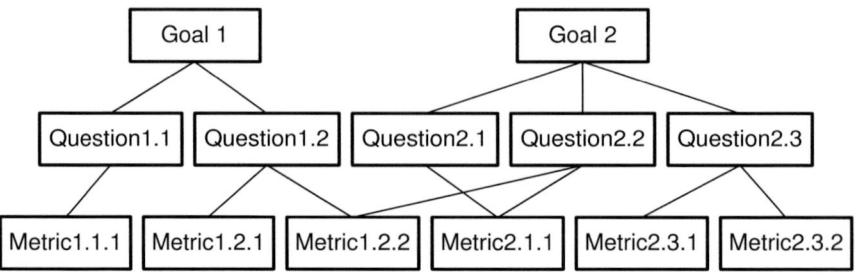

Figure 7.1.: GQM structure as defined by Basili [BCR94].

constructs in the view type definitions. The purpose of this goal is to evaluate to which extent the features of view based modelling were applied by the language engineers that executed the case study. The results for these metrics will give hints on the degree of willingness of language developers to exploit the features of view-based modelling also in textual languages.

Goal 1: Purpose: Evaluation of usage

   Object: View type definitions

   Issue: Usage of view specific constructs

   Viewpoints: Language engineer

Question 1 is related to the willingness of language engineers to split aspects of modelling into different view types:

Question 1.1: How big is the amount of view type overlaps in the developed view type specifications?

To answer this question, this thesis defines the following metrics:

M1.1.1: The *amount of classes* in the metamodel for which the view types are defined. This metric will serve as basis that defines the general size of the modelling language under consideration. The larger the number the more complex is the language and the more aspects have to be considered in the creation of the view types.

M1.1.2: The *amount of view types* that are defined for the given metamodel. This number gives a hint on how many different aspects and/or levels of detail the language uses. The more view types a language constitutes, the higher the degree of specialisation on a certain aspect.

M1.1.3: The *amount of templates within a view type* determines the expressiveness of a view type. The computation of the *average* of this numbers gives an overview on how expressive the view types are. The higher this average number is the more can be expressed in the view types.

M1.1.4: The *amount of properties and templates for which the* selective *attribute has a value other than the default.* This metric should give hints on whether the selectivity of textual view types actually finds application in practice.

M1.1.5: The *percentage of attributes and references that are actually shown by a template.* This metric allows to see to which extent the projection feature of view-based modelling is used to hide information that should not be accessible from within a certain view.

M1.1.6: The *amount of intra view type overlaps* is given by how many templates (with different modes) exist for a given metamodel class:

$$IntraViewTypeOverlap = \frac{templatesForClass}{classesOfViewType}$$

where $classesOfViewType$ is the amount of distinct classes for which templates exist in a view type and $templatesForClass$ is the total number of templates of a view type. This number gives hints on how many different aspects of the same element types are exploited from a certain view type. The computation of the *average* of this number gives an overview on the overall usage of intra view type overlap feature.

M1.1.7: The *inter view type overlap of a view type* gives the degree of overlap between this view type and other view types and is computed as follows:

$$InterViewTypeOverlap = \frac{\sum\limits_{c \in M_{VT}} overlappingClassesOccurences}{classes}$$

where $overlappingClassesOccurences$ is the amount of occurrences of a class of a given view type VT in other view types and $classes$ is total number of classes for which a template exists in any of the view types.

The second question is concerned with the *automatability* of newly introduced view constructs:

Question 1.2: How good is the OCL inversion approach with respect to real world view type definitions?

To answer this question, this thesis defines the following metrics:

M1.2.1: The *overall amount of OCL queries* used in a language.

M1.2.2: The *amount of OCL queries that could be automatically inverted by* FURCAS*' OCL inversion approach.* This metric evaluates the applicability of the OCL inversion approach in practice. The higher the percentage of automatically inverted queries the more applicable is the approach in practice.

Based on this plan, the gathering of the respective metrics that help to answer the posed questions were be evaluated for the case studies described below.

7.3.2. The Runlet Language at SAP

The *Runlet* language was created with the goal of defining a base language featuring static and dynamic aspects of a multi-purpose language for the development of business applications. The development approach was driven by iteratively creating new language features and trying to realise them with the given means of FURCAS. Starting from a core language that defines concepts such as classes, associations as well as method signatures further aspects were added step by step. Finally, a total of 5 different view types were defined where the metamodel has a total of 233 classes.

The programming model of *Runlet* defines a fundamental type system consisting of (entity and value) classes as well as associations between them, an expression language over this type system, an action language, language modules for analytics, durable and time-dependent storage and retrieval, as well as binding functionality to REST-like [Fie00] HTTP ports. Key aspects are the explicit support for side effect free functions and methods that facilitate parallel execution, e.g., on multi-core systems, and the support for what is called multi-objects which is Runlet's approach to collection-like types, only tighter integrated with the programming model. For example, a method can be invoked on a multi-object which results in the invocation of that method on each single object of the multi-object, collecting the results again in a multi-object. This has proven helpful in mass data operations such as those known from SQL or other data or set manipulation languages.

The development approach of the *Runlet* language was driven by its metamodel. The creation of the metamodel only relied on the business needs of the domain and was not restricted by the capabilities of the concrete syntax. This is an important aspect of domain engineering [Ara89] where a clear separation between abstract (the metamodel) and the concrete syntax should be kept [Fow05].

For executing applications created using the *Runlet* language, a specific, extensible interpreter framework was created. The *Runlet* interpreter directly works using the models created using the FURCAS view types. This enables for good debuggability, fast turn-arounds and zero downtime of running applications. For extension scenarios, which were a declared goal of the *Runlet* approach from the beginning, the interpreter framework is build to allow for easy extensions to the basic language. For each new model construct that has a contribution to the behavioural semantics of the language, a separate interpreter class can be defined. The new interpreter class can then simply be registered based on the newly created metamodel element.

7.3.2.1. Description of the Different View Types

As one goal of the *Runlet* case study was to allow different levels of interaction with the system for the different aspects the language incorporates, a multitude of view types was introduced, each with a different purpose but based on a common core. The following view types were all created using FURCAS. However, there are two additional non-textual view types:

- First, a view type using the form of a tree that shows the containment hierarchy of a model which is used for the basic navigation within the model. As this view type is *containment complete* (cf. Section 4.4.3.1), it shows all composite parents and children of a model. Using drag & drop it is possible to interact with the *selective* view types of the textual view types.

- Second, a graphical view type that shows the class and association structure of a model in a diagrammatic way, using boxes and arrows. This view type is quite similar to UML class diagrams and is mostly used for overview purposes.

The main editing environment was supposed to be the textual view types of FURCAS.

The *Class* View Type   The class view type is used to show and create the structural as well as behavioural features of the basic building blocks of *Runlet* which are called *SapClasses*. Figure 7.2 gives an overview on the classes that are involved in this view type from the static part, called *classes*, of the *Runlet* metamodel. This includes the definition of classes and associations between them as well as method signatures.

In this view type the *selective* argument is used to let the developer choose which elementsOfType (refers to association ends) and which ownedSignatures (refers to method signatures) a certain view should display. This resembles somehow the partial class concept that is for example used in C#, where attributes, properties,

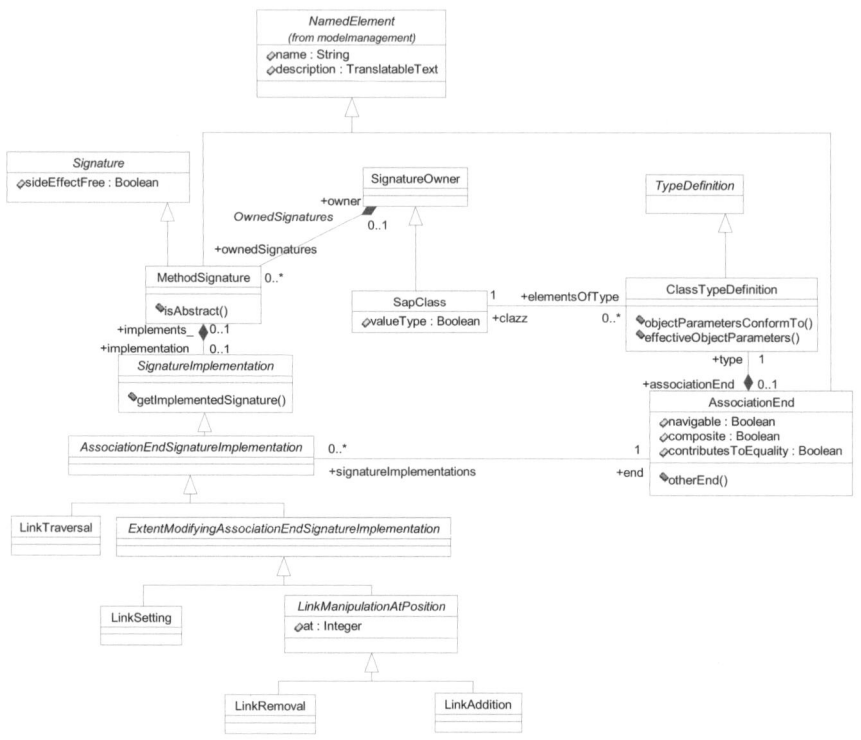

Figure 7.2.: Excerpt from the *classes* package of the *Runlet* metamodel

and methods could be arbitrarily distributes over different concrete syntax units while belonging to the same class. An excerpt of the view type definition of the *class view* is shown in Listing 7.1.

The purpose of the *class* view type is mainly the wiring of SapClasses to each other via the use of associations. Additionally method signatures can be declared. This view type hides some properties that are not of relevance here. The projection rate of this view type is therefore 31.1%, which means that only that percentage of available properties is used in average per class template, the rest is projected away.

For typing the associations and methods, *Runlet* uses so called TypeDefinitions (see Figure 7.2). They are intermediate elements between TypedElements and their referred types, i.e., SapClass. The type definition concept allows for example the

```
1  template data::classes::SapClass main context(root)
2  : (valueType ? "value") "class" name parameterization
3   [[
4    |
5     "|" formalObjectParameters{ forcedLower=1, separator="," } "|"
6   ]]
7   (isDefined(adapters) ? "implements" adapters{ mode=implements,
8         forcedLower=1, separator="," })
9    <space> "{" [
10      ownedSignatures{ selective=addition }
11      elementsOfType{ mode=property, selective=addition }
12   ] "}"
13 ;
```

Listing 7.1: Excerpt from the *class* view type showing the template for `SapClass`

dynamic determination of method call results. For example, assuming a method $m()$ which has a return type with multiplicity $[0..*]$. *Runlet* allows to use method calls also on multiple instances of an class at once. Thus, $m()$ could be called on a set of objects O. Then, however, the return type of the method call expression is not $[0..*]$ anymore but gets a second dimension, as for each element $o \in O$ method $m()$ will be called. A variable receiving the result of such a method call expression would therefore have a multiplicity of $[0..*][0..*]$.

As the `TypeDefinition` construct is used at many places in the *class* view type, the intra view type overlap is quite high: 2.58. The view type consists, in total, of 199 class templates.

These numbers show that, without projection and without the possibility to define intra view type overlaps, this view type would have been much more complex. Recall that the development approach for the underlying metamodel was completely independent from the definition of the concrete syntax. Thus, a different approach for specifying the concrete syntax would find the same metamodel as basis.

The *Actions* View Type   The behaviour of `SapClasses` can be specified using the *actions* view type. *Runlet* therefore provides a complete set of statement (cf. Figure 7.3) and expression (cf. Figure 7.4) language constructs. With these elements *Runlet* is Turing-complete and can be used to define arbitrary programs.

A special feature of *Runlet* is furthermore the possibility to define object queries directly in the language. This feature is achieved by the use of the Object Query Language (OQL) [Cat93] as defined by the ODMG. For the result sets of such queries explicitly

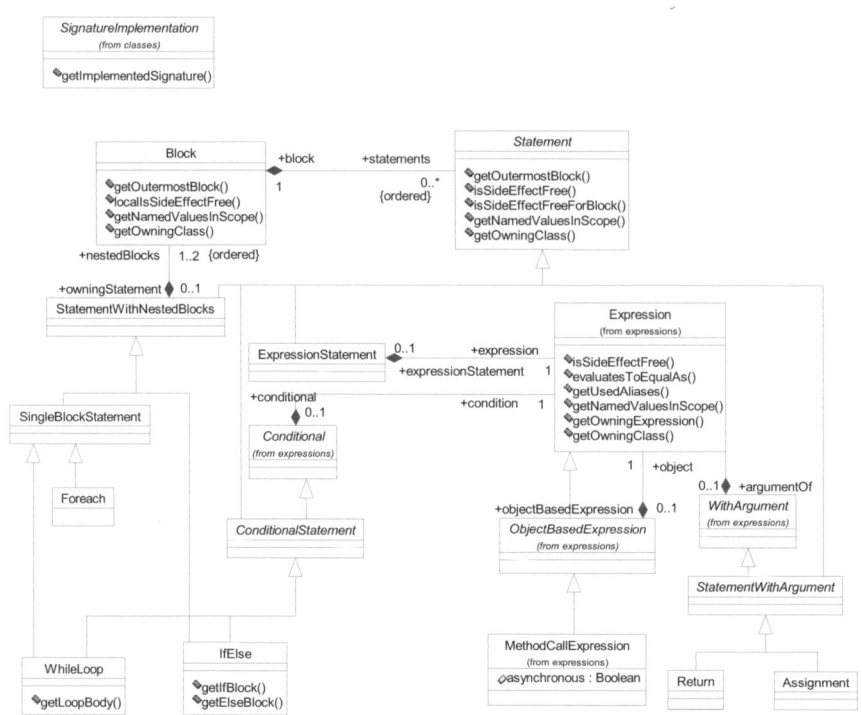

Figure 7.3.: Excerpt from the *behavioral* package of the *Runlet* metamodel

typed classes are created in *Runlet*. The templates for this heavily rely on the advanced model element construction rules as introduced in Section 5.3.4. With the use of these constructs no additional model transformation on the resulting model is required to produce the desired elements. This reduced the effort of defining the language tremendously, as neither additional languages such as QVT nor additional artefacts such as a separate model transformation were required to build the language. An excerpt from the definition of the OQL constructs in the *actions* view type is shown in Listing 7.2. The template for `Iterator`, for example, makes use of the *foreach* construct of FURCAS as introduced in Section 5.3.4.2 to create the type definitions and classes for the result set of a query.

The *action* view type overlaps almost 100% with the *class* view type as method implementations can be edited either directly using the *class* view type or using the dedicated

324

```
 1  template OqlQuery context(oqlQuery)
 2  : [[ -- explicit select
 3      "select" selected { as=identifier,
 4       query=self.fromClause.fromClauseOfOqlQuery
 5           .fromClauses.alias->select(i|i.name=?),
 6         separator=","}
 7    | -- implicit select; constructs tuple from FROM aliases
 8      {{ selected=OCL:self.fromClauses.alias }}
 9    ]]
10    "from" fromClauses{separator=","}
11    "where" condition{forcedLower=1}
12    ownedTypeDefinition{mode=oqlQueryResult, forcedLower=1}
13  ;
14
15  template FromClause
16  : fromExpression "as" alias{mode=fromClause}
17  ;
18
19  template Iterator #fromClause context(iteratorFromClause)
20  : name
21    {{ ownedTypeDefinition = foreach(
22    if self.fromClause.fromExpression.getType()
23      .oclIsKindOf(NestedTypeDefinition) then
24     self.fromClause.fromExpression.getType()
25      .oclAsType(NestedTypeDefinition).type
26    else
27     self.fromClause.fromExpression.getType()
28    endif",
29        mode="iteratorFromClause") }}
30  ;
```

Listing 7.2: Excerpt from the *actions* view type showing the templates for the definition of OQL queries.

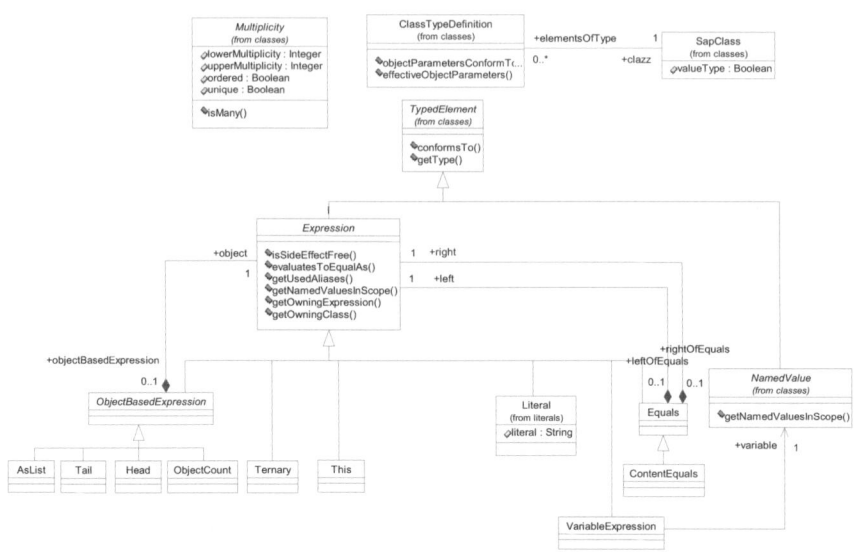

Figure 7.4.: Excerpt from the *expressions* package of the *Runlet* metamodel

actions view type. The total number of templates for this view type is 143. The intra view type overlap is, also due to the extensive use of specific type definitions for the types of the different expressions quite high: 2.1. Due to the similarity to the *class* view type also the projection rate of the *action* view type is quite similar: 22.9%.

The *Adapter* View Type A strong type system is one of the key features of the *Runlet* case study. However, for several reasons the type system is different than those of the most, prominent programming languages.

Assuming a type A conforms to a type B, objects of type A may be used anywhere an object of type B is expected. This concept is also known as assignment compatibility. Different languages define different conformance rules. In Java, for example, conformance is explicit and must be declared by the conforming class or interface by means of an extends or implements clause. The compiler checks the validity of the conformance specification. Other languages use what is called structural conformance, sometimes sloppily referred to as *duck typing*. An advantage of duck typing is its non-intrusiveness, which avoids the strong binding that intrusive conformance declaration styles such as that of Java lead to.

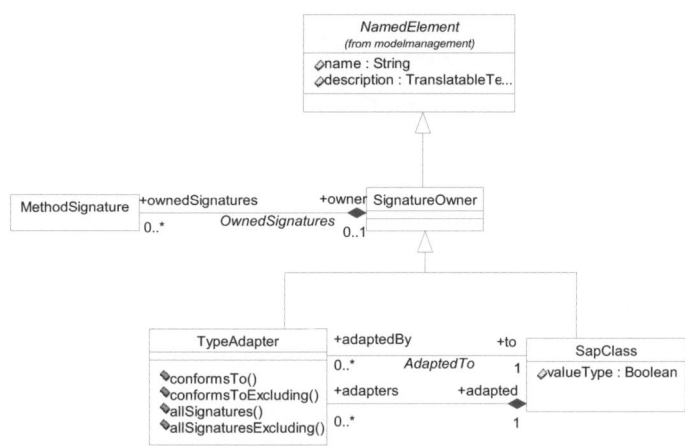

Figure 7.5.: Excerpt from the *classes* package of the *Runlet* metamodel showing the type adapter concept

```
1  template data::classes::SapClass main context(root)
2    : (valueType ? "value") "class" name parameterization
3      [...]
4        (isDefined(adapters) ? "implements" adapters{
5          mode=implements, forcedLower=1, separator=","})
6        [...]
7      "}"
8    ;
9
10 template TypeAdapter #implements
11   : to{as=identifier,
12     query=SapClass.allInstances()->select(c | c.name = ?) }
13   {{ name = 'From_'.concat(self.adapted.name)
14        .concat('_to_').concat(self.to.name) }}
15   ;
```

Listing 7.3: Declaration of the type adapter syntax in the *class* view type

```
 1  template TypeAdapter main context(root)
 2    : "adapter" name "from"
 3      adapted {query=SapClass.allInstances()->select(c | c.name = ?)}
 4      "to"
 5      to { query=SapClass.allInstances()->select(c | c.name = ?) }
 6      [[
 7        ";" -- no signatures
 8        |
 9          "{"
10            ownedSignatures
11          "}"
12      ]]
13    ;
```

Listing 7.4: Declaration of the type adapter syntax in the *adapter* view type

```
 1  class Customer implements Contact {
 2    Address getAddress();
 3  }
 4
 5  class Contact {
 6    Address getContactAddress();
 7  }
```

Listing 7.5: Declaration and use of a type adapter in the *class* view type.

However, duck typing can lead to accidental conformance and makes it harder for development tools to understand the conformance relations that exist in a large software application. The decision for *Runlet* was therefore to introduce the notion of explicit *type adapters* that make conformance explicit (cf. metamodel excerpt shown in Figure 7.5 and view type definition in Listing 7.4). Type adapter are still non-intrusive with respect to both, the conforming class and the class it conforms to. Type adapters have their own life cycle and can live in separate model partitions. Introducing, modifying and deleting a type adapter does not have to mean a modification of the conforming class or its model partition.

Listings 7.5 and 7.6 show the use and the declaration of a type adapter respectively. Note that both view types work on the same level of precedence. If a type adapter has not been declared yet its declaration is also done by the use given in a certain class. This is a good example for where overlapping view types can be used productively to define different aspects on an element with a different focus.

The projection rate of the *adapter* view point is 23.5% whereas its intra view type overlap is 2.1 while the view type consists of a total of 144 templates.

```
1 adapter From_Customer_To_Contact
2   from Customer to Contact {
3     Address getContactAddress() {
4       return this.getAddress();
5     }
6 }
```

Listing 7.6: Declaration and use of a type adapter in the *class* view type.

```
1  template HttpGetBinding main
2    : "binding" name urlPattern "-->" function
3    ;
4
5  template UrlPattern abstract;
6  template SimpleUrlPattern
7    : baseUrl{as = stringSymbol}
8    ;
9
10 template behavioral::actions::Block context(block)
11   : "{" [
12     ( isDefined(statements) ? statements
13       {separator = ";", forcedLower=1} ";" ) ]
14   "}"
15   ;
16
17 template StringTemplate
18   : "<$"
19     [ (isDefined(expressions) ? expressions{separator = ";"} ";") ]
20   "$>"
21   ;
```

Listing 7.7: Excerpt from the *binding* view type

The *Binding* View Type   To provide easy integration of *Runlet* applications within GUI frameworks, a template like view type was introduced, which is called *binding*. This view type uses similar constructs to other template languages like JSP or ASP.Net to include HTML constructs into functions or vice-versa. Figure 7.6 shows the corresponding excerpt from the *Runlet* metamodel. The basic constructs of the view type are shown in Listing 7.7.

For providing the behavioural aspects of the *binding* view type, the contents of functions that are provided by a `Binding` using the statements and expressions parts also used in the *actions* and *class* view points was reused. Therefore, the projection and intra view type overlap metrics for the *binding* view type are quite similar to those of these

329

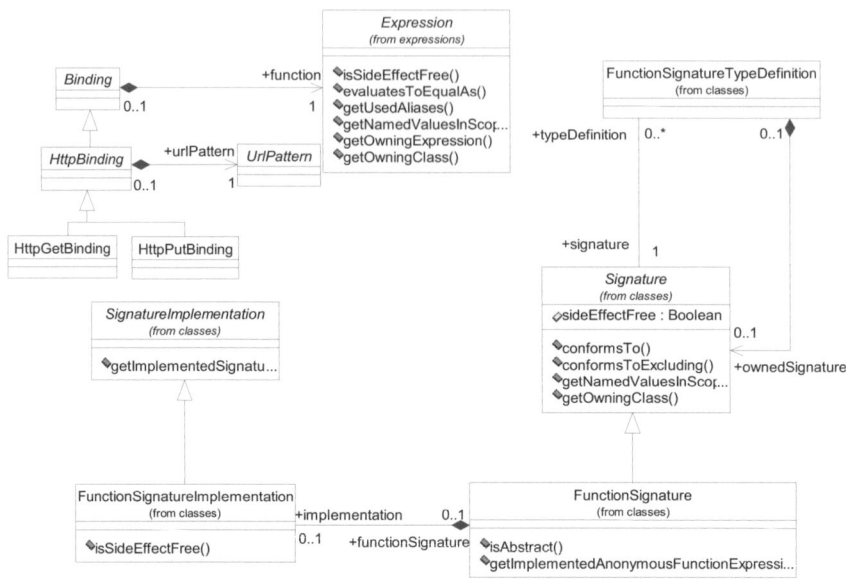

Figure 7.6.: Excerpt from the *binding* package of the *Runlet* metamodel

view types. The intra view type overlap metric has a value of 2.43 where the projection rate is 24.2% and a total number of 146 templates reside within this view type.

The *Package* View Type   The *package* view type is responsible for dealing with the modularisation structure of *Runlet*. This structure is mainly resembled by the definition of Packages and their containing sub packages, classes and associations. This structure allows to define the modularisation of a business system and the associations between classes.

The view type therefore mainly contains structural information, such as: which package contains which sub-packages, classes and associations, etc. Therefore, the view type only contains 7 templates. As only the name and containment structure of packages, classes and associations is represented within this view type, the projection rate of this view type is quite low concerning these elements. However, in contrast to most of the other view types which make massive use of the type definition concept for which mostly templates with only property inits and no textual representations are used, the projection rate is still a lot higher than in those other view types: 62.6%. The only intra view type overlap that occurs in the *package* view point is the existence of two templates for the local and remote association end. Consequently, the metric for intra view type overlaps is only: 1.16.

7.3.2.2. "Opportunity Management" an Application built with the *Runlet* Language

To evaluate the *Runlet* language itself, some case study applications where built with this language using the FURCAS generated editors. The most complex application is the "Opportunity Management" application. Opportunity management is the process of generating, managing, controlling and distributing sales opportunities with customers and related information. Each sales lead is annotated with information such as source, type, worth, status, likelihood of closure etc. An application for opportunity management is furthermore responsible for giving an overview on the progress of several of these opportunities during an amount of time. The opportunity management application built with *Runlet* supports this purpose by allowing for so called "timetravelling". This feature allows to see how the sales opportunities were at a certain point in time and see how they developed over time. Additionally, this application allows for creating reports across several dimensions such as time, revenue, phase or customer. The interaction with the application itself is done using a web interface which is directly connected to the interpreter framework running in a OSGi container included in a web server.

Listing 7.8 shows an excerpt of the textual representation of a part of the application showing mainly the analytics part of the application. Figure 7.7 depicts the user interface of the applications showing a report on aggregated values of different sales opportunities. With the creation of real-world applications using a language created using FURCAS also the applicability of on this layer of modelling could be shown.

7.3.2.3. Conclusions Concerning the Runlet Case Study

Within the *Runlet* case study it was demonstrated how a comprehensive programming model can be developed using FURCAS. The programming model was based on classes (entity and value) and functions as the basic abstractions. *Runlet* incorporated ideas like multi-objects, concurrency, persistence, analytics, declaration and check of side-effect functions/methods. All these features made this case study quite complex. With a metamodel of 233 classes, 5 different view types and hundreds of templates *Runlet* proved that even a large, industrial scale domain specific modelling language can be

```
1  value class Reports {
2    const Amount getExpectedRevenueByMonthAndPhase(Opportunity*
3      opportunities, MonthAndYear monthAndYear, String phase)
4    {
5      return this.getExpectedRevenueByMonthAndPhaseCube()
6        (opportunities, monthAndYear, phase);
7    }
8
9    const function const (Opportunity* opportunities,
10        MonthAndYear monthAndYear, String phase)
11        : Amount getExpectedRevenueByMonthAndPhaseCube() {
12      return aggregate Opportunity* by
13      month: MonthAndYear {
14        return value Calendar().getMonth(fact.expectedCloseDate);
15      },
16      phase: String { return fact.phase; }:
17      key   Amount 1..1 {
18        return fact.expectedSalesVolume.times(fact.probability); }
19      Amount {
20        return value Amount(val: 0,
21          currency: value Currency(code: "USD")).plus(values); };
22    }
23    [...]
24  }
```

Listing 7.8: Excerpt from the *Reports* of the opportunity management application class displayed in the *class* view type

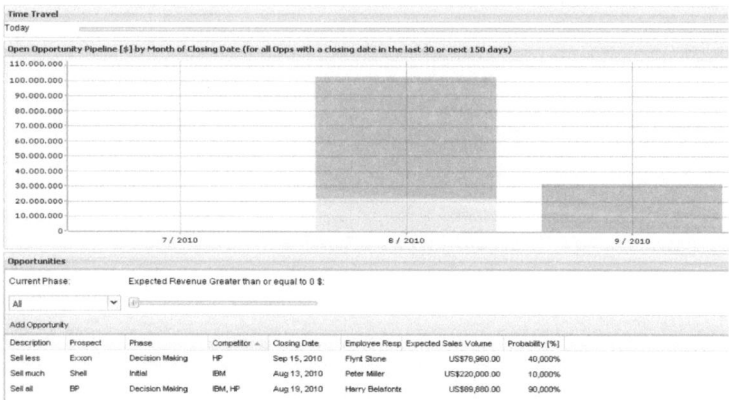

Figure 7.7.: Sceenshot of the user interface built for the "Opportunity Management" application that was built using the *Runlet* language.

developed using the view-based textual modelling approach propagated by this thesis. At several points within this case study new challenges occurred also for FURCAS itself. In the course of the project the experiences from applying FURCAS in such a large setting was fed back and let to continuous improvement of the usability and applicability of FURCAS.

Another dimension that was evaluated in the course of the *Runlet* case study was the usability of the generated editors for the defined textual view types. Applications, such as the "Opportunity Management" showed that it is feasible to work with this kind of editor. The overall development turnaround time from defining or modifying the different view types to working with the language itself can be considered relatively low. As FURCAS not only allows to quickly modify and re-generate the employed view types but also provides means that help to migrate the existing instances of the view types, an average turnaround cycle was only about 30 to 60 minutes. This includes several steps:

1. Modification or extension of the metamodel.

2. Adoption or extension of the respective view types.

3. Extension of the interpreter framework.

4. Migration and testing the applications built with the language.

This allows for rapid development and modification of languages which gives language engineers to possibility to work on new languages in an agile way. Especially in the development of domain specific languages where a close collaboration with domain experts is crucial, this short roundtrip is advantageous.

7.3.3. The Coghead Language at SAP

Coghead [wik] was a company that provided an easy to use and easy to develop *Software as a Service (SaaS)* platform. Users could easily develop applications by modelling their data schemas, in Coghead speak named *Collection*, using a web based platform. The SAP AG acquired Coghead in 2008 to extend their Software as a Service (SaaS) portfolio.

The development of these *Collections* was mainly done using a form based web interface including some graphical editors for the structural parts of the applications. Using this approach, Coghead achieved a low entrance hurdle for new customers which could easily create new and simple applications. However, once applications get larger and more complex, this way of development evolved to be more and more impractical. Therefore, a textual representation including enhanced editors seemed to be a step towards handling this problem. For prototyping a language for *Coghead*, supporting the different views of the *Coghead* platform, FURCAS was used.

The insights gained during development of this case study were mainly to see how steep the learning curve is for a developer who is inexperienced w.r.t. the FURCAS approach. In contrast to the *Runlet* case study, which aimed in the direction of evaluating the expressive power of the FURCAS approach, in the *Coghead* case study the focus was more on the understandability and applicability of FURCAS. One important difference to the *Runlet* case study was furthermore that people that were not involved in FURCAS developed the language. They were given a short introductory workshop on how to create FURCAS view types. Based on this initial training and and some further guidance, they developed the view types described in the next section.

7.3.3.1. Description of the Different View Types

Two view types were created for the *Coghead* case study. One for creating the structure and schema definitions for the *Collections* and one for defining permissions on different levels for the applications. The former view type is therefore called *Collection* whereas the latter is called *Permissions*. The total amount of classes in the metamodel is 108.

The *Collection* View Type   The data schema of a *Collection* within *Coghead* is defined with the *Collection* view type. Here, the structural aspects, such as fields and groups of fields form the data structures. In addition, expressions for default values or constraints can be attached to these fields. The expressions language is based on the *XPath* [CD] language that was originally designed for querying elements within XML documents. Actions, that can be defined for a *Collection* resemble the dynamic aspects of the language. This part of the language contributes to the Turing-completeness of *Coghead* programs.

An excerpt from the main metamodel constructs used in the *Collection* view type is depicted in Figure 7.8. The corresponding view type definition is sketched in Listing 7.9. Listing 7.10 finally illustrates the usage of this view type with a simple example.

The metrics for this view type are quite different from those gathered for the *Runlet* language. *Coghead* does include less implicitly created elements, in contrast to the massive use of the type definition constructs within *Runlet*. This fact is mainly reflected

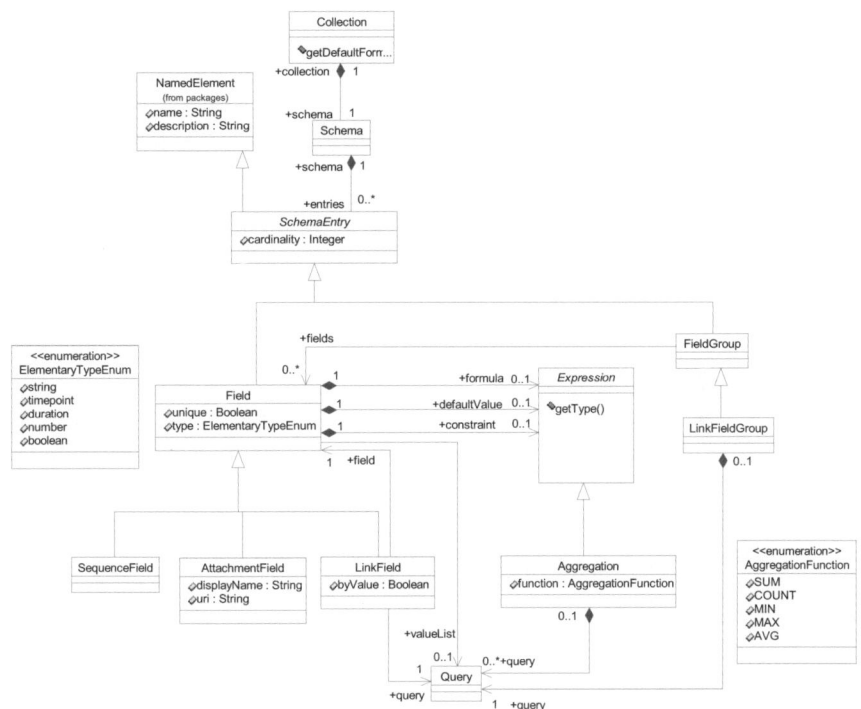

Figure 7.8.: Excerpt from the *structure* package of the *Coghead* metamodel

in the projection rate, which is 55.3 %. Also the intra view type overlap is quite low: 1.1. This view type contains a total of 29 templates.

The *Permissions* View Type   Another important feature of the *Coghead* approach is the ability to define fine grained permissions on the create applications. Figure 7.9 shows the metamodel constructs for this concept. Starting from application level, over account level down to per *Collection* level, permissions can be defined. For this purpose, the *permissions* view type was created. Listing 7.11 shows an excerpt form the view type definitions for this view type. It shows the use of OCL queries for the resolving of accounts for which certain permissions should hold. Finally, Listing 7.12 exemplifies the use of this view type by providing some simple permissions for a given *Collection*.

```
1  template Collection main context(env)
2    : "collection" name "{"
3        schema
4        actions
5      "}"
6    ;
7
8  template Schema
9    : entries{separator=";"} (isDefined(entries) ? ";")
10   ;
11
12 template SchemaEntry abstract;
13
14 template FieldGroup context(FieldGroup)
15   : "group" $cardinality name "{"
16        fields{mode=inFieldGroup, separator=";"}
17     "}"
18   ;
19
20 template Field
21   : (unique ? "unique") type $cardinality name
22     (isDefined(defaultValue) ? "default" defaultValue)
23     (isDefined(formula) ? "formula" formula)
24     (isDefined(constraint) ? "constraint" constraint)
25   ;
```

Listing 7.9: Excerpt from the *collection* view type

The intra view type overlap of the *permissions* view type is as low as possible: 1.0. The projection rate 58,7% with a total of 14 templates in the view type.

7.3.3.2. Conclusions Concerning the Coghead Case Study

As the view types of the *Coghead* case study where created by developers that have no experience with the FURCAS approach the usability and learnability of FURCAS could be evaluated in this context. It turned out that in general inexperienced developers could deal well with the template constructs, whereas special constructs such as context handling and operator templates were more difficult to handle. The view-specific constructs turned out to be quite intuitively usable.

Furthermore, this case study showed that FURCAS also allows to define view-based textual modelling languages for existing setups with a fixed metamodel and a predefined context.

336

```
1  collection Drinks {
2    string name;
3    number quantity default 6;
4    group supplier {
5      string name;
6      string email;
7      string address
8    }
9    buyDrinks ( Guests ) : Drinks {
10     ...
11   }
12 }
```

Listing 7.10: Example for a view using the *collection* view type

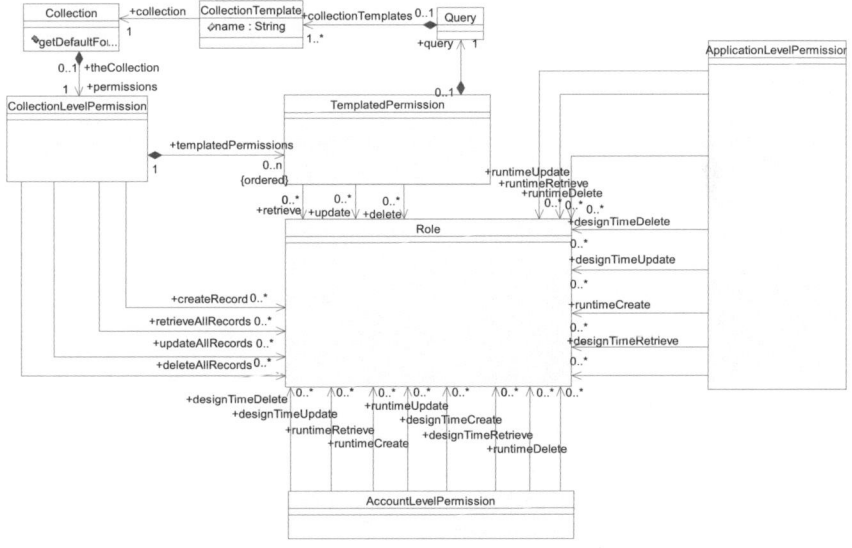

Figure 7.9.: Excerpt from the *permissions* package of the *Coghead* metamodel

```
1  template coghead::CollectionLevelPermission main context(Perm)
2  :
3    "collection" "permissions" "{"
4    "default" "{"
5      (isDefined(createRecord) ?
6        "create" ":" "(" createRecord{ separator=",",
7          query=#context(Perm).theCollection.getApplication()
8            .myAccount.roles->select(r | r.name= ?)}
9        ")" " ;"
10     )
11     (isDefined(retrieveAllRecords) ?
12       "retrieve" ":" "(" retrieveAllRecords{ separator=",",
13         query=#context(Perm).theCollection.getApplication()
14           .myAccount.roles->select(r | r.name= ?)}
15       ")" " ;"
16     )
17     (isDefined(updateAllRecords) ?
18       "update" ":" "(" updateAllRecords{ separator=",",
19         query=#context(Perm).theCollection.getApplication()
20           .myAccount.roles->select(r | r.name= ?)}
21       ")" " ;"
22     )
23     (isDefined(deleteAllRecords) ?
24       "delete" ":" "(" deleteAllRecords{ separator=",",
25         query=#context(Perm).theCollection.getApplication()
26           .myAccount.roles->select(r | r.name= ?)}
27       ")" " ;"
28     )
29     "}"
30     (isDefined(templatedPermissions) ?
31       "data-driven" "{"
32         templatedPermissions{separator=";"}
33       "}"
34     )
35     "}"
36  ;
37  [...]
```

Listing 7.11: Excerpt from the *permissions* view type

```
1 collection permissions {
2   default {
3     create : (Users,Support);
4   }
5   data-driven {
6     [ from Drinks as d where quantity = 100 ]
7       update(Admins)
8   }
9 }
```

Listing 7.12: Example for a view using the *permissions* view type

7.3.4. Additional Case Studies

In addition to the two case studies presented in detail above, two more case studies were performed using FURCAS. First, another language for business information systems, this time with focus on the financial sector, called *Finex* and second a language to create and modify metamodels themselves, including support for OCL expressions.

7.3.4.1. The FINEX Language at SAP

FINEX stands for FINancial EXpressions, which is a domain specific language developed using the FURCAS approach as a further real-world, industrial case study. The *Finex* language was designed to create business objects responsible for financial business information systems that are, for example, performing dunning runs or calculating balances.

The insights that this case study brought for the FURCAS approach is to get a feeling for the effort for developing a language using the FURCAS approach. These insights were gathered by letting experts estimate the effort which they would initially predict for developing the language using a traditional language engineering approach and comparing it with the results that where gathered during the actual development of the language with FURCAS.

It turned out that the experts estimated at least two person weeks for the initial prototype. However, this initial version could already be delivered after three days. In the course of refining the prototype and adding new functionality to the language very short roundtrips from defining new requirements to presenting the prototype could be achieved.

7.3.4.2. The MofClass Case Study

Creating and modifying metamodels using a textual representation has been tackled with different textual modelling approaches in the past. For example, *KM3* created by Jouault et al. [JB06a] included a textual notation for specifying metamodels using the TCS approach. Furthermore, the *Emfatic* tool [Dal05] allows to define metamodels for EMF in a textual way using Gymnast [GS07]. However, all these approaches do not explicitly deal with the different aspects of a metamodel, namely package hierarchy, classes and associations as well as OCL constraint and other OCL based expressions. A metamodel in the textual representations of these approaches is therefore mostly one huge text without further structuring or view building. Furthermore, OCL is only weakly supported by these approaches.

Therefore, also due to the fact that metamodelling is an essential precondition for the application of FURCAS, three different textual view types were developed for the creation of metamodels using FURCAS. The first view type is responsible for the static structure using classes, attributes and associations of a metamodel. This is the one that also the other textual metamodelling approaches support quite well. Additionally, a view point for the outline of the package hierarchy was created. In this second view type packages and classes as well as associations as first level entities can be edited on a coarse grained level. Finally, a third view type was created for to be able to edit OCL expression-based constructs such as constraints, attribute derivation rules and operation body definitions.

Especially for large metamodels, such as the *Runlet* metamodel consisting of several hundred classes the existence of an additional coarse grained view type turned out to be useful. Furthermore, as large metamodels such as the *Runlet* metamodel also tend to employ a decent set of more or less complex OCL constraints as well as other OCL-based constructs, the explicitly supported OCL view-type was also widely used.

7.3.5. Metrics Gathered for the Case Studies

Table 7.1 combines the metrics gathered for the different case studies to average numbers. A closer look on these number reveals that the case studies vary in many aspects such as the size of the mapped metamodel, the amount of view types and templates therein. The derived metrics M1.1.5 to M1.1.7 indicate an overview on the use of the special view based features of FURCAS. Especially the two different overlap rates show that this property of view based modelling was extensively used. Also the ability to hide

Metrics	Runlet	Coghead	Finex	MOF
M1.1.1: classes	233	108	63	82
M1.1.2: view types	5	2	1	3
M1.1.3: avg. templates	127.8	21.5	63	19
M1.1.4: avg. selective temp.	1.3	0.5	1	0.33
M1.1.5: % projection	31.1%	57.0%	28.1%	29.0%
M1.1.6: intra VT overlap	2.1	1.1	1.8	1.5
M1.1.7: inter VT overlap	2.8	0.15	0	0.23

Table 7.1.: Results for metrics defined for question 1.1.

Metrics	Runlet	Coghead	Finex	MOF
M1.2.1: amount of queries	76	13	8	12
M1.2.2: invertible	76	13	8	10

Table 7.2.: Results for metrics defined for question 1.2.

certain properties of a model in one view type while showing them in other view types, indicated by the projection rate, was used frequently. Only one case study lies above 50% of non-hidden properties, the three others lie around 30% which means that, in average, 70% of the properties are hidden.

The inter view type overlap also varies to a great extent depending on the language is structured. Especially in the *Runlet* language this value is rather high (2.8). This is due to the fact that the actions and expressions part is re-used in several different view types (actions, type adapter, class and binding). It also indicates that a language modularisation technique such as, for example, propagated by the MontiCore approach [KRV07b, Kra10] may be useful to extract the common parts into a common base language. Language modularisation is currently not supported by FURCAS which leads to an increased maintainability effort in the case of the *Runlet* language.

Table 7.2 shows the resulting values for question 1.2 which was to evaluate the extent to which the OCL queries used in the view type definitions could be automatically inverted. Automation is perceived to have a positive impact on the maintainability of a system. Therefore, we can say that, the higher the amount of automation, the better is the maintainability of a system. As the values of Table 7.2 indicate, the automation rate for the inversion of OCL queries was very high. Except for the MOF language were two

341

very complex OCL queries, FURCAS could automatically invert all queries used in the view types of the different languages.

7.3.6. Conclusions Drawn from the Case Studies

In general, the case studies themselves as well as the metrics gathered for the case studies show that it is possible to create complex multi-view textual languages with FURCAS. Even Turing-complete languages with extended features such as a complex type system, integrated query languages and GUI bindings can be created using the approach. The realised languages made use of the view-based concepts to a certain extent. The most used feature was the ability to project properties away in one view and show them in a different view. The selectiveness feature, on the other hand, was not used at many places. Maybe selective modelling is only sensible in very specific places within a textual language. The models resulting from the modelling with FURCAS were used in interpreters or translated to a different runtime environment, but by and large were used in a productive environment without need for additional modifications by external tools.

Chapter 8.

Conclusion

This section gives a summary of the contributions presented in this thesis. Furthermore, it discusses current limitations of the FURCAS approach in Section 8.2. Section 8.3 presents open questions that give hints to future possible extensions and improvements of the approach.

8.1. Summary

This thesis presented several contributions to different areas of model-driven engineering and language engineering. First, the *RetainmentPolicy* approach enables transformation developers to define explicit rules on how to handle external target model changes. Second, the FURCAS approach allows for the definition of textual view types that may be partial and/or overlapping w.r.t. their underlying metamodel. Third, on view level FURCAS contributes the TextBlock-decorator approach that can handle arbitrarily scoped textual views which includes selective views and views that overlap w.r.t. their underlying model. Finally, this thesis presents a view synchronisation approach that is tailored for the FURCAS approach and features retainment of format and temporarily inconsistent parts over round-trip transformations made during the modelling process.

8.1.1. Retainment Policies

The retainment policies approach is targeted at scenarios where a transformation's target models are at the same time subject to other external modifications. These modifications might either come from manual changes made by a modeller, or by other model transformations that do, e.g., refinements on these target models. With traditional model transformations, such changes would either be overwritten by the transformation, once it is re-executed, or, in the case of a bidirectional transformation synchronised back to the source model. This might not be the outcome the transformation developer wanted to realise.

To enable transformation developers to easily specify retainment behaviour this thesis provides the retainment policies approach. An extensive analysis and classification of changes that might occur in a target model as well as the possible reactions of a transformation to these changes was performed. Based on this analysis, for each possible type of change a retainment kind was defined. With the combination of a retainment kind and one or more transformation rules or a certain area in the target model to which it is applied, this forms so-called retainment policies.

With the use of the retainment policies approach, transformation developers can easily configure their standard transformations to become target model change aware. As the retainment policies are annotated within the comments of the original transformation definition, the transformation can also still be used without the retainment policies extension.

The QVT based realisation of the retainment policy approach allows for a broad adoption of the approach in practice, as QVT is the OMG standard for model to model transformations. Furthermore, this enables the approach to be used for already existent transformations and, by annotating them, making them aware of target model changes.

Being formulated on a solid formal basis the retainment policies approach has well defined formal semantics. Properties such as completeness were proven based on the formal representations of transformations and the retainment policies.

8.1.2. Definition of Textual View Types using FURCAS

Defining textual view types on models that may be partial and/or overlapping w.r.t. the used metamodel(s) was not supported by any textual modelling approach, yet. In contrast to textual view points, however, graphical view types already support this in many ways. This results in a gap between the applicability of graphical and textual models on the same level. With the use of a template based view type declaration language FURCAS closes this gap. With explicit model constructs for defining the scope of a view type as well as advanced model construction rules, which employ OCL as their main language, FURCAS leverages textual views to the same level of abilities as graphical modelling languages.

FURCAS bases on an existing template based approach called TCS and extends TCS's concepts with constructs for the view-based modelling paradigm as well as OCL based lookup and creation rules. With the use of OCL, FURCAS reuses a language that language engineers would use anyway in the construction of a metamodel's constraint system. Therefore, no new language needs to be learned which improves the willingness of language engineers to use the approach as well as lowering the time needed for the initial learning phase of the FURCAS view type definition language.

In order to keep the OCL expressions bidirectional, which is required to retain the ability of TCS to specify mappings from text to model as well as from model to text in one definition, an OCL inversion mechanism is introduced. This approach automatically derives inverse expressions for the OCL queries of a FURCAS view type specification. Only a small set of OCL expressions cannot be automatically inverted and require a manual specification of the inversion expression.

A formal validation of the properties a view-based modelling approach may support showed that FURCAS enables view-based modelling for textual languages to a nearly feature complete extent. Additionally, the industry scale validations of FURCAS show that it is possible to define complex, real-world view-based languages using FURCAS. Furthermore, it showed that the special view building constructs where used to a reasonable extent.

8.1.3. Non-Intrusive Textual Views using FURCAS TextBlocks-Models

Keeping the representation and layout information of views decoupled from the actual models was possible in graphical modelling languages, but they were tightly coupled in textual modelling languages. The TextBlocks approach introduced in this thesis resolves this coupling and allows to non-intrusively annotate models with their textual representation. This approach also features the storage of custom layout as well as temporary inconsistency in the textual representation.

To achieve this kind of non-intrusive textual representation, FURCAS includes the TextBlocks metamodel which can represent arbitrary textual structures. In combination with the view type definition, the special FURCAS editor allows for the interaction with the textual view representation featuring all kinds of productivity enhancing component.

Extensive editor support for the TextBlocks approach, including refactoring tools and a generic auto-completion approach enables users of the view-based approach to efficiently interact with textual views on their models. As incomplete work is retained, also fast view switching for increased productivity [FKN+92] is possible.

The case-studies performed as validation for the approach showed that it is possible to use a feature rich and complex textual modelling language to create domain specific applications.

8.1.4. View Synchronisation for Textual Views

Whenever multiple views simultaneously represent a model and are at the same time editable, synchronisation challenges arise. In the special case of textual views research could not present a satisfying solution, yet. Especially support for temporarily inconsistent textual representations and retainment of textual layout information was missing.

This thesis introduced an incremental, element retaining and bidirectional update mechanism that is specifically tailored to the use of textual views. With the use of the retainment policy approach, introduced early in this thesis, this update mechanism is capable of retaining layout information as well as temporarily inconsistent states of a model's textual representation.

Due to the incrementality of the approach, the FURCAS editor can update the model in the background, while the modeller is still working on the model. This raises the productivity as no additional time is required for the view to model update transformation.

Formal validation of the synchronisation properties of the FURCAS approach ensures that certain requirements for view-based modelling are met.

8.2. Limitations

The assumptions and limitations of the retainment policy approach have already been discussed at the end of the corresponding chapter in Section 3.4 and 3.12 respectively. Therefore, this Section will only discuss the limitations of the FURCAS approach itself.

8.2.1. Determination of Domain Completeness for OCL Queries not Supported

As discussed in Section 5.3.2.1, currently the view types of FURCAS cannot be checked for domain completeness on the level of their included OCL queries. Brucker et al. [BDW06], identify that reasoning on the total scope of an OCL expression is still an unsolved challenge. They say that this is mainly due to the fact that the OCL specification [Obj10a] is "based on naive set theory and an informal notion of *model*" and "it assumes a universe for values and objects and algebras over it without any concern of existence and consistency".

Therefore, one limitation of the view type approach of FURCAS is that the scope of the view type cannot always be completely determined. However, as queries can only narrow the selection made in a template rather than widen it, the scope determined by FURCAS may only be a superset of the actual scope. Thus, no elements will be considered out of scope, if they are actually within the scope if the OCL query is considered.

A solution to this problem could be the use of a stronger semantic definition of OCL, as also proposed by Brucker et al. [BDW06]. Based on this definition, the domain completeness determination could be extended to the complete expressive power of OCL.

8.2.2. Mergeability not Guaranteed

In the course of editing a textual representation of a model it is inevitable that in some cases view and model are out of sync. If during this time, modifications to the underlying model, e.g., through other views, are performed FURCAS may need to merge these changes, once the view is again in a consistent state. As these changes may also conflict with each other, a completely automatic merge is not always possible. In these cases FURCAS will provide an interactive merge, based on the textual representation of the model. However, as actually more than just the textual information is present, i.e., there is also the underlying model, this may not always be the best solution. An integrated merge which uses both, information from the textual merge as well as from a merge on model level could improve this process.

8.2.3. Respect to Access Control

Respect to access control is one of the properties that is requested by the view synchronisation properties presented in Section 4.5.3.2. However, the validation of FURCAS against this property (cf. Section 7.1.2.9) showed that there is one case in which this property does not hold. This is the case when an element that is deleted through a view contains elements in its containment hierarchy and the current view type is not *downwards containment complete*. According to the semantics of containment, defined in the MOF specification [Obj06], all transitively contained elements will be deleted once their parent element is deleted. This contradicts with the requirement for access control which says that only access to those elements should be granted that are shown in the view. Modellers need to be aware of this limitation when they use FURCAS.

8.2.4. Deletion of Partially Viewed Elements

One of the main challenges that the FURCAS approach had to face was the ability to retain partially viewed elements during editing. As, at least in theory, using textual interaction a modeller could first delete a whole textual view using textual deletion and then re-type the very same constructs later-on. If these actions occur within a larger period of time in between, the limitation of the *undo* action stack (cf. Section 7.2.3.3) may avoid a revert of the deletion action using the *undo* action. Then the parts of the element that were not viewed in the current, manually re-typed view will be lost.

8.2.5. Trade-Off Between Evolution of Concrete And Abstract Syntax

One of the main differences between FURCAS and other textual modelling environments is that FURCAS stores primarily the abstract syntax, the underlying model. It keeps the concrete syntax, the textual views, loosely coupled to the actual model. This gives advantages in evolution scenarios when the concrete syntax evolves faster than the abstract syntax. While the underlying model may stay unchanged, for a new version of the concrete syntax only the corresponding templates in the view types need to be changed. As the instances of a view type, which are represented as a TextBlocks model are directly connected to their corresponding view type model, changes to that view type model can directly be reflected in the TextBlocks model, too. For example, if a language engineer changes the keyword `bo` to `businessObject`, all connected `LiteralRefs` will find the new value and update their textual representation accordingly.

On the other hand, the evolution problem is now shifted towards the metamodel evolution and model co-evolution problem. Metamodel changes now require a migration of all instance models as well as the view types. For the area of metamodel evolution and model co-evolution, recently a set of promising approaches emerged [BGGK07, Wac07, HBJ08, BG10]. With the use of such an approach also the language evolution approach in FURCAS could be handled.

In the end the language engineer has to decide on this trade-off, which is influenced by what is anticipated to change more frequently – the abstract or the concrete syntax.

8.3. Open Questions and Future Work

This section gives an overview on possible areas of future research based on the results of this thesis.

8.3.1. Hybrid Model Merge

As outlined in the limitations section, there are cases where it becomes inevitable to merge changes from a view with those coming from external sources applied to the same underlying model. The current merge approach that FURCAS employs is solely based on the concrete textual syntax and uses standard techniques for that. However, as in FURCAS not only the textual but also the abstract model representation as well as a version history of the textual representation is available, this task could by improved. Merge techniques that take the semantics of the merged text into account became available some years ago [Men02]. The EMF framework on which FURCAS' implementation is based, also came up with an approach for merging models called *EMF Compare* [Bru10]. A hybrid approach for merging changed textual views with their modified underlying model could alleviate the merge problem tremendously. As most of the time, due to the given links between view and model, there are already existing correspondences, these could be exploited to improve the merging process [PB03].

8.3.2. Recovering of Deleted Model Elements

Recovering of deleted, partially viewed elements is not always possible. The limitations section already mentioned that there may be cases where having the possibility to undo unintended changes by using an IDE's undo stack may also not always be possible.

However, an idea to get rid of this problem would be to introduce an approach that tries to revert unintended deletions of partially viewed elements. This could be achieved by trying to get a complete image of the deleted element by its remains in different, still existing view instances. Analysing the context of the remaining textual representations and matching it according to the view type definitions might give enough information to be able to reconstruct a deleted model element completely.

8.3.3. Modular Development of View Types

Having different view types for the different aspects of a model element enables for better separation of concerns. However, there are still cases where multiple view types share a common part of a syntax definition. Especially core constructs, such as an expression system, strive to be reused. The case studies performed with FURCAS also showed that it is a valid use case to have a larger core language that is reused several specific languages that extend the base language only slightly.

To be able to maintain such core components in a better way, it is inevitable to extract them into an external, reusable module that can then be imported by the using view types. Krahn [Kra10] introduced a module concept for the MontiCore approach for textual modelling. Also Kleppe [Kle09] mentioned the use of an interface language to ease extensibility of software languages.

Still, FURCAS with its extensions to explicit view-based modelling, extensive use of OCL expressions would need a more specialised approach for modularisation. For example, in order to reuse OCL queries one could introduce the notion of generic type system for OCL [Kya05] to these queries. This would allow to write generic base expressions that could then be specialised in the using view types and bound to a certain type.

Appendix A.

Cheat Sheet

Symbol	Description	Pg.
	Basic Definitions	
$\perp$	denotes the undefined state	20
$\mathbb{N}^+$	denotes the set of positive natural numbers including ∞ and excluding 0.	
$\mathbb{N}_0^+$	denotes the set of positive natural numbers including ∞ and 0.	
$\mathbb{N}^\perp := \mathbb{N}_0^+ \cup \perp$	denotes the set of positive natural numbers including 0, ∞ and an undefined state.	
$\mathbb{B} := \{true, false\}$	denotes the set of logical values.	
$\mathbb{D} := \{first, second\}$	denotes a set of values for the distinction between the first and the second end of an association.	
$proj_n(x_1, ..., x_n, ..., x_m) = x_n$	denotes the n-th element in a given tuple.	
$\mathcal{P}(X)$	denotes the powerset of a given set X	
$\mathcal{B}(X)$	denotes set of all multi-sets over a given set X	
$\#(X)$	denotes the cardinality of a given set or tuple X	
$\#_y(X)$	denotes the cardinality of element y in a given multi-set X	
r^*	denotes the reflexive transitive closure of a binary relation r and a set-valued function (which is another representation of a binary relation)	
r^+	denotes the transitive closure of a binary relation r	
$e \in T$	where T is a tuple means $e \in \bigcup_{n=1..\#(T)} (proj_n(T)$, if $proj_n(T)$ is a set; $\varnothing$, else$)$	
$\exists e_1 \in E_1, ..., e_n \in E_n\|...$	is shorthand for $\exists e_1 \in E_1\|(...\|\exists e_n \in E_n\|(...)...)$	

Symbol	Description	Pg.
	Models and Metamodels	
MM	Metamodel	20
C	is the finite set of classes	
A	is the finite set of associations (for sake of brevity, I consider all associations as navigable in both directions)	
P	is the finite set of attributes	
$first : A \rightarrow C$	is the mapping of associations to their first end	
$second : A \rightarrow C$	is the mapping of associations to their second end	
$attributes : C \rightarrow P$	is the mapping of classes to their attributes	
$isComposite : A \times \mathbb{D} \rightarrow \mathbb{B}$	returns the information whether an end of a given association is a composite end or not	
M	Model	21
$O \subset O_{MM}$	denotes the finite set of the model's object IDs	
$L \subset L_{MM}$	denotes the finite set of the model's link IDs	
$V \subset V_{MM}$	denotes the finite set of the model's attribute values	
$class : O \rightarrow C$	returns the class $c \in C$ of a given object $o \in O$	
$association : L \rightarrow A$	returns the association $a \in A$ of a given link $l \in L$	
$attribute : V \rightarrow P$	returns the attribute $p \in P$ of a given attribute value $v \in V$	
$firstObject : L \rightarrow O$	returns the first object $o \in O$ for a given link $l \in L$	
$secondObject : L \rightarrow O$	returns the second object $o \in O$ for a given link $l \in L$	
$compositeLinks : O \rightarrow \mathcal{P}(L)$	returns the links in which a given object acts as composite object	
$childObjects : O \rightarrow \mathcal{P}(O)$	returns all child objects for a given composite object	
$compositeParent : O \rightarrow \mathcal{P}(O)$	returns the composite parent object for a given child object	
$value : O \times A \rightarrow \mathcal{P}(O)$	returns the attribute value for a given object and attribute	
$orderL \subseteq L \times L$	is a strict partial order on L where $(l_1, l_2) \in orderL \iff l_1$ occurs directly before l_2	
$orderV \subseteq V \times V$	is a strict partial order on V where $(v_1, v_2) \in orderV \iff v_1$ occurs directly before v_2.	
$Models_{MM}$	denotes the set of all (consistent) models for a given metamodel MM	

Symbol	Description	Pg.
	Changes	
δ_o^+	creating an instance o	23
δ_o^-	deleting an instance o	
δ_{l,o_1,o_2}^+	creating a link l between instances o_1 and o_2	
δ_{l,o_1,o_2}^-	deleting a link l between instances o_1 and o_2	
δ_{l_1,l_2}^o	change of ordering of a link l_1 which is swapped with l_2 if $association(l)$ is ordered at its first or second end	
$\delta_{o,a,v}^s$	setting attribute a of instance o to value v	
$\delta_{o,a,v}^u$	unsetting attribute a of instance o for value v	
δ_{o,a,v_1,v_2}^o	change of order of value v_1 of attribute a of instance o which is swapped with v_2 if $isOrdered(a) = true$	
$element : Changes_{MM} \rightarrow Models_{MM}$	yields the element under change	
Δ	Complex change	23
∇_δ	Consistent change in order to keep a model consistent after change δ occured	67
$consistentChanges$: $\mathcal{P}(Changes_{MM}) \rightarrow \mathcal{P}(Changes_{MM})$	yields the consistent changes of a given set of changes	

Symbol		Description	Pg.
		Transformations	
$leftModelPattern_T$ $proj_1(T)$	:=	yields the left model pattern of a transformation T	25
$rightModelPattern_T$ $proj_2(T)$	:=	yields the left model pattern of a transformation T	
lmp_T $leftModelPattern(T)$	:=	shorthand for $leftModelPattern$	
rmp_T $rightModelPattern(T)$	:=	shorthand for $rightModelPattern$	
$\leadsto_T$		Application of transformation T	26
$\leadsto(M_s, M_t)$		Yields the set of changes applied to M_t through the transformation.	
$rules$ $Transformations_{MM} \rightarrow \mathcal{P}(Transformations_{MM})$	:	yields the rules contained in a rule based transformation	69
$Trace$		Trace model	70
Θ		Set of tracelinks	
$source : \Theta \rightarrow \mathcal{P}(M_l)$		yields the set of source elements of a trace link	
$target : \Theta \rightarrow \mathcal{P}(M_r)$		yields the set of target elements of a trace link	
$rule : \Theta \rightarrow rules(T)$		yields the rule from the transformation that was responsible for the creation of the trace link	
$orderT \subseteq \Theta \times \Theta$		is a strict partial order defined on Θ where $(\theta_1, \theta_2) \in orderT \iff \theta_1$ occurs directly before θ_2. This defines the order in which the model objects, links or values where set in the target model according to the transformation.	
$projectOrderL : \Theta \times \Theta \rightarrow L \times L$		projects the order as given in the tracelink to a strict partial order of links.	
$projectOrderV : \Theta \times \Theta \rightarrow V \times V$		projects the order as given in the tracelink to a strict partial order of attribute values.	

Symbol	Description	Pg.
	Retainment Policies	
⊥	is the `NotSet RetainmentKind`	87
∅	is the `never RetainmentKind`	
►	is the `targetChangedExclusively RetainmentKind`	
◄	is the `sourceChangedExclusively RetainmentKind`	
■	is the `sourceAndTargetChanges RetainmentKind`	
◄►	is the `sourceXorTargetChanged RetainmentKind`	
■►	is the `targetChanged RetainmentKind`	
◄■	is the `sourceChanged RetainmentKind`	
◄■►	is the `always RetainmentKind`.	

Appendix B.

Complex Ocl Inversion Example

The following example will show that also rather complex OCL expressions can be inverted by the approach presented in Section 5.3.3. Listing B.1 shows the expressions that should be inverted. This purpose of this expression is to lookup MOF classes in their namespaces by a given qualified name that is represented by a string separated by double colons, such as e.g., $A::Test$. In this example, we want to invert this expression to get from a given class with name "Test" that resides in a package "A" to the qualified name $A::Test$.

```
236  MofClass(name='Test', container=MofPackage(name='A')) :=
237    let t=Sequence{1..?(3).size()}->select(j|?(3).subString(j,j+1)='::')
238      ->iterate(i; acc:Tuple(pos:Integer,ns:Set(Namespace),qn:String)=
239        Tuple{pos=1, ns=null, qn=''} |
240      let namePart=?(2).subString(acc.pos, i-1) in
241        Tuple{pos=i+2,
242          ns=if acc.ns=null then
243            Namespace.allInstances()->select(
244              ns2 | ns2.container->isEmpty() and ns2.name=namePart)
245          else
246            acc.ns.contents->select(ns2 | ns2.name=namePart)->asSet()
247          endif,
248          qn=acc.qn.concat('::').concat(namePart)}) in
249    t.ns.contents->select(c | c.name=?(1).subString(t.pos, ?(1).size()))
```

Listing B.1: Building the inverse of a complex OCL expression: the source expression

The inversion will tackle the three different occurrences (1), (2) and (3) of the "?"-expression. Listing B.2 inverts occurrence (1) while Listing B.3 handles occurrence (2) in the iterator body. Occurrence (3), in the source of the iterator is inverted in Listing B.5

```
250 (1) MofClass(name='Test', container=MofPackage(name='A'))_{t.pos,?.size()}
251     := t.ns.contents->^select(c | c.name=?)   --source rule-->
252 (1) Set{MofClass(name = 'Test',
253         container = MofPackage(name= 'A'))_{t.pos,?.size()}}->any(true) :=
254     c.name=?
255 (1) MofClass(name = 'Test',
256         container=MofPackage(name= 'A'))_{t.pos,?.size()} :=
257     c.name=?   --property rule-->
258 (1) 'Test'_{t.pos,?.size()} := ?
259 (1) => ?_{t.pos,?.size()} := 'Test'
260 => t.pos = ?.size() - 4
```

Listing B.2: Inverting occurrence (1) of the "?" literal.

```
261 (2) MofClass(name = 'Test', container=MofPackage(name= 'A'))_{1,t.pos} :=
262 let t=Sequence{1..?.size()}->select(j|?.subString(j, j+1) = '::')
263 ->iterate(i;
264     acc:Tuple(pos:Integer, ns:Set(Namespace), qn:String) =
265         Tuple{pos=1, ns=null, qn=''} |
266     let namePart=?.subString(acc.pos, i-1) in
267     Tuple{pos=i+2,
268         ns=if acc.ns=null then
269             Namespace.allInstances()->select(
270             ns2 | ns2.container->isEmpty() and ns2.name=namePart)
271         else
272             acc.ns.contents->select(ns2 | ns2.name=namePart)->asSet()
273         endif,
274         qn=acc.qn.concat('::').concat(namePart)}).ns.contents
275             --replace namePart with init of let expression -->
276 (2) MofClass(name = 'Test', container=MofPackage(name= 'A'))_{1,t.pos} :=
277 let t=Sequence{1..?.size()}->select(j|?.subString(j, j+1) = '::')
278 ->iterate(i;
279     acc:Tuple(pos:Integer, ns:Set(Namespace), qn:String) =
280         Tuple{pos=1, ns=null, qn=''} |
281     Tuple{pos=i+2,
282     ns=if acc.ns=null then
283     Namespace.allInstances()->select(
284     ns2 | ns2.container->isEmpty() and
285         ns2.name=?.subString(acc.pos, i-1))
286     else
287         acc.ns.contents->select(ns2 |
288         ns2.name=?.subString(acc.pos, i-1))->asSet()
```

358

```
289   endif,
290   qn=acc.qn.concat('::').concat(?.subString(acc.pos, i-1))})
291   .ns.contents
292      --navigating backwards form c to container-->property rule-->
293
294 (2) MofPackage(name= 'A')_{1,t.pos} =
295 let t=Sequence{1..?.size()}->select(j|?.subString(j, j+1) = '::')
296   ->iterate(i;
297      acc:Tuple(pos:Integer, ns:Set(Namespace), qn:String) =
298         Tuple{pos=1, ns=null, qn=''} |
299   Tuple{pos=i+2,
300    ns=if acc.ns=null then
301      Namespace.allInstances()->select(
302      ns2 | ns2.container->isEmpty() and
303        ns2.name=?.subString(acc.pos, i-1))
304    else
305      acc.ns.contents->select(ns2 |
306        ns2.name=?.subString(acc.pos, i-1))->asSet()
307    endif,
308    qn=acc.qn.concat('::').concat(?.subString(acc.pos, i-1))})
309    .ns
310      --replace ns at last iteration index last_i and replace ns -->
311 (2.last) MofPackage(name= 'A')_{1,last_i+2} =
312 let t=Sequence{1..?.size()}->select(j|?.subString(j, j+1) = '::')
313 ->at(last_i)
314 ->iterate(last_i; acc:Tuple(pos:Integer,ns:Set(Namespace),qn:String)=
315   Tuple{pos=1, ns=null, qn=''} |
316    Tuple{pos_{last_i}=last_i+2,
317      MofPackage(name= 'A')):=if acc.ns_{last_i}=null then
318        Namespace.allInstances()->select(
319        ns2 | ns2.container->isEmpty() and ns2.name=?.subString(
320         acc.pos_{last_i}, last_i-1))
321      else
322        acc.ns_{last_i}.contents->select(ns2 |
323          ns2.name=?.subString(acc.pos_{last_i}, last_i-1))->asSet()
324      endif,
325      qn=acc.qn_{last_i}.concat('::').concat(
326        ?.subString(acc.pos_{last_i}, last_i-1))}).ns
```

Listing B.3: Inverting occurrence (2) of the "?" literal.

Now we can investigate the ns property of the tuple as it contains the substituted model element as well as an ?-expression.

```
327  (2.last.ns) MofPackage(name= 'A'):=
328  if acc.ns_last_i=null then --if then rule
329    Namespace.allInstances()->select(
330      ns2 | ns2.container->isEmpty() and
331        ns2.name=?.subString(acc.pos_last_i, last_i-1))
332  else
333    acc.ns.contents->select(ns2 |
334      ns2.name=?.subString(acc.pos_last_i, last_i-1))->asSet()
335  endif
336
337  (2.last.ns.then)
338  MofPackage(name= 'A')  :=
339    Namespace.allInstances()->select(ns2|ns2.container->isEmpty() and
340      ns2.name=?.subString(acc.pos_last_i, last_i-1)))
341      --property rule
342
343  (2.last.ns.then)
344  MofPackage(name= 'A').container->isEmpty() = true and
345    --condition to be set to true!
346    'A' := ?.subString(acc.pos_last_i, last_i-1))
347  ?_acc.pos_last_i,last_i-1  = 'A'
```

Listing B.4: Determination of the ns property of occurrence (2) of the "?" literal.

We can omit else part as this evaluates to true, therefore we need to ensure that the condition is set to true. This is achieved by setting $acc.ns = null$. Next we insert this part into parent expression, as this is the initial value of acc. There we get $Tuple\{pos=1, ns=null, qn=''\}$ which is the intial state of the iterate expression and which lets us assume that the reverse iteration can be stopped at this point. From that we can conclude that: $acc.pos_{last_i} = 1$ and therefore: $?_{1,last_i-1} = 'A'$ and finally $last_i = 2$.

The value of first segment of ? is thus $?_{1,1} = 'A'$.

The `acc.pos` for the $last_i$ can then be determined as:

$$\text{pos}_{last_i} = 2 + 2$$

$$\Rightarrow \text{pos}_{last_i} = 4$$

Then we can insert $\text{pos}_{last_i} = 4$ in the formula for occurence (1):

$$\Rightarrow ?_{.\text{pos}_{last_i},?.\texttt{size}()} := \texttt{'Test'}$$

$$\Rightarrow ?_{4,?.\texttt{size}()} := \texttt{'Test'}$$

from that we find that:

$$\Rightarrow ?.\texttt{size}() = 7$$

For the last segment of ? we get $?_{4,7} := \texttt{'Test'}$. Thus, the last missing segment of ? is $?_{2,3}$.

Furthermore, we can insert $last_i = 1$ and `?.size()` = 7 into the source expression of the iterate expression:

```
348  (3)  Sequence{1..7}->select(j|?.subString(j, j+1) = '::') := {2}
349        --j = 2
350  (3)  ?.subString(2, 2+1) := '::'
351  Which leads to the last segment of ?:
352  ?2,3 = '::'
```

Listing B.5: Determination of the ns property of occurrence (3) of the "?" literal.

Putting all segments together results in the final value for ?:

$$? = \texttt{'A'} + \texttt{'::'} + \texttt{'Test'}$$

$$? = \texttt{'A :: Test'} \quad q.e.d.$$

Bibliography

[AHK06]   Michael Altenhofen, Thomas Hettel, and Stefan Kusterer. Ocl support in an industrial environment. In *MoDELS Workshops*, pages 169–178, 2006.

[Ara89]   G. Arango. Domain analysis: from art form to engineering discipline. *SIGSOFT Softw. Eng. Notes*, 14(3):152–159, 1989.

[AS07]   C. Amelunxen and A. Schürr. Formalizing Model Transformation Rules for UML/MOF 2. *IET Software Journal*, 2(3):204–222, June 2007. Special Issue: Language Engineering.

[AS08]   Colin Atkinson and Dietmar Stoll. Orthographic modeling environment. In José Luiz Fiadeiro and Paola Inverardi, editors, *FASE*, volume 4961 of *Lecture Notes in Computer Science*, pages 93–96. Springer, 2008.

[Bar08]   Christian Bartelt. Consistence preserving model merge in collaborative development processes. In *CVSM '08: Proceedings of the 2008 international workshop on Comparison and versioning of software models*, pages 13–18, New York, NY, USA, 2008. ACM.

[BCD+89]   Patrick Borras, Dominique Clément, Thierry Despeyroux, Janet Incerpi, Gilles Kahn, Bernard Lang, and Victor Pascual. Centaur: The system. *SIGPLAN Notices*, pages 14–24, 1989.

[BCR94]   V. Basili, G. Caldeira, and H. D. Rombach. *Encyclopedia of Software Engineering*, chapter The Goal Question Metric Approach. Wiley, 1994.

[BDW06]   Achim D Brucker, Jürgen Doser, and Burkhart Wolff. Semantic issues of OCL: Past, present, and future. *Electronic Communications of EASST*, 5:213–228, 2006.

[BG10]   Erik Burger and Boris Gruschko. A change metamodel for the evolution of mof-based metamodels. In *Modellierung*, volume 161 of *LNI*, pages 285–300. GI, 2010.

[BGGK07]   Steffen Becker, Thomas Goldschmidt, Boris Gruschko, and Heiko Koziolek. A Process Model and Classification Scheme for Semi-Automatic Meta-Model Evolution. In *Proc. 1st Workshop MDD, SOA und IT-Management (MSI'07)*, pages 35–46. GI, GiTO-Verlag, April 2007.

[BMS08]   Claus Brabrand, Anders Möller, and Michek I. Schwartzbach. Dual syntaxes for XML languages. *Information Systems*, 33(4-5):385–406, 2008.

[Bru10]   Cédric Brun. Diff, merge and patch your models with helios. `http://model-driven-blogging.blogspot.com/2010/03/diff-merge-and-patch-your-models-with.html`, 2010. Last retrieved 2010-08-21.

[BW02]   Achim D. Brucker and Burkhart Wolff. HOL-OCL: Experiences, Consequences and Design Choices. In *UML 2002: Model Engineering, Concepts And Tools, Number 2460 in Lecture Notes in Computer Science*, pages 196–211. Springer, 2002.

[Cat93]   R Cattell. The object database standard: ODMG-93, 1993.

[CD]   James Clark and Steve DeRose. XML Path Language (XPath). `http://www.w3.org/TR/xpath/`.

[CH06]   Krzysztof Czarnecki and Simon Helsen. Feature-based survey of model transformation approaches. *IBM Systems Journal*, 45(3):621–646, 2006.

[Cle03]   Paul Clements. *Documenting software architectures: Views and beyond*. SEI series in software engineering. Addison-Wesley, Boston, Mass., 2003.

[Cod91]   Edgar F. Codd. *The relational model for database management: Version 2*. Addison-Wesley, Reading, Mass., reprinted with corr. edition, 1991.

[CT05]   Jordi Cabot and Ernest Teniente. Computing the relevant instances that may violate an ocl constraint. In Oscar Pastor and João Falcão e Cunha, editors, *CAiSE*, volume 3520 of *Lecture Notes in Computer Science*, pages 48–62. Springer, 2005.

[CT09]   Jordi Cabot and Ernest Teniente. Incremental integrity checking of uml/ocl conceptual schemas. *J. Syst. Softw.*, 82(9):1459–1478, 2009.

[CW01]   Phil Cook and Jim Welsh. Incremental parsing in language-based editors: user needs and how to meet them. *Software: Practice and Experience*, 31:1461–1486, 2001.

[Dal05]   C. Daly. Emfatic language for EMF development. http://wiki.eclipse.org/Emfatic, 2005. last visited: 13/08/2010.

[DC01]   Kees Dorst and Nigel Cross. Creativity in the design process: co-evolution of problem-solution. *Design Studies*, 22(5):425 – 437, 2001.

[Des84]   Thierry Despeyroux. Executable specification of static semantics. In *International Symposium on Semantics of Data Types*, volume 173 of *Lecture Notes in Computer Science*. Springer, 1984.

[DGHKL84] Veronique Donzeau-Gouge, Gerard Huet, Gilles Kahn, and Bernard Lang. *Programming Environments Based on Structured Editors: The MENTOR Experience*. McGraw-Hill, 1984.

[Dim05]   Sergey Dimitriev. Language oriented programming: The next programming paradigm. *onBoard Magazine*, 2, 2005.

[DJL88]   P. Deransart, M. Jourdan, and B. Lorho. *Attribute Grammars: Definitions, Systems, and Bibliography*, volume 323 of *LNCS*. Springer-Verlag, 1988.

[DQPvS03] Remco M. Dijkman, Dick A. C. Quartel, Luis F. Pires, and Marten J. van Sinderen. An approach to relate viewpoints and modeling languages. In *7th International Enterprise Distributed Object Computing Conference (EDOC 2003), Proceedings*, pages 14–27, Los Alamitos, Calif., 2003. IEEE Computer Society.

[Ecl10a]   Eclipse Foundation. Eclipse Java Development Tools (JDT) Subproject. http://www.eclipse.org/jdt/, 2010. Last retrieved 2010-07-06.

[Ecl10b]   Eclipse Foundation.   Graphical Modeling Framework Homepage. `http://www.eclipse.org/gmf/`, 2010. Last retrieved 2010-07-06.

[Ecl10c]   Eclipse Foundation. The Eclipse Modelling Project. `http://www.eclipse.org/modeling/`, 2010. Last retrieved 2010-07-06.

[EHTE97]   Hartmut Ehrig, Reiko Heckel, Gabi Taentzer, and Gregor Engels. A combined reference model- and view-based approach to system specification. *Int. Journal of Software and Knowledge Engeneering*, 7:457–477, 1997.

[Ern99]   Johannes Ernst.   What is metamodeling, and what is it good for?   `http://infogrid.org/wiki/Reference/WhatIsMetaModeling`, 1999. Last retrieved 2010-08-18.

[EWH07]   Matthias Erche, Michael Wagner, and Christian Hein. Mapping Visual Notations to MOF Compliant Models with QVT-Relations. In *SAC '07: Proc. of the 2007 ACM Symposium on Applied Computing*, pages 1037–1038, New York, NY, USA, 2007. ACM.

[FCS+10]   Robert M. Fuhrer, Philippe Charles, Stanley Sutton, Jurgen Vinju, and Oege de Moor. IMP: The IDE Meta-Tooling Platform. `http://www.eclipse.org/imp/`, 2010. last retrieved: 2010-07-08.

[FGM+07]   J. Nathan Foster, Michel B. Greenwald, Jonathan T. Moore, Benjamin C. Pierce, and Alan Schmitt. Combinators for bidirectional tree transformations: A linguistic approach to the view-update problem. *ACM Trans. Program. Lang. Syst.*, 3, 2007.

[Fie00]   Roy Thomas Fielding. *Architectural styles and the design of network-based software architectures*.   PhD thesis, University of California, Irvine, 2000.

[FKN+92]   A. Finkelstein, J. Kramer, B. Nuseibeh, L. Finkelstein, and M. Goedicke. Viewpoints: A framework for integrating multiple perspectives in system development. *International Journal of Software Engineering and Knowledge Engineering*, 2, 1992.

[Fon07]   Frédéric Fondement. *Concrete syntax definition for modeling languages.*
              PhD thesis, Ecole Polytechnique Fédérale de Lausanne, 2007.

[Fou]   Eclipse Foundation. Eclipse textual modelling framework. `http://`
              `www.eclipse.org/modeling/tmf/`. Last retrieved 2010-08-20.

[Fou10]   Eclipse Foundation.   Eclipse XText Website.   `http://www.`
              `eclipse.org/Xtext/`, 2010. Last retrieved 2010-07-06.

[Fow05]   Martin Fowler.   Language workbenches: The killer-app for do-
              main specific languages?   `http://www.martinfowler.com/`
              `articles/languageWorkbench.html`, 2005.

[Gar08]   Miguel Garcia. Bidirectional synchronization of multiple views of soft-
              ware models. In *Proceedings of the Workshop on Domain-Specific Mod-
              eling Languages (DSML-2008)*, volume 324 of *CEUR-WS*, pages 7–19,
              2008.

[Gar09]   Miguel Garcia. *On the Formalization of Model-Driven Software Engin-
              eering.* PhD thesis, Technische Universität Hamburg-Harburg, Hamburg,
              Germany, 2009.

[GBU08]   Thomas Goldschmidt, Steffen Becker, and Axel Uhl. Classification of
              Concrete Textual Syntax Mapping Approaches. In *Proceedings of the
              4th European Conference on Model Driven Architecture - Foundations
              and Applications*, volume 5059 of *Lecture Notes in Computer Science*,
              pages 169–184. Springer-Verlag Berlin Heidelberg, 2008.

[GBU09a]   Thomas Goldschmidt, Steffen Becker, and Axel Uhl. FURCAS: Frame-
              work for UUID-Retaining Concrete to Abstract Syntax Mappings. In
              *Proceedings of the 5th European Conference on Model Driven Architec-
              ture - Foundations and Applications (ECMDA 2009) - Tools and Con-
              sultancy Track*. CTIT, 2009.

[GBU09b]   Thomas Goldschmidt, Steffen Becker, and Axel Uhl. Textual views
              in model driven engineering. In *Proceedings of the 35th EUR-
              OMICRO Conference on Software Engineering and Advanced Applic-
              ations (SEAA)*. IEEE, 2009.

[GBU10]   Thomas Goldschmidt, Steffen Becker, and Axel Uhl. Incremental Up-
            dates for Textual Modeling of Large Scale Models. In *Proceedings of the
            15th IEEE International Conference on Engineering of Complex Com-
            puter Systems (ICECCS 2010) - Poster Paper*. IEEE, 2010.

[GHJV95]   Erich Gamma, Richard Helm, Ralph Johnson, and John Vlissides.
            Design Patterns: Elements of Reusable Object-Oriented Software.
            Addison-Wesley, 1995.

[Gol06]   Thomas Goldschmidt. Grammar based code transformation for the
            model driven architecture. Master's thesis, Hochschule Furtwangen Uni-
            versity, Furtwangen, Germany, August 2006.

[Gol08]   Thomas Goldschmidt. Towards an incremental update approach for con-
            crete textual syntaxes for UUID-based model repositories. In Dragan
            Gasevic, Ralf Lämmel, and Eric van Wyk, editors, *Proceedings of the
            1st International Conference on Software Language Engineering (SLE)*,
            volume 5452 of *Lecture Notes in Computer Science*, pages 168–177.
            Springer-Verlag Berlin Heidelberg, 2008.

[GRW08]   Thomas Goldschmidt, Ralf Reussner, and Jochen Winzen. A Case Study
            Evaluation of Maintainability and Performance of Persistency Tech-
            niques. In *ICSE '08: Proceedings of the 30th international conference
            on Software engineering*, pages 401–410, New York, NY, USA, 2008.
            ACM.

[GS07]   Miguel Garcia and Paul Sentosa. Generation of Eclipse-based IDEs
            for Custom DSLs. Technical report, Software Systems Institute (STS),
            Technische Universität Hamburg-Harburg, Germany, 2007.

[GWR07]   Thomas Goldschmidt, Jochen Winzen, and Ralf Reussner. Evaluation of
            Maintainability of Model-driven Persistency Techniques. In *IEEE CSMR
            07 - Workshop on Model-Driven Software Evolution (MoDSE2007)*,
            pages 17–24, 2007.

[HBJ08]   Markus Herrmannsdoerfer, Sebastian Benz, and Elmar Juergens. Cope:
            A language for the coupled evolution of metamodels and models. In

Proceedings of the 1st International Workshop on Model Co-Evolution and Consistency Management, 2008.

[Het10]   Thomas Hettel. *Model Round-Trip Engineering*. PhD thesis, Queensland University of Technology, 2010.

[HG09]   Robert Wagner Holger Giese. From model transformation to incremental bidirectional model synchronization. *Software and Systems Modeling*, 8:21–43, 2009.

[HLR08]   Thomas Hettel, Michael Lawley, and Kerry Raymond. Model synchronisation: Definitions for round-trip engineering. In *1st International Conference on Model Transformation, ICMT 2008*, pages 31–45, 2008.

[HLR09]   Thomas Hettel, Michael Lawley, and Kerry Raymond. Towards model round-trip engineering: An abductive approach. In *ICMT '09: Proceedings of the 2nd International Conference on Theory and Practice of Model Transformations*, pages 100–115, Berlin, Heidelberg, 2009. Springer-Verlag.

[HR04]   David Harel and Bernhard Rumpe. Meaningful modeling: What's the semantics of "semantics"? *Computer*, 37:64–72, 2004.

[Hud98]   P Hudak. Modular domain specific languages and tools. In *ICSR '98: Proceedings of the 5th International Conference on Software Reuse*, pages 134–142. IEEE Computer Society, 1998.

[IEE00]   IEEE. *IEEE Std 1471:2000 – Recommended practice for architectural description of software intensive systems*. Los Alamitos,CA: IEEE, 2000.

[JB06a]   Frédéric Jouault and Jean Bézivin. KM3: A DSL for Metamodel Specification. In *8th IFIP WG 6.1 International Conference on Formal Methods for Open Object-Based Distributed Systems*, pages 171–185, 2006.

[JB06b]   Frédéric Jouault and Jean Bézivin. On the specification of textual syntaxes for models. In *Eclipse Summit Europe 2006*, 2006.

[JBK06]   Frédéric Jouault, Jean Bézivin, and Ivan Kurtev. TCS: a DSL for the spe-
             cification of textual concrete syntaxes in model engineering. In *GPCE
             '06*, pages 249–254, New York, NY, USA, 2006. ACM Press.

[Jet]   JetBrains. Meta Programming System. `http://www.jetbrains.
             com/mps/`. last retrieved 2010-07-06.

[JP08]   Jan Jancura and Daniel Prusa. Generic framework for integration of
             programming languages into netbeans ide. In *PEPM '08: Proceed-
             ings of the 2008 ACM SIGPLAN symposium on Partial evaluation and
             semantics-based program manipulation*, pages 123–124, New York, NY,
             USA, 2008. ACM.

[Kah87]   G. Kahn. Natural semantics. In *Symposium on Theoretical Aspects of
             Computer Sciences (STACS)*, volume 247 of *Lecture Notes in Computer
             Science*, pages 22–39. Springer, 1987.

[Kar07]   Martin Karlsch. A model-driven framework for domain specific lan-
             guages. Master's thesis, University of Potsdam, Hasso Plattner Insitute,
             2007.

[Kle09]   Anneke Kleppe. *Software Language Engineering: Creating Domain-
             specific Languages Using Metamodels*. Addison-Wesley, Upper Saddle
             River, NJ, 2009.

[KP88]   G E Krasner and S T Pope. A description of the model-view-controller
             user interface paradigm in the smalltalk-80 system. In *Journal of Object
             Oriented Programming*, pages 26–49, 1988.

[KPKP06]   D S Kolovos, R F Paige, T P Kelly, and F A C Polack. Requirements
             for domain-specific languages. In *In Proceedings of the First ECOOP
             Workshop on Domain-Specific Program Development, co-located with
             ECOOP'06*, 2006.

[KPP06]   Dimitrios S. Kolovos, Richard F. Paige, and Fiona A. C. Polack. Merging
             models with the epsilon merging language (EML). In *Model Driven
             Engineering Languages and Systems*, pages 215 – 229, 2006.

[Kra10]   H. Krahn. *MontiCore: Agile Entwicklung von domänenspezifischen Sprachen im Software-Engineering.* PhD thesis, RWTH Aachen, 2010.

[KRV07a]   Holger Krahn, Bernhard Rumpe, and Steven Völkel. Integrated definition of abstract and concrete syntax for textual languages. In Gregor Engels, Bill Opdyke, Douglas C. Schmidt, and Frank Weil, editors, *MoDELS*, volume 4735 of *Lecture Notes in Computer Science*, pages 286–300. Springer, 2007.

[KRV07b]   Holger Krahn, Bernhard Rumpe, and Steven Völkel. Efficient editor generation for compositional dsls in eclipse. In *Proc. of the 7th OOPSLA Workshop on Domain-Specific Modeling (DSM' 07), Montreal, Quebec, Canada*, 2007.

[Kya05]   Marcel Kyas. An extended type-system for ocl supporting templates and transformations. In *In M. Steffen and Gianluigi Zavattaro (Eds), Formal Methods for Open Object-Based Distributed Systems (FMOODS 2005), Lecture Notes in Computer Science, number 3535*, pages 83–98. Springer-Verlag, 2005.

[LHT07a]   Dongxi Liu, Yhenjiang Hu, and Masato Takeichi. Bidirectional Interpretation of XQuery. In *Proc. of the 2007 ACM SIGPLAN symposium on partial evaluation and semantics-based program manipulation*, pages 21–30. ACM Press, 2007.

[LHT+07b]   Dongxi Liu, Yhenjiang Hu, Masato Takeichi, Kazuhiko Kakehi, and Hao Wang. A java Library for Bidirectional XML Transformation. *JSSST Computer Software*, 2:164–177, May 2007.

[Li95]   Warren X. Li. A simple and efficient incremental ll(1) parsing. In *SOFSEM '95: Theory and Practice of Informatics*, pages 399–404, 1995.

[LP88]   T.F. Lunney and R.H. Perrott. Syntax-directed editing. *Software Engineering Journal*, 3(2):37–46, Mar 1988.

[LS93]   B Logan and T Smithers. *Creativity and design as exploration.* Lawrence Erlbaum Associates Inc, 1993.

[MCnt]   S. L. MacGregor Mathers and A. Crowley. *The Goetia: The Lesser Key of Solomon the King*. 1904; 1995 reprint.

[Men02]   T. Mens. A state-of-the-art survey on software merging. *IEEE Trans. Softw. Eng.*, 28(5):449–462, 2002.

[MFJ05]   Pierre-Alain Muller, Franck Fleurey, and Jean-Marc Jézéquel. Weaving executability into object-oriented meta-languages. In Lionel C. Briand and Clay Williams, editors, *MoDELS*, volume 3713 of *Lecture Notes in Computer Science*, pages 264–278. Springer, 2005.

[MG06]   Tom Mens and Pieter Van Gorp. A taxonomy of model transformation. *Electronic Notes in Theoretical Computer Science*, 152:125–142, March 2006.

[MH05]   Pierre-Alain Muller and Michel Hassenforder.   HUTN as a bridge between modelware and grammarware - an experience report. In *WiSME 2005 4th Workshop in Software Model Engineering*, 2005.

[MHN⁺07]   Kazutaka Matsuda, Zhenjiang Hu, Keisuke Nakano, Makoto Hamana, and Masato Takeichi. Bidirectional transformation based on automatic derivation of view complement functions. In *Proc. of the ICFP 2007*, pages 47–58. ACM Press, 2007.

[Mod07]   ModelWare. Information Society Technologies (IST) Sixth Framework Programme: Glossary. `http://www.modelware-ist.org/index.php?option=com_rd_glossary&Itemid=55`, 2007. last retrieved: 2010-08-18.

[MP99]   V. Menon and K. Pingali. A case for source-level transformations in matlab. In *Proceedings of 2nd Conference on Domain-specific Languages*, pages 53–65, 1999.

[Muc97]   Steven Muchnick. *Advanced Compiler Design and Implementation*. Morgan Kaufmann, 1997.

[Nag96]   Manfred Nagl, editor. *Building tightly integrated software development environments: the IPSEN approach*. Springer-Verlag New York, Inc., New York, NY, USA, 1996.

[Niv04]   Gabriel Nivasch. Cycle detection using a stack. *Information Processing Letters*, 90(3):135 – 140, 2004.

[Obj]   Object Management Group. Architecture Driven Modernization (ADM). http://www.omg.org/adm/.

[Obj02]   Object Management Group. Meta Object Facility (MOF) Specification Version 1.4 (formal/02-04-03), 2002.

[Obj04]   Object Management Group. Human-Usable Textual Notation (HUTN) Specification (formal/04-08-01), 2004.

[Obj06]   Object Management Group (OMG). MOF 2.0 Core Specification (formal/2006-01-01), 2006.

[Obj10a]   Object Management Group. Object Constraint Language (OCL) Specification Version 2.2 (formal/2010-02-01), 2010.

[Obj10b]   Object Management Group (OMG). Unified Modeling Language Specification: Version 2.3, (formal/2010-05-03), 2010.

[Obj11]   Object Management Group. Meta Object Facility (MOF) 2.0 Query/View/Transformation (QVT) (formal/2011-01-01), 2011.

[PALG08]   Francisco Pérez Andrés, Juan Lara, and Esther Guerra. Domain specific languages with graphical and textual views. In *Applications of Graph Transformations with Industrial Relevance: Third International Symposium, AGTIVE 2007, Kassel, Germany, October 10-12, 2007, Revised Selected and Invited Papers*, pages 82–97, Berlin, Heidelberg, 2008. Springer-Verlag.

[PB03]   Rachel A. Pottinger and Philip A. Bernstein. Merging models based on given correspondences. In *VLDB '2003: Proceedings of the 29th international conference on Very large data bases*, pages 862–873. VLDB Endowment, 2003.

[Pep79]   P. Pepper. A study on transformational semantics. In *Program Construction*, volume 69 of *Lecture Notes in Computer Science*, pages 322–405. Springer Berlin / Heidelberg, 1979.

[Plo04]   Gordon D. Plotkin. The origins of structural operational semantics. *Journal of Logic and Algebraic Programming*, 60-61:3–15, 2004.

[PQ95]   Terence Parr and Russell Quong. Antlr: A predicated-ll(k) parser generator. *Journal of Software Practice and Experience*, 25(7), 1995.

[RT84]   Thomas Reps and Tim Teitelbaum. The synthesizer generator. *SIGSOFT Softw. Eng. Notes*, 9(3):42–48, 1984.

[RT89]   Thomas W. Reps and Tim Teitelbaum. *The Synthesizer Generator Reference Manual*. Springer, 2nd edition, 1989.

[RTD83]   Thomas Reps, Tim Teitelbaum, and Alan Demers. Incremental context-dependent analysis for language-based editors. *ACM Transactions on Programming Languages and Systems (TOPLAS)*, 5(3):449–477, 1983.

[Sch90]   Andy Schürr. Progress: A vhl-language based on graph grammars. In Hartmut Ehrig, Hans-Jörg Kreowski, and Grzegorz Rozenberg, editors, *Graph-Grammars and Their Application to Computer Science*, volume 532 of *Lecture Notes in Computer Science*, pages 641–659. Springer, 1990.

[Sch07]   Markus Scheidgen. Textual editing framework. `http://www2.informatik.hu-berlin.de/sam/meta-tools/tef/tool.html`, 2007. Last retrieved 2010-07-06.

[SE06]   Mehrdad Sabetzadeh and Steve Easterbrook. View merging in the presence of incompleteness and inconsistency. *Requirements Engineering*, 11:174–193, 2006.

[SH86]   Gregor Snelting and Wolfgang Henhapl. Unification in many-sorted algebras as a device for incremental semantic analysis. In *POPL '86: Proceedings of the 13th ACM SIGACT-SIGPLAN symposium on Principles of programming languages*, pages 229–235, New York, NY, USA, 1986. ACM.

[Shi93]   J.J. Shilling. Incremental ll(1) parsing in language-based editors. *Software Engineering, IEEE Transactions on*, 19(9):935–940, Sep 1993.

[SHT06]   Pierre-Yves Schobbens, Patrick Heymans, and Jean-Christophe Trigaux. Feature diagrams: A survey and a formal semantics. *Requirements Engineering*, 0:139–148, 2006.

[Sim07]   Charles Simonyi. Intentional software. http://www.intentsoft.com/, 2007.

[SLT91]   Marc H. Scholl, Christian Laasch, and Markus Tresch. Updatable views in object-oriented databases. In C Delobel, editor, *Deductive and Object-Oriented Databases*, volume 566 of *Lecture Notes in Computer Science*, pages 189–207, Berlin, Heidelberg, Springer,, 1991.

[Sne91]   Gregor Snelting. The calculus of context relations. *Acta Informatica*, 5:441–445, 1991.

[SS71]   Dana Scott and Christopher Strachey. Toward a mathematical semantics for computer languages. In Jerome Fox, editor, *Proceedings of the Symposium on Computers and Automata*, volume XXI, pages 19–46, Brooklyn, N.Y., April 1971. Polytechnic Press.

[Sta73]   Herbert Stachowiak, editor. *Allgemeine Modelltheorie*. Springer, Wien [u.a.], 1973.

[Tid05]   Jenifer Tidwell. *Designing Interfaces*. O'Reilly Media, illustrated edition edition, November 2005.

[TR81]   Tim Teitelbaum and Thomas Reps. The cornell program synthesizer: a syntax-directed programming environment. *Commun. ACM*, 24(9):563–573, 1981.

[Uhl07]   Axel   Uhl.   Model-driven   development   in   the   enterprise. https://www.sdn.sap.com/irj/sdn/weblogs?blog=/pub/wlg/7237, 2007. Last retrieved 2010-07-06.

[Uhl08]   Axel Uhl. Model-driven development in the enterprise. *IEEE Software*, 25(1):46–49, 2008.

[vdBHvD+01] Mark van den Brand, Jan Heering, Arie van Deursen, Hayco de Jong, Merijn de Jonge, Tobias Kuipers, Paul Klint, Leon Moonen, Pieter

Olivier, Jeroen Scheerder, Jurgen Vinju, Eelco Visser, and Joost Visser. The ASF+SDF Meta-Environment: a Component-Based Language Development Environment. In *Proc. of Compiler Construction (CC) 2001*, volume 2102 of *Lecture Notes in Computer Science*, pages 365–370. Springer, 2001.

[vDK98]   Arie van Deursen and Paul Klint. Little languages: little maintenance. *Journal of Software Maintenance*, 10(2):75–92, 1998.

[vDKV00]   Arie van Deursen, Paul Klint, and Joost Visser. Domain-specific languages: an annotated bibliography. *ACM SIGPLAN Notices*, 35(6):26–36, 2000.

[Wac07]   Guido Wachsmuth. Metamodel adaptation and model co-adaptation. In Erik Ernst, editor, *ECOOP 2007 - Object-Oriented Programming*, volume 4609 of *Lecture Notes in Computer Science*, pages 600–624. Springer Berlin / Heidelberg, 2007.

[Wag98]   Tim A. Wagner. *Practical Algorithms for Incremental Software Development Environments*. PhD thesis, University of California at Berkeley, 1998.

[wik]   wikipedia.org. Article on Coghead at wikipedia.org. http://en.wikipedia.org/wiki/Coghead. Last retrieved 10/08/2010.

[WK05]   Manuel Wimmer and Gerhard Kramler. Bridging grammarware and modelware. In *Satellite Events at the MoDELS 2005 Conference*, pages 159–168, 2005.